DATE DUE

GAYLORD			PRINTED IN U.S.A.

POLICING
PROSTITUTION
in Nineteenth-Century Paris

POLICING
PROSTITUTION
in Nineteenth-Century Paris

o o o

JILL HARSIN

PRINCETON UNIVERSITY PRESS

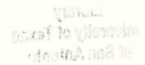

Copyright © 1985 by Princeton University Press
Published by Princeton University Press,
41 William Street, Princeton, New Jersey 08540
In the United Kingdom:
Princeton University Press,
Guildford, Surrey

Library of Congress Cataloging in Publication Data
will be found on the last printed page of this book
ISBN 0-691-05439-8

Publication of this book has been aided by a grant from the
Ira O. Wade Fund of Princeton University Press

This book has been composed in Linotron Granjon with Caslon Open

Clothbound editions of Princeton University Press books
are printed on acid-free paper, and binding materials
are chosen for strength and durability.

Printed in the United States of America
by Princeton University Press
Princeton, New Jersey

TO MY PARENTS

Contents

CONTENTS

Tables

Preface

I FIRST became interested in the history of prostitution in Paris after reading Parent-Duchâtelet's remarkable 1836 study. After several years of studying and writing about his subject, I am still amazed by his work, and so perhaps I should begin my list of acknowledgments with him.

Research for this study was supported in large part by a grant from the American Association of University Women. I should also like to thank the staffs of the following archives and libraries: the Archives nationales, Archives de la Préfecture de police, Bibliothèque nationale, Bibliothèque de la ville de Paris, and the University of Iowa Library and Health Sciences Library.

The study has benefited greatly from the help, advice, and encouragement of numerous friends and colleagues. My greatest thanks go to Alan B. Spitzer, my advisor throughout graduate school, for his kindness, his help, and his shrewd historical insight. I should also like to thank Laurence Lafore, who tactfully corrected my early excesses of style; Sarah Hanley, who provided friendship and moral support as well as practical advice on virtually everything; Linda Kerber, who went out of her way to be helpful and encouraging; Ralph Giesey and the late Pierre de Saint-Victor, who graciously served on my dissertation committee; and John B. Henneman, who employed me as a research assistant early in my studies.

Finally, I owe special thanks to my parents, Duane and

Margaret Harsin, who remained cheerful and supportive throughout my graduate work. My deepest gratitude goes to my mother, who typed every single version of this manuscript, from its earliest rough draft as a doctoral thesis to its final, finished form. After all that, we are still friends, and that is a remarkable achievement.

Colgate University
Hamilton, New York
December 1983

Introduction

"THE city of Paris," wrote an enthusiastic observer in 1840, "distinguishes itself among the capitals of civilized nations, as the one where order, morality, and public health are the most fully guaranteed against the influences of prostitution."[1] It was the proud boast of the Prefecture of Police of Paris that they were the pioneers in prostitution control, a claim which had far more resonance then than it has today. The early nineteenth century marked the beginning, in much of Europe, of the interest in public hygiene and sanitation, and the officials in charge of cleaning up the cities extended their concern to troublesome individuals as well. It was no accident that Parent-Duchâtelet, one of the leading public hygienists of the period, an expert in sewage and waste disposal, was also the foremost European authority on prostitution.

In the nineteenth century the policing of prostitution was undergoing a revolution of massive proportions. The *fille publique,* once viewed primarily as an outcast, had been redefined as a threat to public health. Administrators, motivated by a new sense of responsibility for the well-being of the citizenry, rationalized the control of prostitution to a remarkable degree. They established municipal guidelines, registration systems, and venereal examinations, under the general heading of the *police des moeurs,* so that the prostitute could remain within society and under its control.

[1] H. A. Frégier, *Des classes dangereuses de la population dans les grandes villes,* 2 vols. (Paris: J.-B. Baillière, 1840), I:153.

The system began very quietly and unobtrusively in France. It originated in Paris, stemming from a simple administrative decision in 1802 to provide facilities for examining public prostitutes for venereal disease. Shortly thereafter, the examination was made mandatory and, to ensure compliance, the police began to keep an inscription list of all prostitutes. The system was regarded as something of a compromise, preserving society from the worst effects of venereal disease and preserving the prostitute from meaningless harassment. To be sure, what she gained in acceptability she lost in mystique; the dark secrets of the *femme perdue* could scarcely survive the onslaught of police statisticians busily figuring the number of syphilitics per hundred.

The system was not completely new. The broad outlines of toleration, an implicit coexistence of prostitutes and municipal authorities (who reluctantly acknowledged them as a "necessary evil"), had been sketched out during the old regime. Yet the linking of toleration with an organized method of disease control was a genuinely innovative manner of handling prostitution, one that was copied by other major European cities; it provided the inspiration, if not the exact model, for the Contagious Diseases Acts in England. Unfortunately, something went badly wrong. Instead of the orderly procedures envisioned by the creators of the system, the *police des moeurs* gave rise to a system of repression directed not only against prostitutes but against women of the working classes in general.

The difficulties suffered by *filles publiques,* by women who were registered prostitutes, were inherent in the system itself. The legality of prostitution was left conveniently vague; women were, however, allowed to engage in the trade so long as they followed police regulations governing their conduct. Violation of the rules resulted in something euphemistically referred to as "administrative detention," or imprisonment without trial.

These arbitrary actions, indefensible from any legal stand-point, were nevertheless theoretically confined to women who had put themselves "outside the law" by their registration with the police.

Such theoretical limits did not hold in practice. The subjection to this system of other working-class women developed slowly but surely, expanding from a minor loophole in the regulations of the *police des moeurs*. The police did not get, nor did they expect, voluntary registration on the part of all prostitutes. Consequently, it was decided early in the regime that if sufficient presumption of prostitution existed, the prefecture could register a woman "by office," that is, against her will, making her subject to all the rules. From this policy there developed a necessary accompaniment, the concept of the "clandestine" prostitute, a woman who engaged in prostitution without police supervision of any sort; any woman was potentially clandestine, particularly if her conduct was "irregular." To this mixture was added the self-expanding mandate of the *police des moeurs*. This creeping bureaucracy was founded on the basis of a few apparently trivial administrative decisions, with the modest ambition of ensuring that all registered prostitutes reported for their medical examinations. It ended as an administrative department with a budget of over 100,000 francs a year and a self-defined mission of purging society of its impure elements. "The police do not have a social mission of public moral reform," one of their critics reminded them at the end of the century. But by then it was too late.[2]

By the late 1800s there had developed a virtual mania over prostitution. Arrests in Paris alone numbered in the thousands every year. Women were gathered in with relentless determination, singly and in groups. One prefect of police at the

---

[2] Louis Fiaux, *La Police des moeurs devant la Commission extraparlementaire du régime des moeurs,* 3 vols. (Paris: Félix Alcan, 1910), I:37.

end of the century, who claimed to have reformed the policy, explained how the mass arrest had formerly been conducted: "These nighttime expeditions generally took place between midnight and 1:00 a.m. on the boulevards and consisted of barring the thoroughfare and then, by an immense casting of the net, of driving into the arms of the agents all the unfortunate women found within the perimeter. . . . It is understandable that, when the group of agents of the Sûreté launched themselves with loud cries into the middle of the unfortunate women there, they could have encountered some honest women who were distinguished from the others too late."[3] Senator René Bérenger early in the twentieth century suggested one explanation for these wild forays: "I consider that the agents who fulfill the difficult duty of assuring the morality of the streets have the greatest integrity; but they live in a special milieu, and although they are recruited with the greatest care, they finish by seeing prostitutes everywhere."[4]

The tendency to "see prostitutes everywhere" was allowed to develop as far as it did, and for as long as it did, because those being arrested shared two important characteristics. First, they were members of the working classes, made vulnerable by their economic powerlessness in the growing industrial capitalism of nineteenth-century France. Like all poor people, they sometimes found that the law judged them more harshly than it did those with some means. But even more important than social class was the fact that those being arrested were women; in no other area did their legal invisibility cut so deeply.

The virtual civil nonexistence of women under the law had been confirmed by the Napoleonic Code of 1804. Because of Napoleon's determination to protect his notion of the family,

---

[3] Edouard Dolléans, *La Police des moeurs* (Paris: Librairie de la Société du recueil général des lois et des arrêts, 1903), pp. 28-29.
[4] Fiaux, *Commission extraparlementaire*, III:34.

the most serious prohibitions fell upon married women. Without her husband's permission, a wife could not maintain a separate residence, attend school, or hold a job; her husband had unconditional control over family property, as he did over any wages or royalties her work might bring. The Civil Code included women in the category of unfit persons, along with minors and ex-convicts; women were declared incompetent to witness certificates of marriage, birth, or death.

Probably the best known provisions of the Civil Code were those involving sexual relations. The code prohibited the filing of paternity suits, for fear that some men might be falsely accused. In cases of adultery, an erring wife was liable to imprisonment for three months to two years, while a guilty husband was subject only to a fine; this was fairly consistent, since those without sufficient independent financial resources—wives, the poor, members of the working class—were always punished by imprisonment. A husband, moreover, could be charged with adultery only if he brought his mistress into the family home. Divorce, possible from 1792 to 1816, was not allowed again until 1884.

To these specific legal disabilities were added other, less tangible ones. Judicial decisions, following the climate of the times, tended to be rendered against women. One court ruling, noted in a recent study, stated that a husband could open his wife's mail on the grounds that she might be plotting to commit adultery.[5] The sexual anxiety revealed in this decision did not translate into universally prohibitive judgments, for courts could also choose to ignore certain statutes if they interfered with accepted sexual practices. Article 334 of the Penal Code provided severe penalties for those who "excited

[5] Patrick Kay Bidelman, *Pariahs Stand Up! The Founding of the Liberal Feminist Movement in France, 1858-1889* (Westport, Conn.: Greenwood Press, 1982), p. 6. See Bidelman, pp. 3-32, for a full discussion not only of legal restraints but also of institutional, cultural, and economic inequalities.

minors to debauchery"; this was rarely, and only in exceptional circumstances, used against authorized bordellos, even though much of their business depended upon providing very young women to customers.[6]

Many of the legal disabilities of women had direct relevance only to the middle and upper classes. It goes without saying that poor women had no property to worry about, and it took the wages of husband and wife together to ensure the survival of the family. Poor women could scarcely be faulted for believing that their greatest problems were economic. Nevertheless, the struggle for civil rights was not a matter to concern only the bourgeoisie. The denial of full citizenship to women of all classes made it easy for the Paris police, by simple administrative fiat, to dispense with the most basic civil rights of prostitutes and eventually of many working-class women who were not prostitutes. Such dispensations were not legal, as the police themselves admitted, and such actions could not have been taken against men of any social class, as the police also admitted; but there was no one ready to protest the illegality of their actions against women, at least not until the late nineteenth century.

And, too, the lack of legal rights was a symptom of a more deeply rooted commitment to the subordination of women. All the vague fears, tensions, anxieties, and misogyny of the nineteenth century got tangled up in the control of prostitution, as normally stalwart officials found themselves unable to contemplate the idea of extending to prostitutes the rights granted to ordinary criminals. "How would civil tribunals judge infractions of this nature?" wrote Henri-Joseph Gisquet, a prefect of police during the 1830s. "How would they proceed in a multitude of cases where the lawyers as well as the witnesses would feel an invincible repugnance to discuss

---

[6] Charles-Jerôme Lecour, *La Prostitution à Paris et à Londres, 1789-1871*, 2nd ed. (Paris: Asselin, 1872), pp. 163, 165.

the case? It would be a perpetual scandal, and almost all the material proofs would be lacking for the conviction." But the problems went even deeper than this, as he perhaps imprudently revealed:

> One of the greatest disadvantages would be the insubordination that this state of affairs would create among the women. From the moment the administration would have no direct control over their conduct, and the punishment would not immediately follow the crime, they would mock all recommendations, injunctions, and prohibitions made by the police; then they would offer on the public thoroughfares the disgusting spectacle of their turpitudes; it would be impossible to assign a limit to their outrages. The salutary curb that maintains them in this absolutely necessary condition of dependency would be broken, and the contagion could extend to a greater number of persons of their sex.[7]

It was not entirely clear, in that last sentence, whether Gisquet was worried about the contagion of prostitution or of insubordination. The two were linked, in any case: the administrative name for the registered prostitute who obeyed all the rules was the *fille soumise*.

Police policies did not go entirely unchallenged in the course of the century. Abolitionism, dedicated to the elimination of the regulatory system, began early in the Third Republic. This movement was in part inspired by Josephine Butler's crusade against the Contagious Diseases Acts; it took particular energy from the wave of republican idealism that followed the fall of the Second Empire, and it had some links

---

[7] Henri-Joseph Gisquet, *Mémoires de M. Gisquet, ancien préfet de police, écrits par lui-même,* 4 vols. (Paris: n.p., 1840), IV:354-355.

with organized feminism.[8] Abolitionists, fighting a battle against "sanctified custom," were forced to paint their arguments as boldly as possible, and the defenders of the regulatory system responded in kind. Printed attacks on both sides became increasingly hysterical. The police official Charles-Jerôme Lecour warned that the prominent abolitionist Yves Guyot was seeking, in his attacks on the regulatory system, to destroy the Prefecture of Police itself.[9] Abolitionists answered with the listing of increasingly well-documented cases of police "errors." These cases of mistaken arrest were hard to refute; the Prefect Louis Andrieux could only defend his agents by attacking the virtue of the arrested women, a tactic that offended nineteenth-century sensibilities.[10] A later prefect, Louis Lépine, sensed the public relations problem now faced by the police: "*Réglementaristes* cut a bad figure, play the villain's part; it is up to them to prove the utility of regulation, and to prove it in two respects, from the medical point of view and from the point of view of order."[11] The problem of public relations eventually became critical, and it was perhaps felt the more strongly because the *police des moeurs* had existed for so long without challenge.

[8] Bidelman, *Pariahs,* p. 61. Maria Deraismes, one of the leading feminists, was vice-president of the Association française pour l'abolition de la prostitution réglementée.

[9] Charles-Jerôme Lecour, *La Campagne contre la Préfecture de police* (Paris: Asselin, 1881), pp. 99-100.

[10] See, for instance, Andrieux's discussion of the Eyben affair, the case of a widow arrested while waiting for her children. Along with numerous insinuations about her apparent lack of an occupation, Andrieux made the following remark: "Je ferai seulement remarquer combien était mal choisi le lieu où Mme Eyben avait coutume d'attendre ses enfants. Depuis longtemps le passage des Panoramas était signalé à l'attention de la police des moeurs, de nombreuses arrestations y avaient eu lieu, surtout dans le voisinage de la rue des Panoramas, où se trouvait un hôtel dont la réputation était fâcheuse." Louis Andrieux, *Souvenirs d'un préfet de police,* 2 vols. (Paris: Jules Rouff, 1885), II:110-115.

[11] Fiaux, *Commission extraparlementaire,* I:379.

The tensions of the nineteenth-century middle classes have been well aired and are almost as familiar to us as our own. What have been less well examined, however, are the concrete structural difficulties these tensions created. The intrusion of public authority into the private lives of individuals (particularly those of the working classes and particularly those who were women) was a common phenomenon of this era.[12] In the case of prostitutes, this intrusion came out of a frequently articulated anxiety over venereal disease, social revolution, and "immorality," however defined; and all this was combined, sometimes, with genuinely humanitarian impulses. The desire to save society from prostitutes and to save prostitutes from themselves was not an unworthy goal. The fact that women lacked so many aspects of full citizenship—legal equality, economic power, a political voice—allowed the system to develop without check. The control of prostitution, what became known as the *chasse à la femme,* was for the most part born of essentially decent motives, but those who directed the regulatory system had far too much power, able by minor administrative changes to affect the lives of thousands of women and never called to account for their actions. It was almost inevitable that the system would become abusive.

This book encompasses the entire nineteenth century— appropriately, since the *régime des moeurs,* with its overlapping, contradictory goals, its institutionalization of the double standard, the sexual tension apparent in its very structure, was so clearly a product of the nineteenth century. Also appropriately, the regime as originally constituted lasted almost

---

[12] A number of recent works have examined this phenomenon. See, for example, Michel Foucault, *The History of Sexuality* (New York: Vintage Books, 1980); Jacques Donzelot, *La Police des familles* (Paris: Editions de minuit, 1977); and Judith R. Walkowitz, *Prostitution and Victorian Society: Women, Class, and the State* (Cambridge: Cambridge University Press, 1980).

exactly a hundred years; its dismantling began in 1903. The regulatory system, a perfect microcosm of the society and economy, the intellectual ideals, and the moral strictures of the 1800s, was an anachronism in the twentieth century. Despite my attempt in this book to follow the regime through its entire course, my major emphasis is on the evolution of the regulatory system in the early nineteenth century, when it was first coming into existence and when the significant decisions that would guide the regime through the rest of its existence were being made.

My purpose is twofold. The first is to examine one set of consequences of the legal inequality of women. No one could have predicted the enormous growth of the *police des moeurs* from the fact of women's subordination; but the fact that women had no legal barriers to throw up before them allowed the system to grow as it did. The second and in one sense contradictory purpose is to try to defend the *police des moeurs* or, perhaps better, to reconstruct the theories, assumptions, and fears that lay behind their actions.[13]

Part One examines the administrative structure and legal bases for the regime. An analysis of Parent-Duchâtelet is included here, for he was the self-appointed defender of the *police des moeurs*; ironically, his work quite uninten-

---

[13] This work has benefited from a number of important recent studies of prostitution, especially Walkowitz, *Prostitution and Victorian Society,* and Alain Corbin, *Les Filles de noce: misère sexuelle et prostitution aux XIXe et XXe siècles* (Paris: Aubier Montaigne, 1978). See also Frances Finnegan, *Poverty and Prostitution: A Study of Victorian Prostitutes in York* (Cambridge: Cambridge University Press, 1979); Mark Thomas Connelly, *The Response to Prostitution in the Progressive Era* (Chapel Hill: University of North Carolina Press, 1980); and Ruth Rosen, *The Lost Sisterhood: Prostitution in America, 1900-1918* (Baltimore: Johns Hopkins University Press, 1982). This study was also enriched, particularly in the formative stages, by the work of Joan Scott and Louise Tilly. See especially Scott and Tilly, "Women's Work and the Family in Nineteenth-Century Europe," *Comparative Studies in History and Society* 16 (Winter 1975).

tionally undermined the ideological basis of the system. Part Two examines, through the use of official records, the practical functioning of the system and its effects on the women who were caught up in it. The women portrayed in this section necessarily had their stories filtered through the reports of the police and other governmental agencies, but many of their own ambitions, motives, and assumptions were also apparent. Finally, Part Three examines the chief problems that developed from the regulatory system, the obsession with clandestinity and the uneasy relationship with the bordello. These represented the opposite poles of the regime: clandestinity was uncontrolled, anonymous, and anarchic, while bordello prostitution was the most fully organized, the most nearly professional. The last chapter examines the resolution of these two problems, and of the system itself, early in the twentieth century.

PART ONE

The Foundations of the
Régime des Moeurs

o o o

○ 1 ○

Bringing Order into Disorder

Virtuous women have nothing to fear from the
morals police.
Chief of the Brigade des moeurs, 1879[1]

THE alleged sins of the agents of the Morals Brigade seemed
to have caught up with them in the late 1870s. The brigade,
an agency of the Prefecture of Police devoted to the control
of prostitution, had long been fending off rumors about its
manner of operation. It was admittedly arbitrary in its dealings with prostitutes, sending arrested women to prison without benefit of trial or appeal. Many citizens had seen a *razzia,*
or *rafle,* in which the brigade secretly surrounded an area
and, at a given signal, gathered up all the women within.
The desire of the police to restrict prostitution to houses was
well known, and rumor had it that certain officers were in
the pay of brothelkeepers. Most serious of all was the charge
that young working women were picked up indiscriminately
for prostitution by agents anxious to fill their daily quota of arrests. Poor and ashamed, the women were afraid of the notoriety of a protest and allowed the injustice to pass in silence.

Some credence was given to the charge of unsubstantiated
arrests in late 1876, when a well-known actress was picked

[1] Conseil municipal de Paris, *Procès-verbal de la Commission de la police
des moeurs* (Paris: n.p., 1879), p. 27.

up for soliciting in a public place. The furor aroused by this
obviously mistaken catch gave new fire to the anti-Moeurs
crusade during the next few years; the abolitionist movement
(devoted to eliminating police regulation of prostitution) was
fanned by pamphlets, newspaper campaigns, and the publicized trial of an antibrigade activist. Finally, in 1879, the
inquiry into the activities of the prefecture shifted from the
newspapers to the city government of Paris.[2]

The investigation of prostitution and the police conducted
by the Paris Municipal Council in 1879 was remarkable only
for the degree to which it failed to shed any light on the
controversy. The issues and areas of dispute had by this time
been largely clarified; the questioners on the council, on one
side, and the police, on the other, were polite adversaries
exchanging lines from a well-worn script. There was surprise
neither in the questions nor in the answers; nor was there
any attempt by the councilors to press further, to challenge
the official responses. One councilor worried about the unsubstantiated arrest. Is it true, he wondered, that during a
razzia "the agents have the authority to arrest all the women
they find in a designated area?" The prefect was reassuring:

There is a general misunderstanding of the true character
of these so-called *razzias*. The administration is asked

---

[2] An account of the events leading up to the 1879 inquiry can be found
in many places, including the introductions of most books written by Louis
Fiaux; see especially Fiaux, *La Police des moeurs en France et dans les
principaux pays de l'Europe* (Paris: E. Dentu, 1888), pp. 11-23. A different
view of the situation is to be found in Andrieux, *Souvenirs,* I:14-22. The
activist, sentenced to six months in prison, was Yves Guyot, who had been
charged with "defaming" government agents in the performance of their
duties; his hopes of turning the trial into a forum for debate over the
Bureau des moeurs were thwarted, and he entered prison in April 1877.
Two years later Guyot was elected to the Municipal Council, and he
remained active in the antiregulatory (abolitionist) cause for the rest of the
century.

from time to time to make a special surveillance of areas which serve as a gathering place for many clandestine prostitutes. . . . When some of the *insoumises* are arrested, a general panic ensues . . . and some regrettable and involuntary errors are committed.[3]

Would the prefect like to increase the number of *maisons de tolérance* in Paris? The answer was engagingly frank:

The activity of the administration is much more efficacious with regard to women gathered in houses of prostitution than with regard to *filles isolées*. We cannot, then, rejoice over the decrease in the number of these houses during the past several years, which has corresponded to a marked increase in clandestine prostitution. It would not, however, be exact to say that the administration instigates or encourages the establishment of new houses of prostitution.[4]

The questions for Coué, head of the Morals Brigade, were equally random, and the answers went equally unchallenged. Was it true, asked a member, that a married woman had been arrested on the streets just moments after parting from her husband? Yes, but the woman had contributed to the mistake by her "equivocal behavior." No, an *insoumise* was not subjected to the *visite sanitaire* after her first arrest. Yes, a few of the older houses of prostitution were authorized to have a *marcheuse* outside the house. No, the *tolérance* was not granted only to married women. Yes, the 36 (of 127) houses of prostitution authorized to receive independent prostitutes received only *filles en carte*.[5]

The shared esoteric vocabulary indicated the extent to which

---

[3] Conseil municipal de Paris, *Procès-verbal,* p. 6.
[4] Ibid., p. 8.
[5] Ibid., pp. 21-27.

the thinking of both friends and foes of the system had been molded by the administrative structure. The *maison de tolérance* was a technically illegal but officially tolerated house of prostitution, established with the permission of the police; the *tolérance* was the permission to run such a house. The *fille en carte* was a prostitute who was "inscribed," or registered, with the police and was given a card issued by the prefecture. The *fille de maison* worked in a house, the *fille isolée* lived outside a tolerated house and found her own customers; both were *en carte*. The *marcheuse* (or *bonne*) was an older woman who stood outside the house and hawked its wares to the passers-by. *Prostitution clandestine* was practiced by women who eluded police surveillance; they were referred to as *insoumises*. The *visite sanitaire* was the examination for venereal disease conducted by doctors who worked for the Dispensaire de salubrité, or dispensary.

A vast administrative edifice, as well as a solid ideological construction, had been in place since the first decade of the nineteenth century. The structural framework for the regime had been created by the circulars and ordinances from the Empire, Restoration, and July Monarchy; these prefectural decrees are the subject of this chapter. The system, which began to be implemented in 1810, can be summed up quickly. Every prostitute was required to register with the police. Inscription carried with it an implicit authorization for the prostitute to conduct her illegal trade in a relatively unhampered manner. In return, she had to submit to regular medical examinations for venereal disease and, if found ill, to treatment within the prison hospital. She also had to submit to certain regulations which determined where and when she could solicit.

The prostitute was arrested if she broke a regulation, or did not appear for a medical examination, or caused a disturbance. The police asserted that the prostitute was "outside the law"; thus her arrest led her away from the regular judicial track and into a "court" within the prefecture. There was no way to appeal a decision of this "court" because, strictly speaking, it was not a court, and what she had was not a trial but a hearing. The presiding officer was the chief of the Morals Brigade, who sentenced her to a relatively short stay in the Petite Force prison. "The Petite Force . . . usually has about four hundred prostitutes incarcerated there," wrote a spokesman for the prefecture in 1822. "This considerable number proves the necessity for this administrative correction."[6] The first prefect of the Restoration, the Comte d'Anglès (1815-1821), was not so certain: "A slight punishment after continual relapses into crime is equivalent (for this crowd of ne'er-do-wells who make a game of it) to impunity. A lot of women have been sent to the prison workshops fifteen times, twenty times, sometimes even thirty times, although they are still young."[7] Effective or not, this was the system; and though all they could do, as the prefect Guy Delavau (1821-1828) complained, was "send them to the Petite Force," there were a variety of ways to do this.[8]

The Dispensary

The origin of the dispensary, unlike that of most of the regulatory system, can be precisely dated. An *arrêté* of 12 Ventôse Year X (3 March 1802) decreed the medical examination of prostitutes for venereal disease. This decree was given some substance by an *arrêté* of 1 Prairial Year XIII (21 May 1805) which established the dispensary itself. In its ear-

[6] AN F⁷ 9304, report, c. 1819 and 1822.
[7] AN F⁷ 9305, letter of 20 September 1817 from the prefect of police to the minister of the interior.
[8] AN F⁷ 9305, letter of 7 September 1822 from the prefect of police to the minister of the interior.

liest form the dispensary was a traditional French sinecure rather than a modern municipal institution. The two doctors in charge, Colon and Teytaut, were named in the text of the *arrêté;* they had previously had the lucrative privilege of examining prostitutes in their homes (*visites à domicile*) on behalf of the city. Now they were given the right to establish a dispensary in "a convenient location," to see that it was well supplied with "linen, drugs, and other necessities," and to pay the other doctors who would be associated with them; all payments were to be made from the revenues provided by the examinations.[9]

This method of organization swiftly brought some apparently deserved criticism. It was alleged that the doctors examined only those women who were able to pay the 3-franc fee, to the neglect of all the rest. Indeed, it was worse than this; it was reported that they had hired two medical students to perform the examinations, while they occupied themselves with the collection of money. They even demanded payment from women who were in the hospital, on the grounds that the doctors had gone to the trouble of making a house call and should thus be repaid. Colon and Teytaut were allowed to resign, each with a yearly pension of 3,000 francs, and the institution was reorganized.[10] The *arrêté* of 24 December 1810 instituted mandatory examinations for all prostitutes on the inscription list, thus removing the matter of who was to be examined from the discretion of the doctors.[11]

The fall of the Empire allowed the dispensary to become

---

[9] PP DB 408, *arrêtés* of 12 Ventôse Year X and 1 Prairial Year XIII.

[10] Alexandre-Jean-Baptiste Parent-Duchâtelet, *De la prostitution dans la ville de Paris,* 2 vols., 3rd ed. (Paris: J.-B. Baillière, 1857), I:623, 628.

[11] See AN F⁷ 9305, *Compte rendu sur la prostitution publique,* for a discussion of the establishment of the clinic in 1810.

firmly established; the stationing of foreign occupation troops outside Paris during the first years of the Restoration brought about a predictable explosion in the numbers of prostitutes and of cases of venereal disease. The obvious need for some kind of public health measure, however, did not quite erase the tainted early history of the dispensary. Sensing the controversial character of the establishment, Anglès made repeated attempts to put the dispensary on a firmer legal footing, either by means of a law or by a royal ordinance. A proposal for such an ordinance, submitted to the Ministry of the Interior in 1817, was returned to the prefect with a note stating that "the minister believed it pointless to pass an ordinance; if someone attacks the dispensary in the Chamber he will defend it."[12] And with that precarious justification the prefect had to be content, at least until 1820, when Anglès decided to try another route to legality. He asked the Paris Municipal Council to take over the funding of the dispensary in order to give it the character, as he expressed it, of a "true municipal

[12] The ministerial comment was reported in AN F⁶ II Seine 19, *Note pour Monsieur le Directeur général*, 15 January 1821. A trial *ordonnance* was actually drawn up but never passed. As the text (AN F⁷ 9305) indicates, it would simply have legitimized the existing state of affairs:

Art. 1ᵉʳ: L'établissement formé à Paris, par les soins du Préfet de Police sous le titre de Dispensaire de salubrité pour la surveillance et la visite des femmes publiques est confirmé.

Art. 2ᵉ: L'organisation et les attributions de ce Dispensaire seront déterminées par un règlement qui sera arrêté par le Préfet de police et soumis à l'approbation de Notre Ministre Secretaire d'Etat au Département de l'Intérieur.

Art. 3ᵉ: Les dépenses auxquelles donne lieu la visite des femmes publiques continueront d'être à leur charge suivant les fixations qui seront réglées par le Préfet de Police. Il sera formé des rétributions payées un fonds commun dont la repartition sera déterminée par le Préfet de Police qui en soumettra le Compte chaque année à notre Ministre secretaire d'Etat au Département de l'Intérieur.

establishment." The council, professing to see no difficulty with the system as it was, turned him down. They understandably saw no reason to saddle themselves with an expense that was already running up to 70,000 francs per year.[13]

As Anglès realized, money was the key to the early difficulties of the dispensary. Though it had been removed from the control of individuals and taken under the wing of the Prefecture of Police, it was still funded entirely by prostitutes. Independent prostitutes, ordered to report once (later twice) a month, were charged 3 francs a visit. Madams, beneficiaries of a group rate, paid 6 francs twice a month; this covered weekly visits to the brothel by dispensary doctors.[14] These charges had at first been regarded as the solution to the vexing problem of finance, a problem because the dispensary represented an expense that was regarded as both necessary and yet expended for the unworthy. Legal experts were quick to find justification for the assessment. The fee, they argued, was simply another municipal tax, similar to the one placed on public coaches. Those uneasy with this explanation could choose to regard it as a special revenue exacted for establishments of public health, or—and this was the explanation preferred by Anglès—it could be regarded as nothing more than a doctor's fee paid for services rendered. The fee was

[13] AN F⁶ II Seine 19, *Extrait du registre des procès-verbaux des séances du Conseil général du département de la Seine,* session of 7 January 1821. Also AN F⁶ II Seine 19, letter of 20 April 1821 from the director general to the prefect of police, summing up the motives behind the request: "En faisant cette proposition vous aviez principalement en vue de donner à l'établissement du dispensaire une existence légale, de le consolider et de le mettre ainsi à l'abri des préventions outrageantes et des imputations calomnieuses dont il a été ou pourrait encore être l'objet."

[14] AN F⁷ 9305. See any of the budgets (*Compte sommaire en deniers du Dispensaire de salubrité*) for the years 1819-1826.

paid to the dispensary rather than directly to the doctors because it would be "humiliating" for doctors to accept money from prostitutes and could, in fact, result in "repulsive" disputes between them.[15] The presumed humiliation of the doctors was not the primary reason for this method of operation, for it took money to rent the building, to buy equipment, to support the clerks, and to pay the twelve-man Brigade des moeurs. So long as all of this was paid for by prostitutes, the organization remained entirely self-contained and self-supporting, and, it was assumed, free also of public criticism.

This latter hope was a bad calculation of the public mentality, for criticism came even after the institution had been reformed. Anglès was stung by the imputation that the payment of the fee led the police to encourage the growth of prostitution in Paris so that they could increase the revenue.[16] More to the point, and more difficult to deny, was the charge that the doctors and the police were examining many more women than they reported and were splitting the hidden profit among themselves. The prefects were not in on this diversion of "immense sums," according to an anonymous report of 1822, but there were many middle-level employees who had made "considerable fortunes."[17] More explicit were

[15] AN F⁷ 9305, report of October 1817 from the Bureau de secours to the minister of the interior.

[16] AN F⁶ II Seine 19, report of 27 December 1820 from the prefect of police to the minister of the interior. Anglès stated that "la calomnie s'était attachée à cet établissement, comme elle s'attache trop souvent à ce qui est utile et que la malveillance tentait de donner le charge sur la nature d'une institution dont les éléments ne pouvaient être rendus publics; que l'intrigue, en un mot, en exagérant audelà de toute idée les resources annuellement très bornées sur lesquelles est fondée l'existance du Dispensaire, essayait de la présenter dans l'opinion publique sous l'apparence d'une exploitation lucrative."

[17] AN F⁷ 9304, *Rapport,* 1822.

the charges made in an anonymous note against Noël, the *officier de paix* who headed the Morals Brigade. It was alleged that Noël kept two sets of books. His secret accounts supposedly revealed that he took in 648,000 francs per year (from 18,000 prostitutes who each paid 3 francs per month), spent 60,000 francs to maintain the dispensary operations, and stole the remaining 588,000 francs. It was further charged that Noël's corrupt example had undermined the entire dispensary:

> Prostitutes who have not paid the taxes for three months are imprisoned at the Petite Force or Madelonnettes, and they only leave after paying 15 francs of which 6 francs are shared among the officer of the peace for the attribution of morals and the agents. In 1811, and in the following years, madams paid a restaurant near the prefecture to cater dinner daily to the Bureau of Morals. . . . Girard, employee at the prefecture, first clerk in the Bureau of Buildings, can give some more information.[18]

Charges like this are now impossible to prove but, significantly, even acknowledged practices were beginning to draw criticism. Anglès found himself in the uncomfortable position of having to explain to the minister of the interior why the dispensary budgets for 1814-1816 balanced each other exactly (in 1816, for example, the income and the expenses each came to the identical sum of 66,302.97 francs). His explanation was rather involved, but when the facts were untangled it ap-

[18] AN F⁷ 9304, probably dates 1816-1817. Noël and Ducarroy (or Ducourez) were apparently in charge of the Brigade des moeurs from its inception; they survived into the Restoration. A novel written in 1845 provides an interesting look back at their manner of operation. See Sir P. Robert, *Oeuvres complèts: les confessions de Pied-de-Fer* (Paris: Bureau du journal *La Nation*, 1845), pp. 122-129.

peared that the doctors had simply split up the surplus among themselves.[19]

After this minor flap, the dispensary began to donate its excess funds to various *maisons de refuge,* or homes of assistance for young girls who wished to leave prostitution. The practice required strict accountability, and it was discovered that the dispensary was running in the black to an almost embarrassing extent. Its surpluses ranged from a high of 15,000 francs in 1822 to a low of over 9,000 francs in 1826. They would have been even greater, had the payroll not been padded with a number of clerks who were correctly suspected to be unnecessary.

The dispensary had not been created as a profitmaking organization. Moreover—strange as it may seem—the charitable refuges as they were then constituted could not absorb the extra funds. With the single exception of a 2,000-franc donation in 1823 to an assistance fund for women just released from prison, all the donations went to charities organized along the conventual principle: the "repentant" girls, supervised constantly, were held to a strict regime of religion and work, with the goal of inculcating the habits of hard labor and the duties of religion. The amount of good the charities could do was limited by constraints of space. A proposal to

---

[19] "A la fin de chaque exercice, lorsque le produit des visites a été connu, et que, sur le montant de la somme, les frais du matériel de l'établissement et les frais de surveillance pour l'exécution de toutes les mesures sanitaires ont été payés, on a reparté, entre les médécins, comme complément de leurs traitements, et en proportion du tous où ils avaient été fixés, ce qu'il pouvait y avoir d'excédent de la recette sur la dépense." AN F⁷ 9305, letter of 11 October 1817 from the prefect of police to the minister of the interior. The extra sum, 4,050 francs, was subsumed under the heading of "Indemnités eventuelles." As a result of this financial miscue, Anglès ordered that the excess every year should go to a charity for repentant prostitutes, and this was confirmed during the term of the next prefect. AN F⁷ 9305, *arrêtés* of 10 August 1818 and 29 October 1822.

build an 80,000-franc shelter for *repenties,* to which Anglès lent his support, was rejected, and by 1852 the principal shelter held only forty girls.[20]

Louis Debelleyme (1828-1829) took over the prefecture in early 1828. On his proposal, the Municipal Council (which had earlier refused a similar request by Anglès) agreed to take over the funding of the dispensary and of the Brigade des moeurs. Basing their considerations on the fat budgets of the early years, they voted a year's credit of 75,000 francs. By means of a reorganization and by the elimination of certain jobs, the dispensary budget was soon trimmed down; but the public commitment in this era to the control of prostitution can be measured by the fact that for a number of years expenditures for the *police des moeurs* were roughly comparable to, and often exceeded, those of the services of surveillance, the policing of mendicity, and the Sûreté combined.[21]

The high budget led to a pressure for results; what the prefecture wanted to see was a decrease in the incidence of venereal disease. Consequently the figuring of disease statistics took on a special significance, for it was important to present the work of the dispensary in the best possible light. Statistical

[20] The Société de patronage des jeunes filles liberées et abandonnées was founded in 1838 to assist young girls arrested for prostitution, and it soon became the favored public charity. The society attempted to reconcile the girls with their families and place them in apprenticeship. In 1841 only twenty young girls were cared for, each of whom stayed in the institution for two years; by 1852 the number had grown to forty, and the yearly budget was 11,680 francs. PP DB 408: letter of 14 October 1841 from the minister of the interior to the prefect of police; letter of 24 November 1841 from the prefect of police to the minister of the interior; letter of 3 November 1852 from the prefect of police to the members of the Conseil général of the Seine.

[21] *Compte d'administration des dépenses de la Préfecture de police,* annual report (Paris: Lottin de Saint-Germain, 1818-1845). From 1837 on, the budgets of the Sûreté grew while those of the dispensary remained fairly steady at 33,000-35,000 francs per year.

clumsiness may have gotten in the way of even the best intentions. The reports of the Conseil général de salubrité, whether deliberately or not, misstated its finding for 1821, asserting that only one of every fifty-one prostitutes had contracted venereal disease. The "one in fifty-one" result was figured on 46,654, the total number of examinations conducted during the year, rather than on 2,913, the population of registered prostitutes. The total number of *malades* (458 discovered for the last five months of 1821 alone) was greater than the dispensary reports led people to believe. The Conseil acknowledged this error in calculation a year later, admitting that it would be "false security" to assume that only a small percentage of registered prostitutes was ill.[22]

An additional problem stemmed from the fact that the figures could not measure the constantly changing personnel in the ranks of the inscribed prostitutes. There was a hard core of regulars, but many of the prostitutes examined by the dispensary were of the periphery, either as part-time prostitutes or as so-called *insoumises,* who may or may not have been prostitutes, examined for the first time. The yearly total of 2,913 registered prostitutes given for 1821 was merely an average of the monthly totals, which showed considerable variation, ranging from a high in October of 3,065 to a low

[22] The admission was printed in *Le Moniteur universel,* 18 September 1822. Not surprisingly, the retraction contained an error; they apologized for stating that one in forty-nine was ill. They stated that about half of the roughly six hundred (so they claimed) women sent for treatment were sent twice in the course of the year. The dispensary examination figures can be found in the yearly budget prepared by the police for the minister of the interior (AN F⁷ 9305); in the daily prefectural bulletin, which was also destined for the minister of the interior (AN F⁷ 3875); and in V. de Moléon, ed., *Rapports généraux sur la salubrité publique,* 2 vols. (Paris: Bureau du recueil industriel, 1840-1841). These reports never seemed to agree with each other.

of 2,760 in February.[23] Even these numbers did not indicate
the full extent of the changes; every prostitute who disappeared for three months, from the dispensary and from the
arrest reports, was dropped from the rolls. The police might
"lose" 100 women a month; but if they found 100 new *insoumises,* their monthly total was unchanged.

The idea of absolute police control over an unchanging,
clearly delineated group of prostitutes was a false one, as critics
began to point out. A further challenge was made against the
efficacy of the examination. The number of prostitutes to
appear at the dispensary was "nearly the same each day of
the month," according to the report of the Conseil.[24] That
statement was flatly contradicted by the bulletins for the last
five months of 1821 (unfortunately the only months of that
year complete enough to use) which showed that prostitutes
tended to flood the dispensary at the end of each month. (See
Appendix A, Table 28.) In part this must have resulted from
a natural desire to put the examination off as long as possible,
but contemporaries throughout the nineteenth century credited prostitutes with a certain degree of cunning as well; minor
eruptions, or symptoms masked by rice powder, were more
likely to pass through undetected when the doctors were
rushed. Dr. Corlieu of the dispensary disputed allegations of
inefficiency, evoking at the same time a rather curious assembly line:

[23] Parent-Duchâtelet, *De la prostitution,* I:32. The inscription rate fluc-
tuated, but a time-series analysis showed an average annual increase (for
the period 1816-1848) of sixty-three prostitutes per year, which helps to
put these figures into perspective. The year 1827 had a total inscription of
2,472; 1828, 2,663; 1829, 2,843; 1830, 3,028; 1831, 3,261; and 1832, 3,558.
The increases were due primarily to the relatively lax enforcement of
Delavau compared with the more stringent enforcement of his successors.
The figures come from Parent-Duchâtelet, *De la prostitution,* I:32. For the
total inscription figures (1812-1854, 1872-1900) see Appendix A, Table 27.
[24] Moléon, *Rapports généraux,* I:251.

The girls wait in a large room under the surveillance of special agents, are called in groups of four to six into the examining room where there are two special *lits-fauteuils*. Since everything is arranged, not an instant is lost. The girl climbs onto the *fauteuil* in order to submit to the examination with a speculum, which has been prepared and washed by the woman charged with this duty; there are several speculums. It does not take long for a doctor accustomed to these exams to examine the cervix, then the urethra and the anal region. The girl climbs down from the chair and the doctor examines the mouth with the tongue depressor, then the hands, in order to ensure that she has neither scabies nor psoriasis. During this examination of the mouth and hands, another girl has already taken her place on the examining chair. In this way, there is not a minute unoccupied and the examination can be *complete* and *rapid*.[25]

There were several brief attempts during the Restoration to submit courtesans, the prostitutes who served the upper classes, to the examination. In 1817, the police had enlisted the services of one "M. V——" to help them find *femmes galantes*, who never walked the streets or appeared in the cabarets; ultimately they arrested about sixty women and forced them to submit to venereal examinations, a procedure that led to so many complaints from their protectors that the attempt was dropped.[26] On 8 September 1820 the prefecture tried again with the *petite dispensaire*, a special examination room for women (about seventy of them) who were thought to require special consideration. The policing of these women was put entirely in the hands of a well-mannered police agent,

[25] Auguste Corlieu, *La Prostitution à Paris* (Paris: J.-B. Baillière, 1887), pp. 56-57.
[26] Parent-Duchâtelet, *De la prostitution,* I:642.

whose duties consisted solely of social calls to remind them of their medical obligations; his assignment aroused so much jealousy among his fellow officers that the courtesan duty had to be divided up among all the inspectors, a procedure that soon destroyed the experiment. The ordinary morals agents, "not understanding the women they were seeking, used harshness and brutality; they made the women known for what they were in the law-abiding buildings in which they lived, which led to their immediate expulsion."[27] The *femmes galantes* began to resist all efforts to police them, and the *petite dispensaire* had to be suppressed in October 1822.[28]

Another attempt to invade the demimonde was made in 1827, when the dispensary set aside a special day and time for women who did not want to mix with the rest; this also had to be abandoned.[29] Early in 1830 Prefect Jean-Claude Mangin attempted to make a distinction once again, dividing all prostitutes into two classes and setting separate times for their examinations. The smaller, first class would consist of women who "dressed elegantly or even simply properly"; the second class would be composed, as Parent-Duchâtelet later summarized it, of "disgusting prostitutes, badly dressed and in *sabots*."[30] This experiment was unsuccessful, and courtesans remained unpoliced for the rest of the century, ironically depriving the upper classes entirely of what slight security the examination provided.

[27] Ibid., I:643-645.

[28] AN F⁷ 9305, *Dispensaire de salubrité: compte sommaire en deniers, de l'exercice 1822.* "Une salle particulière de visite, succursale du Dispensaire, avait été ouverte dans un quartier de l'établissement pour y recevoir les filles publiques dite femmes galantes qui paraissaient repugner à se présenter aux salles communes. Elle a été supprimée vers la fin de 1822 comme jugée peu utile."

[29] Lecour, *Paris et Londres,* p. 75.

[30] Parent-Duchâtelet, *De la prostitution,* I:647.

Names and Numbers

The inscription had the deceptive appearance of a harmless bureaucratic measure. Its date of origin is difficult to pinpoint; the published reports of the lieutenant-general of police Antoine Gabriel de Sartine (1759-1774), for example, listed the names, activities, and favored companions of certain prostitutes. After 1789 Pierre Manuel, a disgruntled former employee of the administration, stated that the police had habitually spied on certain women who had attracted the attention of members of the court.[31] The shifting of interest from the courtesan to the lowly *femme publique* occurred gradually. Prostitution expert Parent-Duchâtelet believed that the keeping of the list of prostitutes began, in a regular manner, in 1796; but this list betrayed traces of the voyeurism of the old reports, including not only the names and addresses of the women but also their favored lovers.[32] It was not until the establishment of the dispensary in 1810 that the inscription list became necessary, and consequently it became more fixed and orderly, including not only the woman's name, age, birthplace, address, and occupation but eventually (beginning in the later Restoration) her birth certificate as well.

The police liked to claim that the prostitute's inscription was usually voluntary. The procedures involved in the prostitution arrest suggest that inscription was not so much voluntary as inevitable, for women faced a legal Catch-22 the minute they were arrested. A woman could only hope to disprove the charge of prostitution in a court of law, but once

---

[31] L. Larchay, ed., *Journal des inspecteurs de M. de Sartine* (Paris: E. Dentu, 1863). No reference can be singled out here; but look for the reports on the *soupers,* the nightly assignations of notorious prostitutes. And see Pierre Manuel, *La Police de Paris dévoilée,* 2 vols. (Paris: J.-B. Garnery, Year II [1794]), I: 327-329.

[32] Parent-Duchâtelet, *De la prostitution,* I:225-226.

she was arrested for prostitution she was automatically exempted from the regular legal track. Such was the substance of the following official clarification:

> Article 484 of the Penal Code maintained in use all the old regulations on prostitution; it must from that be recognized that prostitution is prohibited, and that women recognized as prostitutes are subject to the consequences of this offense. The only formality that our laws require in this matter is the legal establishment of the offense; *but when the police officer has established the facts of the case by an official report* [procès-verbal] *of the offense, the women thus legally recognized as being prostitutes find themselves placed outside the law,* and subject to those of the measures still in force that the magistrates judge applicable, in the current state of our customs, to apply to them, and which are generally only expulsion from cities if they are not native-born, or to incarceration by administrative decision.[33]

Thus a woman might get arrested on the street for solicitation by means of an *oeillade* (a provocative look) or a *geste lascif.* Her arrest depended upon the judgment of the arresting officer and of the *commissaire* who took her statement. Once the report was written, the woman was established as a prostitute and was thus exempted from legal formalities; she had no chance to disprove the charge. Her hearing before the chief of the Bureau of Morals was a mere matter of procedure which resulted in an inevitable term in the Petite Force or, later, in Saint-Lazare prison. Her term was not likely to be

---

[33] AN F⁷ 9304, report, c. 1819 and 1822. I believe this to be the report on the history and legal basis of the dispensary referred to by Delavau in a letter, dated October 1822, to the minister of the interior. The report was drafted under Anglès and endorsed again by Delavau.

long, but the fact remained that, in the prostitution offense, guilt was sufficiently established by accusation.

The *arbitraire* stretched even further than this, also encompassing registered prostitutes accused of any crime whatsoever. Prefect Gisquet (1831-1836) created a rogue's gallery of "prostitutes of low degree" who were also known to be thieves. An artist made quick sketches of them during their dispensary examinations; these sketches were shown to men who had been robbed by prostitutes. Punishment for the prostitute in question was certain from the moment the identification was made, though the manner of punishment was left to the victim. "When they agreed to make a formal complaint," wrote Gisquet in his memoirs, "I had nothing more to do with the case except to ensure the proper execution of the legal forms." But action within the law meant that the men involved would have to undergo the public embarrassment of appearing as witnesses in court. Gisquet was sympathetic to such reluctance. "When a very natural repugnance caused them to prefer purely administrative action, I myself condemned the guilty ones [that is, the prostitutes identified from the sketches] to a year's imprisonment, the maximum penalty that, according to sanctified custom, prefects have the right to pronounce against prostitutes."[34]

The continuing practice of exempting prostitutes from the legal procedures was joined by greater efficiency, fed by greater manpower and by an increasingly effective routine. A small, single-minded bureaucracy developed, devoted solely to the apprehension of prostitutes. They had their own printed forms and model *procès-verbaux* which indicated some of the more common reasons for arrest:

The woman ＿＿ who appeared before us, arrested at (time) in (place); (in a flagrant act of prostitution) (solic-

[34] Gisquet, *Mémoires,* IV:352-353.

iting passers-by) (without authorization in a house of prostitution) (found in bed in a lodging house with an individual whom she does not know and who does not know her name) (having been surprised in intimacy with an individual in a room in a public establishment). She was asked her name, her address, her means of livelihood, and her previous record.

For the *insoumise,* the line of questioning was meant to lay the groundwork for her future registration:

Passing (place) at (hour), we noticed in the street a woman soliciting passers-by, either by words or by gestures (of such and such a nature). When questioned, she told us she was not inscribed and consequently we told her to accompany us to the Commissariat which she did (without resistance and without difficulty) (after first refusing with more or less determination to go). We searched her and found (the objects herein) (nothing suspicious) ... If there was active resistance constituting rebellion, the official report should reveal this. If the girl was found in a *maison de tolérance* or caught in bed in a *maison garnie* with a man unknown to her, if she was found in a *maison publique* giving herself up to debauchery with an unknown but in a place private enough to avoid the *délit* of outrage to public morality, the *procès-verbal* should mention it thus: having entered, in accordance with our duty, (the *maison de tolérance* situated ____) (the *maison garnie* kept by ____ rue ____) (the public establishment kept by the Sieur ____ rue ____) we were informed that there was a prostitute who gave herself up to prostitution. We entered a room which was locked but was opened for us by ____, and we found there (in such and such a position) a man and a girl who, when questioned, declared themselves to be unknown to each other. This girl having admitted that she is not inscribed, we have brought her before the *commissaire.* She was interrogated as follows: Your name? How long have you lived at your present address? Where do you work? How long have you lived in this part of the country? You are charged with (the complaint mentioned above). What have you to say? If the girl denies the charge, question her again, pointing out the unlikelihood of her response. Also question her separately on each point mentioned.[35]

After her apprehension by the gendarmerie or an agent, the prostitute was sent to the *commissaire* of the *quartier* in which she had been found. He filled out a document called the *interrogatoire et ordre d'envoi;* as he took her statement he was simultaneously filling out the form that would accompany her to the prefecture. ("Are you inscribed? What are your means of livelihood? At the moment of your arrest, what were you doing? Have you ever been arrested?") The prefecture and dispensary emitted a number of printed forms, including the "information taken at the moment of registration" (social rank, parents, children, state of health, length of time in Paris, profession, primary education); the registration form itself, which included a physical description of the woman; the form certifying the state of health of a *fille de maison,* and a similar one for a *fille isolée;* the form to verify the presence of a prostitute in the hospital; the registration form for the *maîtresse de maison,* as well as one to report any offense committed by her; and a *bulletin de recherche* for a prostitute who had not appeared at the dispensary.

The most decisive in its effects on the prostitute's life was the following formula, read to her after it was determined that she had engaged in behavior characteristic of prostitutes:

[35] PP DB 409, *Formules.*

Whereas the woman _____ is charged with prostitution without being registered, it is consequently in the interest of public health that her state of health be established and that she be submitted to the administrative regulations.[36]

The inscription list was not necessarily final, for a woman had the right to renounce prostitution and request that her name be expunged. Removal from the list was immediate in the cases of marriage, serious illness attested by the dispensary doctors, or the return (for non-Parisians) to one's native department. The expunging was delayed in other cases: when the prostitute declared her intention of living in concubinage with someone, when a respectable person accepted responsibility for her, or when she found a job. In these three cases the removal from the list could be held up for several months to a year. During this time, police kept her under a surveillance which included questioning her neighbors and employers about her habits and standard of living. During her probation she had to report regularly to the dispensary. Many prostitutes chose simply to stay out of the way of agents and avoid the dispensary; if they eluded capture for three months they were automatically dropped from the list and joined the ranks of the *disparues*.[37]

The police had an absolute certainty of their right to inscribe women above the age of twenty-one and to submit them to the dispensary examination. They were far less certain about the morality of inscribing legal minors, and the changes and refinements in their policy reflected this uneasiness. And yet the issue came up. Parent-Duchâtelet's study of the inscription

[36] Ibid.
[37] Parent-Duchâtelet, *De la prostitution,* I:388-395.

list from 1816 to 1832 revealed that half of the women had been inscribed before the age of twenty-one.[38] Indeed, Parent's list included a few examples of children inscribed at ages ranging from ten to fifteen years. Two police officials of the Second Empire, editors of an 1857 edition of Parent's study, felt obliged to set the record straight:

> Until 1828 *filles* were inscribed without information on their *état civil,* their family and their antecedents, and it happened that girls of ten to fifteen years, whose figure and precocious development suggested a more advanced age, and whom bordello madams coached or provided with false papers, were inscribed; but this fraud could not continue up until the period covered by the table in question, in that, on the very admission of Parent-Duchâtelet, birth certificates were required under M. Debelleyme (1828). Moreover, M. Mangin, who succeeded to M. Debelleyme (1829) proscribed in an absolute manner the inscription of *filles mineures,* and *had minors arrested for acts of prostitution conducted by the gendarmerie back to their families.*[39]

The explanation was not entirely successful. Before 1828, they argued, children had been inscribed because they had deceived the prefecture about their ages (which did not explain how Parent-Duchâtelet had found them out); after 1828, children had not been inscribed because the practice was "formally prohibited."

In fact, official policy was far more flexible than the police

[38] Ibid., I:364. From 1816 to 1832, 12,550 *filles* were inscribed, of whom 6,274 were younger than twenty-one.
[39] Note by Adolphe Trébuchet and Poirat-Duval, in Parent-Duchâtelet, *De la prostitution,* I:96.

[25]

wanted to admit. A regulation of 20 Vendémiaire Year XIII (12 October 1804) stated that "no girl who does not appear to be nubile will be registered."[40] This vague directive had been translated into a general practice of not registering girls before the age of sixteen; even this fragile barrier had been violated on occasion. An 1817 dispensary report to the prefecture revealed the officers' recent discovery of a young girl, "of a very frail constitution," who had been registered for eighteen months; she had not yet reached the age of sixteen. Subsequent investigation had found "a dozen girls of about fourteen years" on the dispensary lists; the officers had placed them in protective detention, and expressed their determination to tighten up the rules once again.[41] In the midst of such relapses and reinvigorations of the policy, sixteen remained the lowest acknowledged age of inscription until 1823, when Delavau became prefect. "Religious considerations" prompted him to raise the age of inscription to eighteen; on 20 March 1828, the dispensary committee decided to lower the age again to seventeen, and it soon was lowered back to sixteen.[42] Since fifteen was the age at which a woman could be legally married, sixteen remained the age boundary, unless special cases seemed to require special dispensations.[43]

The prefecture usually advanced two reasons for the inscription of minors: one was the danger to public health; the other was the possibility of moral reform. The danger to public health was obvious. A girl already involved in prostitution would simply continue to prostitute herself "clan-

[40] AN F⁷ 9305, letter of 15 May 1841 from the prefect of police to the minister of the interior. See also Lecour, *Paris et Londres,* pp. 163-165.

[41] AN F⁷ 9305, letter of 15 May 1841 from the prefect of police to the minister of the interior.

[42] Ibid. and Lecour, *Paris et Londres,* pp. 163-165.

[43] Note by Trébuchet and Poirat-Duval, in Parent-Duchâtelet, *De la prostitution,* I:380.

destinely," without registration, and thus without benefit of regular medical examinations. In addition, her clandestinity would prevent the prefecture from having any future influence on her conduct. F. F. A. Béraud, an officer in the Bureau of Morals during part of the Restoration, suggested that all applicants, no matter what their age or condition, be inscribed upon request; the prefecture would then be able to contact them if it were decided that they could benefit from the efforts of charitable societies.[44] Fathers also had the right to request that their daughters be held in Saint-Lazare prison for a time, in the hope that they might be reformed.

In practice, the prefecture divided minors into two categories: those whose parents lived in Paris and those whose parents did not. Girls in the former category were not registered until the parents had formally declared their intention to do nothing more for them.[45] Even when the parents attempted to prevent the inscription of a daughter, the prefecture might decide to proceed with her registration anyway, if there were indications of a lack of family supervision: "Two girls of fifteen, both arrested eight or ten times, were always reclaimed by their relatives. They did not inscribe one of them because she slept under the paternal roof; the other was inscribed because she lived in a *garni* [lodging house]."[46]

Young women whose families lived outside Paris, considered likely candidates for deportation, were placed in detention until the prefecture contacted their parents, usually through the local mayor. The prefecture's efforts were serious; the case of a young Englishwoman was referred to her government, an inquiry which elicited a bored and somewhat as-

[44] F. F. A. Béraud, *Les Filles publiques de Paris, et la police qui les régit,* 2 vols. (Paris: Desforges, 1839), II:168-169.
[45] AN F⁷ 9305, letter of 15 May 1841 from the prefect of police to the minister of the interior.
[46] Parent-Duchâtelet, *De la prostitution,* I:375.

tonished response from the British ambassador to France.[47] If the parents wanted them back, they were given a mendicity passport with aid and itinerary, an official identity paper that guaranteed them food and lodging in the places named on their route back to their homes. (Occasionally the prefecture was able to arrange a half-price fare in the public coaches.) Bordello madams who used "fraudulent maneuvers" to attract young girls to Paris—through the promise of another kind of job, usually domestic service—had to send them back immediately to their families, "at their own expense," and regardless of criminal charges that might be pending.[48]

The prefecture had a number of persuasive reasons for inscribing minors, and in some cases there was clear evidence that the authorities attempted to act in a humanitarian way. The one compelling reason for not registering minors, however, was that it appeared to be in violation of one of the few laws that applied to prostitution. The problem lay in the fact that many inscribed minors found their way into *maisons de tolérance,* with the madam incongruously placed in the role of guardian; children in a state of vagabondage, as young prostitutes were considered to be, could not be left to wander the streets.

This left madams in apparent violation of Article 334 of the Penal Code, which forbade "the habitual excitation of minors to debauchery." But madams had nothing to fear from

[47] The case concerned Mathilda Smith, nineteen years old, who was brought to the prefecture to be inscribed by her madam. Smith declared herself to be an orphan who had fled to Paris to escape her former lover. Neither her brother, a soldier, nor her uncle, a jeweler with a large family, was able to help her. "Je ne pense pas avoir assez d'autorité," the British ambassador wrote, "pour pouvoir intervenir utilement dans l'affaire dont il s'agit," and so she was inscribed. AN F⁷ 9305, correspondence of 27 June 1837 and 11 August 1837 between the minister of the interior and the British ambassador to France.

[48] AN F⁷ 9305, letter of 15 May 1841 from the prefect of police to the minister of the interior.

the law. "Definitively, Article 334 of the Penal Code can be applied to *maîtresses de maisons de tolérance* who keep minor girls," wrote Lecour, head of the Bureau of Morals later in the century, "but practical necessities and the important considerations attaching to the repression of prostitution discourage legal pursuits in these cases . . . unless there are special incidents involving the corruption of minors." Article 334 was just as likely to be invoked for the protection of boys; occasionally the courts witnessed a solemn condemnation of bordello madams who had violated the purity of young customers.[49]

Later in the century, some critics of the regime would assert that the prefecture itself was in violation of Article 334, aiding in the corruption of minors by the very fact of inscription. This was, indeed, the position taken by Prefect Mangin, who decided that prostitutes would no longer be registered before the age of twenty-one. By taking this position, he caused a serious rift between the prefecture and the Special Commission of the Dispensary. Such a split might have had serious consequences for the future of the Bureau of Morals—except for the date. The disagreement between Mangin and the commission did not come into the open until the session of 24 June 1830. After Mangin (and the dynasty) fell, the prefecture reverted to its old practice of inscription at the age of sixteen, regarded, according to Parent-Duchâtelet, as the "legal" age at which this could be done.[50]

It is impossible to know how many cases of false arrest and

---

[49] Lecour, *Paris et Londres,* pp. 163-165. One example of the protection of minor boys: "Il est arrivé qu'une maîtresse de maison a été expulsée du département, par application de la loi du 9 juillet 1852, pour avoir recélé un mineur et lui avoir fait dépenser en orgies de tous genres une somme importante qu'il avait dérobée à son patron, lequel n'a pas voulu porter plainte en justice." Note by Trébuchet and Poirat-Duval, in Parent-Duchâtelet, *De la prostitution,* II:266.

[50] AN F⁷ 9305, letter of 15 May 1841 from the prefect of police to the minister of the interior; Parent-Duchâtelet, *De la prostitution,* I:368.

unjustified inscription occurred, for minors as well as for adults, for none had to stand the test of the judiciary. Almost from the beginning of the regulatory system, the police had warned of the distinctions to be made between women who were prostitutes and women who were merely guilty of moral lapses; it seems likely that this distinction was often ignored.[51] What was certain, however, was that the inscription process in the early nineteenth century provided few safeguards for women, a fact made clear by the two general guides to prostitution arrest and inscription during the nineteenth century. The first was the *instruction réglementaire* of 16 November 1843, which codified the existing procedure. It was replaced with the *règlement* of October 1878, probably issued to blunt criticism from the Municipal Council investigation which was to begin three months later.

The 1843 regulation urged the police to act with "great circumspection" in regard to clandestine prostitutes but was comfortably vague about the circumstances in which an arrest of an *insoumise* could take place. Women encountered on the street had to be followed into a house of prostitution, or into the home of a prostitute, before the arrest could be made. Officers could not arrest a woman in a notorious red-light district unless they caught her in the act of soliciting. She could be arrested if she were caught leaving a house of prostitution or if she were found walking with known prostitutes. If none of these situations occurred, she could be arrested after a "prolonged surveillance" had convinced the agents that her behavior was suspicious. Arrest because of a denunciation was also possible. If she lived in a lodging house "with

[51] "On concevra facilement qu'il ne lui était pas permis de franchir, quelque faiblement indiquée qu'elle fût la plupart du temps, la ligne de démarcation qui existe entre la dissolution et la prostitution publique." *Compte d'administration des dépenses de la Préfecture de police* (1819), p. xxx. See also PP DB 407, *instruction réglementaire* of 16 November 1843.

a bad reputation" and had been denounced as a clandestine prostitute (or even if someone had denounced her as a carrier of venereal disease), the officers were to question her neighbors. All *insoumises* were to be taken directly to the *commissaire,* who would interrogate them in the manner illustrated by the model *procès-verbaux.*[52]

In contrast, the 1878 rules "absolutely forbade" the use of the model *procès-verbaux* in the case of the *insoumise,* and they were in most regards more scrupulous about the circumstances in which women were taken. The rules applicable to a woman found in a notorious red-light district repeated, word for word, those of the 1843 regulation; this allowed for her arrest on the word of a man who claimed she had been soliciting him, but in no other case was denunciation considered sufficient grounds. The arrest of a woman on the street could take place only "after the establishment of precise and multiple facts of solicitation," a directive that still left unclear the nature of the offense.

The innovation of this regulation lay in its establishment of a semblance of due process in the matter of inscription. The chief of the Bureau of Morals now had the duty, after examining the evidence, to decide if the woman should be subjected to the physical examination; before this, the examination had been done automatically. Moreover, if the woman refused to sign the inscription list, or if she were a minor, she would be granted a hearing before a board composed of the prefect (or his delegate), the chief of the first division (the administrative superior of the chief of the Bureau of Morals), and the *commissaire* in charge of interrogations. Both she and the arresting officers would be heard.[53]

[52] PP DB 407, *instruction réglementaire* of 16 November 1843.

[53] BN [Bibliothèque nationale] 8° Z. Le Senne 14255, *règlement* of October 1878.

This supposed protection for the *insoumise* was satisfactory
to no one. The "multiple acts of solicitation" necessary for
an arrest called for surveillance and required manpower, which
the police did not like to expend in this way. The woman's
attempt to dispute the testimony of an arresting officer carried
no more weight than it ever had. Nevertheless there was a
perceptible difference between the two codes. The 1878 regulation, in contrast to the earlier one, revealed a clear emphasis
on "personalizing" the arrest; the intention in 1843 was to
make it more routine. The differences were reflective of the
different contexts in which each regulation was designed to
operate. The police in 1878 had (rather grudgingly) admitted
the need to be sensitive to civil liberties; the police in 1843,
who firmly believed that prostitutes were "outside the law,"
were concerned primarily with making sure that not a single
guilty prostitute escaped—even if one hundred innocents had
to suffer.

The Lodging House and the Bordello

The most troublesome question for the prefecture throughout
the century was the location of prostitution. This was a problem largely because the police seemed determined to thwart
debauchery in the very places to which it most naturally
gravitated. One of the earliest regulations on the subject, in
1815, prohibited tavernkeepers from maintaining *cabinets noirs*
in their back rooms. If policemen discovered such profitable
side enterprises, they were to "seize the moment when the
cabinets were occupied by *personnes de mauvaise vie*" so they
could bring them to justice as well.[54] This regulation, based

[54] Circular of the director general of police, 11 February 1815, repeated
as an instruction of the prefect of police on 1 August 1819, in Elouin,
A. Trébuchet, and E. Labat, *Nouveau dictionnaire de police,* 2 vols. (Paris:
Béchet Jeune, 1835), I:283-284.

on a police ordinance of 8 October 1780, was finally given teeth by Louis Napoleon's decree of 29 December 1851. The prefect, according to this new regulation, had the power to grant licenses, without which taverns could not open, and could revoke the licenses at will. Louis Napoleon issued the decree because of his fear of political gatherings, but the Bureau of Morals was able to turn this power to its own purpose. The threat of revocation of license was far more serious than the 100-franc fine prescribed by the old 1780 ordinance.[55]

In addition to the back rooms of public houses, prostitution also naturally gravitated to the lodging house. The so-called *maison garnie,* or *hôtel garni,* was home for much of the population of Paris. Furnished rooms, rented for a short term, were occupied by migrant workers, by the ubiquitous *malfaiteurs,* by those too poor to afford something more permanent—and by prostitutes, who often fit all of these categories. A bureau within the prefecture had the responsibility for the supervision of *garnis,* as did each *commissaire,* and a weekly bulletin kept track of the movement of population within.[56]

The basis of lodging-house regulation was the pre-Revolution ordinance of 6 November 1778. By its terms, proprietors were to keep a register of all their tenants, including

[55] The decree stated, in part, that "ces établissements sont devenus, en grand nombre, des lieux de réunion et d'affiliation pour les sociétés secrètes, et ont favorisé d'une manière déplorable les progrès des mauvaises passions." Parent-Duchâtelet, *De la prostitution,* I:518.

[56] The surveillance of *hôtels garnis* was the duty of the First Bureau of the Second Division, which was charged also with the following responsibilities: "les assassinats, vols et escroqueries; la fabrication des fausses monnaies ou des faux en écriture; la recherche des évadés; la surveillance des hôtels garnis et des maisons de prêts, la répression du vagabondage et de la mendicité." Jean Tulard, *Paris et son administration* (Paris: Commission des travaux historiques, 1976), p. 134. In the police mind, at least, there seemed to be a close connection between *garnis* and crime.

birthplace, address, profession, and the dates of each arrival and departure. Lodging-house keepers were apparently remiss in this matter, for there were frequent exhortations from the prefecture to maintain these registers. Even the registration book was scarcely sufficient, "for hotel keepers... inscribe prostitutes on their registers as *ouvrières* [workers], according to the declaration they make, of any profession whatever." The prefect Gisquet spoke of the "facility with which men, the majority of them homeless and jobless, spend the night with prostitutes in lodging houses without appearing on the registers."[57] The lodging house may have seemed a natural place for such assignations, but the law was clear. Article 4 of the 1778 ordinance enjoined lodging-house keepers "to allow inside no vagrants or debauched women engaged in prostitution, to put men and women in separate rooms, and to rent to no so-called married couples unless they can show proof of their marriage."[58]

This provision, all three clauses of it, was widely violated by proprietors and tenants alike. But it was not allowed to fall into disuse; rather, it was subject to massive periodic enforcement. The *garni* keepers could be exhorted constantly; that did not alter the fact that renting to prostitutes was profitable because of the high turnover and the possibility of

[57] All the circulars before 1882 can be found in the *Recueil officiel des circulaires émanées de la Préfecture de police*, 2 vols. (Paris: Imprimerie Chaix, 1882). The archives of the Prefecture of Police also have copies in DB 407-410. The discovery that prostitutes lied is in the circular of 25 July 1818, *Recueil des circulaires*, I:69; Gisquet's lament is in the circular of 25 August 1832, *Recueil des circulaires*, I:219.

[58] Ordinance of 6 November 1778, in François-André Isambert, *Recueil général des anciennes lois françaises, depuis l'an 420 jusqu'à la Revolution de 1789*, 29 vols. (Paris: Belin-Leprieur, 1821-1833), XXV:448-450.

renting the same room several times in an evening.[59] The prefecture's solution to the violation of lodging-house rules was what was delicately termed the *visite de nuit,* or *exploration nocturne.* Late in the nineteenth century a journalist was allowed to accompany a Paris *commissaire* on one of these midnight raids. The strong impression made on him by this event is reflected in the vividness of his account:

> A woman—milliner, said the hotel register—unemployed and engaging in clandestine prostitution, claimed the inspectors' reports. She made some difficulties about opening. There was a man with her. She affected indignation and so did he. They spoke of abuse of power, of violation of domicile, of outraged honor.... The *commissaire* listened patiently to this torrent of words. Then without answering them, he said curtly:
>
> "Get up and get dressed."
>
> "Are you going to let him take me away like this?" cried the woman in an explosion of sobs.
>
> "Sir, this woman is my mistress; I answer for her!"...said the man with an air of perfect dignity.
>
> "Ah! Very well, sir, that is different. Your name, profession, address?"
>
> "What for?"
>
> "Well! If you are answering for her, we must know with whom we are dealing, also if your moral situation will allow us to take your word...when this little in-

[59] The National Guard was called one night at 11:30 by a lodging-house keeper; they arrested a prostitute, Augustine Veronique Renoul, "qui fesait de bruit dans la maison, et menaçait de casser les vitres croyant par ce moyen de se soustraire au payement de la location d'une chambre qu'elle avait occupée, alleguant qu'elle n'avait pas passé la nuit entière, et qu'elle ne devait, par conséquent, rien, quoiqu'ayant couché dans le lit de la chambre." It was duly noted that she had a soldier for company. AN F^7 4181, report of 27-28 October 1821.

vestigation is finished, we will have only to apologize to you for the inconvenience we have caused."

"B-b-but, sir," he stuttered.

"I thought so! Do you have any papers on you, to prove your identity? That would simplify matters."

"It is just that I do not want anyone to know. . . ."

"Well then, be quiet and let us do our job."

The man got back in bed and the girl had to get dressed and leave. The same scene, or nearly, was renewed in ten other rooms. . . . It was a strange sight, at the same time seductive and repulsive, to see these girls, some of whom were magnificent creatures, get out of bed clad only in nightgowns and get dressed in the sight of a dozen men, in these miserable slums, by the light of three candles.[60]

Such a visit was legal. *Commissaires* were allowed to enter lodging houses between sunrise and 11:00 p.m. without a warrant; nighttime raids required a *mandat* obtained on the basis of prior surveillance or information.[61] As the reporter indicated, there was little regard for the privacy or dignity of the arrested woman, though few women challenged this. One of the few reported complaints of brutality was brought by Victoire Choublis, a domestic servant, who stated that she had been surprised in bed by a group of officers who had searched her and then forced her to dress in front of them. The prefect, after investigating the complaint—that is, he asked the arresting officer—concluded that her "lying report"

[60] Georges Grisson, *Paris horrible et Paris original* (Paris: E. Dentu, 1882), pp. 319-322.

[61] Elouin, Trébuchet, and Labat, *Nouveau dictionnaire,* I:71-72. See also the *instruction réglementaire* of 16 November 1843 and the *règlement* of October 1878.

had been motivated by vengeance, and nothing further was done.[62]

The natural desire of lodgers to remove themselves from the threat of sudden police intrusion took several forms. One was the development of what were referred to as "clandestine" *garnis*. These furnished rooms, whose landlords had falsely declared them to be unfurnished rooms that had been furnished by the tenants (and were thus permanent domiciles, not temporary shelters), were mentioned in an 1824 circular ordering the *commissaires* to stamp them out.[63] The tenant could also deal with the situation by buying his own furniture and renting an apartment on a long-term basis. An apartment furnished by the tenant was a home, a permanent domicile, and was thus not subject to sudden police intrusion. Prosti-

[62] Choublis' situation was described in this way:

La fille Choublis était, . . . soupçonnée du vol d'une montre en or, commis quelques jours avant, sans aucune effraction, dans la chambre à coucher de la Dame Turbout, tenant maison garnie rue Saint-Honoré n° 329, et les soupçons se dirigeaient sur elle, parce que, logeant dans cette maison garnie et étant sans place depuis longtems, elle était entrée deux fois, le jour du vol, dans la chambre à la cheminée de laquelle la montre était suspendue, et parce qu'elle paraissait avoir plus d'argent que sa position ne le permettait.

The *commissaire*'s version of Choublis' arrest was different, but even his account gave her some grounds for complaint:

Je me suis transporté le 20 7ᵇʳᵉ à 6 heures du matin chez la demoiselle Choublis, . . . arrivé à la porte de sa chambre, je frappai & me nommai. La demoiselle Choublis ouvrit après 10 minutes. Elle avait passé une robe & mis des bas. Je lui donnai connaissance du mandat. Après la perquisition dans la Chambre je lui demandai si elle n'avait rien sur elle. Elle me répondit que non, qu'elle n'avait d'autre argent que le 25 francs renfermés dans une bourse sur sa commode. Sachent qu'elle ne disait pas la vérité, je lui annonçai qu'on allait la fouiller. L'Inspecteur porta la main sur ses seins & sentit une ceinture qu'elle ôta elle-même, en disant: *On veut donc me voler mon argent.* Je la prévins qu'elle devait nous suivre. Je sortis de sa chambre avec les inspecteurs, pour lui laisser la liberté de s'habiller. Cela fait, elle nous suivit.

[63] Circular of 10 July 1824, *Recueil des circulaires,* I:109.

tutes were sometimes victimized in their desire to elevate themselves; one prostitute who rented a room from a tavernkeeper made an agreement with him to purchase some furniture on an installment plan. She paid 5 francs a day for three months, missed one day and returned home, according to the *commissaire*'s report, to find "a buyer of used furniture holding a bill of sale for her property."[64]

The great expense involved in reaching this level of stable and inviolable tenancy proved a great obstacle for most would-be tenants; a further complication for prostitutes was added by the fact that the ordinance of 1778 decreed that proprietors and landlords, as well as lodging-house keepers, were forbidden to rent to known *filles*. Like the lodging-house keepers, landlords were subject to sporadic prosecution. A decision by the Cour de cassation closed the loophole of subletting by upholding the conviction of a man who had taken a prostitute's apartment in his own name. One prostitute who had failed to declare herself as such to the landlord was expelled from her apartment on the complaint of her neighbors, as was another woman, nominally an embroiderer, whose life style made her suspect; both these expulsions stood up in court.[65]

These two instances were unrepresentative, for cases only made it to court when the expelled prostitute was willing to expose herself to the notoriety of a lawsuit. The frequency with which prostitutes were evicted can perhaps be better gauged by the existence of an 1838 police circular which described the procedure to be followed by landlords who

---

[64] PP DB 408, complaint of 8 July 1845. The complaint was filed by Victoire Pierrette Bourgay, a twenty-two-year-old native of Paris. Her rent was 600 francs a year, and her furniture had been bought for 500 francs down and 5 francs a day.

[65] PP DB 408, *arrêts* of 11 and 18 February 1846, Cour de cassation; PP DB 408, report of March 1854.

wished to rid themselves of prostitutes; the terms of the circular suggested that such evictions were not uncommon.[66] To be sure, prostitutes were not the best neighbors. Two fellow tenants of a certain Denoyelle complained of the "constant comings and goings of men and women . . . of carriages parked for prolonged periods of time in front of the door, of mysterious receptions at the doorsill of the apartment, soon followed by significant noises which reveal the perpetual party inside." The two tenants, who had lived in "perfect tranquility" until she came, were successful in their suit against her.[67]

The one place prostitutes could be certain of a welcome was in a tolerated house. The *maison de tolérance* was not necessarily a brothel; rather, it was simply a place to which the police granted dispensation from the 1778 regulation, tolerating the existence of prostitution there so long as the holder of the tolerance obeyed certain rules. The regulations governing the tolerance remained essentially the same throughout the nineteenth century. The house could not be established too near a church, school, or public building. It had to be shuttered and equipped with curtains or glazed windows. Each madam had to make certain that all her inmates—that is, the women who actually lived in the bordello—were inscribed with the police; she had twenty-four hours to report each new arrival and departure to the prefecture. Each madam had to have all her women—again, only those actually domiciled there—present during the weekly medical examination, a house call made by a dispensary doc-

[66] Circular of 14 June 1838, *Recueil des circulaires*, I:318.

[67] *Gazette des tribunaux*, 6 August 1884. The eviction of this particular prostitute, who had already been evicted twice before, followed a court decision abrogating that part of the 1778 ordinance which denied proprietors the right to rent to prostitutes. Denoyelle was evicted not because she was a prostitute but because the terms of her lease did not allow her to establish a business in her home.

tor. She could admit neither minors of the male sex nor young men wearing the uniform of one of the Grandes Ecoles. (This regulation was enforced, occasionally, as one madam discovered in 1845.) Each woman had to have her own bed, a regulation motivated not by hygiene but by the fear of lesbianism.[68]

In addition to these special rules, tolerances had to follow the rules generally applied to *garnis,* particularly in the keeping of the *livres de police.* Each person who slept there, "even for a single night," had to be inscribed on the register; this allowed the police to keep track of *isolées* who brought their customers to tolerances, as well as the customers themselves.[69] Even more important was the fact that the police were allowed to enter tolerances at any time and with no legal formalities; a 1791 law gave the police the right to enter at all times "places notoriously given over to debauchery."[70] The instant accessibility was the most valuable quality of the tolerance, providing the police, or so they thought, with immediate entry into the activities of the lower classes; madams cooperated or risked losing their special dispensation. And the police, finally, preferred on the whole to have a *maîtresse* rather than a *maître de maison,* preferring a madam who had some experience as a prostitute rather than a man who would likely be involved in more serious criminal activities. Prostitution was the only business that the authorities tried to leave in the control of women.

---

[68] The *tolérance* rules were reported in a number of places, including the 1843 instruction and the 1878 *règlement.* The delinquent madam was reported in the *Gazette des tribunaux,* 8 June 1845. She was sentenced to two years, the prostitutes to fifteen months and thirteen months, for receiving teenagers; this came under Article 334 of the Penal Code, contributing to the delinquency of a minor. The "one bed, one prostitute" rule was established in 1824, according to Parent-Duchâtelet, *De la prostitution,* I:167.

[69] Elouin, Trébuchet, and Labat, *Nouveau dictionnaire,* II:410-411; note the ordinance of 15 June 1832.

[70] The Law of 22 July 1791, ibid.

The three prefects who dominated the 1820s, Delavau, De-belleyme, and Mangin, were jointly responsible for the century's one major attempt to bring all prostitution into tolerated areas which could be easily kept under surveillance by the police. This policy was, at least at first, no more than a simple determination to enforce all regulations to the letter, since prostitution was already theoretically confined to *maisons de tolérance*. Delavau began this tougher policy in June 1823 with a statement that served in many ways as a kind of justification of the *maison de tolérance* for the rest of the century. The statement was directed to the *commissaires,* who had been discouraging the applications of those who wanted to establish tolerances in their *quartiers* and thus naturally showing "the repugnance that they feel in allowing these refuges of corruption and libertinage in the neighborhoods." Prostitution, however, was ineradicable; and given that, it was obvious that the least of all evils was to confine it to areas that could be carefully watched. "The police," the circular stated, "would consider itself to have done a great deal in favor of morality and public order, if it succeeded in enclosing prostitution in tolerated houses, in which its action could be constant and uniform, and could not escape surveillance."[71]

A serious attempt to enclose prostitution entirely within the tolerance was not to be made until the late 1820s. In 1823, Delavau was primarily interested in discovering what the current situation was, and so he asked all *commissaires* to evaluate their neighborhoods and draw up three lists. One list would contain the names of lodging houses which catered to prostitutes as well as to travelers (a "scandalous mélange," and a practice he wanted to end); a second would list all lodging houses which received only prostitutes, in effect undeclared houses of prostitution, which were possible candi-

[71] Circular of 14 June 1823, *Recueil des circulaires,* I:103-105.

dates for a tolerance; and the third would list all tolerated houses.[72]

Delavau's efforts at first were directed almost entirely toward the establishment of more *maisons de tolérance*. While the total number of houses of prostitution increased, however, the average number of inmates per house decreased, falling to an average, from 1822 to 1825, of a little over one prostitute per house. The *maisons de tolérance* were becoming *maisons de passe,* or lodging houses that catered to the prostitution trade.[73] Though there are no figures available to determine how many lodging houses changed their designation officially to houses of prostitution, the advantages to such a move were obvious. A lodging-house keeper was fined 200 francs for allowing prostitutes to use his establishment; the keeper of a house of prostitution was freed from the fear of such a fine, and her (or his) responsibilities were minimal when only one or two prostitutes lived there.

The situation began to change under the energetic prefect Debelleyme. He had been active in suppressing mendicity, attempting to clear the streets of beggars by large-scale arrests. His street-cleaning mentality extended to prostitution as well, for he wanted above all to make it less conspicuous. A circular of 27 April 1829 prohibited prostitutes from "walking together, standing around in the streets, forming groups, taking up the sidewalks, soliciting passers-by, and provoking scandals by their free discourse and indecent dress."[74]

Prefect Mangin (1829-1830), who served during the last

[72] Ibid.

[73] AN F⁷ 3838, report of 9 February 1816. The report stated that too many authorizations to operate *garnis* were being issued by the police, and "ces permissions sont presque toutes accordées à des femmes qui esperent trouver, par là, des occasions de se prostituer en secret."

[74] Circular of 27 April 1829, *Recueil des circulaires,* I:163-164. Debelleyme's mendicity regulations were discussed in M. Bertin, *Biographie de M. De Belleyme* (Paris: Durand, 1863), pp. 26-29.

days of the Restoration government, decided to end the possibility of scandal once and for all, issuing on 14 April 1830 the century's most radical pronouncement on the subject of prostitution. Mangin had two apparent purposes. One was to avoid disorder by removing all evidence of prostitution from the sight of the public. All soliciting on the streets was absolutely prohibited, and prostitutes were forbidden to appear on the boulevards, thoroughfares, or in public gardens "on any pretext," a rule that made them virtual prisoners. Mangin's second purpose was the creation of intermediaries between the police and the people; this had been foreseen in Delavau's 1823 regulation, in which he had expressed his desire to "concentrate the evil in houses known [to the police] and directed by women who are responsible for the conduct of the girls they receive in their establishments." Consequently, bordellos were to be given a monopoly on the business of prostitution. Madams were for the first time given the right to serve liquor in their establishments, a concession designed to enable them to compete more successfully with *cabinets noirs*. The ordinance fell most heavily on the independent prostitute. She could not make her way to the tolerance until 7:00 p.m., she could not change houses during a single night, and she had to be back in her own room by 11:00 p.m. Her working hours were thus severely curtailed, and she was at the mercy of whatever price the madam wished to exact.[75]

The new ordinance was strict, although it made few genuine innovations. Theoretically, at least, prostitution had always been restricted to special tolerated areas and to the evening hours. The clause that denied prostitutes access, at any time, to certain public places (foreshadowed in Debelleyme's 1829 circular) represented a decided change, for Delavau had earlier stated unequivocally that prostitutes could

[75] PP DB 407, ordinance of 14 April 1830.

not be arrested for appearing anywhere in public, so long as they did not solicit.[76] Yet this change, too, was more apparent than real. In practice the subjective conditions of the prostitution arrest had made women always vulnerable anywhere, particularly when the police had decided to clean up a particular area. Mangin's ordinance was largely symbolic, reflective more of a change in attitude and consequently in enforcement practices rather than of a real change in the system. It served as a signal to the officers that more arrests would be acceptable, or, as one satirical pamphlet said to the prefect, "When you say 'Kill!' your agents say 'Destroy!'"[77]

Mangin's tenure in office was to be shorter than he anticipated, and his enforcement policy barely made itself felt; but as a symbolic gesture the ordinance attracted much attention from the penny pamphleteers in the Palais Royal. Some of the pamphlets were openly frivolous; others, though frivolous in style, were quite serious in their criticism, cloaking in satire what would later be said openly and in all earnestness later in the century. One pamphlet shrewdly saw in the new regulation a continuation of the increasingly restrictive policies of the prefect Debelleyme; a so-called response to other petitions criticized, by pretending to defend, the encroaching authority of the prefect, slyly mocking Debelleyme's "arsenal of ordinances" for every imaginable contingency, as well as

[76] AN F⁷ 9304, letter of 7 September 1822 from the prefect of police to the minister of the interior: "On se plaint que les filles publiques se permettent de paraître dans les rues et promenades même en plein jour. Aucun règlement n'a jamais pu être fait pour les en empêcher; tout ce qui peut faire la police, c'est d'empêcher qu'en plein jour, les filles publiques provoquent les passans et les gens honnêtes."

[77] *Pétition des filles publiques de Paris à M. le Préfet de police* (Paris: chez les libraires du Palais Royal, 1830), p. 4.

Mangin's attempts to control prostitution by restricting it:

> Yes, there will be houses of prostitution, but see how easy it will be to oversee them. The number of their priestesses will be regulated, and if one of them is missing from the fold during a police invasion, one will immediately be able to *write a report, arrest her,* and *immure her,* unless there is a receipt from a hospital, or a notice of imprisonment from the Depot or the Force, attesting the presence of the missing one. Thus, you see that these demoiselles can still, in a strict sense, take the air, though only on the way to the prison and the hospital.[78]

The *maison close* policy encountered immediate resistance, not only from the public (at least as represented by the pamphleteers) but also from certain officials within the police force. Opinions differed about both the practicality and the morality of the *maison close,* and minor adjustments were made throughout the 1830s and early 1840s. Probably the most extreme decision—more radical, in its way, than Mangin's 1830 pronouncement—was the decision by Prefect Gabriel Delessert (1836-1848) in 1842 to begin restricting the places where prostitutes were allowed to live. The circular of 8 August 1842 prohibited prostitutes from sharing their lodgings with anyone else, either male or female, and declared that no more than one *isolée* could live in any building. The situation was further complicated by a restriction that forbade them to live in certain areas including establishments—mostly lodgings—which were "specially prohibited." The point of the circular was clearly stated: "This measure cannot help

[78] *Le Tocsin de ces demoiselles, ou mémoire à consulter, addressé à tous les barreaux de France* (Paris: chez les marchands de nouveautés, 1830), p. 5; *Réponse de M. Engin, aux pétitions des filles publiques* (Paris: chez les marchands de nouveautés, 1830), pp. 8-9.

but bring a notable change in the current state of prostitution, forcing prostitutes to re-enter the tolerances they have been leaving for some time and isolating from each other those able to have a private domicile."[79] This decision was soon modified by a further decision of 5 July 1843, which authorized *filles publiques* who, "because of their age or their infirmities, cannot place themselves in tolerances," to live in *garnis*. This decision, Delessert later explained, had no purpose except to ensure women in this category of a place to live; it did not amount to an authorization to practice their trade in their homes, and women found with men through *visites de nuit* would be arrested.[80]

But, in what seemed to be standard procedure for the prefecture, the various clarifications worked at cross-purposes with each other, each one issued in the heat of a particular problem with little regard for already existing policies. Despite further discussions of the rights of prostitutes to live in places other than *maisons de tolérance,* the *maison close* policy was abandoned as a goal—it had never come close to working in practice—in a circular of 26 December 1842. This circular was a discussion of the madam's right to rent *chambres de passe* to women outside her bordello:

It has been expressly recommended to these *maîtresses de maison* to receive only the women they know, and who are provided with their card, and to watch them in such

[79] Circular of 8 August 1842, *Recueil des circulaires,* I:419. As Lecour has pointed out, the Mangin regulation was effectively abrogated by a decree of 7 September 1830 that prohibited prostitutes from appearing in public "de manière à s'y faire remarquer" outside the hours between dusk and 11:00 p.m. Lecour, *Paris et Londres,* p. 112.

[80] PP DB407, *instruction réglementaire* of 16 November 1843 and circular of 5 July 1843.

a manner as to ensure, before their departure, that they have not stolen anything from the men they brought there.

But this was only a recommendation; madams were also given explicit permission to rent to unregistered prostitutes, so long as they later turned them in to the police.

It has been thus enjoined to the *maîtresses de maison* only to receive those whose physical appearance suggests that they have reached at least their seventeenth year, and to take sufficient information about them to allow the administration to find them again.[81]

For all practical purposes, this ended the period of experimentation in the control of prostitution. From this point on, the problem of clandestinity—the search for unregistered women—would outweigh all other concerns, including the concern for public decency. Nevertheless, the police continued to make attempts, as they expressed it, to put some order into the disorder.

The relation of the house to the neighborhood—that is, the degree to which it became intrusive—underwent a few changes over the years, in large part due to regulations from the prefecture. One of the more puzzling manipulations of the police involved the *marcheuse*. Until 1829, madams were allowed to station two prostitutes outside to attract customers. A circular of 27 April 1829 ended this practice, on the grounds that the prostitutes were often surrounded by crowds of young men who caused scandalous scenes. Madams were then allowed to substitute an elderly domestic servant on the doorstep to lure men inside. The prefect Delessert later saw fit to

[81] Circular of 26 December 1842, *Recueil des circulaires,* I:414-415.

modify this rule in a circular of 20 September 1842. Madams who had five or fewer inmates were now allowed to have a domestic servant at the door. Madams with six or more were allowed one domestic at the door *and* a prostitute outside making a circuit of the neighborhood. The circuit could be as wide as she wished (so long as she did nothing to disturb the peace) but her madam had to be careful to send her off in a direction opposite that taken by a woman from a neighboring brothel.[82]

Such minor tinkering with the regulations left the prefecture constantly open to ridicule. And, despite police efforts to distance themselves from the business, it was evident that they were greatly concerned with the interior management of the places. The capital outlay involved in setting up a house gave *tenancières* a certain claim on the police. One madam, a widow responsible for the support of her "poor orphaned children," wrote to protest when her tolerance was suddenly refused; she had already paid the rent and furnished it with the profits from her previous brothel, and she feared that she would be thrown into destitution.[83] For the rest of the century

---

[82] Circular of 27 April 1829, *Recueil des circulaires,* I:163; circular of 20 September 1842, *Recueil des circulaires,* I:409.

[83] AN F⁷ 9305, letter of 15 February 1841 from the widow Nedy to the minister of the interior:

La veuve Nedy prends la respectueuse confiance d'exposer très humblement à votre Excellence, qu lorsqu'elle eut le malheur de perdre son mari, elle restat avec plusieurs enfants en bas âge, sans fortune et sans état et que pour se soustraire à la misère qui la menaçait elle établit à Lille rue de la Hallotiree n° 24 une Maison de plaisir, forcée de quitter cette maison, elle vient d'en louer une rue du Dragon [Paris] et sans penser qu'elle aurait rencontrée le moindre obstacle à ses projets elle a sacrifiée le fruit de trois années d'économies pour faire bail et la faire arranger convenablement: mais voici que la police lui défend d'ouvrir cette maison pour l'usage auquel elle la destine, et la met dans la position la plus critique en l'exposant à perdre toutes avances qu'elle a faites et à se voir réduit à la mendicité elle et ses trop malheureux enfants.

the police were in a quandary, torn between their desire to remain aloof from prostitution as a business and their need for the tolerated house as a means of control. They continued as they had begun, ameliorating certain aspects of the tolerance in order to make the principle itself more palatable.

Despite the difficulties surrounding the tolerated house, the 1778 ordinance, prohibiting prostitution in lodging houses, remained durable. It was upheld by the Cour de cassation in 1840. An 1866 ruling by the same court upheld the principle of the law but vitiated its effect, diminishing to almost nothing the penalty for violation. This devastating decision was shortly followed by a prefectural directive advising agents to take heart and to continue to enforce the ordinance.[84] Nightly visits to lodging houses continued, but now, more than ever, the focus was on the search for clandestine prostitutes rather than for erring innkeepers. That part of the 1778 ordinance which prohibited landlords from leasing to prostitutes was destroyed in 1884, when a court decision pointed out the obvious illogic of such a law: "Prostitutes being tolerated in Paris, and therefore authorized to reside in Paris, proprietors or landlords have incontestably the right to rent to prostitutes."[85] This decision was less painful than it might have been earlier; by the 1880s the focus of the prefecture had substantially shifted.

[84] "Est légal et obligatoire, au moins à l'égard des logeurs en garni, l'arrêté municipal qui fait défense à tous propriétaires ou locataires de louer aucune chambre à filles ou femmes débauchées et de les loger ou recueiller chez eux." *Bulletin des arrêts de la Cour de cassation* (Paris: n.p., 1840), XLV:391. This referred to an *arrêté* in Sedan dated 23 October 1834. The ordinance of 6 November 1778 was judged in the Cour de cassation in December 1866. The 200-franc fine, it was decided, should be replaced by a *peine de simple police* and determined by the Tribunal de simple police. An 1867 circular, noting that the matter of prostitutes in lodging houses concerned "faits complexes de moralité," urged officers to remain vigilant. Circular of 10 April 1867, *Recueil des circulaires,* II:250-260.

[85] *Gazette des tribunaux,* 29 March 1884.

CONTROL OF THE STREETS

The brief attempt to segregate all prostitutes from the rest of the population was the logical counterpart of the prefecture's concern with the clearing of the streets. The desire to sweep the streets clean had moral, sanitary, and even aesthetic foundations; it was dependent also on the belief that prostitution was a contained problem, restricted only to a relatively small number of *femmes perdues* who could be conquered by sufficiently energetic policing. Early in the century the ambitions of the newly formed Morals Brigade had sometimes outstripped reasonable boundaries. In the autumn of 1813, as the Empire's borders were constricting, the prefecture became worried about inadequate policing in Versailles. Ducourez of the Bureau of Morals led a successful invasion into this neighboring city (much to the anger of the prefect of the Seine-et-Oise), capturing thirty-two prostitutes. In his slow procession home he also cast a wide net: "There was a lot to do here; the routes of Saint-Cyr, of Viroflay, of Ville d'Avray, of Montreuil and the forests of Satory are infested with transient and completely revolting women. I have even been assured that several sleep in the forests and gather on the roads during the day." Of the fifty-three women he ultimately captured, thirty-three were found to be "more or less" afflicted with venereal disease. The mission was considered a success, and all the participating gendarmes were given bonuses.[86]

A few years later, a prefectural *arrêté* of 19 August 1816 was promulgated to "purge Paris as much as possible" of unruly elements. It declared that all *filles publiques* not born in Paris and known as "thieves, vagabonds, and without fixed domicile" would be sent from the capital, "without any ex-

[86] Reports of 28 September and 8 October 1813, cited in Louis Fiaux, *La Police des moeurs en France: son abolition,* 2 vols. (Paris: Félix Alcan, 1921), I:725-729. Ducourez received 100 francs, and his two immediate subordinates each received 52 francs.

ception and without any consideration." The expulsion, conducted under armed escort of the gendarmerie, was final; if
they were discovered in Paris again as prostitutes, they would
be set to hard labor for six months. (Native-born Parisians
could not be expelled, but the police nevertheless attempted
to discourage them by a decision in 1816 to imprison for a
year at hard labor all those arrested more than twenty times.)
But the practice of forced expulsion, a remnant of the old
regime, was dying out even by the end of the Restoration.
"Without alleging that this method was illegal," wrote Delessert in 1841, "it must be admitted that it was often of an
excessive severity, because of the distance to be traveled, or
the weak constitution of the subject."[87] Those escorted from
the city also had a tendency to return the moment they were
free, drawn by the same forces that had led them to Paris in
the first place.

Through a slow, gradual, and often contradictory process,
the police of the Restoration and July Monarchy changed the
focus of their enforcement. From the simple goals of clearance
and containment, which had dictated the *maison close* policy,
they shifted to a more sophisticated concept of control, based
on the *arbitraire* of the prefect of police. The arbitrary power
of the prefect over prostitutes, exercised through his agents,
came to be regarded as a positive virtue, as a system of infinite
flexibility, able to respond at need to the requirements of
public order and public health and unconstrained by the slower
pace of the courts. The *arbitraire* became more necessary as
the scope of the problem grew. The policy of containment
could only be considered seriously if there were a limited
population of prostitutes; their own experience with Mangin's
reforms, and the social insights provided by Parent-Duchâtelet
and others, showed that prostitution in the nineteenth century

[87] AN F⁷ 9305, letter of 15 May 1841 from the prefect of police to the
minister of the interior.

was maintained by an ever-growing army of recruits. All they could hope to do was to ameliorate the worst excesses of this group through their ability to respond instantly to specific problems. What they required to do this was unhampered accessibility, both to places and to persons, as well as the power to punish instantly, proportionately, and without publicity.

The arbitrary powers of punishment, unchallenged through the first half of the century, were triggered by a cat-and-mouse game of street regulations, a set of virtually universal prohibitions which were only enforced selectively. A *mémoire* from the 1820s detailed the circumstances in which a prostitute might be arrested, even when she was not engaged in any specific actions of prostitution:

> They are arrested when, after 11:00 p.m., they are found in the streets, cabarets, etc.
>
> They are arrested if they are found at dusk in the courtyard or the garden of the Tuileries, or near the Tuileries, or in the courtyard of the Louvre.
>
> If they are not among the women allowed to live in the Palais Royal, they are arrested if they are found in the garden of the Palais Royal, at any time. They are arrested when they are standing together in a large group, at any hour of the day or night.
>
> They are arrested outside the barriers when they are involved in any kind of riot.
>
> They are arrested when they insult passers-by in a public place.
>
> They are arrested when they walk by or stand on the place Vendôme, the boulevard des Capucines, the place des Victoires, the place du Palais Royal, the place Louis XV, in the Luxembourg gardens, near the Luxembourg gardens, in the church and the place Sainte-Genevieve, and on the Champs Elysées.

They are arrested when they are found at any time of the day on the bridges, quais, the public places, in the taverns near the Palais de justice, and finally, when they exercise their métier on the streets.[88]

A list drawn up in 1833 added that they could not appear in public "in such a manner as to make themselves noticed" before the street lights were lit; they had to be dressed decently. They could not stand at their doors or sit at their windows "at any time or because of any imaginable pretext." They could not be in crowds—they were prohibited from "standing on the streets, forming groups, walking around together, or pacing in too small an area"—nor could they be alone. "They are equally forbidden to frequent deserted and obscure streets and areas, as well as cabarets and other public establishments, or private homes which favor clandestine prostitution."[89] A circular of 1841 added "covered passageways" to the list. In addition, they were not allowed to speak to men who were accompanied by women or children, nor were they to address any one "in a loud voice or with insistence."[90] None of the prohibitions was ever specifically revoked.

Limited manpower made the control of prostitution sporadic, dependent upon daily decisions (which were often based on local complaints) to clean up a particular area. But when the decision was made to concentrate on an area, it was a poor policeman indeed who could not find a pretext for arrest. There was no direct evidence that the police ever exploited the obvious potential for corruption in this system, though there was a report of a man arrested for impersonating a police officer. In this guise he had arrested several prostitutes,

---

[88] AN F⁷ 9304, undated *mémoire*, probably mid-1820s.
[89] AN F⁷ 9305, letter of 7 August 1833 from the prefect of police to the minister of the interior.
[90] Circular of 10 February 1841, *Recueil des circulaires,* I:370-373.

as the report stated with breathtaking directness, "so that he could extort money from them."[91]

By the middle of the century the *police des moeurs* was in good working order, as yet unmarked by serious criticism. The hesitations, the experiments, the stop-gap measures, and the contradictions of the early period had ended; in their place was a settled bureaucracy whose upper ranks, at least, shared a strong sense of purpose. They did not expect to end prostitution, but they were convinced that they could keep it within reasonable bounds.

They based the regulatory system on two foundations, on moral as well as on sanitary prophylaxy. The system had begun during the Empire; it had been viewed primarily as a means of fighting venereal disease at a time when the up-heavals caused by Napoleon's wars had led to severe out-breaks. During the Restoration had come the idea of using the *police des moeurs* as an agency of moral reform. In 1822, a new supervisory position had been created for an officer with the duty of proposing modifications "that he will judge necessary not only for the functioning of the service but also all those which could contribute to public decency or to the amelioration of morals."[92] It was the determination to "contribute to public decency" that had led to many of the experiments of the early years.

The regulatory system was successful in a limited way, in imposing a modest sort of order on an inherently disorderly situation. The prostitutes were sufficiently conditioned so that a substantial number of them reported voluntarily each month for the examination. The prefecture's categories and definitions of prostitution had imposed themselves on the public mentality. And it was not, after all, the lack of policing that

[91] AN F⁷ 4172, report of 27-28 February 1825; AN F⁷ 3879, report of Saturday, 8 October 1825 ("... pour en estorquer de l'argent").
[92] AN F⁷ 9304, *arrêté* of 20 August 1822.

made the regulations a source of grievance, but rather the sporadic nature of their enforcement. The street regulations were not all enforced all the time—there was not sufficient manpower for that—but some were enforced some of the time, at the prefecture's discretion.

But the power of the regulatory system was often illusory. Prefectural ambitions for the system always overreached its practical operating limits, both in the matter of disease control and in the maintaining of public tranquillity. These enlarged goals were bound to fail, but in attempting to achieve them the police effectively left prostitutes in the old regime; no other single group was bypassed so completely by the reforms of the revolutionary era. Prostitutes in the nineteenth century were dealt with as arbitrarily as they had been in the eighteenth century—with one difference. The modern police were more efficient.

˚ 2 ˚

Prostitution, Toleration, and the Law

LATE in the nineteenth century a prefect of police was subjected to unfriendly questioning by a group hostile to the regulatory system. They doubted the legality of the regime; they challenged him with increasing persistence to justify it. Finally, the prefect became angry and was reported to have stated, to the amusement of all present, that he based himself "on the capitularies of Charlemagne!"[1] The story may well be apocryphal, but it contains an element of truth nonetheless. One of the thorniest problems of the *régime des moeurs* was its shaky legality. The Revolution had swept away all the old laws, and the new laws were virtually silent (the few exceptions will be discussed) on the matter. Article 484 of the Penal Code had left in force all ordinances not specifically abrogated;[2] this proved a comfort to generations of prefects who

---

[1] Yves Guyot, *Etudes de physiologie sociale: la prostitution* (Paris: G. Charpentier, 1882), p. 13. The statement was made by Félix Voisin during an 1876 investigation by the Conseil municipal.

[2] A discussion on Article 484 took place on 10 February 1810; "la police des maisons de débauche et de jeu" was specified as one of the matters that would be affected by the article. However, as reformists later in the century would point out, Article 484 left such matters to the courts. ("En tout ce qui n'est pas réglé par le présent Code en matière de crimes, délits, et contraventions, les cours et tribunaux continueront d'observer et de faire exécuter les dispositions des lois et des règlements actuellement en vigueur.") See *Le Moniteur universel,* 18 February 1810.

were thus able to cite historical precedents reaching back to Charlemagne and even beyond.

The story of the legal basis of the control of prostitution in the nineteenth century is a story of expediency over justice, of the strength of custom and tradition over the letter of the law. In its continuity prostitution resembled many other aspects of French society. At the same time the Revolution clearly had an effect, if only because those who policed prostitutes were now forced to find new justifications for their administrative decisions. The surface modernity of the nineteenth century regime—the dispensary, the regular exam, the registration system—should not obscure the fact that its broad outlines and conceptual framework had been established long before. Or rather, the police were predisposed to take certain kinds of action rather than others because of the ways in which prostitution had been handled in the past. In the nineteenth century the control of prostitution became a matter of deliberate decisions to violate systematically the rights of prostitutes as well as women who were merely suspected of prostitution. Arbitrary methods were used against prostitutes because, throughout most of the century at least, the lack of public outcry allowed the police to get away with them. But it was the outcry (when it finally came) and not the *arbitraire* that was the genuine innovation; throughout the historical past of France, prostitutes had been treated as outcasts unworthy of the protection of the law.

THE ROYAL ORDINANCES

Prefects had a millennium of experience on which to draw, for Charlemagne had indeed issued an ordinance in the year 800, banishing prostitutes as well as those who gave them shelter.[3] This was unhelpful, for banishment did little to solve

[3] Nicolas Delamare, *Traité de la police,* 4 vols. (Amsterdam: n.p., 1729), I:441.

the problem. The earliest significant ordinance quoted by those intent on justifying the regime was usually one dating from 1254 which warned that "women and girls who prostitute themselves will be driven out, from the towns as well as the hamlets"; and "after they have been warned, and prohibited from continuing their evil commerce, their property will be seized . . . and they will be despoiled of their clothing." Landlords were prohibited from renting to them.[4] In 1256 an "ordinance for the utility of the kingdom" ordered that all *foles femmes et ribaudes communes* be driven from the cities, away from "holy places such as churches and cemeteries." Those who rented to them and received their custom were to be punished by the loss of rent for a year.[5] Both of these had been issued by Saint Louis, a fact that tended to disarm criticism. Just before leaving for the Crusades in 1269 he had issued yet another ordinance, announcing his intention to purge the kingdom of *malfaiteurs* and *scélérats;* prostitutes were again ordered from the cities.[6]

Where they went was no mystery. The *bordeaux* were just

[4] Royal ordinance of December 1254, in Isambert, *Anciennes lois françaises,* I:345-348; Delamare, *Traité,* I:441.

[5] Royal ordinance of 1256, in Isambert, *Anciennes lois françaises,* I:276. Delamare placed this ordinance in 1254, as did a report issued in 1819 by the Prefecture of Police. Both Delamare and the prefecture's report saw this ordinance as a softening of the earlier banishment, since it merely ordered that prostitutes should not live in private homes, within the city walls, or near churches and schools. In addition, "Baillifs, Prévôts, Maires, Juges," and other royal officials were forbidden to frequent *bordeaux,* in itself an acknowledgment of tolerated havens for prostitution. See Delamare, *Traité,* I:442, and AN F[7] 9305, *Compte rendu à Son Excellence le Ministre de l'intérieur sur la prostitution publique.*

[6] Royal ordinance of 1269, in Isambert, *Anciennes lois françaises,* I:345-348. Saint Louis' hatred for debauchery was illustrated by Joinville's often-quoted account of his treatment of a knight found in a bordello. The guilty knight was given two choices: "ou que la ribaude le menroit par l'ost [host, army], en chemise, une corde liée aux genetaires; ou il perderoit son chevel et s'armeure, et le chaceroit l'on de l'ost." The knight chose to leave. Joinville, *Histoire de Saint Louis* (Paris: Hachette, n.d.), chap. XCIX.

beyond the city walls, but not beyond the community's reach. They were so close, in fact, that the expansion of the city walls in Paris sometimes had the effect of repatriating bordellos and their inhabitants. Sometimes they were expelled again,[7] but by the fourteenth century a policy of toleration had developed. An ordinance of the Prévôt of Paris on 18 September 1367 enjoined "all women of dissolute life to live in the *bordeaux* and public places designated for them." A list of streets followed, effectively condemning certain areas to prostitution for centuries to come; the police reports of the nineteenth century recorded incidents that occurred in these same areas. This ordinance, like virtually all the others, attacked landlords as well as prostitutes. Except on the designated streets, property owners were neither to sell nor to rent to prostitutes under penalty of losing rent revenues.[8]

The same streets were designated in ordinances of 1415 and 1419, but prostitution continued to spread beyond these invisible barriers and into neighboring streets.[9] The Saint Merry Church, a frequent haven for prostitutes because of its proximity to certain *rues chaudes,* was ruled out-of-bounds in 1424.[10] Royal *lettres patentes* of Charles VI on 3 August 1381,

[7] The rue Chapon had been designated as a street for prostitutes, but after its enclosure within new city walls it became populated with respectable people; in 1368 the king ordered it closed to *filles. Lettres patentes* of 3 February 1368, in Delamare, *Traité,* I:443.

[8] Ordinance of the Prévôt of Paris, 18 September 1367, in Delamare, *Traité,* I:442-443. The streets were Abreuvoir Maçon (rue de la Harpe), Boucherie, Froidmantel(-eau), Glatigny (parvis Notre Dame), Cour Robert de Paris (rue du Renard), Baillehoe (rue Brisemiche), Tiron, Chapon, and Champfleury (rue de Rivoli). All street names from here on are from Jacques Hillairet, *Dictionnaire historique des rues de Paris,* 2 vols. (Paris: Editions de minuit, n.d.).

[9] Ordinances of the Prévôt of Paris, 8 January 1415 and 6 March 1419, in Delamare, *Traité,* I:444.

[10] Royal ordinance of April 1424, in Isambert, *Anciennes lois françaises,* VIII:684-686. Isambert noted (VIII:685) that the *chanoines* of Saint Merry had already opposed the expulsion of prostitutes in 1386 because they paid high rents.

repeating the penalties of the ordinance of 1254, forbade proprietors from renting their houses to women of "dissolute life" on certain streets that were also (though the intention was the reverse) identified as havens.[11] Geographical separation was reinforced by the regulation of hours. An ordinance of the Prévôt of Paris on 30 June 1395 ordered prostitutes back into their bordellos by 6:00 p.m. in the winter and 7:00 p.m. in the summer, marked by the sounding of the curfew.[12] Violations of these ordinances resulted in imprisonment in the Châtelet as well as seizure of one's property; the arresting officers received a cut. Arrests were made on the basis of a complaint by two neighbors or, in the 1415 and 1419 ordinances, by "two virtuous women."[13]

It was commonly supposed that prostitutes were driven by love of luxury as well as debauchery, so it made sense to attempt to dictate dress; at the very least, this kind of regulation ensured that those who embraced vice would be denied one of its few rewards. On occasion these rules ordered that a particular symbol or article of clothing be worn so that virtuous women would not be mistaken for prostitutes.[14] It was more frequent, however, for regulations to dictate what prostitutes could *not* wear. An early ordinance denounced

[11] *Lettres patentes* of 3 August 1381, in Isambert, *Anciennes lois françaises,* VI:559, and in Delamare, *Traité,* I:443. The supposedly forbidden streets were Beaubourg, Geoffroy Langevin, des Jongleurs, Simon-le-Franc (with the closely connected Fontaine Maubuée), and Saint Denis de la Charte (rue de la Cité).

[12] Ordinance of the Prévôt of Paris, 30 June 1395; an earlier ordinance of the Prévôt of Paris, on 17 March 1374, had set the curfew at 6:00 p.m. and ordered a fine of 20 sous each time a violation occurred. For both, see Delamare, *Traité,* I:443.

[13] Ordinances of the Prévôt of Paris, 8 January 1415 and 6 March 1419, in Delamare, *Traité,* I:444.

[14] Prostitutes of Toulouse were ordered to wear a distinctive mark on their dresses. Letter of Charles VI, December 1389, in Isambert, *Anciennes lois françaises,* VI:685-686.

filles et femmes de mauvaise vie who had the "boldness" to wear on their dresses and hoods "decorations of gauze or embroidery, slashes of silver, white, or gold, pearls, furred cloaks."[15] An *arrêt* of Parlement in 1420, perhaps responding to new fashions, forbade dresses with upturned collars and trains, gilded belts, and headdresses.[16] An *arrêt* of 1426 forbade scarlet dresses.[17] Such fashions were prohibited even in the tolerated areas. Arrest resulted in imprisonment and seizure of the clothing.[18]

These prohibitions were punitive, but there was a symbolic importance attached to clothing as well. The strict rules governing the dress of the repentant prostitutes who entered the Maison du Bon Pasteur, the refuge that came under the king's official protection in 1698, seemed unnecessarily copious.[19] As a substitute for the furs, pearls, and elaborate gowns of the unrepentant, penitents wore pleated gowns of coarse brown cloth, belted with a strip of black leather that fastened with a blackened iron clasp. Sleeve lengths were regulated, as were the numerous pleats and folds, and much attention was given to the mobcap, which was made of a certain material, folded in a certain way, and weighted with a bit of buckram to keep it in place. Since the cap was light, the shaved heads of the

---

[15] Ordinance of the Prévôt of Paris in 1360, in Delamare, *Traité,* I:442. Delamare found entered in the accounts of Paris the proceeds from the sale of goods confiscated from prostitutes, including the fur-trimmed cape, black silk dress, and various other items taken from the *femme amoureuse* "Jehannette, widow of the late Pierre Michel." *Traité,* I:444.

[16] *Arrêt* of Parlement, 26 June 1420, in Delamare, *Traité,* I:444.

[17] *Arrêt* of Parlement, 17 April 1426, in Delamare, *Traité,* I:444.

[18] Ibid.

[19] The Maison du Bon Pasteur was started as a private institution by one Madam de Combé to provide a place for those who wanted to leave prostitution; it was taken under the king's protection in 1698, several years after the founder's death. The *lettres patentes* stated that the refuge "recevoit gratuitement les filles que le libertinage ou la nécessité avoit engagées dans le désordre, lors qu'elles venoient dans la resolution d'y faire penitence." Delamare, *Traité,* I:450.

women were kept warm with large woolen bonnets.[20] The purpose of the bulky outfit was to "banish entirely the spirit of the world"; the days were designed to that end as well, every minute being filled with prayer and meditation or work. Blind obedience was required: "a complete mortification of the senses, a continual abnegation of the self." The rules warned would-be postulants that the life to be lived in Bon Pasteur was "hard, poor, and very withdrawn"; they were also warned, in a rather disconcerting concession to reality, not to spit on the curtains.[21]

Ordinances of the kings almost from the first reflected a policy of limited tolerance, sometimes even of protection.[22] The most radical divergence from this policy issued from a meeting of the Estates General in 1560. Landlords had long been forbidden to rent to prostitutes, except in tolerated areas; by the new decree, innkeepers were forbidden to shelter them longer than a single night, and bordellos were prohibited altogether.[23] Nicholas Delamare asserted that the decree resulted in the closing of all houses in the kingdom, although one in Paris, on the rue de Heuleu (Hurleur), resisted for five years. Its neighbors finally had recourse to the king, who

---

[20] Ibid., I:451.

[21] Ibid., I:450, 456.

[22] For one of the few explicit protections extended to prostitutes, see the royal ordinance of 13 February 1424, in Isambert, *Anciennes lois françaises,* VIII:695-698. Brundage has shown that toleration of prostitution was a longstanding policy among Catholic theologians, even as they condemned prostitution on moral grounds; this split also characterized the thinking of the lawmakers. See James A. Brundage, "Prostitution in the Medieval Canon Law," *Signs* 1 (Summer 1976):825-845.

[23] "Défendons à toutes personnes de loger et recevoir en leurs maisons plus d'une nuit, gens sans aveu et inconnus, leur enjoignons de les dénoncer à justice, à peine de prison & d'amende arbitraire. Défendons aussi à tous bordeaux, berlans, jeux de quilles & de dez, que voulons être punis extraordinairement sans dissimulation ou connivence des Juges." *Arrêt* of Estates General at Orleans, January 1560, in Delamare, *Traité,* I:445.

ordered it closed in March 1565, thus ending, according to reports, three hundred years of tradition in that spot.[24]

The closing of all houses, by far the most extreme reform ever attempted, proved unworkable and was allowed to fall into disuse. A police ordinance of 1619 reverted to the old policy of "driving out" prostitutes from the city (they had twenty-four hours to get out of town) and punishing greedy landlords. Bordellos were denounced as frequent sites of robbery, murder, and manslaughter, and citizens of the town were ordered to lend force of arms to the officers of the Châtelet, even to the extent of arresting the lawbreakers and bringing them to jail themselves.[25] A chance for redemption was offered by an ordinance of the Prévôté of Paris on 30 March 1635; prostitutes were ordered to get a job within twenty-four hours or leave town, under threat of being "shaved and banished forever, with no other legal formality." This ordinance, along with the usual admonition to landlords, also warned tavernkeepers and lodging-house keepers against receiving or serving prostitutes.[26] An ordinance of 17 September 1644 was aimed directly at landlords, giving them three days to empty their houses of disorderly tenants, male and female; after the houses were emptied, the doors were to be barred and the houses shut up for a period of time,[27] an action that

---

[24] *Lettres patentes* of 24 March 1565, in Delamare, *Traité*, I:445. Dufour's account of the establishment on Hurleur suggests a rather remarkable enterprise. Presided over by Mother Gardine, it apparently encompassed a number of houses on the rues du Grand and du Petit Hurleur. Dufour points out, moreover, that Gardine had enough money to hold out against the *arrêt* for five years through various legal proceedings; it finally took the authority of the king to close down her business for good. Pierre Dufour, *History of Prostitution,* 3 vols. (Chicago: Covici, 1926), III:275-276.

[25] Ordinance of the police, 19 July 1619, in Delamare, *Traité,* I:445; Isambert, *Anciennes lois françaises,* XVI:130.

[26] Ordinance of the Prévôté of Paris, 30 March 1635, in Delamare, *Traité,* I:446.

[27] Ordinance of the police, 17 September 1644, in Delamare, *Traité,* I:446.

meant a loss of revenue but was also, perhaps, a kind of exorcism.

Aside from the momentary confusion that must have been caused by the decision of the Estates General to "abolish" all houses of prostitution, the treatment of prostitutes throughout the medieval and early modern period was rather consistent. Fierce ordinances spoke of "driving" women from the towns; with each new ordinance prostitutes packed their bags and moved to the bordellos outside the walls, and just as surely crept back inside. The royal government and the city administration capitulated, granting them certain streets—and capitulated further by declaring that prostitutes must be inside the tolerated areas by curfew, thus indirectly acknowledging their presence outside at other times. Justice in these cases was summary, but hardly more so for prostitutes than for all *gens sans aveu*. Indeed, prostitutes could even boast of a "representative" at court. The so-called *roi des ribauds,* an officer of the king's household and army in the medieval period, was primarily charged with clearing the king's household of extraneous guests; however, as other members of the king's household sponsored various trade groups, so did the *roi des ribauds* sponsor prostitutes, madams, and *souteneurs.* At Tournai, he collected a regular weekly sum from *filles de joie* and from their madams. In Paris, his authority as a royal officer conflicted with the local authority of the Prévôté of Paris; this body's determination upon the local control of prostitution was a telling presage.[28]

The introduction of venereal disease into Europe at the beginning of the sixteenth century would ultimately be the

[28] Anne Terroine, "Le Roi des ribauds de l'hôtel du roi et les prostituées parisiennes," *Revue historique de droit français et étranger* 56 (avril-juin 1978):257-259, 263-264.

decisive factor in the treatment of prostitutes, though the authorities apparently did not react directly to it at first.[29] Prostitutes were eventually targeted, in a natural if not entirely logical way, as the chief carriers of the disease. The desire to protect society from this sickness became entangled with the general movement toward *enfermement,* or the phenomenon of isolating from society those perceived to be dangerous. Enclosure was decreed for certain types of vagabonds and mendicants in a series of royal ordinances.[30]

The problem of prostitution was handled in this new way by an ordinance of 1684 which ordered Parisian prostitutes to be confined and enclosed in Salpêtrière Hospital. They were to be treated for venereal disease if the examination (imposed on all prostitutes) revealed that they were infected; the length of imprisonment was entirely discretionary and dependent upon the decision of the lieutenant-general of police. The traditional arbitrariness evident in the imprisonment should not obscure the fact that this policy marked an important break with the past. The imposed quarantine reflected

---

[29] Jacques Rossiaud, "Prostitution, jeunesse et société dans les villes du sud-est au XVᶜ siècle," *Annales E.S.C.* 31 (mars-avril 1976):313.

[30] Gutton has noted that enclosure was regarded as the "miracle solution" for vagabondage and mendicity in the sixteenth and seventeenth centuries because the authorities could force the inmates to work, end their licentiousness and give religious instruction, and prevent the "contagion" of vagabondage. Jean-Pierre Gutton, *La Société et les pauvres: l'exemple de la généralité de Lyon, 1534-1789* (Paris: Société d'édition, 1970), p. 305. The four most important "enclosure" ordinances for vagabondage and mendicity are the ordinances of 25 July 1700 (Isambert, *Anciennes lois françaises,* XX:366-367), 27 August 1701 (ibid., XX:394, cited only), 18 July 1724 (ibid., XXI:271-273), and 3 August 1764 (ibid., XXII:404). These are briefly discussed in Gutton, *La Société,* pp. 438-441, and at greater length in Camille Bloch, *L'Assistance et l'état en France à la veille de la Révolution* (Paris: 1908). The works of Michel Foucault have explored the meaning of enclosure or, as he has called it, the "Grand Renfermement," or institutionalization of various marginal groups.

not a changing perception of prostitutes—for they had always been regarded as apart from the rest of society—but rather a changing perception of the sort of peripheral relationship they could occupy in regard to society. However contradictory it may seem, quarantining represented the recognition of a link between prostitutes and the society that had temporarily expelled them.

Prostitutes had long been regarded as *femmes perdues,* as women who were lost to society. They were marginal characters, allowed to practice the trade within limits defined or at least tacitly acknowledged by the authorities. A kind of spiritual alienation had set them apart. Previous ordinances had merely ordered prostitutes from one place to another, revealing no interest in why they had come to be or in what they were going to become.

In contrast the 1684 ruling revealed the beginning of a policy of recognition and rehabilitation. Prostitutes were to labor in the Salpêtrière, performing tasks as difficult, and for as long a time, as their strength permitted. Books of piety and the catechism were to be read aloud to enliven their working hours. Repentance (presumably to be induced by the hearing of inspirational messages) was rewarded with less difficult work, a fact that undoubtedly led to many spontaneous conversions.[31] Repentance and a virtuous life were now regarded as goals possible of attainment by institutional methods; this was the essential meaning behind these provisions as well as those relating to the refuge Bon Pasteur, founded around the same time. Bon Pasteur was not to be regarded as a permanent home; the worldly goods of repentant prostitutes were to be kept for them in a box and returned when they left.[32]

[31] Royal ordinance of 20 April 1684, in Isambert, *Anciennes lois françaises,* XIX:441-445.

[32] Delamare, *Traité,* I:451. Bon Pasteur took over the functions of the *filles*

Yet it was in the attempt to diagnose and prevent prostitution that the ordinance was most noteworthy, for the Salpêtrière also took in wayward girls, those "girls who have been debauched or who are in evident peril of being debauched." Entry into the prison could be requested by fathers or by young girls who wanted to save themselves from disorder. Prostitutes, or in this case future prostitutes, were for the first time officially identified by class as the "children of the artisans and of the poor inhabitants of Paris and its suburbs."[33]

Camp followers were also subjected to incarceration and enforced hospitalization during this period, practices that gradually replaced the stigmatizing punishments prescribed by the first ordinances to deal with this ancient problem. An ordinance of 1684 followed the traditional pattern of punishment and expulsion. It was written in response to a complaint that *filles de mauvaise vie* were seducing the troops stationed at Versailles, inciting quarrels that had resulted in deaths among the soldiers. In spite of floggings they had continued to flock to the camps; any woman found there after publication of the ordinance was to have her nose and ears clipped.[34]

---

penitentes, a religious order composed of former prostitutes. The set of rules provided in 1497 reveals that this convent had the unusual problem of actually provoking debauchery in some cases; as a result, "les postulantes seront obligées de jurer, sous peine de damnation éternelle,... qu'elles ne s'étoient point prostituées à dessein d'entrer un jour dans cette congrégation." Not all ex-prostitutes wanted to join a religious order, and so Bon Pasteur was founded as a kind of halfway house. Boucher d'Argis, "Prostitution," in *Encyclopédie méthodique* [ed. by Diderot] (Paris: Panckoucke, 1787), vol. 27, pt. 7: "Jurisprudence," pp. 52-53.

[33] Royal ordinance of 20 April 1684, in Isambert, *Anciennes lois françaises,* XIX:441-445. Young male delinquents were also to be imprisoned, in a separate ward.

[34] Royal ordinance of 31 October 1684, in Isambert, *Anciennes lois françaises,* XIX:464, cited only.

This must have been ineffective, for yet another ear-splicing ordinance for Versailles was issued on 18 March 1687.[35] "This girl, although an imbecile, has given herself up to libertinage since her earliest youth, and she has no resources" was the description of one of these women. The calculating sirens envisioned by the language of the army proclamations could seldom be found in reality.[36]

The desire to punish was replaced by a more practical concern for the health of the soldiers of France. An ordinance of 1 March 1768 gave the military the authority to arrest any troublesome camp follower. Women arrested by military authority were to be kept in prison for three months on bread and water, then transferred to a *maison de force* for an undetermined stay. The plan immediately ran into a roadblock, for *maisons de force* were not established in all parts of France. The provisions were almost immediately modified as early as August of the same year. Because of the strongly felt need for the measure, the plan was not, as were so many ill-conceived projects, allowed to lapse. The new destination of the *filles* became the recently established *dépôts de mendicité;* the women were to be kept there at 5 sous a day, a sum to be charged to the Department of War. This quick modification caused some initial confusion but seems to have been regarded as a practical solution, even an advantageous one, since it permitted the treatment of venereal disease to begin immediately in the depot instead of after a stay in prison. An official pointed out the similarity between the prostitutes and those for whom the depot was originally planned, "these girls being precisely in the same situation as vagabonds, libertines, and *gens sans aveu.*" They were to remain in the depots for

---

[35] Ordinance of 18 March 1687, in Isambert, *Anciennes lois françaises,* XX:20.
[36] AN F[15] 2811, statement from the mendicity depot at Auch, 23 September 1791.

at least the three months originally prescribed, "in order to follow literally the spirit of the ordinance."[37]

This plan foreshadowed the regulatory system of nineteenth-century Paris—in the concern to limit venereal disease, in the mandatory treatment of the disease, and in the imprisonment for an indefinite period according to a determination by the authorities, who were in this case military rather than civilian. Prostitutes (in practice if not in theory) were no worse off than the average vagabond or mendicant, for all were in danger of being summarily arrested. The particular disadvantages suffered by prostitutes arose from the fact that they were women, as the report of one intendant indicated:

> It almost always happens that those detained twenty-five or thirty *lieues* from the [mendicity] depot are locked up there three or four months after their arrest, and sometimes longer.... The men and women are kept in the same prison, and it always happens that those who were not pregnant when they were arrested, always are when they arrive at the depot. The prisons are usually unhealthy, and it often happens that most of those detained are sick when they leave.[38]

The Law of 8-10 July 1791 absolved the army of the responsibility for the *filles à soldat;* they were now to be turned

---

[37] Royal ordinance of 1 March 1768, in Isambert, *Anciennes lois françaises,* XXII:476 (cited only). And in AN F¹⁵ 2811, see correspondence in the *filles publiques* file, especially the letter of 21 August 1768 from the Duc de Choiseul to the controller general and the letter of 15 October 1768 from the Duc de Choiseul to the commandants general of the provinces.

[38] Copy of a letter of 17 August 1785 from M. de Bertrand to the controller general, cited as AN H556, *pièce* 8, in Christian Paultre, *De la répression de la mendicité et du vagabondage en France sous l'ancien régime* (Paris: J.-B. Sirey, 1906), pp. 468-471.

over to the police of the nearest town, to be judged, so it was said, according to law. If only there had been nationwide laws (to say nothing of uniform laws) this would have held the promise of a reform of sorts. The revolutionary government, faced with the task of revising French legislation, overlooked prostitution. The anonymous author of a report on the subject observed that one was still faced with the problem of what to do with prostitutes and where to put them. The depots had been established solely for the benefit of vagabonds and beggars, thus making doubtful the power of the local police to send prostitutes there as well; and if they did have the power, the report continued, then the funds allocated to the mendicity problem should be substantially increased. The questions raised were not settled, at least not nationally, as the issues of vagabondage and mendicity were; each community was left to find a local solution to the problem.[39]

Imprisonment in a hospital was only one aspect of the nineteenth-century system that first appeared during the old regime. Another was the *maison de tolérance*. The origin of the tolerated house in its nineteenth-century form has been set in the mid-eighteenth century. From that time on, the lieutenants-general of police in Paris had informal arrangements by which madams were allowed to carry on their lucrative trade in return for keeping order within their establishments and furnishing the police with information.[40]

[39] AN F[15] 2811, letter of May 1788 from the controller general to the Comte de Brienne. Though prostitution received little legislative attention, vagabondage and mendicity were dealt with rather quickly. Vagabondage received legal definition in the laws of 19-22 July 1791, tit. 1, art. 3, and of 10 Vendémiaire Year IV, tit. 3, art. 7. Penalties were decreed by the Law of 24 Vendémiaire Year II, tit. 4, arts. 3 and 4. The Law of 24 Vendémiaire Year II also defined mendicity and discussed the penalties that would be imposed.

[40] Alan Williams, *The Police of Paris, 1715-1789* (Baton Rouge: Louisiana State University Press, 1979), pp. 100-102.

Yet in this as in so many aspects of the prostitution regime, it is difficult to pinpoint a beginning, for the ordinances suggested that the policy of tolerated houses was a longstanding one. Delamare, writing in 1729, even used the term *tolérance* to refer to such an establishment.

The idea of mandatory medical care dates back at least to the 1684 ordinance, though the women who were thus forcibly cured were captured randomly. The idea of regular medical examinations for all was in the air in the eighteenth century; a recommendation to begin such exams was submitted to the government in 1762.[41] Restif de la Bretonne had made regular exams a part of his prostitute utopia, described in *Le Pornographe;* and an anonymous reply to *Le Pornographe* recommended in 1775 a system, which eventually became established, of regular, scheduled examinations by police-appointed doctors.[42]

Imprisonment on the charge of prostitution without benefit of "formalities" was also a well-established part of the system. The old ordinances had allowed for imprisonment on the basis of denunciation. Even more specific was the 1684 ordinance, which had set down guidelines for the imprisonment of prostitutes in the Salpêtrière. Women tried in court for other crimes could be sent to the Salpêtrière (whether guilty of the main charge or not) by their judges. In all other instances it was explicitly stated that the lieutenant-general was to act as a "judge of last resort"; this power, conserved

[41] Hyppolite Mireur, "Historical Note" to Nicolas-Edme Restif de la Bretonne, *Le Pornographe, ou idées d'un honnête homme sur un projet de règlement pour les prostituées* (Brussels: Gay & Doucé, 1879), p. xix.

[42] The reply to Restif was the *Code, ou nouveau règlement sur les lieux de prostitution dans la ville de Paris* (London: n.p., 1775), pp. 150-153. An apocryphal law, supposedly issued by Queen Jeanne of Naples in 1347, echoed these demands by providing for a municipal bordello and regular medical visits. See the *Encyclopédie méthodique,* vol. 27, pt. 7, pp. 50-51.

throughout the rest of the old regime, left prostitution in the rather arbitrary hands of the police.[43]

A faint note of caution was sounded in the ordinance of 26 July 1713. This procedural clarification promised stern punishments in addition to prison. Prostitutes who had been the subject of complaint were enjoined to vacate their apartments or, if they had been the subject of several complaints, to leave the city. If they delayed, their furniture was to be thrown into the streets and confiscated for the profit of the poor in the Hôpital général. At the same time, however, the regulation established guidelines for taking complaints from neighbors and warned against denunciations that might be inspired "by the hatred of individuals rather than by the love of the public good."[44] Such cautionary notes were rare. The control of prostitution during the old regime was harsh, arbitrary, punitive—and tolerant.

THE REVOLUTION AND ITS EFFECTS

Restoration officials were quick to blame the Revolution for the moral chaos they perceived in the nineteenth century. It was true, they argued, that the eighteenth century had been a period of great libertinage, but one confined to the aristocracy. During the old regime, according to one police report, the people had respect for work, family life, and moral virtues. When anarchy (revolution) appeared on the horizon, these old virtues disappeared. Households broke up, workshops became disorganized, artisans developed "soldieresque" tastes. Prostitution, freed from all the old ordinances, had "raised

[43] Royal ordinance of 20 April 1684, in Isambert, *Anciennes lois françaises,* XIX:441-445.
[44] Royal ordinance of 26 July 1713, in Isambert, *Anciennes lois françaises,* XX:603.

its head," and venereal disease was now serious enough to threaten the nation.[45]

The prostitution expert Parent-Duchâtelet was no great friend of the old regime, but he was a staunch regulationist. He deplored the lack of method and order, which he traced to the period of the Revolution: "The prostitutes were delivered from all surveillance, assimilated to those who practiced any other trade, and free in their actions." Through the oversight of the Constituent Assembly, he continued, "they had found themselves emancipated, a favor that they have perhaps never enjoyed in any time and in any country."[46] Parent-Duchâtelet's statements were exaggerated, for prostitutes continued to be arrested during the Revolution for traditional reasons, as surviving records show.[47]

Nevertheless, Parent-Duchâtelet's argument was not unfounded; the situation was necessarily different after the Revolution, though the change was not immediately apparent. During the Reign of Terror, the arrest and imprisonment of prostitutes had passed easily with the rest. As the government had acquired stability and conditions returned to normal, it became clear that the ordinances that had formerly governed prostitution were now tainted, and had not yet been replaced. At least one attempt was made to fill this gap in the new legislation. In 1796, Jean-François Rewbell of the Directory sent a message to the Council of Five Hundred, pointing out the dangers of libertinage to the health and republican character of the nation and asking them to prepare legislation to

[45] AN F⁷ 9305, *Compte rendu* of 12 May 1819; and see a similar lament in *Compte d'administration des dépenses de la Préfecture de police* (1819), p. xxvii.

[46] Parent-Duchâtelet, *De la prostitution,* II:301.

[47] For example, see the *commissaire*'s reports summarized in the fifth volume of Alexandre Tuetey, *Répertoire général des sources manuscrites de l'histoire de Paris pendant la Révolution française,* 11 vols. (Paris: Imprimerie nouvelle, 1900).

curb prostitution. Proposals were never even discussed; Parent-Duchâtelet believed that the legislators found the subject to be too inconsequential, or too ignoble, to be accorded the dignity of legislative action.[48] The resulting legal vacuum forced the prefecture (as the natural heir of the abolished lieutenant-generalship) to step in. The elaborate regulatory structure was entirely an administrative creation; no written law authorized the system.

Though it had no practical effect, Rewbell's message was not without significance. Rewbell had wanted prostitution defined as an offense rather than as a *qualité*. Legal definition would rest on a number of different bases: the arrest *en flagrant délit;* public notoriety; and recidivism, or repeated suspicious actions or arrests. Definition was necessary because women arrested as *filles publiques,* on no specific charges, usually claimed to practice other trades and even found people willing to pose as their employers; such ruses could not work if the police were prepared with specific allegations. While Rewbell's main concern was to prevent guilty women from escaping, the establishment of clear-cut offenses (however loosely worded in the preliminary proposal) would have forced arresting officers to come up with specific examples of wrongdoing rather than the sweeping charges they had always used. (Women were commonly arrested as *femmes de mauvaise vie* or as "known prostitutes.") Finally, Rewbell wanted prostitution cases to go through the Tribunal de police correctionnelle or the Tribunal de simple police, according to the severity of the case. Punishment would be assessed as a fine or, because of the poverty of those involved, imprisonment.

[48] Rewbell's message of 17 Nivôse Year IV was reprinted in Parent-Duchâtelet, *De la prostitution,* I:20-23. Parent's research had also yielded a refusal to consider the issue of prostitution that had apparently carried the day: "Les vues qu'on nous propose sont petites, minutieuses, indignes, ce me semble, du corps législatif." See *De la prostitution,* I:24, and *Le Moniteur universel,* 12 Germinal Year V.

Such proposals would have assimilated prostitution to other crimes and would have integrated it into the criminal justice system. The refusal of the legislators to act on the matter in 1796 allowed regulation to develop from police initiative. The system became entrenched in the last years of the Empire, and it worked fairly well. Indeed, from the police standpoint it was better than a law would have been. When legislators again tried to draft a law on prostitution, early in the Restoration, they met this time with resistance from police officials anxious to preserve the status quo.

The idea of a prostitution law or ordinance was raised in 1819, dropped, and then revived again in 1822. The Garde des sceaux, initiator of both proposals, wished to regularize the treatment of prostitutes.

> The discretionary power that the municipal authority has enjoyed up to the present . . . is founded on custom rather than on any precise disposition of law, and . . . it would be essential to remedy this disadvantage by collecting the dispositions relative to prostitutes which are found in the old general police regulations, by modifying them as necessary according to present-day needs, and by making prostitution the object of a new ordinance that would sketch out definite rules and end conflicts that are often raised on this subject between magistrates and functionaries of the administrative order.[49]

[49] AN F⁷ 9304, letter of 24 April 1822 from the Garde des sceaux to the minister of the interior. See also the letter of 7 May 1822 from the minister of the interior to the prefect of police. Attempts were made by the national administration to formulate uniform regulations in 1811, 1816, 1819, 1822, and 1848, all to no purpose. A law introduced in May 1895 by Senator René Berenger also fell through. Felicien Hennequin, "Annex II: Rapport de M. Lépine, préfet de police sur la réglementation de la prostitution à Paris et dans le département de la Seine," in Hennequin, *Annexes au rapport général présenté par M. F. Hennequin, . . . sur les travaux de la Commission extraparlementaire du régime des moeurs* (Melun: Imprimerie administrative, 1908), p. 6.

The attempt to draft an ordinance met with a lukewarm response from Delavau, who replied in 1822 with the curious defensiveness that seemed to characterize his dealings with the Ministry of the Interior on this issue:

> Your Excellency, by his letters of 7 May, 20 June, 4 September, and 13 October, has done me the honor of asking for information on the regulations, old and new, on public prostitution and to furnish all the necessary materials to allow the Garde des sceaux to draw up a royal ordinance on this important object. . . . A similar demand . . . was made of my predecessor, on 7 April 1819. . . . This report was delivered to the bureau headed by M. Rosan, who signed a receipt for it which I have in my office; but the changes that have taken place in the ministry now confided to your Excellency, could make the search too difficult, so I have just had a copy made which I have the honor to send you.[50]

The report, drafted in 1819 during the tenure of Anglès, was both an extensive survey and a blatant argument for the policy of toleration. "The experience of fifteen centuries" had shown that the wisest legislator was one who recognized his own inability to stamp out debauchery. The capitularies of Charlemagne and the 1560 edict of the Estates General had been disastrous in their severity, for in attempting to outlaw prostitution they had succeeded only in driving it underground, away from the watchful eyes of the police. The tested method of effective control was tolerance, by which prostitutes were not prosecuted for prostitution itself but were held to a certain standard of behavior.[51]

The key to control was the power to punish, and in this

---

[50] AN F⁷ 9305, letter of October 1822 from the prefect of police to the minister of the interior.

[51] AN F⁷ 9305, *Compte rendu . . . sur la prostitution publique.*

the prefects stood firmly on the old prerogatives of the lieutenant-general of police. A law that made only certain types of behavior illegal was also undesirable; common decency alone made it difficult even to frame such a law, let alone to try individuals in open court, as Delavau insisted:

> On the question of whether the rules relative to prostitutes could not be regularized by a law, it has generally been recognized that a law on this matter was impossible to make, either because of the nature of the object; or because of the infinite details into which the law would have to enter, without the assurance of covering every case that could arise in the repression of crimes or simple abuses; or finally because of the powerlessness to which the magistrate would be reduced by the necessity of following the rules of law in regard to women who, having put themselves voluntarily outside common law, would find themselves raised from their degradation by that law itself.[52]

Even if lawmakers got over the hurdle of defining the offense, it would be impossible to establish that a crime had been committed according to the forms required by the Penal Code. Soliciting, the most visible aspect of prostitution, was merely the "first act"; a check at the lodging houses of captured streetwalkers would find them registered as "workers," and there would be no sure way to distinguish prostitution from simple debauchery.[53]

Finally, if the police managed after all to bring a case to court, it was likely that the judges would dismiss such an offense as beneath their dignity. The complaint of the police on this point, part of a timeless policeman's lament, was that

---

[52] AN F⁷ 9304, letter of 22 June 1822 from the prefect of police to the minister of the interior.

[53] AN F⁷ 9304, report, c. 1819 and 1822.

courts negated the efforts of the constables by refusing, for various mysterious reasons, to fulfill their functions. A law would ensure prostitutes "the most complete immunity," stated one report: "I am speaking of the custom introduced in the magistrature of the *première instance* of Paris to reject as unworthy of it cases of this type. It can even be observed that they stubbornly refuse to pronounce sentence on the crime of vagabondage, although it is rather clearly defined, and the penalties rather positively pronounced by the Penal Code." The judges of Paris had made this refusal the "palladium of their dignity and independence," and remonstrances were futile.[54]

All these rather too numerous protestations meant that the prefecture had become accustomed to the luxury of not having to prepare court cases against prostitutes, and they were not about to give it up. The idea of writing a conventional kind of law, outlawing prostitution and prescribing penalties for it, quickly ran into opposition from the entrenched regime of the prefecture; but it also went against the body of custom and tradition that had decreed the toleration of prostitution within prescribed limits. It would be repeated by various writers and officials throughout the century that prostitutes were, because of the repugnance that their profession inspired, "outside the law." But this was an after-the-fact justification. There was no intrinsic reason why prostitutes could not have been brought, along with vagabonds and mendicants, into the shelter of the courts. Rewbell's message had made the assumption that this would be the normal course of events. A directive from the Communal government of Paris in 1793 was unsurpassed in its denunciation of prostitutes, the "monsters" who were corrupting youth and endangering the re-

[54] Ibid.

public, but it merely threatened them with arrest and trial.[55]

One could not, in the nineteenth century, wholeheartedly embrace the goal of abolishing all prostitution in the same way that one might advocate the abolition of vagabondage or theft or murder, for prostitutes performed a service that was recognized, with however much real or feigned reluctance, by society. Preventing the occurrence of prostitution took a distant second place to the need to keep Paris safe from the "dangerous classes," and the two goals were thought to be incompatible. Officials believed that prostitutes were the natural consorts of vagabonds and thieves. It was administratively convenient to believe, conversely, that the consorts of vagabonds and thieves were all prostitutes. Large-scale prostitution arrests disrupted the criminal activities in a given area. The arrests of nonprostitutes required the establishment of an offense in a manner suitable for a court of law; in addition, such offenses generally entailed a certain minimal sentence, if they were to be cost-effective, and limited prison space cut down the number of people who could be locked away. In contrast, many prostitutes could be arrested and kept for a short time, a practice that had the effect of breaking the continuity of their activities without straining the prison system.

In short, the prefecture had little interest in any kind of law that would have limited its ability to arrest prostitutes by defining the offense more precisely. Anglès, as we have seen, favored a royal ordinance recognizing the dispensary; in his report to the Interior, drafted in 1819, he seemed receptive to the idea of a royal ordinance on prostitution. The apparent receptiveness was in reality quite limited. What Anglès had in mind was either an ordinance confirming the regulatory

[55] PP DB 407, report of the Conseil général de la Commune de Paris, session of 4 October 1793. The office of lieutenant-general had been abolished, and the prefecture had not yet been established.

system as it then existed or an ordinance that would have given the prefect of police discretionary power over prostitutes, thus making him (as in the 1684 ordinance) their "judge of last resort."[56] This is what the prefect was in fact, through his subordinates; it was apparently not considered expedient to write this practice into an ordinance.

Legal Foundations

No law on prostitution was passed in France in the nineteenth century. Nevertheless, prostitution was policed and controlled throughout the country. Paris had provided the model for other French cities. The prefecture received requests for copies of the Parisian regulations from all over Europe, some of them unofficial (one, for example, from the son of the director of police of Rotterdam, who thought his father might be interested).[57] To all of these the prefecture responded with

[56] AN F⁷ 9305, *Compte rendu . . . sur la prostitution publique.* See also AN F⁷ 9305, report of 20 September 1817 from the prefect of police to the minister of the interior: "Autrefois les femmes publiques dont l'indiscipline est si opiniâtre aujourd'hui, étaient autrement contenues par la crainte. Le Magistrat de police investi d'un pouvoir judiciaire avait une latitude suffisante pour proportionner les peines aux fautes, car c'étaient les peines qu'il appliquait. . . . Ses pouvoirs à cet égard étaient en quelque sorte illimités; . . . A défaut de cette ancienne juridiction la police a dû pour le maintien de l'ordre et dans l'intérêt de la morale publique, tendre à la répression du scandale par ses seuls moyens administratifs; mais la crainte d'outrepasser ses pouvoirs ne la laisse pas maîtresse d'opposer au torrent une digue suffisante." As noted in Chapter 1, Anglès was not happy with the contemporary procedure of imprisoning many prostitutes for short periods of time; however, he accepted this, for his own solution (imprisoning great numbers of prostitutes for long periods of time) was financially impossible. Essentially he looked back to the good old days, when prostitution had supposedly been less serious.

[57] AN F⁷ 9305, letter of September 1836 from the prefect of police to the minister of the interior. There are also similar letters in this file from the ambassador of Sardinia, from the Vicomte de Carreira of Portugal, and from a number of French cities.

some pride. Anglès had dreams of future glory for the dispensary ("the precious institution of the Dispensaire de salubrité, which other capitals of Europe will perhaps someday take as a model").[58] It was only with the establishment of the Third Republic, in a movement coinciding with Butler's drive against the Contagious Diseases Acts, that opposition to this regulatory activity arose.[59]

Even the British abolitionists might have felt discouraged by the magnitude of the problem in France. The regulatory system proved a very elusive target indeed, for there was no single law, or set of laws, whose revocation would automatically have ended the arbitrary treatment of prostitutes. Instead, the system was based on the imaginative interpretation of the provisions of a variety of laws, some of them fundamental to the French government and none concerned specifically with prostitution.

The French legal situation was so far removed from the British, in fact, that the French government had no clear idea of the extent of the regulatory system in France. The first nationwide survey of the matter was not published until 1908, by Felicien Hennequin, an official in the Ministry of the Interior. It grew out of a 1902 circular sent to departmental prefects, urging them to send copies of all local regulations as soon as possible. Despite the urgency (a mystery, since the French government had left the issue alone for a hundred years) the prefects were unable to reply immediately. The policing of prostitution was one of the few areas of the gov-

---

[58] AN F⁶ II Seine 19, letter of 27 December 1820 from the prefect of police to the minister of the interior.

[59] For a brief discussion of the repeal campaign against the Contagious Diseases Acts, see E. M. Sigsworth and T. J. Wyke, "A Study of Victorian Prostitution and Venereal Disease," in Martha Vicinus, ed., *Suffer and Be Still* (Bloomington: Indiana University Press, 1972), pp. 77-99. A fuller study of prostitution and reform movements in Britain is Walkowitz, *Prostitution and Victorian Society.*

ernment to be explicitly decentralized (by a circular dated 23 April 1859)[60] and there had been no inquiries on the matter, as Hennequin noted, since "time immemorial." The survey eventually encompassed the 445 communes in France (for a total population of 8.3 million) having one or more regulations concerning prostitution; virtually all large cities, with some notable exceptions, had a regulatory system. The greatest extension of the regulations throughout France had coincided with, and perhaps stimulated, the abolitionist movement; 429 of the 470 regulations dated from 1870 on.[61]

Perhaps of greatest utility was Hennequin's evaluation of the legal foundations of prostitution control. Faced with a multitude of separate systems, he simply counted the *visas (Vu la loi de ____),* or legal bases, invoked at the beginning of each regulation. Certain laws, ordinances, *arrêtés,* and even ministerial directives appeared more frequently than others, and so he was able to establish a list of the eighteen most frequently quoted legal justifications. Hennequin regarded the list as too long. "Nothing," he said, "could better betray the uncertainties and hesitations of the municipalities about the foundation of their powers."[62]

The Prefecture of Police, whose regulatory system served as a model for the rest of France, felt no such uncertainty, and generations of prefects had cited the multiple justifications that appeared in the report as proof of the ample legal foundation of the regime. Hennequin's summary, in its emphasis on the old laws of the Revolution and Empire that had shaped

---

[60] PP DB 407, ministerial circular of 23 April 1859. This is reprinted in Felicien Hennequin, "Annex III: Rapport sur la réglementation de la prostitution en France," in Hennequin, *Annexes,* pp. 4-5.

[61] Hennequin, "Annex III," pp. 7, 20-21.

[62] At the same time Hennequin recognized that it was customary for local regulations of all types to be encumbered with every conceivable kind of justification. Ibid., p. 27; his list of laws and commentary can be found on pp. 25-35.

the prefecture's system, revealed the extent to which most other cities must simply have copied Paris.

The Law of 19-22 July 1791 held first place as the law most frequently invoked. It was a lengthy and complicated establishment of police powers and seemed to touch upon prostitution in several places. The most apparently clear-cut reference established penalties for those who "outraged the modesty of women" and minor children by selling obscene publications or as panderers; however, the fact that this was not considered a sufficient deterrent to prostitutes was indicated by subsequent attempts to frame a prostitution law.[63] The Law of 16-24 August 1790 was the third most frequently cited, and like the first it was a long and complex constituent law, in this case on the foundation of judicial powers. The relevant passages gave municipal bodies the right to take steps to control "calamitous scourges," mentioning fires and human and animal epidemics as examples.[64] Venereal disease was held to be sufficiently epidemic to qualify, and the dispensaries and

[63] Law of 19-22 July 1791, tit. 2, art. 8, in Jean Baptiste Duvergier, *Collection complète des lois, décrets, ordonnances, règlements, et avis du Conseil d'état*, 30 vols. (Paris: Guyot, 1834-1838), III:114-126. "Ceux qui seraient prévenus d'avoir attenté publiquement aux moeurs, par outrage à la pudeur des femmes, par actions deshonnêtes, par exposition ou vente d'images obscènes, d'avoir favorisé la débauche ou corrompu des jeunes gens de l'un ou de l'autre sexe, pourront être saisis sur-le-champ et conduits devant le juge de paix, lequel est autorisé à les faire retenir jusqu'à la prochaine audience de la police correctionnelle. . . ." Parent-Duchâtelet did not believe this law was meant for prostitutes: "Il est évident que le législateur de cette époque n'a voulu atteindre que ces êtres qui débauchent les jeunes gens de l'un et de l'autre sexe pour les prostituer à un individu. Ne disant rien de la prostitution, il paraît qu'il la regarde comme un métier que chacun avait le droit d'exercer, et qu'un règlement à cet égard serait un attentat contre la liberté individuelle." Parent did not make this comment with approval; he believed the resultant lack of legal restraint had led to complete license. *De la prostitution*, II:300-301.

[64] Law of 16-24 August 1790, tit. 2, art. 5, in Duvergier, *Collection*, I:310-333.

mandatory examinations were based on this power. A related law of the same vintage, and the fifth most frequently cited, was the Law of 14-22 December 1789 on the powers of municipalities. Article 50 granted such bodies the right to allow inhabitants to enjoy the advantages of a "good police," notably in the matters of cleanliness, hygiene, and tranquillity in public places.[65]

These laws, written during the early years, indeed the early months, of the Revolution, had at best an implicit connection to prostitution and did not rule on prostitution as a crime in itself. Similar in type was the second most frequently cited *visa,* an "organic law" (5 April 1884) on the powers of the municipality. It superseded in whole or in part previous laws of the same type, including the Municipal Law of 18 July 1837, the seventh most frequently cited law; the Law of 5 May 1855 on municipal organization, the sixteenth most frequently cited; and the laws of 24 July 1867, 2 Pluviôse Year IX, and 18 November 1814, which shared eighteenth place.[66] Most of these laws had been written too late to have any real influence on the Parisian system, except in the sense that they reinforced the rights of muncipalities to take necessary measures in the matter of public health and public order.

The Penal Code figured as the fourth most commonly cited source. Paris tended to emphasize Article 484, which kept in force all ordinances of the old regime not specifically abro-

---

[65] Law of 14-22 December 1789, art. 50, in Duvergier, *Collection,* I:63-71.

[66] Hennequin, "Annex III," pp. 25-27, 35-36. Hennequin stated that the legal base of regulation "réside tout entière, aujourd'hui, dans la loi du 5 avril 1884 et qu'il n'est pas nécessaire de viser d'autres lois dans les arrêtés municipaux." The relevant passages of the law, as summarized by Hennequin, seemed a rather fragile base: Article 91 gave the mayor control of the Police municipale; articles 94 and 95 gave him the right to make "permanent or temporary" *arrêtés* on matters under his control; and Article 97 charged him with ensuring "le bon ordre, la sûreté et la salubrité publique."

gated or replaced. Provincial regulations quoted the articles beginning with 330 on *attentats aux moeurs* and "public outrages to modesty"; Article 471, an outline of the sanctions against violations of mayoral edicts; and the articles beginning with 269, on the punishments of vagabonds and *gens sans aveu*. Article 471, like so many of the citations, had no explicit connection to prostitution. Article 330 was, like the Law of 19-22 July 1791, a prohibition against "debauching" minors through seduction or rape. Finally, prostitutes tended not to be treated as vagabonds in French law (and were not so treated even by the communities who invoked these powers) and so these articles were largely irrelevant.[67]

To find an explicit reference to prostitution it was necessary to go back to the most popular *visa*, the Law of 19-22 July 1791, which authorized the police to enter places "notorious" for debauchery.[68] The *arrêté* of 5 Brumaire Year IX, number six on the list, determined the functions of *commissaires;* they were charged, among their other duties, with "the surveillance of *maisons de débauche* and those who frequent them."[69] The phrasing in both these laws acknowledged the existence of such places and even, in the case of the second, suggested a kind of tolerance for them. Similar in nature, but relevant only to Paris, was the 1800 law that established the Prefecture of Police. The terms of this law were similar to the others: the prefecture was authorized to keep under surveillance "the houses of prostitution, and those who reside there or are found there."[70] The prefecture used all these provisions as part of the justification for the rather elaborate set of rules governing

[67] Ibid., pp. 30-31.

[68] Law of 19-22 July 1791, tit. 1, art. 10, in Duvergier, *Collection,* III:114-126.

[69] Law of 5 Brumaire Year IX (27 October 1800), art. 8, in Duvergier, *Collection,* XII:319-323.

[70] Law of 12 Messidor Year VIII (30 June 1800), sec. 2, art. 9, in Duvergier, *Collection,* XII:250-254.

the *maisons de tolérance,* but some officials elsewhere in France found the limits of authority to be rather ambiguous. One departmental prefect lamented the lack of clarity: "The Law of 22 July 1791 authorized *police officials to enter at any time places notoriously given over to debauchery* without explaining further the power of these functionaries. However they enter there for something, apparently."[71]

To go through all the remaining eighteen *visas* individually would be pointless. It is enough to say that the others were procedural or organizational in nature, or had a restricted or improper reference to *filles publiques;* one, for example, was the already cited Law of 8-10 July 1791 concerning the arrest of prostitutes found in military encampments, and two others referred to vagabondage.[72] Yet another, the decree of 24 Vendémiaire Year II, reflected an interesting state of affairs, if not a clear mandate. The relevant article stated that "persons imprisoned for [having] venereal disease will be sent, at national expense, into hospitals."[73] Upon careful examination, Hennequin did not find that this law provided a clear-cut justification for the imprisonment of those with venereal dis-

---

[71] AN F⁷ 9305, letter of 21 February 1833 from the acting prefect of the Department of Haute Marne to the Ministry of the Interior.

[72] Law of 8-10 July 1791, tit. 3, art. 52, in Duvergier, *Collection,* III:82-98. "Toutes femmes ou filles notoirement connues pour mener une vie débauchée, qui seront surprises avec les soldats dans leurs quartiers lorsqu'ils seront de service, ou après la retrait militaire, seront arrêtées et remises sans delai à la police civile, pour être jugées conformément aux lois." The vagabondage laws were the imperial decree of 23 Fructidor Year XIII (10 September 1805) and the decree of 10 Vendémiaire Year IV (2 October 1795), in Duvergier, *Collection,* XV:258-259 and VIII:301-303. The remaining legal justifications uncovered by Hennequin, and not mentioned elsewhere, were the following: the Law of 28 Pluviôse Year VIII, concerning the responsibilities of municipal governments; Article 1384 of the Civil Code, concerning the responsibilities of property owners; and the ordinance of 29 October 1820, on the duties of the gendarmerie.

[73] Decree of 24 Vendémiaire Year II (15 October 1793), tit. 2, art. 8, in Duvergier, *Collection,* VI:229-230.

ease, as it seemed to do. Instead, it merely stated that people who were imprisoned for such cause should be cured, and made no reference to any law authorizing their arrest and detention. In Hennequin's view, the article "only revealed a situation of fact"—that is, acknowledged that *vénériens* were being imprisoned—and "does not have the constituent force that one seeks."[74] Arbitrary practices of the old regime, continued through the Revolution, accounted for the imprisonments.

Another *visa* worthy of note was the ordinance of 6 November 1778, the oldest justification cited and the only holdover from the old regime. This has been mentioned before as the basis for the policing of lodging houses. It was the culmination, and can be considered as the replacement, of all previous injunctions against landlords who rented to prostitutes. Under its terms, landlords were fined 500 livres for renting apartments to prostitutes, and lodging-house keepers were fined 200 livres for allowing them to stay overnight. This law received sporadic enforcement at best, and it was finally abrogated. As Hennequin pointed out, it should not have been on the national list at all, for it concerned only Paris. Even Parisian officials preferred to ignore its barbaric first article, which stated that prostitutes found on the streets or at their windows would be seized and have their heads shaved, and might even be subject to corporal punishment.[75]

Finally, two of the justifications cited (they shared eleventh place) were found only through detective work by Hennequin; they had apparently been used by generations of mayors

[74] Hennequin, "Annex III," pp. 33-34.
[75] Royal ordinance of 6 November 1778, in Isambert, *Anciennes lois françaises,* XXV:448. Usually associated with this was an ordinance that prohibited tavernkeepers from serving or sheltering prostitutes; it too was considered to have survived the Revolution. Royal ordinance of 8 November 1780, in Isambert, *Anciennes lois françaises,* XXVI:396.

who had never in fact read them but had merely copied them from other regulations. These were the ministerial directives of 17 October 1814 and 28 August 1833. The 1814 directive ratified the system already in existence in Paris, including the right of the authorities to imprison prostitutes without trial:

> Civil laws neither authorize nor protect the establishments of prostitution. One tolerates them in populous cities *to avoid a greater evil;* and it is to this consideration alone, that the *maisons de tolérance* owe their existence.... The municipal authority has similarly the right to make all the regulations relative to these houses which it judges necessary, or simply useful. It can order their closing, when they compromise public tranquillity, *administratively punish the prostitutes who bring it on by their conduct,* and submit them to a regime that considerations of public health may require.[76]

Except in the matter of administrative punishment, this directive remained valid throughout the century. Ministerial opinion had changed by the July Monarchy, and the 1833 directive categorically denied the possibility of administrative detention:

> By the terms of the old ordinances, prostitutes found themselves by the very fact of their prostitution outside common law, but this can no longer be the case under our constitutional regime. However, if one cannot apply to them the dispositions of the old edicts, the civil authority has nevertheless kept the right to submit them to the police regulations, such as the localities require, on the maintenance of order and the care of public health.... But the civil authority neither can punish nor cause them to be punished administratively, nor imprison

[76] Hennequin, "Annex III," p. 41.

[88]

them, nor cause them to be conducted by the gendarmerie to their birthplace, so long as they have not been sentenced in the Tribunal de police correctionnelle, in conformity with Article 330 of the Penal Code, for indecent behavior (*outrage aux moeurs*).[77]

This directive was clear enough. While upholding the right of municipalities to register prostitutes and subject them to medical exams, it explicitly denied their power to imprison prostitutes arbitrarily. Why, then, did this not immediately affect the Paris regime? Because there was one document that even Hennequin's detective work did not turn up, and it was the most revealing of all.

Two months after the directive just cited was written, an unknown functionary in the Ministry of the Interior roughed out a letter to be sent to the prefect of police in response to a copy (sent by request of the ministry) of the prostitution regulations. The author of the letter approved the regulations generally, but expressed the same reservations about the Parisian practice of arresting and imprisoning prostitutes without trial:

> In effect, prostitutes are not exempted from common law, and in no case does the civil authority have the right to punish them by administrative measures; legally, under Article 471, Section 15 of the new Penal Code, it can only place their cases in the charge of the public ministry if they act contrary to police regulations; but no incarceration can take place without a judgment of the Tribunal de simple police or Tribunal correctionnel, according to the case.
>
> It is in this sense that it is necessary to change the regulations that you have sent me; and, save this indis-

[77] Ibid., pp. 41-42.

pensable modification, I see no drawbacks to the system you have described at Paris.

All of the above was scratched out; written above it, in a different hand, was the final draft:

> In effect, prostitutes in Paris are considered (if not legally) as individuals outside common law, and I believe that such a regime, so long as its legality has not been contested, is useful to maintain, in that the efficacy of police measures depends on the promptness with which they can be carried out. We must, then, avoid compromising this salutary jurisprudence by urging the mayors of other cities of the kingdom to adopt it; because court cases could arise on the legality of administrative detention, and it is feared that the tribunals could rule in a manner contrary to the system established in Paris.[78]

Not only did the Prefecture of Police act illegally in imprisoning prostitutes "administratively," but it and the Ministry of the Interior knew that such actions were illegal. Their prime concern was to act with discretion, at least in Paris, even if prostitutes in the rest of France were as a result treated somewhat more benignly.

There is no evidence that this almost refreshingly cynical piece of work was ever formally copied and sent to the prefect of police, but the sentiments expressed were transmitted successfully. The prefecture continued its practice of "administrative detention," while prostitutes in other cities of France were generally sent before the Tribunal de simple police, a

---

[78] AN F⁷ 9305, rough draft of letter, dated 5 October 1833, from the Ministry of the Interior to the prefect of police.

court established to deal with simple contraventions of police regulations. The punishments that this court was allowed to administer were minor and uniform.[79] Administrative detention remained the only significant difference between the individual systems of Paris and the other cities in France. There were numerous minor variations in the frequency of mandatory exams, in the policy toward legal minors, in the definition of streetwalking offenses. Aside from that, all French cities with prostitution control featured some form of inscription and mandatory medical examination; usually, as in Paris, there was a distinction made between house prostitutes and *isolées*.[80] The frequent similarity of phrasing is explained by the fact that most municipalities seem to have used the same guide when drawing up their regulations: Eloi-Marie-Mathieu Miroir's *Recensement méthodique des dispositions législatives et réglementaires,* first published in 1834 as a how-to book for local bureaucrats.[81]

Opinions on the regimes were not always uniform. Local courts sometimes found in favor of prostitutes arrested under the terms of the police regulations. When that happened, local authorities, fearful that their power base might be eroded, often sent the case to the Cour de cassation for a judgment on the point of law. The Cour de cassation almost always

[79] Imprisonment imposed by this court could not be less than one day or more than five; fines ranged from 1 to 15 francs. Henry S. Sanford, *The Different Systems of Penal Codes in Europe* (Washington, D.C.: Tucker, 1854), p. 26.

[80] Regulations in France are filed in alphabetical order by department in AN F⁷ 9304 and 9305. The 1857 edition of Parent-Duchâtelet includes a lengthy appendix of essays on regulatory systems in a number of French and other European cities. Guyot, *La Prostitution,* has the results of an informal survey of regulatory systems throughout France, conducted by Guyot himself. Finally, there are many monographs on the regulatory systems of various cities.

[81] Hennequin, "Annex III," p. 44.

upheld the right of the *mairie* to place arbitrary restrictions on prostitutes, on the grounds that the mayor had the right to ensure the safety and tranquillity of his constituents.

Typical of these cases was a suit brought on the basis of a decision by the Tribunal de simple police in Chartres. The city of Chartres had a regulation that prohibited prostitutes from stationing themselves in public to attract customers and that ordered prostitutes off the streets after 7:00 p.m. Marguerite Rousseau and Victorine Lecomte had been found "standing and circling" in a public place after hours. The facts of the case were not in question, for they had indisputably been in the area at a late hour, and "it is nowhere a matter of doubt that [they] . . . are known by the police as professional prostitutes." Nevertheless the police court had found in their favor, on the grounds "that their presence on this public promenade is contrary neither to public order nor to morality, for they did nothing to attract passers-by to them; and that the prohibition in question is not obligatory, no authority having the right to prevent anyone from leaving his home for any licit cause." The police *commissaire* appealed this, and the Cour de cassation overturned the lower court's judgment on the grounds that the decision had "arbitrarily restrained" the power of the municipality to make regulations on this matter.[82]

A similar case in 1847 upheld the municipality's right to subject prostitutes to a medical exam. Once again it was the *commissaire*, having been defeated in the Tribunal de simple police by a decision favorable to the prostitutes, who carried the matter to the highest appellate court. And once again it was the municipality's right to ensure the "public tranquillity" and, in this case, the health of the community, that was judged

---

[82] *Arrêt* of 23 April 1842, in *Bulletin des arrêts de la Cour de cassation rendus en matière criminelle* (Paris: n.p., 1842), XLVII:158-159.

paramount.[83] The women involved in these cases had little interest in challenging them, both because of the mildness of the penalties involved and because of the natural desire to avoid notoriety. It was the municipal establishments who appealed for clear rulings from the court, and they were usually satisfied; court decisions throughout the century upheld different aspects of the regulatory system.[84] Administrative detention, practiced in Paris alone, was apparently not challenged in court, as the Ministry of the Interior had predicted; and of course, the Cour de cassation reviewed court decisions, and the administrative hearing given prostitutes left no judicial trace.

In light of the string of decisions that upheld the regulatory system, it was small wonder that prostitutes or their families expected little help from the judiciary.[85] Yet the prefectural archives preserved the record of at least one judgment, stemming from a decision of the Tribunal de simple police of Nîmes, that went against the regulatory system. One Virginie Castagnier, arrested as a "clandestine prostitute," had been released by the tribunal on the grounds that she was innocent of the charge. The *commissaire* appealed the decision. His

[83] *Arrêt* of 3 December 1847, summarized in *Documents fournis par M. le Préfet de police sur le prostitution publique* (Paris: n.p., 1878), pp. 35-39. The laws cited as the basis for such decisions were the Municipal Law of 18 July 1837, the Law of 16-24 August 1790, and the Law of 19-22 July 1791.

[84] For a list of the most relevant Cour de cassation cases, see Hennequin, "Annex III," pp. 35-36.

[85] One sister of a minor in a house of prostitution complained bitterly about the court's exoneration of her sister's madam: "[Si elle] avait été la fille d'un riche sûr & certain qu'elle aurait été punie. Comme c'est la fille d'un ouvrier, et que la patronne de l'établissement est riche c'est pour cela que l'affaire ne marche pas." The *procureur général* claimed in response that the girl "avait trompé la bonne foi de la femme Mondan, de la police d'Uzes, et du médecin de l'établissement" in allowing them to believe she was twenty-one. AN BB[18] 2156, letters of March and April 1900.

appeal was rejected on the grounds that the determination of guilt or innocence was one of the functions of the court.[86]

OLD IDEAS, NEW RULES

The legal relationship between prostitutes and government in Paris could easily be summed up in a single word: *tolérance*. Administrators received the policy as a legacy of the old regime, and subsequent revolutions did not prompt the slightest questioning of it. A circular from April 1848 spoke of the recent "interruption of surveillance" caused by the February Revolution and ordered all "citizen-*commissaires*" to begin once again to repress the disorders created by public prostitution; several months later, after the June Days, the citizen-prefect introduced reforms into the regulatory system of such Draconian severity that they had to be abandoned less than a year later.[87] The Communal government in 1871 passed a law against prostitution and drunkenness,[88] but prostitution control in this period was most affected by the group resignation (led by Clerc, the *médecin en chef*) of all the doctors of the dispensary. "No one has the right to cause . . . the disorganization of a public service," stated this first of all communist governments, and a warrant was put out for Clerc's arrest.[89] The regime was fully reinstated, without much delay, after the fall of the Commune. Regulationists throughout the nineteenth century continued to insist, at first complacently but then with growing urgency, that prostitutes were "outside the law." Such an assertion was absurd; a law that could accommodate assassins, sheep stealers, forgers, and Corsican

[86] PP DB 408, *arrêt* of 30 July 1875.
[87] PP DB 407, note of 27 April 1848; *Le Moniteur universel,* 10 October 1848. For discussion of the failure of the second reform, see Lecour, *Paris et Londres,* pp. 81-82.
[88] PP DB 407, *Journal officiel de la Commune,* 18 May 1871.
[89] PP DB 408, *Paris Journal,* 11 May 1871.

vendettists could make room for prostitutes. Medieval authorities, with whom the expression originated, had given it literal meaning by sending prostitutes outside the city walls. Taken out of context, as it was in the nineteenth century, the expression marooned prostitutes in an indefinable place: if they were not within the boundaries encompassed by the law, then where were they?

They were, apparently, in "tolerance." *Tolérance* was itself hard to define, a nether region between legality and illegality. Prostitution was "tolerated," which meant that it was not authorized or protected or prosecuted. Normally lucid administrators became confused and uncertain in their attempts to invoke this concept for the uninitiated, to explain why a law on prostitution was not only impossible but undesirable. By the simplest definition, tolerance meant that, although prostitution could be regarded as illegal (if not in itself, then in certain aspects inseparably related to it) the authorities would not bring the force of law to bear upon it; they could, however, at any moment choose to exercise their power. The result was a situation of great tension, harboring much potential for abuse. Despite the obvious problems, the concept of tolerance was virtually sanctified by time, by legal traditions dating back to Saint Louis and beyond. The nineteenth-century system had come into being by virtue of the imaginative recasting of new rules onto old ideas; the very familiarity of the regulatory system obscured the fact that it was, within the legal environment of the nineteenth century, a complete anachronism.

° 3 °

Parent-Duchâtelet:
Theorist of the Regime

In the first decade of the nineteenth century, a young Parisian
medical student was struck by what he regarded as incon-
gruous behavior on the part of prostitutes brought into his
classroom. He later recalled the occasion:

> I took the course taught by Michel Cullerier some twenty
> years ago, and I have not forgotten the profound impres-
> sion made on the prostitutes by the examination and dem-
> onstration of their maladies before a large audience. All,
> without exception, even including the most shameless,
> would blush; they would hide themselves and regard as
> torment the examination to which they were submitted.[1]

Subsequent experience only confused him further. Arrested
prostitutes, he discovered, firmly refused to appear before the
commissaires until they were fully dressed; if they had been
in a brawl the night before, their modesty occasioned a delay
as they were forced to borrow from others. He found that
when he entered the prison while they were dressing, "one
sees them instantly cover themselves or cross their arms over
their breasts."[2]

This bemused intruder seems an unlikely candidate to write

[1] Parent-Duchâtelet, *De la prostitution,* I:119-120.
[2] Ibid., I:119.

a study of prostitutes, much less a brilliant study; nevertheless, the publication of *De la prostitution dans la ville de Paris* marked the first occasion that prostitution had been treated as a serious social problem. The author, Dr. Alexandre-Jean-Baptiste Parent-Duchâtelet, had enjoyed modest renown before the 1836 publication of his two-volume study. Fame had eluded him, for it is difficult to become famous by writing, as he did, about clogged sewers, polluted rivers, dead horses, and other problems of public health. He was a member of the Paris Conseil général de salubrité, from 1825 to 1836, and a founding editor (1829) and frequent contributor to the *Annales d'hygiène publique et de médecine légale,* the most prestigious French journal in its field. He wrote monographs on a variety of topics, often acting as reporter to various specially formed subcommittees of the Conseil général. His publications were utilitarian, not meant to entertain, but nevertheless made palatable by his easy style.

It was only with *De la prostitution* that Parent seemed consciously to strive toward a more ambitious goal. The research and writing of the book had occupied him for eight years, beginning in 1828; it was undertaken in addition to his regular work for the council and his medical practice, which by this time was taken up entirely by charitable work for the poor. By its very nature the study of prostitution was a project that involved some danger, considerable embarrassment, and frequent difficulties. Nevertheless he continued, acquiring something of the persistence displayed by so many nineteenth-century writers—Marx, Macaulay, Michelet, for example—who became obsessed with a topic, researched it doggedly, wrote feverishly, and sent forth a stream of huge volumes. (Parent-Duchâtelet wrote only two huge volumes, but he also had an active professional career.) He visited the depths, fathomed their mysteries, wrote his book—and died. *De la prostitution* was a posthumous publication, and it was believed that the forty-five-year-old physician had killed himself with overwork.[3]

His apparent self-sacrifice was not without meaning. He became, by virtue of this single work, the chief authority on prostitution in the nineteenth century. His findings, though based on Paris, were accepted and adapted to circumstances throughout Europe. He was, at the same time, the chief apologist of the regulatory system. His work added immeasurably to the prestige of the *police des moeurs;* indeed, one might almost say that he created a respectable image for this generally despised service.

Yet despite his preeminence, Parent's entry into the field of prostitution by his own account was involuntary. A friend, described as a worthy man of modest means, had become interested in the reformation of prostitutes and had apparently made some attempts in that direction before discovering his complete ignorance of the lower classes. He had asked Parent-Duchâtelet to investigate prostitutes for him, and Parent apparently felt that he could not refuse, even though this simple request for aid would occupy eight years of his life and contribute to his death. Still, Parent could not have anticipated that, and neither could the anonymous friend, who died before the project was fairly started. With the death of its instigator Parent might have dropped the plan, but he felt bound to

[3] Parent became a doctor in 1814 but had given up the regular practice of medicine (for all except the poor) by 1821. He became a member of the Bureau central of the charity hospitals and, in 1823, became an *agrégé* of the Ecole de médecine, a position for which he had not applied. Parent's timidity, according to his biographer, prevented him from ever giving a single lesson and virtually incapacitated him when it came to examining a candidate. François Leuret, "Notice historique sur A.-J.-B. Parent-Duchâtelet," *Annales d'hygiène publique et de médecine légale* 16 (1836): v-xxiv. Leuret's essay was reprinted in the 1857 edition of *De la prostitution,* I:ix-xxiii. See also Ann Fowler La Berge, "A.-J.-B. Parent-Duchâtelet: Hygienist of Paris, 1821-1836," *Clio Medica* 12 (December 1977):279-301.

continue in the man's memory. And, too, at that point a belief in the importance of the task had led to enthusiasm: "It was no longer an obscure man who desired information on the prostitutes of Paris, it was my fatherland and, if I can so express it, all civilized governments. What a powerful stimulus for my zeal!"[4]

Parent also had an opportunity, as he realized, to overturn established stereotypes with solid proof. The regulatory system was in full operation by the time he began his studies and, like all bureaucracies, was in the business of collecting information; not the least of Parent's innovations was his recognition of the value of government statistics.[5] His carefully documented study in fact preserved much information that otherwise would have disappeared. By his own account, he barely finished his research in the police archives before the

---

[4] Parent-Duchâtelet, *De la prostitution,* I:2-3, 5. The importance that Parent attributed to his task can be seen by the fact that his will included a clause requesting that Louis-René Villermé, C.-E.-S. Gaultier de Claubry, and François Leuret see to the publication of his study in the event of his death. Fiaux, *Son Abolition,* II:144.

[5] The *Compte général de l'administration de la justice criminelle en France* began publication in 1825, providing statistics on the types of crimes committed, the verdicts, the sentences, and other pertinent data as well as personal statistics on those arrested. Lecuir has discovered an eighteenth-century study compiled by Montyon from the 10,021 cases sent to the Parlement of Paris during the years 1775-1786. Montyon divided his data according to the sex, age, and profession of the accused, the nature and location of the crime, the decision of the Parlement and the punishment exacted. Though this work was never published, its existence suggests that the idea of turning to statistics was in the air. Jean Lecuir, "Montyon, statisticien du Parlement de Paris," *Revue d'histoire moderne et contemporaine* 21 (juil.-sept. 1974):445-493. For an account of Parent-Duchâtelet's contemporaries, also statisticians, see Terence Morris, *The Criminal Area: A Study in Social Ecology* (London: Routledge & Kegan Paul, 1957), pp. 37-64. See also Yale Levin and Alfred Lindesmith, "English Ecology and Criminology of the Past Century," in Harwin L. Voss and David M. Peterson, eds., *Ecology, Crime and Delinquency* (New York: Appleton-Century-Crofts, 1974), pp. 47-64.

order was given to destroy the prostitution files.[6] Even before this wholesale destruction the police had not extracted any information except that which was administratively useful, such as inscription figures or disease rates. Parent was the first to try to collect bits of sociological information from the inscription books, volumes of such magnitude that he believed they would have frightened most people—indeed, if anyone had ever thought of looking. But, "more intrepid than others, I began the work; more persevering, I finished it."[7]

As Parent had realized, an important aspect of *De la prostitution* stemmed from his insistence upon bringing the scientific method to the study of people. He repeated his principles endlessly, in the hope of impressing them upon his fellow doctors and hygienists. He asserted that he made a "religion" of accuracy, a worship that was evident both in his observations and in his careful collection of statistics. Terms like "a great many," "often," and "very often" were not suitable for scientific discourse in the nineteenth century. Medicine did not satisfy him because it had not been practiced as a science; doctors had not, up to this time, collected methodical records that would allow them to generalize.[8] His goal in broad terms (though he could scarcely have expressed it in this way) was to extend the scientific method to the social sciences, which had long been dominated by armchair philosophers who composed utopian plans.[9]

The primary stage in any social reform was the gathering

---

[6] Parent-Duchâtelet, *De la prostitution,* I:12.

[7] Ibid., I:38.

[8] Ibid., I:14, 18, 238. Medicine, Parent believed, had the potential to be the most positive of the natural sciences by the use of the *méthode numerique.*

[9] Parent criticized those who, as he put it, "saisissent la plume, se renferment dans leur cabinet, font travailler leur imagination, et sans recueillir aucun fait, sans s'informer de ce qui existe, elles parviennent, dans l'espace de quelques jours, à composer un livre qu'elles distribuent à leurs amis." Ibid., I:8-9.

of facts; such patient labor may have been less glamorous than theorizing, but it was work to which he (with both modest and self-satisfied disclaimers) gladly devoted himself.[10] Parent's goals and purity of method did not prevent him from making some absurd mistakes; he apparently had a habit of launching himself into major statistical projects before he had thought them through. He sorted through eleven years of charity hospital reports, and performed lengthy calculations, to come to the completely fortuitous conclusion that patients with sores on their right legs tended to spend five days longer in the hospital than patients with sores on their left legs.[11] This mistake was less interesting than his most notoriously bad table, a hair/eye/eyebrow color chart listing the various hues of all the registered prostitutes in Paris. He himself disavowed this work, but for the wrong reasons. Parent had divided the prostitutes according to their origin in large cities, towns, or the countryside. He had assumed that the differences in environment would be expressed in coloring, but of course his tables yielded no such result. He concluded that prostitutes, coming as a rule from impoverished families, were not a fair measure of the effects of each area, and he decided to await a profile of the entire population before drawing conclusions.[12]

Parent tried to do justice to all the evidence he uncovered,

[10] "Si elle [the statistical method] a maintenant des détracteurs c'est qu'elle exige du travail, et que les travailleurs sont plus rares que les hommes d'esprit, même parmi les médicins." Ibid., I:19.

[11] Parent-Duchâtelet, "Recherches sur la véritable cause des ulcères qui affectent fréquemment les extrémités inférieures d'un grand nombre d'artisans de la ville de Paris," *Annales d'hygiène publique et de médecine légale* 4 (1830):268.

[12] This was based on information on 12,600 prostitutes. Parent-Duchâtelet, *De la prostitution,* I:190-197. He also included a chart on the height of prostitutes, reasoning that such a chart was useful because women were not subjected to administrative formalities (as men were in the army) that required measurement. I:197.

and he realized that he often presented a contradictory or incomplete portrait. "All this appears rather vague to some people," he wrote of one aspect of his discussion, "but I cannot create or invent information."[13] He was, as it turned out, far too modest in his estimation of the effect of his work. Given Parent's determination to overturn unproved assumptions, it was indeed ironic that his analysis of prostitutes was almost immediately granted the status of truth; for, despite Parent's insistence upon the need for observation, verification, and criticism, his conclusions were for the most part adopted wholeheartedly by those who came after.[14] Unfortunately, his work was also vulgarized, his tentative conclusions transformed by later writers into dogma, his arguments stripped of their refinements and exceptions. The nineteenth-century view of the prostitute was essentially that of Parent-Duchâtelet; few duplicated or added to his detailed research, preferring simply to copy his assertions (whether credited to him or not) as fact.

Parent-Duchâtelet's massive work had a double-edged result, in both cases different from what he had intended. Parent's preeminence in the study of prostitutes meant that he effectively defined the proregulatory position for the rest of the century. In general, he simply approved what the prefecture had done; he and several generations of regulationists (including many physicians and lawyers) would lend their prestige and professional approval to the policies of inscription, involuntary examination, and administrative detention in the hospitals and prisons. He also gave the stamp of or-

[13] Ibid., I:149.
[14] As Corbin has pointed out, not only were Parent's conclusions adopted but his methods and organization set the pattern for subsequent studies; his description of the various categories of prostitution "s'est imposée avec tant d'autorité qu'elle a obscuri la vision des enqueteurs ultérieurs." Corbin, *Les Filles de noce,* pp. 36-37, 18.

thodoxy to the policy of the *maison close*.[15] Though the prefecture soon abandoned the hope of enclosing all prostitutes within bordellos—indeed, repudiated the policy even before Parent's death—the regulatory system continued to be associated with the policy of physical enclosure and segregation. This point would become important later in the century, when the regulationist-abolitionist controversy was diverted into a debate of "closed" versus "open" prostitution.

Parent-Duchâtelet's second and more important achievement was his proletarianization of prostitutes, his transformation of them from the picturesque characters found in the works of Mercier and Restif de la Bretonne into the drab working-class figures of the nineteenth century. Parent's role as a transitional figure was reflected in the ambiguity of his presentation. He began by viewing prostitutes as guilty (because of their own proclivities) and ended by seeing them as innocent (because of their helpless economic position). He began by viewing prostitutes as creatures apart in a physiological sense, a kind of biological complement to their status "outside the law"; his studies of their coloring and height, his assessment of their personal and emotional qualities, his examination of their sexual organs, were all attempts to find some sort of identifying characteristic. He ended by seeing them as ordinary working-class women, though more unfortunate than most, for whom prostitution was only a passage in life. The two viewpoints merged and contradicted each

[15] "Ce milieu clos doit demeurer constamment sous le regard de l'administration. Invisible pour le reste de la société, il est parfaitement transparent pour ceux qui le contrôlent. La volonté de panoptisme, soulignée par Michel Foucault à propos de la prison, se traduit d'une manière quasi obsessionnelle dans le réglementarisme." Ibid., p. 25. This passage is insightful but perhaps a bit overstated: the Bureau des mœurs was not wedded to the policy of enclosure, nor did Parent-Duchâtelet seem to advocate enclosure, the *maison close* policy, for any but the most practical reasons of public order and safety.

other throughout his work, as they did in prostitution studies by those who came after. Not all those who followed Parent-Duchâtelet were able to match his essential honesty and freshness of vision, but all absorbed his conclusion: he had irrevocably transformed the prostitute from a *fille de joie* to a member of the urban proletariat.

THE SEWERS OF PARIS

Who was this pioneer, and why did he study prostitutes? A glance at his biography and writing reveals Parent-Duchâtelet as a recognizable French type, a politically neutral bureaucrat (viewing politics in the strictest sense of the word) from a family of neutral bureaucrats. He was born in Paris in 1790, the oldest of five children. The Parent family had for three hundred years held a minor office, which was suppressed, along with the accompanying seigneurial rights, in the Revolution. Aside from their large financial loss, the family was not endangered by the Revolution, and they retired peacefully from Paris to a country estate called Châtelet. Parent's biographer, no doubt indulging in a bit of hagiography, averred that he was serious even as a child: he "almost never played, but was always engaged in something useful"; he collected birds and insects. In 1806 he returned to Paris to study medicine, a career undertaken in deference to the wishes of his parents. It turned out to be a fortunate choice, for he had a scientific bent and found that his degree gained him ready entry to the field of public health. This was a new field, not yet fully defined. Parent himself defined it frequently as the study of problems that emerged from *réunions d'hommes,* or agglomerations of people; his opportunities for useful work were thus virtually unlimited.[16]

[16] Leuret, "Notice historique," pp. ix-xxiii. Parent was encouraged to enter the field by Jean Noël Hallé, at that time the distinguished occupant of

The Revolution was not an emotional watershed for Parent, as it was for many of his contemporaries. He regarded it, rather, as an annoying *bouleversement général,* the period when the administration had been interrupted and everything had been turned upside down. It had been an age of heroism, just as the eighteenth century had been and the nineteenth century would be, an era of intellectual giants. Parent consciously rejected heroism and genius to embrace the golden mean, both of intellect and achievement:

> That man who, through duty or self-sacrifice feels called upon to correct the abuses that he glimpses in the social order, and to throw some light on an obscure subject, should, above all, consult his strength, and see if it is equal to the scope of work that he proposes to undertake; he should examine his character and know if he is capable of struggling against the unavoidable obstacles that are confronted everywhere; he should be persuaded that perseverance and tenacity in this case replace genius, and that with the aid of these qualities, a very mediocre man may render services to his country that one would await in vain from the eloquence and brilliant dissertations of those who value only the productions of their own minds. These dazzle, and enjoy honors during their lives; the other remains in obscurity, but he does good work, and he knows it. Sometimes his memory is respected.[17]

He cared little for politics. Of his many casual comments about the Revolution of 1789—he seldom had occasion to

---

the chair of public hygiene. Erwin H. Ackerknecht, "Hygiene in France, 1815-1848," *Bulletin of the History of Medicine* 22 (March-April 1948):117-155.

[17] Parent-Duchâtelet, *De la prostitution,* I:10-11

refer to it directly—perhaps none was more revealing than his complaint that "political events" and the attention they had attracted had slowed the establishment of public health councils in the major cities of France. His belief that the councils would have continued their inevitable march onward, had not men's minds been absorbed by war and Napoleon, revealed his strong belief in the significance, the power, and the permanence of the administration.[18] For his own part, he felt no hesitation about serving whatever regime was in power; for although he had been appointed to the General Health Council by a Restoration prefect, he quickly became preoccupied—"shortly after the reestablishment of the prefecture"—with a sanitation problem involving the disposal of corpses left from the July Revolution.[19] He had, in short, an astute appreciation of the importance of the bureaucracy and of the middle-level officials who largely controlled local events. His research for *De la prostitution* spanned the Restoration and the July Monarchy; the exchange of one dynasty for another was scarcely mentioned by him, but the differences between various prefects of police were outlined in some detail—and correctly so, for a prefect could give a significant push, one way or another, to the handling of local problems.

Despite his indifference to politics in the strictest sense of the word, Parent was combative in other areas. The council rejected one of his reports, on the disposal of dead horses, because of its intemperate language, and his work as a whole was marked throughout with explanations, apologies, de-

[18] Parent-Duchâtelet, "Quelques considérations sur le Conseil de salubrité de Paris," in *Hygiène publique, ou mémoires sur les questions les plus importantes de l'hygiène,* 2 vols. (Paris: J.-B. Baillière, 1836), I:4. This article was originally published in the *Annales* in 1833.

[19] Parent-Duchâtelet, "Note sur les inhumations et les exhumations qui ont eu lieu à Paris, à la suite des événements du mois de juillet 1830," *Annales d'hygiène publique et de médecine légale* 4 (1830):63-79.

scriptions of failures and triumphs, defensive justifications, and self-congratulations.[20] He kept himself constantly braced for waves of criticism that, in truth, seldom came; he seemed to have been almost universally honored and respected by the professional men who made up his social circle. Still, Parent could become belligerent about the general public's neglect of what was truly important. "How many of the men of Paris," he wrote in the introduction to his study of the sewers, "solely occupied with pleasure or business, pass through all parts of this city without trampling underfoot its most useful monuments, in that these monuments contribute to the preservation of health, and that if for a single instant they ceased to exist or even to be regularly maintained, the city would become uninhabitable?"[21] Sewers, the object of his rhetorical question, were not merely ignored but, in Parent's words, were trampled underfoot. This oddly placed sense of grievance no doubt sprang from the same source as his rather curious attack on genius: he saw both himself and the sewers as doing the unheralded but necessary work of society.

If Parent considered himself to be overlooked, he had only himself to blame; he took a perverse pride in doing things that gave others pause. One of his minor studies, on leg ulcers, was undertaken precisely because of its inglorious utility and utter banality:

We understand very well that [other doctors] regard this part of their art as repulsive and thankless, as incapable

[20] Parent-Duchâtelet, "Des obstacles que les préjugés médicaux apportent dans quelques circonstances, à l'assainissement des villes et à l'établissement de certaines manufactures," in Parent-Duchâtelet, *Hygiène publique, ou mémoires,* I:12.

[21] Parent-Duchâtelet, "Essai sur les cloaques ou égouts de la ville de Paris," in Parent-Duchâtelet, *Hygiène publique, ou mémoires,* I:157. First published in the *Annales* in 1834.

of adding to their celebrity, of raising them above the level of their colleagues, above the herd of practitioners, but we ask if those who confine themselves to internal medicine have more pleasure in caring for consumption, uterine cancer, and this mass of often obscure and bizarre maladies that they can neither ease nor cure?[22]

His justification for studying prostitution was another tribute to his martyrdom:

> If I have been able... to penetrate into the sewers, to handle putrid matter, to spend a part of my time in the refuse dumps, in a sense to live in the midst of the most abject and disgusting products of large groups of people, why would I blush to enter a sewer of another type (a sewer more impure, I swear, than all the others) in the hope of doing some good?[23]

Then, too, his standards were not the standards of others. He reserved his superlatives for works outstanding in their utility; thus his sincere praise of Jacques-René Tenon's "great" work on the hospitals, of J.-N. Hallé's and Baron Dupuytren's "magnificent and beautiful" studies of cesspools.[24] (Even here he found cause for dispute, as he discovered that cesspools had been the object of many studies while sewers had gone virtually unnoticed. "And yet I can affirm ... that sewers are

[22] Parent-Duchâtelet, "Recherches sur la véritable cause," p. 303.

[23] Parent-Duchâtelet, *De la prostitution,* I:6. Such language was possible in pre-Freudian days.

[24] Parent-Duchâtelet, "Cloaques ou égouts," p. 288. Tenon was an eighteenth-century physician who advocated the establishment of public hospitals rather than the private charity hospitals which then predominated, with their limited numbers and strict conditions. Bloch, *L'Assistance et l'état,* pp. 59-60; Parent-Duchâtelet, "Cloaques ou égouts," p. 270. Baron Guillaume Dupuytren was a highly regarded pathologist, active in the administration as well as the author of numerous scholarly papers.

at least as essential as cesspools.")[25] If Parent's enthusiasms occasionally appeared ludicrous, that was at least in part because readers heard only his side of the conversation, only fragments of an ongoing dialogue, his tardy ripostes to challenges made earlier. Parent's public timidity was well known and made him unfit to shine in salons. It also caused him, a married man with children, some embarrassment concerning the choice of his masterwork. As usual he attempted to disarm expected attacks with his own frontal assault:

> Now I ask of everyone . . . if, in the interest of present and future generations, it is or is not useful to study and observe prostitutes, and if the man who devotes himself to this distasteful research, who sacrifices to it his time, his fortunes, and his labor, truly merits the scorn that prejudice, born out of ignorance, has maintained to this day? As for me, who believes himself to see things in their true light, and who knows that the consideration given a work is not always proportionate to the service it renders nor to the difficulties it can involve, I offer myself to the judgment . . .

Of God? That would seem to be the natural conclusion of such a peroration, but it was not. Parent's judges were to be "sensible men."[26]

To the extent that Parent-Duchâtelet figured as a subject of anecdotes—and this could not have been very great—his most amusing moments concerned not prostitutes but sewers. "Parent did not have for sewers the repugnance that these places naturally inspire," wrote his biographer; "I would almost say that he liked them." On one of the few occasions that Parent was persuaded to come to an official function, he was so uncomfortable that he was reported to have confided

[25] Parent-Duchâtelet, "Cloaques ou égouts," p. 158.
[26] Parent-Duchâtelet, *De la prostitution,* I:7.

to a friend that he would "rather be in the sewers."[27] Parent was probably sincere, for he made rather as much a production of going underground as Victor Hugo. In his own eyes at least, Parent's sewer study had represented a triumph of method and will:

> Animated in this work, as in all those which have occupied me up till now, by the importance of the subject, and especially by the desire to make myself useful to my compatriots and to an interesting class of workers, I surmounted without hesitation the repugnance and the dangers inseparable from such studies. I sacrificed my time, my money, and my troubles; I cannot begin to talk of the things I did, the exhaustion I felt, the adversity of all types that I have had to endure. Could it be believed that some persons have refused me information? I conquered, by my perseverance and by my obstinacy, all these obstacles, which are far from honoring those who gave them birth.[28]

The sewers were the subject of Parent's first important independent project (most of the others had been in association with other members of the General Health Council) as well as the field in which he may fairly be said to have served his apprenticeship as a public hygienist. The choice of sewers was absurdly, uncannily appropriate in light of Parent's later work. Saint Augustine's maxim that the prostitute was the "sewer in the palace," the channel by which the gross impurities were removed from society, had long passed as a justification and a defense of prostitution, as Parent was aware.

[27] Leuret, "Notice historique," pp. xii, xiv-xv. "A voir tant de mouvement pour ne rien faire, tant d'empressement pour changer de place ou se montrer, il se rappelait ses précédents soirées si utilement remplies. 'J'aime cent foix mieux, dit-il bien bas à un de ses amis, qui l'avait amené là, aller dans un égout que de venir à cette réunion; on ne me verra plus ici.' "

[28] Parent-Duchâtelet, "Cloaques ou égouts," p. 160.

It was in that spirit that Parent later defended what he feared might be seen as an improper interest in the loose women of society.[29]

The sewer essay was important not merely for its odd resonance with the rest of Parent's work, but also for what it revealed of his investigative methods—his sense of what was important, for example—and for his overall success in discovering how to find out what he wanted to know. It was also clear that this work was, for him, a test of courage and endurance. His walks through the sewers were a significant but surely avoidable part of the research. He did not avoid them, and he listed his symptoms (shortness of breath, light-headedness, a headache that "stayed for several days") almost as evidence of personal failure; the sewer workers consoled him with the assurance that not all men were suited to the work.[30]

This determination to study the sewers from the inside out led Parent to what would become a startling contribution to his prostitution book: he interviewed working-class people and reported their responses. This emphasis upon people was an essential aspect of the work of any hygienist, of course, but Parent took the concern for healthful living conditions one step further, extending it to an interest in the behavior, the aspirations, the life style of the people he studied. His charity hospital work had put him in constant contact with the poor, but those contacts had occurred in a purely medical context; his patients had been suppliants. His relationship with the *égoutiers,* or sewer workers, represented a sustained companionship with members of the lower classes.

Parent's chief contact among the *égoutiers* was an elderly man named Charpian, who had been in the trade since before the Revolution and who appeared rather frequently in the

[29] Parent-Duchâtelet, *De la prostitution,* II:339.
[30] Parent-Duchâtelet, "Cloaques ou égouts," p. 247.

narrative, often as an authority. Parent's suspicion that the health of anyone with venereal disease was aggravated by working in the sewers was seconded by Charpian, who "told me several rather curious facts on this subject, and assured me that he took great care to examine all the young workers who were subordinated to him."[31] (A man who practiced spontaneous inspection was clearly a man after Parent's own heart.) Parent recounted with rather self-conscious pride that he had seen Charpian in his off-duty hours: "I have mentioned this Charpian, who was over seventy years old when I last saw him at his home, and who had worked in the sewers more than forty years."[32] Charpian represented for Parent an association of near equality with the lower classes, the more remarkable when one considers the physical appearance of the man: "On the right half of his face he had a corroding ulcer that had destroyed (on this side) the corner of the lips, the cheek, the lower eyelid, and the teguments of the nose; but one must not judge, in medicine, according to the first appearance, for I heard from this man himself that he had had this ulcer for thirty-six years; the progress had been excessively slow."[33]

Despite his appearance, Charpian had proved to be such a surprisingly intelligent companion that Parent was led into rhapsodic excesses over this group of workers in general, suggesting the existence of a kind of brotherhood beneath the soil. Their need of each other in dangerous work combined with their common poverty to create strong bonds, "and I would not be surprised if one were obliged to seek in the sewers of Paris the model of true happiness, if happiness consists in the certainty of having a true friend, as several

[31] Ibid., p. 256.
[32] Ibid., p. 250.
[33] Ibid., pp. 251-252.

ancient philosophers have thought."[34] To improve this friendship Parent proposed to organize it, by establishing a workers' society that would not only provide help in emergencies but would also monitor behavior: "Is there a better means to avoid vice and practice virtue than to know that there are fifty or one hundred persons who have the right to observe you, to chase you ignominiously from their society?"[35] Some might disagree, but Parent's belief in inspection, organization, and surveillance was reaffirmed in his study of prostitutes.

THE PROSTITUTION STUDY

Parent-Duchâtelet came to the study of prostitution with a great deal of experience in public hygiene and, perhaps just as important, with a reputation that allowed him ready access to police archives. The prefecture's trust was not misplaced. Much of Parent's study was concerned with an examination of the regulatory system, for which he had an almost uncritical enthusiasm, and of the hospitals and prisons that served it. More important was Parent's creative use of police statistics to learn about the prostitutes themselves. He began his study simply by counting. To end the wildly exaggerated contemporary estimates of the number of prostitutes in Paris, Parent compiled a monthly list of inscriptions for the years 1812-1832. This list, which is now the only source for these figures, showed a rather conservative count of registered prostitutes; he realized that there were others but did not share in what would later become a virtual mania over *insoumises*.[36] In opposition to the misconception that prostitutes in Paris were

---

[34] Ibid., p. 258.
[35] Ibid., p. 207.
[36] Parent-Duchâtelet, *De la prostitution,* I:32. The editors of the 1857 edition extended Parent's tables whenever possible; the inscription figures for 1833-1854 are in I:36.

almost all provincial, Parent proved that most of them were from Paris and that the next greatest number came from departments surrounding the Seine, areas whose women were drawn to Paris because of the natural attraction of an economic center.[37] Such findings violated sentimental notions about hordes of country girls seduced in the big city.

Parent's findings on social origins were hardly less startling. He began this part of the inquiry by questioning prostitutes about their families, but the results were unsatisfactory. (Prostitutes often claimed rather exalted family backgrounds.) In order to get the data he wanted, Parent finally had to attempt to initiate a change in the bureaucracy and, whether from his urging or by independent decision, the prefecture began in 1828 to require birth certificates as part of the inscription process. From the certificates he compiled a table on the professions of the fathers; this revealed that prostitutes were mostly the daughters of artisans (and as daughters they could not hope to achieve even the earning power of their fathers or brothers).[38] Parent found that fewer than five of the women he studied could be considered to be of good family, yet the idea of aristocratic and bourgeois prostitutes had some currency. "This shows us," noted Parent, "the tendency men have to generalize what is striking to them, and how many errors one exposes oneself to in reporting observations made out of air, which are based only on memories and which have never been registered in a methodical manner."[39] In apparent

---

[37] Ibid., I:37-52. Parent calculated that annually Paris saw about 298 of its native-born become prostitutes, the largest number furnished by any department. But he did not believe that those departments which furnished only a few women could necessarily congratulate themselves for their superior morality: "car il peut se faire, et il arrive, en effet, que les prostituées nées dans un pays très immoral restent toutes, ou presque toutes, dans le pays, tandis que celles qui habitent des endroits où elles ne sont pas supportées, cherchent à Paris un lieu de refuge." I:49.

[38] Ibid., I:66, 67-68.

[39] Ibid., I:69.

opposition to the notion of well-born prostitutes was another common opinion, that prostitutes were mostly illegitimate. Parent found this to be true of about one-fourth of all Paris-born prostitutes, a percentage four times greater than for those born elsewhere in the Department of the Seine.[40] In this case the stereotype of Paris as a "dangerous" city was upheld.

From the study of families Parent moved to the study of prostitutes themselves. An attempt to compile a list of former occupations yielded nothing more than a table of "truly frightening" length; nevertheless, it suggested the relatively greater danger for those in the unskilled and semiskilled needlework trades.[41] Parent's attempt to gauge the education of prostitutes was a challenge to his ingenuity, one that he finally overcame by studying the signatures on the inscription register. Some signed with only a cross, thus revealing themselves to be "totally ignorant and brutish"; others signed, but shakily, which was for Parent an indication of education begun but not finished; a firm signature thus showed someone whose education had been carried beyond the mere rudiments. He concluded that most prostitutes had little or no education.[42]

There were two tables on age. One showed the ages of women registered as of 31 December 1831, a date chosen arbitrarily in an attempt to reduce the large numbers involved. The ages clustered around the early and mid twenties. A second table, revealing the age at which prostitutes had been

[40] Ibid., I:74-75. Parent's study showed that half of all Paris-born illegitimate prostitutes had been recognized by their fathers. This study, like the previous one, had concerned itself with prostitutes inscribed after the 1828 rule.

[41] Out of a total of 3,102 prostitutes (Parent had taken "the last inscriptions made at the Bureau des moeurs") 1,559, or about 50 percent, were in needlework. Ibid., I:79-80.

[42] Out of Parent's 4,470 Paris-born prostitutes, 52 percent could not sign and 40 percent signed badly. Parent's two editors wondered about his interpretation, reasoning that a well-educated woman would feel more strongly the solemnity of the step she was taking, and thus her hand would be more likely to tremble. Ibid., I:85-89.

inscribed, showed a few children as young as ten or eleven on the roles—an embarrassing revelation, since the prefecture steadfastly denied that it ever inscribed children. It was in this set of tables that Parent first noted—though without, at this point, stressing the fact—that prostitution was a transitory state; his figures showed that, of the same 3,517 prostitutes listed, most had been inscribed for fewer than four years.[43]

Not all information was quantifiable, and Parent's personality sketch of the prostitute was impressionistic, though based on interviews (with prostitutes as well as administrative officials who came in contact with them) and observation. He saw the prostitute as improvident, heedless of the future, and flighty; she was unable to keep her mind on a single subject for any length of time, and had a constant need for noise and movement. She was quick to anger, sometimes moved to violence, but just as quick to forgive. Her behavior was immature, her emotions very close to the surface.[44] Parent found that her off-duty time, especially in the bordello, was spent in idleness. Police inspectors reported that prostitutes played games of lotto for hours at a time; they were also occasionally known to read. They avoided obscene books, an apparent contradiction that Parent attributed to "satiety."[45]

Prostitutes were liars. They began by lying in self-defense, to save themselves from the police or from prosecution, and eventually acquired the habit of lying about inconsequential things as well.[46] They were generous among themselves, gen-

[43] Ibid., I:90-95. Parent had nothing to say about the ten- and eleven-year-olds, but his editors felt that some justification was necessary. Until 1828, they explained, women were inscribed without personal information; thus it could have happened that children of "precocious" development, or with false identity papers, could have been inscribed. This of course does not explain how Parent was able to discover the correct ages from the police registers when the police could not.
[44] Ibid., I:121, 141-142.
[45] Ibid., I:128.
[46] Ibid., I:140-141.

erosity that arose from a recognition that their outcast status made them dependent on each other. They were often markedly enthusiastic about religion, but Parent believed that this was frequently a fanaticism born out of superstitious ignorance rather than genuine faith. He had heard (and this was one of the few bits of information that he passed along without his own verification) that prostitutes frequently helped their parents. He did not know how many made a practice of this, "but I have heard that the number was rather considerable."[47]

Physically, prostitutes seemed to be characterized by extreme obesity and "raucous" voices. While public opinion attributed their excess weight (which, Parent noted, was much less common than most people believed) to the mercury treatments prostitutes were forced to undergo, he attributed it instead to the "great number of hot baths" they took, as well as to their inactive life and their tendency to overeat. "Indifferent to the future, eating every moment . . . not rising till 10:00 or 11:00 a.m., how, with such an animal life, could they not fatten themselves?"[48] He also attributed the raucous voice (which, like obesity, was not universal) to the life style. It seemed to be most common among women who stationed themselves at the doors of cabarets and "who, in drunkenness, have the habit of crying out and vociferating." Parent attributed this rough voice to the all-weather activity of the street-walker as well as to the habit of heavy drinking.[49] Neither characteristic reflected a biological difference between prostitutes and other women.

Nor did they differ from other women in their fertility. Parent's research in the prisons, hospitals, and police registers (prostitutes were exempt from the medical examination two months before and two months after the birth of a child)[50]

---

[47] Ibid., I:142, 117, 143.
[48] Ibid., I:186-187.
[49] Ibid., I:188-189.
[50] Ibid., I:219.

led him to believe that pregnancies among prostitutes were far more common than was generally assumed. They often lost their children to miscarriages, whether recognized as such or not, or to abortions; he had observed a colleague's collection of fetuses, several of which bore perforation marks.[51]

If the children survived infancy, they frequently died later from the various hardships associated with their mothers' trade. Parent-Duchâtelet had heard of one prostitute who had been forbidden to take her child to the Petite Force with her, a fact that had filled her with understandable apprehension about the child's fate: "The sorrow she felt was such that she died a little each day, so that they were obliged, to save her life, to ask the prefect to release her." The commonly held assumption that prostitutes kept their daughters in order to profit from selling them later was regarded with skepticism by Parent: "These persons [who made the assertion], when pressed with questions by me, have never been able to give me the proof of what they advanced."[52] Indeed, many prostitutes did their best to protect their children. Parent cited this story, told him by a prison matron who had questioned a four-year-old girl who accompanied her mother to jail: "I stay by myself in my room; Maman puts me to bed early every day to go look for papa. . . . I have never seen him, but I hear him every evening."[53]

[51] Ibid., I:222-223. Parent questioned Dr. Serres, a physician at the Pitié, who suggested that miscarriages were frequent: "Les pertes abondantes sont rares chez ces femmes, mais les plus jeunes ont souvent des retards dans leurs règles, qui se terminent par l'expulsion de ce qu'elles appellent un *bondon*. Pendant deux années, je ne fis pas attention à cette expression; mais ayant dirigé mes recherches sur l'embryologie, j'examinai avec soin ces productions, et il me fut facile d'y reconnaître tous les caractères de l'oeuf humain; j'ai pu, dans un court espace de temps, en recueillir un grand nombre, qui tous étaient sortis à une époque qui indiquait une conception de quatre à cinq semaines. C'est toujours sur des filles de 18 à 24 ans que j'ai pu faire ces observations."

[52] Ibid., I:144-148.

[53] Ibid., I:149.

Within Parent's generally grim portrait were occasional bits of engaging information. He had, for example, in his research encountered a number of pseudonyms, or noms de guerre, frequently used by prostitutes, and he had (typically) broken them down into categories. The higher levels of prostitutes were likely to call themselves Natalie, Sidonie, Virginie, Aspasie; the lower ranks favored the more descriptive names: La Blonde, Grosse Tête, Belle-Cuisse, Louchon.[54]

Yet Parent's insistence upon an accurate, uncompromising observation of the prostitute prevented any trivializing of her condition. Parent's prostitute was a member of the proletariat—a woman constrained by economic need to practice her trade, not drawn to it by desire. His prostitute was ill-suited to make her way in the world, since she was uneducated or undereducated, unskilled or semiskilled. Romantic literary images of the hetaera could scarcely survive his discussion of head and body lice. (Body lice, he found, were no longer so commonplace as they had once been, though prostitutes were "remarkably negligent" about cleanliness.)[55] His assertion, in this as in everything, rested on personal observation as well as professional testimony.

Parent did not always know what to make of his observations. The camaraderie he had felt for the égoutiers was not carried over into these relationships; he approached prostitutes with reserve. In large part this was unavoidable, for he was fettered by circumstance and propriety. When he went to the maisons de tolérance, he assured his readers, he was "ALWAYS ACCOMPANIED BY AN INSPECTOR," and most of the prostitutes he talked to were in prison or the infirmary.[56] The impenetrable barriers of class and sex led to suspicion. He could not, for example, view friendships among prostitutes with the same philosophical approval he had bestowed on the com-

[54] Ibid., I:134.
[55] Ibid., I:137, 135.
[56] Ibid., I:17.

radeship of the sewer workers, for he always suspected prostitutes of lesbianism. He spoke of *mangeuses,* women observed by prison authorities because they made a habit of sitting together during meals. "Usually these *liaisons de table* are not criminal," he conceded.[57]

Incarceration made prostitutes vulnerable, and so did the fact that they were registered. Inscription made them virtual wards of the administration, subject not only to the whims of the police but also to the occasionally idle curiosity of a doctor. Parent's determination to study his subject in all its aspects did not have to be checked at any point by a concern for the rights of the individual. Thus his research found him examining tattoos on the breast of an imprisoned prostitute—he found thirty—in order to determine their content and variety. (Parent noted that he had seen only one obscene tattoo on a prostitute, "on a cadaver I was using for anatomical research.")[58] His speculations about the physical effects of prostitution led to revelation of a bizarre guessing game played with two of his colleagues in the prison infirmary. These gentlemen picked out certain prisoners to see whether Parent could determine by examination how long they had been prostitutes. "Several times," noted Parent, these men "have had the good nature to let me see some of these young unfortunate creatures; they have been careful to hide from me all the circumstances, so as to try my sagacity, and I avow that I have been grossly mistaken more than once."[59]

Despite the awkwardness of the circumstances, Parent-Duchâtelet found himself increasingly drawn to the prostitutes, to their stories, and to their lives—so alien from his own and yet almost comprehensible through his long experience as a physician to the poor. Their extreme attachment

[57] Ibid., II:151.
[58] Ibid., I:125-126.
[59] Ibid., I:206-207.

to their lovers, for example, was astonishing to him: "I have seen them come to the hospital, their eyes out of their heads, their faces bloodied and their bodies battered by the blows that their lovers, in a state of drunkenness, have given them; but, scarcely healed, they return to them." Or this: "One of them, seeing *her man* return to Paris, completely drunk, followed him from a distance to keep watch; on seeing him fall into a ditch she ran to get help, helped get him back to the road, then instantly turned herself in to the nearest police post *to escape his fury.*"[60] Another woman, whose story Parent verified for himself, had been forced to jump out a window twice within six months to escape beatings from her drunken *souteneur.* Prostitutes' letters to their lovers from prison, which he read, showed "the exaltation of their imagination; nothing dirty, nothing filthy in these letters; they are only protests of love."[61]

Slowly, through scattered details and impressions, he made the prostitute seem more human, her motives more comprehensible. His survey of the causes of prostitution served only to confirm the rest of his portrait. Prostitutes had not been driven to their state through innate peculiarities; economic need was the root cause of prostitution. The largest group of women had become *filles publiques* because of "misery," and the other causes—the loss of a lover or a husband, the need to care for aged parents—were mere variations of that.[62] (See Table 1.)

To be sure, some economic needs were more ignoble than others, tainted with idleness, immoral upbringing, and the fact that all prostitutes had, before entering this state, forgotten their "first duty." Young workingwomen, ashamed to appear in modest dress, were tempted by costume and or-

---

[60] Ibid., I:153-154.
[61] Ibid., I:154.
[62] Ibid., I:107.

TABLE 1
Reasons for Entering Prostitution,
According to Parent-Duchâtelet

Cause	Number of Prostitutes	Percentage of Total
Destitution	1,441	27.8
Loss of parents; expulsion from home	1,255	24.2
Support of old and infirm parents	37	.7
Eldest of the family, responsible for brothers and sisters	29	.6
Widowed, responsible for a large family	23	.4
From the provinces, came to hide and make a living in Paris	280	5.4
Led to Paris and abandoned by soldiers, students, etc.	404	7.8
Domestic, seduced by employer and fired	289	5.6
Concubine, lost her lover	1,425	27.5
TOTAL	5,183	100.0

SOURCE: A.-J.-B. Parent-Duchâtelet, *De la prostitution dans la ville de Paris,* 2 vols. (Paris: J.-B. Baillière, 1857), I:107.

naments. Young girls seduced by the false promise of marriage found themselves cut off from families by shame; others were thrown out of the paternal home, "probably because of their misconduct." A long, financially precarious stay in a hospital or in a lodging house of poor repute fixed the destiny of others, but these too were already likely to have been seduced;

"as for those who are truly virtuous, they always find persons who interest themselves in them, who find them a place or the means to return to their home."[63]

Yet Parent was too honest, finally, to place the onus of prostitution entirely on prostitutes themselves. If they had been truly corrupt, they would have remained in prostitution, for he acknowledged that it was a much easier life. The tendency of women to enter and leave the trade was related to their uncertain financial position:

> Of all the causes of prostitution, particularly in Paris and probably in the other large cities, there is none more active than the lack of work and misery, the inevitable result of insufficient salaries. What are the earnings of our dressmakers, our seamstresses, our menders, and in general all those who occupy themselves with the needle? When one compares the wages of the most able with what the merely mediocre talents can earn, one will see if it is possible for these last to procure the strict necessities; let one compare especially the price of their labor with that of their dishonor, and one will cease to be surprised to see such a great number fall into a disorder that is, so to speak, inevitable.[64]

Parent's study, born out of a friend's humanitarian impulse to save these lost women by inducing them to repent, had defeated the original purpose; such centuries-old religious endeavors had never been successful with more than a few, and immorality was less a problem than poverty. To his own surprise, Parent's study showed that most prostitutes succeeded, eventually, in saving themselves; prostitution was merely a stage of life rather than life in its entirety.[65] And, although

[63] Ibid., I:99-102.
[64] Ibid., I:103-104.
[65] Ibid., I:584-590.

Parent knew only that prostitutes eventually left prostitution, and not exactly what they became, he believed that the conclusion was obvious: "A good many former prostitutes re-enter the world, they surround us, they come into our homes, our households; we are constantly exposed to the chance of confiding our dearest interests to them." For Parent this discovery was a practical justification not only for continued surveillance but also for giving way to charitable impulses: "We have major reasons to watch this population, and not to abandon it as many people advise; to seek to diminish its vices and its faults and, in this manner, to attenuate, as much as possible, the evil they could do to those with whom they would later find themselves in contact."[66] The regulatory system fulfilled this purpose.

PARENT'S RECOMMENDATIONS

Parent was a firm advocate of the regulatory system; or rather, he did not so much advocate it as take it for granted, as a natural stage in the development of public hygiene. The system provided him with a solid data base for his calculations,

---

[66] Ibid., I:585-586. Corbin also quotes this passage, but gives it a slightly different emphasis that perhaps serves to illustrate our differences on the subject of Parent-Duchâtelet: "Elles 'rentrent dans le monde, écrit-il avec angoisse . . . elles nous entourent . . . elles pénètrent dans nos maisons, dans nos intérieurs.'" Corbin views Parent as essentially repressive, "obsessed" with enclosure, analysis, and measurement, bent on disciplining prostitutes primarily through the use of the prison, which inspired a *terreur permanente* in the *fille publique*. *Les Filles de noce*, pp. 16, 30. I prefer to stress the ambiguity of Parent's response to prostitutes, as he found himself drawn to them and repelled by them, determined to solve the health problems they posed and yet aware that the solutions dictated by public hygiene were not, in a social sense, "just." It is worth noting also, as Coleman has done in a recent study of this generation of public hygienists, that Parent's work tended not to be alarmist; his reaction to public health problems was pragmatic, direct, and confident. See William Coleman, *Death Is a Social Disease: Public Health and Political Economy in Early Industrial France* (Madison: University of Wisconsin Press, 1982), p. 296.

and that fact contributed in no small way to his approval. Moreover, it was clear that, for Parent as for others, the act of counting prostitutes—of watching them, of being able to put an exact figure to the number of *malades*—was in itself a satisfying action. Parent's own figures revealed that many *insoumises* were found on examination to have venereal disease.[67] That fact did not shake him in his belief that venereal disease could be controlled solely through the control of prostitution; it merely made him more determined to strengthen the system and bring all the *insoumises* into the fold.

The legal aspects of surveillance troubled him no more than they troubled the police, and he uncritically accepted their justification for it. The prostitute was "outside the law" because of her profession and could thus be legally subject to examination and involuntary treatment.[68] As a physician Parent found further justification for such arbitrary treatment in the fact that venereal disease was worse than a plague in its effects; its chief victims were likely to be the young and virile.[69] Nevertheless, he met with reluctant disapproval a proposal made by the prefecture to include vagabonds and individuals having close ties to prostitution among those who would undergo a mandatory venereal disease examination at the time of arrest. He did not believe that men, no matter how "debauched," could be legally held for treatment, even in serious cases; there would be a public outcry on behalf of "the sacred principle of individual liberty."[70] Parent, despite his sensitive

[67] Parent-Duchâtelet, *De la prostitution*, I:699. The arrests of *insoumises* (from 1816 to 1828) ranged from a high in 1816 of 412 to a low in 1826 of 72.

[68] Ibid., II:236.

[69] Ibid., I:604.

[70] Proposed for the venereal examination were four categories of men: vagabonds "recognized as such"; bad characters who were reputed to live with prostitutes; young men under the age of twenty-one who could give no evidence of employment or family; individuals arrested in the course of raids directed against prostitutes. Ibid., II:234-236.

portrayal of prostitutes, was no more sympathetic to their legal status than anyone else.

His medical training and practice led naturally to his concern for the state of health of prostitutes; his status as a respectable bourgeois, concerned for the wives and children who lived in Paris, led to his equally firm advocacy of the closed bordello. In one section of his study Parent clearly went beyond his self-imposed role as a reporter and social scientist and became an advocate. In the late 1820s and 1830s the prefecture was in the midst of experimenting with the best means to deal with the intrusion of prostitution into the life of the city. It was not an inconsiderable problem, nor were the complaints about the constant presence of prostitutes and their companions a simple product, as might be suspected, of bourgeois hysteria. Most bordellos were concentrated in the center of the city, on the Cité and on both banks of the river. It was a somewhat restricted area, and the concentration of bordellos attracted not only *isolées* but all others who profited from prostitution. They were a genuine public nuisance. "If prostitutes remained isolated, one from the other," Parent commented, "their presence could be tolerated"; but "they have a remarkable tendency to group themselves and, in this state of agglomeration, to take up permanent places at particular points on the street." Unsavory characters inevitably joined them, joking, laughing, making "an insupportable noise," creating dangerous little islands along the sidewalk and forcing ordinary citizens to step into the street.[71]

Two solutions had been proposed as a means of limiting prostitution. One was the medieval plan of quartering prostitutes in special sections of the city, an idea that Parent disliked. It was impossible to go against nature; an attempt to channel prostitution into particular areas would be like

[71] Ibid., I:522.

forcing water to go in a direction it did not flow naturally. It was, instead, necessary to allow prostitution to "settle" wherever it naturally settled in the city; "there are places that repel it, others that attract it."[72] Further, the establishment of a special quarter for prostitution would have the additional unfortunate effect of concentrating all disorder in one place, turning the quarter into a magnet for all the *malfaiteurs* of the capital and putting obstacles in the paths of would-be customers:

> Who would want, in the light of day and even in the night, to enter these streets? What insults would not come to those seen leaving? Who would consent to be pursued by the shouts with which the rascals and the street urchins formerly assailed those who left the Grand, Petit, and Moyen Hurleur, streets that are still today among the most dirty, narrow, and disgusting of Paris, and in which formerly, in centuries past, some prostitutes were cantoned?[73]

Dispersion of bordellos throughout the city was more practical and was likely to be more easily enforceable.

However, the fact that quartering prostitution would not work did not mean that all efforts to control its location would be pointless: "Prostitution, as I have already said several times, is similar to a torrent that one cannot stop, but [one] that it is possible to a certain point to direct."[74] Parent wished to direct it all into the *maison de tolérance,* or rather the *maison close,* which would remove some two thousand registered prostitutes, to say nothing of their associates, from the streets. He had observed for himself the prefecture's attempts to do this. Debelleyme's increasingly restrictive regulations had re-

[72] Ibid., I:336.
[73] Ibid., I:335-336
[74] Ibid., I:336.

moved prostitutes from entire areas, including the Palais Royal. Mangin's 1830 ordinance had been designed to force all prostitutes off the streets during the day and to enclose all prostitution, including that of *filles isolées,* in bordellos; further ordinances had prohibited prostitutes from forming groups in the street.[75] The 1830 revolution had resulted in the easing of the *maison close* policy, though not in its immediate abandonment. The policy had not been taken up seriously since the revolution because, in Béraud's opinion, most of the subsequent prefects had been "political men" rather than true administrators, and had been more interested in street riots and political conspiracies.[76] Parent-Duchâtelet agreed: "It is to be regretted that the administration has relaxed on this point; that a measure so good, which began to produce the most satisfying result, and to which, with a little persistence, prostitutes would have become habituated, has fallen into disuse; let us hope that we will return in this regard to what was done before 1830."[77]

From Bawd to Victim

The police never returned to the strict policies of the late Restoration. They had learned that the stricter their measures against registered prostitutes, the more likely prostitutes were to become *insoumises;* the problem of clandestinity soon overtook all other concerns. Parent's attitude reflected the early period of the prostitution regime, when the police were still confident of their ability to exert absolute control. Ironically, it was Parent's emphasis upon the essential normality of the prostitute that effectively ended whatever hope the prefecture may have had for tracking down and eventually inscribing

[75] See Chapter 1.
[76] Béraud, *Les Filles publiques,* II:8.
[77] Parent-Duchâtelet, *De la prostitution,* I:540-541.

all *filles publiques*. Parent's own discoveries sabotaged his recommendations.

Through his own work and through the studies of those who followed him, Parent had irrevocably transformed the public image of the prostitute from the bawd, cheerfully immersed in the pleasures of life, to that of the victim. His average prostitute was young and probably cut off—by death, geography, or economics—from the support of family and friends; she was uneducated and ill-suited to support herself. He had sketched in the prostitute's past for a society unaccustomed to the idea that her past might be significant.

Just as important, he had suggested the almost universal vulnerability of working-class women to prostitution: "If the young girl seduced by the libertine is without education, and if she belongs to the inferior classes of society, is it not evident, with all that has been said in the preceding chapters, that prostitution will probably be her lot?"[78] Such a combination of circumstances was not uncommon. For later writers prostitution would become not the refuge of rather small numbers of women naturally suited to the trade but instead a trap ready to spring on any working girl. The prefectural conceit of a regiment of regulated prostitutes, viewed as an achievable goal in Parent's time, would dissolve completely before the spectacle of apparently endless numbers of *insoumises,* increasing police measures against clandestinity just as it increased public concern.

As for Parent, he had tried to view prostitution dispassionately, as a problem of public health, but he had not been able to remain detached. The problem of prostitution had seemed a simple one in the beginning: it was a matter of finding all prostitutes (perhaps detecting them through physical characteristics, as he at first thought), segregating them,

[78] Ibid., I:610.

and bringing them back to society through repentance and conversion. None of his assumptions had held, and his essential honesty as a researcher had forced him to report both the original assumptions and the results of his work.

The contradiction between what he had believed and what he found was perhaps most striking in the prison workshops, where the capacity and industry of prostitutes were on display. He observed, with apparently unconscious irony, that most women chose to work in the various kinds of seamstress shops "because they find there, for the most part, occupations to which they have been accustomed." Prostitutes "with neither industriousness nor skill" worked in cleaning the fibers of cotton and wool, or in working with gum arabic, "which they reduce into small fragments." Those incapable of this were put to work at an even simpler task, making carding tools by sticking pins through already-punched holes. "Ah well, would one believe it? There are some creatures incapable of such a simple occupation. I have counted up to fifteen or twenty in the category of imbeciles."[79]

There were others incapable of working because they were almost completely blind: "I will add that, for some, this infirmity was the only reason that they were forced into prostitution." The bureaucracy had no solutions to problems of this kind, and Parent-Duchâtelet was also at a loss. He had backed himself into a corner where misery equaled—had to equal—immorality. "One can only reproach them," he concluded, "for not having had the courage to die of hunger."[80]

[79] Ibid., II:116.
[80] Ibid., II:116-117.

PART TWO

The Effects of the Regime

o   o   o

° 4 °

The Noisy Classes
and Petty Crime

"THE police are, generally speaking, obliged to treat street-walkers with great severity," noted Louis Guyon in 1826. "Each evening, fifty to sixty of them are arrested, although they are registered and have a card to exercise their trade. They are conducted to the depot of the prefecture, and from there to the Petite Force, where, according to the judgment of the *officier de paix,* they remain for one, two, or three months."[1] This was an impression held by many contemporaries concerning the control of prostitutes in Paris, but it was not necessarily the reality. Indeed, it was not even likely; arrests made at this rate would soon have overcrowded the Petite Force, whose population hovered between four and five hundred.[2] Nevertheless, Guyon was going by his impressions, and such observations were virtually the only resource Parisians had with which to judge the scope of these arrests. The police did not publicize their number, and the method

[1] Louis Guyon, *Biographie des commissaires de police et des officiers de paix de la ville de Paris* (Paris: Goullet, 1826), p. 212.

[2] The population of the prisons was reported regularly during the Restoration in the bulletins of the Prefecture of Police. See the series AN F⁷ 3845-3873, filed in order, beginning in about 1800 and finishing with the end of the Restoration.

frequently used—the *rafle,* or mass apprehension of all individuals in a given area—created the impression of great activity. In addition, the arrests did not make their way into court statistics; prostitutes in Paris were exempt from regular judicial procedures and were sent to prison without benefit of trial.

A further problem in evaluating the prostitute's role in crime stemmed from the fact that prostitutes were not, for the most part, involved in crimes serious enough to take all the way to the Cours d'assises; fewer than one hundred prostitutes a year were tried in this court for the nation as a whole. (See Table 2.) Prostitutes tended to be involved in numerous petty crimes: minor thefts, "prowling" at night, inconsequential disputes, all of them problems of the sort frequently settled without recourse to the courts.[3] The smallness of their crimes did not prevent prostitutes from being a major annoyance, and occasional outbursts of prefectural outrage revealed the seriousness with which prostitution was regarded:

> The interests of public security and the health of the citizens require the police to keep a closer eye on prostitutes than on the other classes; and what activity should not be expended to identify, to follow in their tracks, to curb in their outrages, these women who, having renounced all sentiment of modesty, are in intimate relations with individuals who are accustomed to live by theft and rapine; these women who, without this special surveillance, would have finished by goading these bad characters with whom they surround themselves to all sorts of crimes, who would have committed crimes themselves?[4]

[3] The prostitute's exemption from the courts was true only in Paris. In the provinces, prostitutes were brought before the Tribunal de simple police.

[4] *Compte d'administration des dépenses de la Préfecture de police* (1819), p. xxvii.

TABLE 2

Prostitutes Brought before the
Cours d'Assises in France

	1829	1830	1831	1832	1833
Number of prostitutes	33	57	75	97[a]	63
Rural	—	2	2	11	1
Urban	—	55	71	85	62
Without fixed residence	—	—	2	1	—
Crimes against property	33	49	70	93	59
Crimes against people	—	8	5	2	4
Sentenced to forced labor	5	14	6	13	7
Sentenced to reclusion or imprisonment of more than one year	4	6	11	43	25
Imprisonment of less than one year	10	14	25	11	4
Acquitted	14	23	33	30	27

SOURCES: *Compte général de l'administration de la justice criminelle en France pendant l'année 1829* (Paris: Imprimerie royale), p. 34; *Compte général... pendant l'année 1830,* p. 34; *Compte général... pendant l'année 1831,* p. 34; *Compte général... pendant l'année 1832,* p. 36; *Compte général... pendant l'année 1833,* p. 39.

NOTE: Total numbers of defendants for the five years were as follows: 1829, 7,373; 1830, 6,962; 1831, 7,606; 1832, 8,237; 1833, 7,315.

[a] Two of these prostitutes were charged with crimes against public security.

The importance of prostitutes in the criminal activities of Paris, then, was greater than court statistics suggest. It is necessary, in order to examine the role of prostitutes in crime, to go to the lowest level of information available, the daily police record of arrests kept by the Gendarmerie royale.[5]

The maintenance of law and order in Paris rested on diverse kinds of officials with varying degrees of authority. The most important officials locally were the forty-eight *commissaires,* one for each *quartier.* They were required to live in the neighborhoods they administered, a requirement not to the liking of some (such as the *commissaire* of the Cité, who had to preside over a slum),[6] and their hours were long. The commissariat was open from 8:00 a.m. to 10:00 p.m., and though the *commissaires* did not, of course, remain on duty all this time, they were on call at all hours for serious matters. They operated what were, in effect, miniature prefectures, overseeing the same broad range of concerns. They were the chief legal and even judicial officers in their *quartiers,* moderating and settling affairs at this lower level. They concerned themselves with matters of public health and the enforcement of city regulations in public and private establishments, as well as with criminal matters.. Finally, operations conducted in a *quartier* by agents of the prefecture—raids on lodging houses, for example—had to be conducted with the knowledge of and in company with the *commissaire.*[7]

At another level of importance were a varying number of *officiers de paix,* who acted as supervisors of other municipal police. For prostitutes they were the supreme officials; it was

[5] The series begins in 1816 with AN F⁷ 4166 (which was too fragmentary to use) and runs through July 1830 (AN F⁷ 4174); it continues (as the reports of the Garde municipale) through 1846 (AN F⁷ 4179). The reports for the year 1821 were also too fragmentary.

[6] Guyon criticized this *commissaire,* Fleuriais, for leaving the Cité too frequently, declaring that the Cité was "le quartier où la canaille abonde le plus, . . . Sans doute il faut à l'homme des délassemens; mais est-il convenable qu'un magistrat soit sans cesse au café? Et si M. Fleuriais doit y rechercher quelque récréation, est-ce loin de son quartier qu'il devrait choisir le sien?" Guyon, *Biographie des commissaires,* p. 37.

[7] Tulard, *Paris et son administration,* pp. 435-436, 139-145.

an *officier de paix* who interrogated prostitutes and determined their sentences. Finally, there were around five hundred men characterized as employees and agents of the Services extérieurs, a group that included clerks as well as members of the various special forces, including Moeurs, Sûreté, and Hôtels garnis.[8]

The policing and patrolling of the city was accomplished by the Gendarmerie royale, a military force composed largely of former soldiers. The size of the force was set in 1820 at 1,528 men, of whom 630 were mounted.[9] To enter the gendarmerie, a man had to be between the ages of twenty-five and forty; he had to be able to read and write correctly; he had to be able to produce a certificate of good conduct of some sort; and he had to meet a height requirement of at least one and one-half meters.[10] And in the following uniform, dictated by royal decree, he must have been imposing:

> The uniform of the Garde royale of Paris is established as follows: coat of the king's blue, lapels, collar, and cuffs of the same; lining and piping of scarlet; white trousers, hat *à la française,* surmounted with a red plume and a wool pompon of the same color; braid in white thread and aiguillettes of the same for the *sous-officiers* and the *gardes,* and in silver for the *officiers;* a white button with a fleur-de-lis in the middle and the words: Garde royale de la ville de Paris.[11]

[8] Ibid., pp. 436-437, 126-139.

[9] The gendarmerie was founded in 1813 to replace military units detached to guard Paris; it was reorganized and expanded by the ordinance of 10 January 1816 (as the Garde royale) and reorganized again (as the Gendarmerie royale) in 1820. *Compte d'administration des dépenses de la Préfecture de police* (1819), pp. xi-xii. The gendarmerie retained a military organization, and transfers between it and the regular army were provided for in the ordinance of 29 October 1820.

[10] Ordinance of 29 October 1820, in Duvergier, *Collection,* XXIII:143-176.

[11] Ordinance of 14 August 1814, in Duvergier, *Collection,* XIX:166-171.

The gendarmes had responsibility for conducting regular patrols through their *arrondissement,* and they were required to respond to complaints of criminal activity. They frequently became involved with other branches of the police, for agents from the prefecture could leave prisoners at their posts and requisition gendarmes to escort prisoners to the prefecture. For the purpose of this discussion, the most important duty was to send a daily bulletin of their activities to the Prefecture of Police.[12]

The rest of this chapter will be devoted to examining ten complete years (1819-1820, 1822-1829) of reports from the Gendarmerie royale. Only those reports that involved prostitutes are included. The offenses were divided into five categories: assault, theft, disturbing the peace, vagabondage (as *rôdeuses de nuit*), and the contravention of police regulations against prostitution. The police reports provide important insights into the prostitute's role in the street life of Paris. She was often seen primarily as a victim of arbitrary arrest; these reports provide an idea of the extent to which prostitutes were subjected to such harassment. At the same time, the reports show the degree to which prostitutes were involved in genuinely criminal or "disorderly" activities: at least some of the prefectural outrage was well-founded.

ASSAULT AND BATTERY

Incidents of simple assault, of assault and battery, and of disputes that became increasingly more vocal were the life-blood of the police. The causes were often trivial—one police clerk noted with apparent disgust that two individuals had been wreaking mayhem on each other for the sake of "a miserable sum of 15 sous"[13]—but such fights could easily

[12] Ordinance of 29 October 1820, in Duvergier, *Collection,* XXIII:143-176.
[13] AN F⁷ 3875, report of 7 July 1821.

escalate into more serious violence. In no other kind of incident did the peacekeeping forces approach the public more closely, and more helpfully, and at greater risk to themselves.[14]

There were a total of 872 such incidents in the ten-year period studied. In only 78 cases, or 8.9 percent, was the assailant not mentioned; the other 794 cases provided some indication of the types of individuals with whom prostitutes became violently involved. Most of the battles were simple disturbances between a prostitute and one other person. However, 184 incidents, or 21.1 percent of the total, involved more than two people. About half of these involved random attacks by prostitutes against passers-by or against the police. (Only those attacks launched before an arrest are counted here, since many prostitutes fought back during an arrest, whether out of frustration or in an attempt to get away.)

Gendarmes were not empowered to take testimony,[15] so the causes of the disputes seldom appeared in the records. Angry participants sometimes insisted on getting their stories across, and the gendarmes also took note of what might have been mitigating circumstances. Drunkenness was mentioned in only 67, or 7.7 percent of all cases. Only 55 such incidents, or 6.3 percent of the disturbances, occurred after an attempted or alleged theft. In most cases there may well have been no sensible reason for the dispute; these fights were frequently brawls that occurred on the spur of the moment. In only 44 cases, or 5 percent of the total, was a weapon used by any of the parties. The forty-four weapons included thirty knives, five keys (heavy enough to cause serious jolts), two pairs of

[14] Despite numerous injuries, there were only two police deaths in the line of duty during the two monarchies; both deaths occurred in 1832, shortly after the period discussed here, and were attributed to *factieux*. *Compte d'administration des dépenses de la Préfecture de police* (1832), pp. 29-30.

[15] Ordinance of 29 October 1820, in Duvergier, *Collection,* XXIII:143-176.

scissors, one "blunt instrument," one comb, one club, one glass, and one bottle; two soldiers drew their sabers. In 32 of these 44 cases, it was the prostitute who had used the weapon against someone else.[16]

The most surprising factor to emerge from these statistics rests in the settlement of the dispute. Out of 872 incidents, only 82 cases, or 9.4 percent, were sent on to the prefecture, for a hearing, a preliminary investigation, and possibly a trial. The other 790 cases—90.6 percent—ended at the commissariat level. (See Table 3 for the disposition of all categories of offenses.) In many cases, particularly those involving drunkenness or extremely heated arguments, the participants spent some time locked up in the local post until the *commissaire* could find the time to hear them out. For the most part, the role of the gendarmes in such incidents was to pick the battlers up, dust them off, settle them down, and send them on their way. There seems to be no clear-cut reason (evident in the records, at least) why certain cases made it to the prefecture while others did not.

Information on the places where these fights occurred is available for only 307 cases. (See Table 4.) The outside incidents may well have been encountered in the course of a patrol. The Palais Royal, which accounted for a disproportionately large number of the disturbances, was a traditional haven for both the highest and the lowest in society; the

[16] The murder *(meurtre)* statistics for the Department of the Seine for 1826 show that, of eleven murders, one was committed with a saber, three with knives, one with a club, one with an axe, one with a hammer, two by "blows of the feet and fists," and two by unknown methods. In 1827 four murders were committed with knives, one with a pistol, one with a stone, one with an axe, and one with a hammer. Murders were generally committed with whatever was at hand, as were some of the prostitute assaults; but the prostitute assaults, though small in number, suggest that some prostitutes, at least, may have made it a practice to carry knives. *Compte général de l'administration de la justice criminelle en France, pendant l'année 1826* (Paris: Imprimerie royale, 1827), pp. 92-93.

TABLE 3
Disposition of Cases during a Ten-Year Period

Crime	Number Settled at the Post		Number Sent to Prefecture		Total Cases	Percentage of Total
Assault and battery	790	(90.6%)	82	(9.4%)	872	4.2
Theft	664	(86.3%)	105	(13.7%)	769	3.7
Disorderly conduct	1,290	(84.4%)	239	(15.6%)	1,529	7.3
Vagrancy (rodeuses de nuit)	1,508	(100.0%)	—	(—)	1,508	7.3
Contravention	4,667	(29.0%)	11,479	(71.0%)	16,146	77.5
TOTAL	8,919		11,905		20,824	100.0

SOURCE: AN F⁷ 4167-4174, reports of the Gendarmerie royale of Paris (1819-1820, 1822-1829).

galleries housed luxury shops, and the garden and the promenades were crowded with prostitutes and pickpockets. The proximity of the two extremes of society made the Palais Royal one of the most volatile areas in the city, as well as one of the best-lit. This phenomenon may also have accounted for the rather large number of arrests there, for policemen were never far away.[17] The incidents that occurred inside, away from the view of a patrol, suggest that the gendarmerie

[17] A business almanac from 1827 provides an indication of the wealth and variety of the Palais Royal. There were forty-one jewelers and goldsmiths alone, from Lachaume, who sold jewels starting at 3 francs, 50 centimes, to the establishment of Theodore Benoist, whose works combined *"elegance, sturdiness, and good taste."* There were fifteen restaurants (not counting cafés), again ranging from the famous Véry to the Richard, which served 2-franc dinners and attracted those "more endowed with merit and talents than with money." *Almanach historique et commercial du Palais Royal* (Paris: n.p., 1827), pp. 4-9, 58-60.

TABLE 4
Locations of Assault Incidents during a Ten-Year Period

	Number	Percentage
Outside Locations		
Street *(rue)*	68	22.1
Public roadway *(voie publique)*	61	19.9
Palais Royal	27	8.8
Outside a police post	16	5.2
Place	5	1.6
Outside a theater	8	2.6
Quai	4	1.3
TOTAL	189	61.5
Inside Locations		
Marchand de vin	32	10.4
Café, cabaret, or coffee-house	14	4.6
Maison de tolérance	34	11.1
Lodging of a prostitute	16	5.2
Lodging house *(garni)*	15	4.9
Private home	7	2.3
TOTAL	118	38.5

SOURCE: AN F⁷ 4167-4174, reports of the Gendarmerie royale of Paris (1819-1820, 1822-1829).
NOTE: Locations were not reported in all cases.

had been summoned in many cases to clear up the argument; but the gendarmes also had the right to enter any establishment during business hours, and may well have felt it advisable, given the nature of the establishments listed.

The times at which these disputes occurred were given in only 169 cases. Of these, 106 incidents occurred from 10:00 p.m. to 2:00 a.m., for a total of 63.3 percent; an additional 36 incidents were recorded as happening "at night," for a total of 142 cases, or 84 percent. The workday for the prostitute did not start until evening, a fact that unfortunately served to widen the rift between her and other women of her social class. Women out late were automatically suspect and subject to arrest.[18]

Perhaps the most interesting information revealed is the matter of the other participants in the dispute. (See Table 5.) In all, 945 people were mentioned as the opponents of prostitutes; of these, 174, or 18.4 percent, were women, and 771, or 81.6 percent, were men. Men displayed a greater willingness to resort to force of arms in general. At least 249 cases, or 28.6 percent, were not mutual assaults but, rather, physical attacks on prostitutes, launched in almost every case by male antagonists. But the most significant difference between the male and female antagonists rested in their respective positions in society. The female opponents were predominantly marginal: 106, or 60.9 percent, were prostitutes or *maîtresses de maison.* There was a rather large group left undesignated, perhaps indicative of the lack of importance that contemporaries placed on a woman's very real role as breadwinner. Only 6 of the women had trades, and 5 of these were suspect, for they were designated as *couturières,* or dressmakers, a badly overcrowded profession.

While men of the lower and lower-middle classes were apparently less reluctant to become involved with prostitutes, women who were not already "criminal" themselves appeared to avoid public contacts with them—no doubt in many cases out of self-defense, for women seen chatting with prostitutes

[18] There were numerous cases of this sort, but at least one involved a middle-class family. A man briefly left his wife and sister-in-law alone on the street at 11:00 p.m. When he returned, he found them being arrested for prostitution. Explanations persuaded the first policeman to let the women go, but by this time a second officer arrived, and he placed them all under arrest. AN F⁷ 4181, report of 30-31 July 1822.

TABLE 5

Assault Cases, by Profession, during a Ten-Year Period

	Number	Percentage
Male Antagonists		
Bourgeois	45	5.8
Wood trades	53	6.9
Metalworkers	38	4.9
Stone trades (building)	53	6.9
Clothing trades	57	7.4
Other trades	32	4.1
Tavernkeepers, etc.	31	4.0
Food vendors	33	4.3
Sellers (tradesmen)	13	1.7
Clerks	36	4.7
Police, soldiers	160	20.8
Drivers, coachmen	39	5.1
Service (domestics)	25	3.2
Unskilled, marginal labor	108	14.0
Unspecified	48	6.2
TOTAL	771	100.0
PERCENTAGE OF ALL ANTAGONISTS		81.6
Female Antagonists		
Prostitutes	99	56.9
Madams	7	4.0
Workers (ouvrières)	10	5.8
Daily laborers (journalières)	2	1.2
Domestics	3	1.7
Street merchants	10	5.7
Lodging-house keepers	2	1.2
Wives of wine merchants, etc.	4	2.3
Dressmakers (5) and shoemaker	6	3.4
Unspecified	31	17.8
TOTAL	174	100.0
PERCENTAGE OF ALL ANTAGONISTS		18.4

SOURCE: AN F⁷ 4167-4174, reports of the Gendarmerie royale of Paris (1819-1820, 1822-1829).

were themselves vulnerable to arrest as prostitutes simply by association. This also suggests, however, the degree to which the prostitute was cut off from the working-class milieu. Her involvement with working-class men is self-explanatory; her involvement with working-class women, at least according to the official records, was virtually nonexistent.

In contrast, male antagonists had relatively secure positions in society. Of the men, 30.2 percent had trades; many were skilled artisans. The first ten categories of the table, or 50.7 percent of the total, were men who were solid, if often modest, members of society, possessing education or a trade or owning some kind of establishment. Police and soldiers, a category accounting for an additional 20.8 percent, were also firmly integrated into society, though soldiers were notorious and frequent (if not particularly good) customers. Only 14 percent of the men fell into the category of unskilled and marginal labor.

The members of the bourgeois group included a few doctors, lawyers, teachers, and clerks, as well as the inevitable *proprietaires* and *rentiers*. Only 12 students and 1 poet were mentioned, despite the Left Bank's widely publicized obsession with *grisettes*. Among the working classes, all but one of the men listed as craftsmen appeared to be artisans or journeymen; only one was designated as an apprentice. The largest group in the miscellaneous category comprised 10 printers, who had to be at least literate and possess some education. The policemen and soldiers divided almost equally, the soldiers having a slight edge with 84 men, or 53 percent. The men in the unskilled category were primarily those designated as *ouvriers*, or workers (84, or 77.8 percent of the unskilled). The remarkably few unsavory characters were, perhaps unfairly, grouped with these poor but presumably honest laborers. Only 3 men were clearly on the fringes of society: 2 ragpickers and 1 night prowler *(rôdeur)*.

TABLE 6
Men Arrested in Parisian Bordellos during a Ten-Year Period

Occupation	Number	Percentage
Bourgeois	16	1.1
Wood trades	25	
Metalworkers	11	
Stone trades (building)	16	
Clothing trades	23	
Other trades	16	
SUBTOTAL	91	6.8
Tavernkeepers	12	
Food vendors	27	
SUBTOTAL	39	2.9
Sellers (tradesmen)	19	
Clerks	4	
SUBTOTAL	23	1.7
Soldiers	1,015	75.4
Drivers, coachmen	11	
Service (domestics)	10	
SUBTOTAL	21	1.6
Unskilled, marginal labor	36	2.7
Unspecified	105	7.8
SUBTOTAL	144	10.5
GRAND TOTAL	1,346	100.0

SOURCE: AN F⁷ 4167-4174, reports of the Gendarmerie royale of Paris (1819-1820, 1822-1829).

The probability of a predominantly working-class clientele is further confirmed by an analysis of the occupations of men arrested in bordellos during the same ten-year period. (See Table 6.) The reasons for the bordello arrests are not very important in this discussion, revolving almost entirely around the perennial complaint of *tapage,* or disturbance. Sometimes there was an additional notation that the individual in question had broken glasses in the house, attacked the women, or refused to pay his bill. There were also comments to the effect that some of the men had been drinking in the bordellos, an act that was at the time prohibited by the police. The predominance of soldiers stems less from a native propensity to cause trouble than from the fact that the military police rounded them up for various violations of military rules; most soldiers were arrested "by requisition of the military police," and their removal from Table 6 would leave relatively few arrests. Nor does the almost complete absence of bourgeois customers indicate a lack of interest on their part: the middle- and upper-class customers who frequented the luxury bordellos tended not to be arrested, and the women they patronized were usually spared both the inscription and the medical examination. (The efforts of prominent men on behalf of the women of the demimonde were not entirely altruistic, for they had no desire to see their names figure prominently on the registers kept by the madam by order of the police.)

What is left, after the soldiers and the bourgeoisie, is a group of men who shared the same working-class antecedents as the women they patronized; Parent-Duchâtelet confirmed that the fathers of most prostitutes were artisans.[19] The vast majority of inscribed prostitutes were policed and examined for the benefit of men who had begun life, for the most part, in conditions similar to their own. The difference in their circumstances developed as a consequence of their earnings as adults. While some working-class women became prostitutes because of insufficient earnings, many men of their class

[19] Parent-Duchâtelet, *De la prostitution,* I:67-71.

earned enough to pay for a prostitute. A joke making the rounds during the Restoration, though exaggerated, revealed the difference in financial resources and expectations:

"Do you want to come with me?" said an unfortunate creature of the Halle aux blés to a grenadier.

"I don't have any money, I have only 12 sous."

"Come along anyway," answered the girl, "I can make change."[20]

THEFT

Seven hundred sixty-nine prostitutes were arrested as thieves. Only 105 of them, or 13.7 percent, went on to the Prefecture of Police; 664 cases, or 86.3 percent, were settled less formally. (See Table 3.) One example of this kind of informal arrangement (reported because the prostitute reneged on her agreement) suggests the degree to which common sense prevailed in these cases:

Sieur Falavier, carpenter . . . brought to the post yesterday at 10:00 p.m. Josephine Pascal, prostitute, who he claimed had taken 5 francs from his pocket; this girl admitted the charge but said she did not have the money on her; she agreed to bring it back and asked for permission to go get it, leaving her shawl as security, but she did not return. In consequence the shawl has been kept and this morning will be brought to the *commissaire*.[21]

Common sense might also suggest that the prostitution-related theft would very likely be a crime of subsistence, an

[20] *Le Palais Royal et les filles en bon fortune* (Paris: n.p., 1816), p. 97.
[21] AN F⁷ 4182, report of 10-11 October 1823. This report was from the Garde nationale, which policed Paris until early 1827. Tulard, *Paris et son administration,* p. 438.

TABLE 7

Thefts by Parisian Prostitutes during a Ten-Year Period

Item Stolen[a]	Number	Percentage
Amount of 10 francs or less	38	22.2
Amount of 11-50 francs	31	18.1
Amount of 51-150 francs	6	3.5
Amount above 150 francs[b]	5	2.9
Unspecified amount	17	10.0
TOTAL MONEY THEFTS	97	56.7
Watch	41	24.0
Miscellaneous	25	14.6
Jewelry	5	2.9
Food[c]	3	1.8
TOTAL OTHER THEFTS	74	43.3
GRAND TOTAL	171	100.0

SOURCE: AN F⁷ 4167-4174, reports of the Gendarmerie royale of Paris (1819-1820, 1822-1829).

[a] In only 171 cases was the item specified.

[b] One amount was 14,000 francs; another was 2,653 francs.

[c] The three thefts were of *légumes,* a *morceau de sucre,* and a *morceau de pain.*

impression belied by the nature of the stolen items. (See Table 7.) Unfortunately, this list is incomplete—in only 171 of the cases were the stolen items noted—but on this list, money clearly predominated, followed by watches (in those days of pocketwatches, an item very vulnerable to pickpockets), miscellaneous small items, and jewelry. Thefts of food came in a very poor last, with only 3 incidents mentioned. Moreover, 2 of those thefts—a *morceau de sucre* and a *morceau de pain*— seem to have been cases of women who nibbled as they shopped or loitered near a store.

Almost any item a prostitute could get her hands on was of some value, for virtually anything could be sold, if only to the pawnbroker for a few sous. Money had the advantage of being hard to trace and easy to hide. One victim, a shoemaker, captured a prostitute whom he accused of stealing 7 francs. She denied the charge, and an initial search by the police turned up nothing; "but it was soon realized that she had put her larceny in her mouth, a fact not noticed because at the same time she had inserted a plug of tobacco."[22]

The average take from a theft was about 27 francs, a not inconsiderable sum.[23] This high average in part reflects the fact that most of the thefts were committed in the First Arrondissement. It suggests too that prostitutes knew their second profession well. A detailed study of theft, conducted by the prefecture in 1828, revealed that the First Arrondissement accounted for 20 percent of the total value of all goods stolen in the twelve *arrondissements* of Paris during that year.[24]

Prostitutes and thieves had long been seen as virtually one and the same, and the behavior of prostitutes during the Restoration tended to reinforce this perception. During the first decade of the nineteenth century, some of the old confusion of prostitutes and thieves had persisted. Authorities still continued to suggest a link between "debauchery" and criminal behavior, and to an extent they were correct: theft was a logical second occupation for prostitutes.[25] But at the same time, the attitude toward prostitutes was changing.

[22] AN F⁷ 4182, report of 29 February–1 March 1824.

[23] The average was calculated by leaving out the two highest sums, 14,000 francs and 2,653 francs; the highest after those two was 240 francs. AN F⁷ 4168 and F⁷ 4172.

[24] The 1828 survey, an in-depth examination of when and how thefts occurred, revealed that although the First Arrondissement accounted for only 5.6 percent of all thefts that year, the items stolen there nevertheless added up to 20.3 percent of the value of all that was stolen. *Compte général de l'administration de la justice criminelle en France, pendant l'année 1828* (Paris: Imprimerie royale, 1829), pp. 262-266.

[25] Arrests made during the first decade of the nineteenth century are recorded in the series beginning with AN F⁷ 3846.

Administration policy, geared to an increasing differentiation of *filles publiques* from other types of criminals, was reinforced by a growing concern with the visibility of prostitution and a growing emphasis on prostitution as a problem of public health. The new, slowly developing enforcement policy regarded theft less seriously than, for example, evidence that a prostitute had missed her regular examination at the dispensary. The latter was rewarded with several weeks in prison; the former, still regarded as merely an aspect of prostitution, was settled informally.

DISORDERLY CONDUCT

There were many ways to create a scandal. (See Tables 8 and 9.) The gendarmes developed a number of broad descriptive categories to distinguish the different types. The largest single offense was disturbing the peace, and *tapage nocturne* was the variety most often cited. Next came *scandale,* which was a disturbance of the peace with a fillip of indecent or disgusting behavior. Third was drunkenness; as Table 8 indicates, intoxication was a contributing factor in many other offenses as well. The sixth largest offense involved any kind of behavior that attracted a crowd and thus posed a potential danger to public security. The gendarmes claimed that one prostitute had caused an assembly of five hundred passers-by by her "revolting state of indecency."[26] All of these actions (with the partial exception of some cases of intoxication) were highly public kinds of behavior and clearly represented the prostitute's intrusion into the lives of others.

The rest of the offenses were more private ones, involving interaction between the prostitutes and the gendarmes. Many prostitutes, for example, took advantage of the darkness of

[26] AN F^7 4173, report of July 1827.

TABLE 8

Varieties of Disorderly Conduct among Parisian Prostitutes
during a Ten-Year Period

Offense	Prostitutes Arrested	
	Number	Percentage
Disturbing the peace *(tapage)*	157	10.3
Disturbing the peace, intoxicated	59	3.9
Noisy behavior at night	205	13.4
Noisy behavior at night, intoxicated	29	1.9
SUBTOTAL	450	29.5
Scandal	151	9.9
Scandal, intoxicated	88	5.7
SUBTOTAL	239	15.6
Drunkenness[a]	198	13.0
Indecent conduct, prostitution in a public place	92	6.0
Came to the post to ask for refuge	35	2.3
Came to the post to ask for refuge, intoxicated	10	.6
Calling to the gendarmes without motive	15	1.0
Calling to the gendarmes without motive, intoxicated	9	.6
Came to the post, threatened suicide, intoxicated	9	.6
SUBTOTAL	78	5.1
Caused a crowd to gather	28	1.8
Caused a crowd to gather, intoxicated	49	3.2
SUBTOTAL	77	5.0

TABLE 8 (*Continued*)

Offense	Prostitutes Arrested	
	Number	Percentage
Sleeping in public	30	2.0
Sleeping in public, intoxicated	27	1.7
SUBTOTAL	57	3.7
Miscellaneous	338	22.1
GRAND TOTAL	1,529	100.0

SOURCE: AN F⁷ 4167-4174, reports of the Gendarmerie royale of Paris (1819-1820, 1822-1829).

ᵃ These arrests were for drunkenness alone; intoxication was a contributing factor in many other arrests, as noted.

Paris to practice their trade in public; gendarmes occasionally surprised them at it, and the result was an arrest for indecent behavior. Prostitutes bothered gendarmes with what were regarded as frivolous or unmotivated complaints, and these resulted in arrests. Finally, there was a kind of scandalous behavior that was solved by the arrest itself: sleeping on the street, an act arising out of sheer exhaustion, perhaps, or for lack of any other shelter, was rewarded with a night in the police post.

The disorderly conduct cases reveal the same pattern of settlement that resulted with the other categories of offenses. (See Table 3.) Most of the apprehended prostitutes (84.4 percent) were simply released after their offending behavior had been forcibly stopped. Probably the most interesting aspect of these arrests is the rather large portion (39.5 percent) that occurred inside. (See Table 9.) Disorderly conduct was most often a matter of noisy public behavior encountered by the gendarmes in the course of their patrols; the number of inside

TABLE 9

Locations of Disorderly Conduct among Parisian Prostitutes
during a Ten-Year Period

	Prostitutes Arrested	
	Number	Percentage
Outside Locations		
Public roadway *(voie publique)*	288	29.4
Street *(rue)*	161	16.4
Boulevard	32	3.3
Palais Royal	53	5.4
Les Halles	26	2.7
Bridge, *quai,* riverbank	17	1.7
Place	12	1.2
Public toilet	3	.3
Shelter	1	.1
SUBTOTAL	593	60.5
Inside Locations		
Marchand de vin, café, coffeehouse	121	12.3
Lodging house	100	10.2
Police post	52	5.3
Lodging of prostitute	32	3.3
Maison de tolérance	29	3.0
Private home	26	2.7
Theater	6	.6
Hospital	6	.6
Church	5	.5
Restaurant, grocery	5	.5
Shop	3	.3
Public bath	2	.2
SUBTOTAL	387	39.5
GRAND TOTAL	980	100.0

SOURCE: AN F^7 4167-4174, reports of the Gendarmerie royale of Paris
(1819-1820, 1822-1829).

NOTE: Locations were not reported in all cases.

arrests suggests some willingness on the part of citizens to call in the police.

VAGRANCY AND THE CONTRAVENTION

Vagrancy was traditionally an amorphous category designed to catch those who were not doing anything specifically wrong, but who had no money and looked as if they ought to be in jail. There were some guidelines for a vagrancy charge. Those who lacked papers of identity and were unemployed were liable to arrest. In the provinces, strangers who had been in a commune two weeks without finding employment were accounted vagabonds.[27] The scope of the problem in cities made any time limit irrelevant, and whoever happened to be caught without resources was arrested. But, as always, the police found their efforts frustrated by the courts:

> The tribunals are perhaps too indulgent in the application of the law relative to vagabondage. As a result, the police devote much time, care, and effort to find, arrest, and bring to trial a mass of individuals without profession, without papers, without any means of existence other than thefts, swindles, debauchery and disorders of all types, and the courts, when these individuals are not proved guilty of some crime, refuse to find them guilty of vagabondage.[28]

Police in Paris made rather a mystery of vagrancy by their reference to those who were apprehended as *rôdeurs (rôdeuses) de nuit,* or night prowlers. The word "prowling" conveyed a sense of stealth, of activity with a purpose. The purpose was usually presumed to be theft, and the answer to the implied

[27] Law of 10 Vendémiaire Year IV (2 October 1795), in Duvergier, *Collection,* VIII:301-305.
[28] AN F⁷ 3879, report of 26 April 1825.

TABLE 10

Arrests for Vagrancy among Parisian Prostitutes during a
Ten-Year Period

Year	All Arrests		Arrests in Fourth Arrondissement	
	Number	Percentage	Number	Percentage
1819	134	8.9	58	43.3
1820	264	17.5	69	26.1
1822	385	25.5	69	17.9
1823	300	20.0	66	22.0
1824	96	6.4	44	45.8
1825	100	6.6	35	35.0
1826	74	4.9	24	32.4
1827	56	3.7	21	37.5
1828	61	4.0	19	31.1
1829	38	2.5	15	39.5
TOTAL	1,508	100.0	420 (27.8%)	

SOURCE: AN F^7 4167-4174, reports of the Gendarmerie royale of Paris
(1819-1820, 1822-1829).

threat was stepped-up patrols. "The more frequent night
patrols," wrote the prefect in 1824, "will be continued and
extended as much as possible, although this extra service is
fatiguing for the gendarmes and the agents who have scarcely
any time to rest. The shorter nights will also diminish the
number of thefts."[29]

Prostitutes arrested as *rôdeuses de nuit* (see Tables 3 and 10)
were all handled at the post level. A disproportionate number
were arrested in the Fourth Arrondissement, home of the
Paris marketplace. This area had a natural attraction for those
who liked to stay up late; the cafés and restaurants near the
markets stayed open all night for the convenience of those

[29] AN F^7 3878, report of 6 April 1824.

who brought produce in from the countryside. What was notable about the vagrancy arrests, however, was the degree to which they diminished, falling to a low of only 38 arrests in 1829.

There was no single reason for the *rôdeuse de nuit* arrests to decline; vagabondage was, after all, an aspect of prostitution almost by definition. It is probable that the *rôdeuse* arrests began to be subsumed under the heading of contravention, though there is only indirect evidence for this. The drop in the total number of arrests for vagrancy is best understood as reflecting the general transition in the policing of prostitution that occurred during the late Restoration. In part this had to do with the regulations passed by Debelleyme and Mangin, restricting the access of prostitutes to the streets and public places. Vagabondage then became a relatively meaningless distinction, for a prostitute caught virtually anywhere in public was likely to be in contravention of some regulation.

Of central importance in the change, however, was the prefecture's takeover (with the Municipal Council, which voted the funds) of the dispensary in 1828. This takeover, according to a later report by Delessert, had exposed the dispensary to the glare of publicity; officials connected with the Bureau of Morals had suddenly to conduct themselves with "more prudence and circumspection" than they had previously shown.[30] There was a growing tendency to separate prostitutes from other offenders, a result of the public accounting now required of the Bureau of Morals. As the special clientele of the dispensary, prostitutes were increasingly studied not as members of the criminal classes or the poor, but as a distinct group.

The rationalization of the *police des moeurs* was most obvious in the changing styles of police reporting. Early in the century, the clerks at the prefecture had taken some pains to

[30] An F^7 9305, letter of 15 May 1841 from the prefect of police to the minister of the interior.

describe the offense: for example, "prostitutes, standing daily on the place de la Concorde where they attract thieves."[31] If the arrested individual was known to them, they might describe her as a "known prostitute" or "prostitute, known thief"—a description sometimes written in place of a specific charge—but in general they were rather unconcerned with the identity of the offender if she happened to be a prostitute. The report might simply describe the violation as committed by a *fille publique* or even, occasionally, by an *"fp."*

In contrast, during the July Monarchy the exact nature of the prostitution offense was seldom clarified. The variety of offenses reported in the Restoration had been reduced to three categories: *maladie* or *vénérienne*, sometimes specifically syphilis; *insoumise*, which meant that the woman was either unregistered or had missed an examination; and *contravention*, which included every other conceivable offense against the regulations. The prefectural reports were supplemented by the reports of the Gendarmerie of the Seine and by the Garde municipale. The reports of the Garde (which had replaced the gendarmerie) had become as laconic as the prefectural reports, seldom listing as cause for arrest anything more than the uninformative *provocation à la débauche*. The clerks for the Gendarmerie of the Seine were occasionally unwise enough to list an arrest for vagabondage, but this was usually commuted at the prefecture into the all-encompassing "contravention." On those few occasions when a prostitute was arrested specifically for theft or assault, it often meant that the authorities might be planning to bring her to trial on the more serious offense.

This relative lack of interest in the exact nature of the offense was compensated for by a determination to identify the individual; there was an attempt to pinpoint the clients of the dispensary and to keep track of them over time. This

[31] AN F⁷ 3846, report of 6 Thermidor Year XII (24 July 1804).

TABLE 11

Arrests for Contravention among Parisian Prostitutes during a
Ten-Year Period

Year	Cases Settled at the Post	Cases Sent to Prefecture	Total Arrests	Percentage of Total
1819	195	616	811	5.0
1820	188	352	540	3.3
1822	355	579	934	5.8
1823	625	1,144	1,769	11.0
1824	705	1,442	2,147	13.3
1825	588	1,590	2,178	13.5
1826	436	1,846	2,282	14.1
1827	527	1,164	1,691	10.5
1828	716	1,273	1,989	12.3
1829	332	1,473	1,805	11.2
TOTAL	4,667 (29%)	11,479 (71%)	16,146	100.0

SOURCE: AN F⁷ 4167-4174, reports of the Gendarmerie royale of Paris (1819-1820, 1822-1829).

led to some valiant attempts to master foreign names (Eggenschwiller and Fitzgerald, for example, both endured a number of orthographic mutations) and, with Frenchwomen, to a precision that prompted clerks to list as many as four Christian names. One woman had to be reported as La Muette (the Mute) or, in a further attempt to distinguish her, as La Muette de la Cité.

The Restoration, particularly the late Restoration, was the transitional phase between the two styles of police reporting. In a broader sense, the 1820s marked the development of prostitutes as a distinct group, subject to a different kind of justice. The contravention arrest could mean almost anything. Striking, however, is the dramatic rise of contravention arrests (Table 11) and the disposition of such cases (Table 3) compared with others. Only 29 percent were dropped at the post level; 71 percent were sent to the prefecture, and from there to a short "administrative" stay in prison. Arrests in this vague category were more dependent on administrative whim than they were on any real provocation on the prostitute's part. A decision to clean up a particular area, a decision to impress the citizenry by a period of particularly stringent enforcement, even increased night patrols by the gendarmerie were the main factors behind any change in the number of arrests. Nevertheless, it seems clear that the potential of the regulatory system began to be realized in this period. Though it affected women only, it provided an effective way of getting large numbers of people off the streets, if only for a week or so. It was one sure way, not dependent on the whims of the courts, of thwarting the activities of the dangerous classes.

DANGEROUS PARIS

Eugène Sue's *Les Mystères de Paris* was less noteworthy for its wildly improbable plot than for its wonderful, moody descriptions of the underworld of Paris. In one particularly vivid passage he discussed the cabaret Lapin Blanc, the favored neighborhood haunt of thieves and fences. The interior was dark, for the room was sunk below the level of the pavement; the dreariness was increased by the "smoke-blackened" joists, the "lead-plated" counter, the iron bands that encircled the quart jars on the table. A cracked lantern illuminated the message on the door, a message at the same time menacing and inviting: "Ici on loge à la nuit."

The passage was so successful in conveying the Paris of the 1840s that it was later cribbed for the best-selling (but phony) *Mémoires de Monsieur Claude,* the supposed recollections of the famous chief of the Sûreté.[32] Vidocq added to the picture

---

[32] See Claude, *Mémoires de Monsieur Claude,* 2 vols. (Paris: Jules Rouff, 1881), I:39, and Eugène Sue, *Les Mystères de Paris,* 2 vols. (Paris: Charles Gosselin, 1843), I:7-8.

with his four-volume novel, smartly titled *Les Vrais Mystères de Paris,* which also featured humid hovels, open sewers with "nauseating" black sludge, and an area occupied by those whose activities were best conducted in darkness: "There was not a single workshop, not a single store devoted to a business that is conducted in the light of day."[33] The masses of the city came to be regarded as "dangerous classes," as their contemporary H.-A. Frégier dubbed them.[34] Even the police contributed to this imagery with their tantalizing suggestions of areas given over to crimes hidden by darkness: "Around 2:00 a.m., some cries of "Thief! Murderer!" accompanied by groans, were heard in the neighborhood of the post. Two patrols immediately left, but all search was fruitless; nevertheless suspicion has fallen on a house inhabited by prostitutes."[35] Sue, Vidocq, and the rest would have emphasized the disembodied screams in the night for the sake of their atmospheric flavor; perhaps it is time to emphasize the fact that the screams brought an immediate response from the police. Contemporaries and historians alike have tended to emphasize "mysterious" Paris to the detriment of what seems more likely to have been the reality: for the times, Paris was a rather well policed city.

This perception is almost unavoidable when one examines police records rather than other, more customary sources. One of the most effective ways to evaluate crime is to examine court records, and a number of such studies have been done. Some have focused on a particular kind of crime, such as arson, assault and battery, or the theft of provisions, using a single crime as a kind of signpost for the examination of

[33] François-Eugène Vidocq, *Les Vrais Mystères de Paris,* 4 vols. (Paris: Alexandre Cadot, 1844), I:28-29.

[34] Frégier, *Des classes dangereuses,* and Louis Chevalier, *Classes laborieuses et classes dangereuses à Paris pendant la première moitié du XIXᵉ siècle* (Paris: Plon, 1958).

[35] AN F⁷ 4180, report of 24-25 July 1816.

society.[36] Other studies have examined criminal records for a particular area from a global perspective, looking for a pattern or a kind of evolution in the types of crime committed.[37] One problem with these studies, an inevitable one, is the fact that the higher the level of reporting—the higher the courts, for example—the more restricted is the number of cases and the less reflective these cases are of the total picture of crime.[38] Many cases are weeded out along the way for various reasons, and the crimes left may not be the most representative ones; indeed (though there is no way of knowing) the very fact that they were ultimately brought to trial may mean that they were atypical.

An examination of police bulletins alleviates somewhat this problem of attrition (and even here, only those individuals who were apprehended are listed) but a new problem is created, the problem of too much information. Selecting out one particular group, as prostitutes have been selected here, necessarily and unfortunately deprives the study of a view of

[36] For arson, see André Abbiateci, "Les Incendiaires du XVIIIᵉ siècle," *Annales E.S.C.* 25 (janvier-février 1970):229-248. For a study of assault and battery in Paris, see Arlette Farge and André Zysberg, "Les Théâtres de la violence à Paris au XVIIIᵉ siècle," *Annales E.S.C.* 34 (septembre-octobre 1979):984-1012. A long and thoughtful study of the theft of provisions is Arlette Farge, *Délinquance et criminalité: le vol d'aliments à Paris au XVIIIᵉ siècle* (Paris: Plon, 1974). In addition, for a sociological study of vagabondage, see Alexandre Vexliard, *Introduction à la sociologie du vagabondage* (Paris: Marcel Rivière, 1956).

[37] For example, see Véronique Boucheron, "La Montée du flot des errants de 1760 à 1789 dans la généralité d'Alençon," *Annales de normandie* 21 (mars 1971):55-86, for a study of marginal people, and Jean-Claude Gégot, "Etude par sondage de la criminalité dans le bailliage de Falaise," *Annales de Normandie* 16 (juin 1966):103-164.

[38] Thus, "fewer crimes are detected than are committed; fewer people still are indicted for their detected crimes than commit them; and even fewer are actually tried and convicted; finally, only a part of these is ever punished. . . . The best record therefore is the one closest to the crime itself." Carl Hammer, Jr., "Patterns of Homicide in a Medieval University Town: Fourteenth-Century Oxford," *Past and Present,* 78 (February 1978):4-6.

the criminal picture as a whole. An attempt to discern changing patterns, an evolution of crime, as other studies have done,
is defeated.

Nevertheless, police blotters have certain advantages in the
case of Paris. A view of petty crime from the court records
inevitably obscures the amount of rough justice that was meted
out at the street level by the police, who settled many more
crimes themselves than they sent on to the prefecture. This
fact in itself discloses the high degree of police interaction
with the community: their function was not only repression
but also mediation. The police also adjusted their policing
according to the neighborhood, as the record of arrests shown
in Table 12 indicates. While this table is subject to several
interpretations, it seems probable that the variations were due
less to innate differences between *arrondissements* than to enforcement priorities. The bordellos of the wealthy First Arrondissement were not allowed to become intrusive in their
neighborhoods; greater latitude was allowed the Second Arrondissement, location of the Palais Royal and the traditional
nightspot, especially since the Revolution, of Paris. The Fourth
Arrondissement, the location of les Halles, was a particular
worry to the police because of the comings and goings,
throughout the night, of men bringing produce to the next
day's markets. This was the only part of the city in which
the cabarets and restaurants were allowed to remain open
through the night in response to the needs of the market, and
the police were correspondingly active.

Finally, although long-term evolution in crime is not apparent in this kind of study, minor shifts in enforcement—
otherwise obscured by the large picture—become evident.
The sharp rise in the arrests for contravention in 1823 (Table
11) had less to do with an objective increase in the number
of such offenses than with a series of increasingly stern warnings from the minister of the interior to the prefect of police.

TABLE 12

Incidence of Arrest, by Arrondissement, during a Ten-Year Period

Arrondissement	Assault, Theft, and Disorderly Conduct Arrests		Contravention Arrests	
	Number	Percentage	Number	Percentage
First	843	26.5	5,503	34.1
Second	126	4.0	866	5.4
Third	187	5.9	1,822	11.3
Fourth	400	12.6	1,129	7.0
Fifth	55	1.7	269	1.6
Sixth	351	11.0	2,012	12.4
Seventh	451	14.2	1,398	8.6
Eighth	61	1.9	305	1.9
Ninth	346	10.9	1,090	6.8
Tenth	115	3.6	569	3.5
Eleventh	135	4.2	961	6.0
Twelfth	110	3.5	222	1.4
TOTAL	3,180	100.0	16,146	100.0

SOURCE: AN F⁷ 4167-4174, reports of the Gendarmerie royale of Paris (1819-1820, 1822-1829).

These warnings climaxed in late November 1822, when the minister sent a curt note reminding the prefect of "the necessity to carry out rigorously the regulations relative to *filles publiques,* whose license becomes more scandalous every day."[39]

The police bulletins showed the extent to which prostitutes were involved in minor sorts of criminal activities and showed how frequently they escaped official consequences. The bulletins also indicated the very real discrimination to which

[39] AN F⁷ 9305, letter of 22 November 1822 from the minister of the interior to the prefect of police.

prostitutes, as a group, were subjected. The contravention arrest and subsequent short prison term were tempting short-cuts for police officials frustrated by the leniency of the courts. It was little wonder that the police continued to insist that the prostitute was outside the law and that the prefecture had to have arbitrary powers over her in order to police the city properly.

Perhaps the most important fact illuminated by the police records was the high degree of interaction between the gen-darmes and the dangerous classes. Sue and others might per-sist in romanticizing the crime, poverty, and dirt of the city, stressing its essential mystery; a closer look would have re-vealed the tedium of petty disturbances, endlessly repeated. Sometimes the frustration over the prosaic sameness of the incidents was included in the reports; one clerk noted the arrest of two prostitute sisters "for causing scandalous scenes daily."[40] It is likely that the irritation was mutual.

[40] AN F^7 4173, report of 10-11 June 1828.

· 5 ·

Prostitutes and Violence

VIOLENCE was the common denominator. Prostitutes were both victims and perpetrators; they directed their actions against themselves, against society at large, and against those with whom they had personal relationships. Some crimes were acts of defiance, while others were acts of defeat and despair. All reflected the extent to which prostitution meant a break with ordinary life, even beyond their police-imposed segregation from other women. Prostitution could not be regarded as just another line of work:

> She kissed me and said good night. I did not want to sleep, and yet I was tired. But my head was full of my idea, and I roused myself, and seeing that she was sleeping deeply, I got up, and was going to pick up my pruning hook to strike the blow. I do not know if she was awakened by my movement, but at the moment when I was going to strike, she turned and reached for me. I barely had time to throw myself on the bed, my head on the bolster. She embraced me, turned over and fell asleep. I settled myself beside her. A few seconds later I slit her throat. She moved, and wanted to cry out. I struck her again. Then, seizing both her hands, I climbed back on the bed and tied them up with a handkerchief. During

this operation, I pushed her knees on her stomach, and it was in this position that she died. After her last breath, I got up. I searched her room. And when everything was finished, since there was some water in her basin, I used it to wash the blood from my hands and shirt. Then, without waiting for daybreak, I left. That morning, I sold a few of the objects I had taken. After that, I returned to Vaugirard and sharpened my pruning hook. The rest of the day, you know, was Sunday, and I spent it drinking and dancing. Monday, I did the same. [Confession of Guichet, who killed the prostitute Mezeray (La Belle Normande) on 30 September 1821.][1]

Prostitutes were the victims of brutal attack because they were women, because their profession required them to consort with criminals, because they were late-night frequenters of dangerous streets, and because they acquired a certain notoriety. The twenty-year-old gardener who confessed so readily[2] to his crime had planned it well in advance because he knew the woman was prosperous; neighbors later remembered the young man who had been looking for La Belle Normande, and they helped the police to trace him. Another murdered prostitute had advertised her prosperity by keeping a servant (who was killed with her) and by maintaining an

---

[1] Quoted in Eugène-François Vidocq, *Les Voleurs* (Paris: Editions de Paris, 1957), p. 45. Vidocq's report is confirmed by the daily bulletins of the prefecture: "La nommée Mezeray, fille publique, a été trouvée hier soir, assassinée dans sa chambre rue des Frondeurs, volée de ses bijoux et d'une partie de ses effets par un jeune homme de 22 à 25 ans qui avoit couché avec elle. . . ." AN F⁷ 3876, report of Monday, 1 October 1821; and see AN F⁷ 3876, report of Saturday, 13 October 1821, for the report of Guichet's arrest.

[2] Vidocq cheerfully admitted that he had extracted the confession by falsely assuring Guichet that his youth would prevent any serious punishment against him. After the confession was taken down, Vidocq broke the news of his impending execution by telling him that he would never get any older. Vidocq, *Voleurs*, p. 46.

unemployed hairdresser as her lover. The latter was immediately arrested for the crime but was soon released; investigation eventually pinned the deed on a man identified only as a "Neapolitan."[3]

Murder was rather infrequent; violence was routine, and its role in the life of a prostitute needs to be emphasized. Prostitutes caused much of the violence themselves by the injuries they inflicted upon others. They attracted violence by the very nature of their profession. Sometimes they seem to have been random victims of a violence that grew out of the tensions of life in the cafés, the streets, and the shadows their profession forced them to inhabit. Indeed, the world of prostitution required certain kinds of dangerous behavior. The prostitute could not easily blend her marginally criminal existence with the daily routine of the noncriminal working-woman. She could be a prostitute or an "honest woman," and probably was both during the course of her life; but while she was a prostitute, the peculiar requirements of the métier occupied her completely.

She made contacts with the underworld, inevitably; she had to learn how to work the streets, where to take her clients, how to avoid the depredations of thieves who were on the lookout for those with a little money. It was only a small step

---

[3] "Le chef du poste de la Place du Palais Royal . . . a été informé par le Sieur Vignereux, marchand de vin, et principal locataire demeurant rue Pierre Lescot n° 27 qu'un assassinat avait été commis dans ladite maison; il y a de suite envoyé quatre gendarmes, qui à leur arrivée, ont trouvé dans une chambre au 3ᵉ étage, les cadavres des nommées Thérèse Michaud, fille publique, et Constance, sa bonne, qui avaient été assassinées avec un instrument tranchant; la première avait la gorge coupée, et la seconde avait un couteau de table qui lui traversait le coû et plusieurs blessures au bras droit. Avis . . . au commissaire de police du quartier, qui s'est rendu sur le lieux, et a fait arrêter le nommé Fraisse, coiffeur, natif de Narbonne, comme présumé être l'auteur de ce double assassinat. . . ." AN F⁷ 4173, report of 11-12 February 1827. See also AN F⁷ 3881, report of Monday, 12 February 1827; and see AN F⁷ 3881, report of Thursday, 11 October 1827, for the report of the solution to the crime.

for her to become a thief herself. The regulatory system by which prostitution was controlled in Paris made an arrest for petty theft no more costly than a routine prostitution arrest, unless the police decided to make an example in a particular case. Gradually the prostitute established relationships with others who were involved in prostitution, however peripherally. The cabaret owner allowed her inside because she attracted business, and he helped her escape from the police. A madam, or the keeper of a rooming house, came to terms with her over the short-term rental of a room. Another prostitute pointed out to her the greater wisdom and safety of working in pairs. Undoubtedly many prostitutes began by trying to maintain a foothold in both worlds, the shady and the respectable; undoubtedly many found themselves gradually pushed into the shade, joining the dangerous classes.

The criminal actions of *filles publiques* (and against them) provide another perspective from which to view the policing of prostitution. The various regulations, *arrêtés,* and ordinances came from on high and represented statements of policy. In contrast, arrest reports from the gendarmerie and others (available, though not complete, for 1816 to 1846) provide some indication of how these theoretical formulas operated in practice.[4] While the emphasis in the preceding chapter was on the enforcement policies of the police, this admittedly more impressionistic chapter focuses on the lives of prostitutes as revealed in the various police reports.

SUICIDE

Yesterday a prostitute named Anastasie Dor, who had been left at the post Pont au Change, stabbed an inspector, fortunately wounding him only slightly. Asked what mo-

[4] The material for this chapter comes from the series AN F⁷ 4166-4182, reports of the Gendarmerie royale, Garde municipale, and Garde nationale, 1816-1846, and from AN F⁷ 3874-3893, bulletins of the Prefecture of Police, Restoration–July Monarchy.

tivated this action, the girl Dor said she was tired of life
and wanted to die.

Report of 30 August 1821[5]

Suicide was a violent reaction to what were perceived to be
impossible circumstances. Prostitution itself was a manner of
dealing with impossible circumstances, and it might be expected that prostitutes would make up a large percentage of
those women known to have taken their lives. In fact, prostitute suicides were rare (or, perhaps better, were rarely reported) in the thirty years covered in the police reports, though
there were probably numerous examples of marginal women,
pushed beyond their limits of endurance, who chose suicide
as an alternative to prostitution. Between the years 1816 and
1830,[6] the police recorded only twenty-six suicide attempts by
prostitutes, of which only three were successful. Only one
attempt (unsuccessful) was reported during the July Monarchy. Some of the unsuccessful ones were genuine suicide
attempts—what has been called "partial suicide"[7]—and some
were mere threats of suicide that did not seem to reflect a
genuine wish to die. There were distinct contextual differences between suicides, or sincere suicide attempts, and suicide
threats.

[5] An F[7] 3875.

[6] All but one of the suicides mentioned here occurred before July 1830;
the reports for the Restoration are more complete than for the July Monarchy. Many of the suicides undoubtedly went unreported, and many suicides, for one reason or another, did not come to the attention of the
police. The Council of Public Hygiene, in Paris, collected statistics on
suicides for the Department of the Seine that help provide some perspective.
The total numbers for the years 1817-1824 ranged between a low of 317,
in 1822, and a high of 390 in 1823. Men accounted for over half of the
suicides. For a closer look at suicides see Moléon, *Rapports généraux*, I:305.

[7] Otto Fenichel, *The Psychoanalytic Theory of Neurosis* (New York:
W. W. Norton, 1945), p. 401, quoted in George Simpson, introduction to
Emile Durkheim, *Suicide,* trans. by John A. Spaulding and George Simpson
(New York: Free Press, 1951), p. 19.

The most visible of all were the "jailhouse suicides," those attempts made by women in custody. A shared characteristic was their apparent spontaneity. Françoise Jeannot was being escorted across the Seine by several guards when the path was momentarily blocked. She threw herself in the river and was immediately pulled out and sent to a hospital.[8] Marie Vicaire was arrested for assault. She tried twice to hang herself in her cell, the first time with her shawl, the second time with her dress, but did little damage; she was sent to the prefecture for formal charges.[9] Virginie Lequet, arrested for drunk and disorderly conduct in a rooming house, tried to strangle herself with her belt.[10] Thirteen prostitutes were arrested in a routine raid: twelve were sent to the Prefecture of Police, but the thirteenth tried to avoid this by stabbing herself in the stomach nine times; she was sent to the Hôtel-Dieu.[11]

The most detailed story began with a pointless act of destruction. Adelaide Breton was drunk, according to reports, and was walking down the rue de Ponthieu, near the Champs-Elysées, when she saw some flowerpots on a ground-floor window. She smashed them, and became involved in a brawl with the widow who owned the pots and with her two neighbors. After her arrest Breton tried twice to kill herself, first by making a noose of her handkerchief, then by attempting to strangle herself with her own hands. It was only by watching her, the guards noted, that they could keep her from making attempts on her life, but she was sent to the prefecture anyway to be charged with destruction of property.[12]

[8] AN F⁷ 4177, report of 8-9 August 1841.

[9] AN F⁷ 4173, report of 12-13 September 1827.

[10] AN F⁷ 4173, report of 28-29 April 1827.

[11] AN F⁷ 4171, report of 23-24 October 1824.

[12] AN F⁷ 3882, report of 29 June 1828; AN F⁷ 4173, report of 27-28 June 1828.

In at least three of these cases—and possibly in the others as well—the suicide attempt was coupled with a previous act of violence against another. When the women were separated from other targets, self-directed violence became the only release for pent-up hostility. At the same time, it is likely that all six women felt genuine despair. Four who were named had previous criminal records;[13] all were known prostitutes, which greatly lessened the chances that a term in jail could be avoided. At the very least, all faced a day, possibly days, in the Prefectural Depot while they awaited a hearing on their cases. The depot was by all accounts a wretched place; one former prisoner complained that he had been in a "large, sordid, somber room, humid and unhealthy, where he remained confined with the most vile *canaille,* murderers, thieves, and prostitutes, until someone found the time to interrogate him, which . . . sometimes takes several days."[14]

The gloomy aspects of the prefecture were probably not overwhelming to prostitutes, who were not used to creature comforts. Their despair at being arrested stemmed less from the physical discomforts of jail and prison, formidable as they were, than from the threat of even a temporary isolation from

[13] *Anastasie Dor:* AN F⁷ 4167, report of 11-12 June 1819; AN F⁷ 4170, reports of 28-29 March and 20-21 May 1822. *Françoise Jeannot:* AN F⁷ 3898, report of 22-23 August 1843; AN F⁷ 3899, reports of 21-22 January 1845, 13-14 September 1845, 16-17 January 1846, 2-3 February 1846, 7-8 May 1846, and 25-26 November 1846. Concerning Jeannot there is also a court conviction of 2 June 1842 for assault (AN F⁷ 10142) stemming from an arrest in late April 1842 (AN F⁷ 3897). *Marie Vicaire:* AN F⁷ 4170, report of 7-8 October 1822; AN F⁷ 4173, report of 23-24 January 1828; AN F⁷ 4174, report of 27-28 February 1829. *Adelaide Breton:* AN F⁷ 4160, report of 18 August 1826; AN F⁷ 4173, report of 6-7 April 1827.

[14] AN BB18 804, report of the Prefecture of Police to M. Decazes, 24 April 1816. The officer charged with investigating the complaint argued that men and women were kept apart and that all interrogations were made within twenty-four hours after the prisoner's arrival; but he could not deny that the physical surroundings of the place ensured that all individuals detained in the depot were "mal à leur aise."

the outside world. A prison term could entail financial problems: the loss of an apartment for nonpayment of rent, the seizure of goods, the lack of income. There was a human loss as well. Prostitutes had dependents and associates—lovers, children, dogs, even partners in crime—to whom they had varying responsibilities. The contributions of all family members were important for the survival of a family unit. Perhaps the meaning of this long story is captured by the nine-year-old child who asked the police for shelter, "saying that her mother was at the Salpêtrière and her father had disappeared with the determination to kill himself."[15] Prostitutes were given neither the time nor the means to set their affairs in order, and the jailhouse suicide attempts may well have resulted from an understandably bleak appraisal of their sudden change in circumstances.

Suicide attempts made after an arrest were highly visible and thus formed an important part of the whole. Aside from these six, there were only twenty-one other reported suicide attempts and threats between the years 1816 and 1830 (and the word *reported* must be emphasized); of these, only three were successful. One conformed to what was presumed to be the woman's favored method, asphyxiation by charcoal fumes. This method was private, painless and, according to contemporary commentators, preferred by women because it did not leave a disfigured, bloody corpse in public view.[16] Suzanne Desroziers was dignified by the police with the title of *femme entretenue,* or kept woman, a title to which her address on the wealthy rue Lepeletier lent credence. She committed su-

---

[15] "... disant avoir sa mère à la Salpêtrière et son père qui avait disparu avec le dessein de se détruire." AN F^7 4174, report of 26-27 January 1829. And see Olwen Hufton, *The Poor in Eighteenth-Century France* (Oxford: Oxford University Press, 1974), particularly chaps. 1-4.

[16] AN F^7 3839, report of 12 December 1818, and Chevalier, *Classes laborieuses,* p. 350.

icide by jumping out a window of the first floor of her building; the police could find no motive.[17] The final successful suicide for this period was so out of the ordinary that the police were not sure it was a suicide at all. The woman was found on the Cité in one of the narrow dark streets that once surrounded Notre Dame. She was wrapped only in a rough sheet; she had been stabbed twice. The woman was not unknown, for the police identified her as a thirty-six-year-old prostitute. The circumstances were such that the police would probably have ascribed the death to murder had it not been for a note found on the body: "I am called Banage; my brother is an actor at the Gaité." It was a stark epitaph.[18]

The other serious suicide attempts used random methods. A *fille de maison* (Amanda was her nom de guerre) overdosed herself with emetics because of jealousy; her comrades intervened.[19] A woman, Clara, tried to asphyxiate herself with fumes from the charcoal stove.[20] So also did two *femmes galantes* who shut themselves up together in an apartment on the rue de Richelieu; they told the police that they were burdened with debts.[21] One twenty-two-year-old prostitute, previously under treatment for insanity, jumped from a window, breaking all her limbs and suffering head injuries.[22] A second jumper was in despair because of the loss of her lover and threw herself out of a second-story window.[23] A third girl who had recently fled her home jumped from a fifth-floor window to escape her mother.[24]

---

[17] AN F⁷ 3875, report of Saturday, 7 October 1820.
[18] "Je me nomme Banage; mon frère est acteur au Théâtre de la Gaité." AN F⁷ 3838, report of 10 November 1817.
[19] AN F⁷ 3839, report of 14 July 1819.
[20] AN F⁷ 3881, report of Thursday, 18 October 1827.
[21] AN F⁷ 3876, report of Thursday, 17 January 1822.
[22] AN F⁷ 3839, report of 14 October 1819.
[23] AN F⁷ 3875, report of Monday, 21 August 1820.
[24] AN F⁷ 3877, report of Wednesday, 30 April 1823.

The remaining eleven suicide attempts were by drowning and seem to represent a different phenomenon from that of the attempts just noted. All but two were staged on the bridges of the Seine, and only two of the women entered the water.[25] The others merely threatened to jump, loudly enough to give the police a chance to save them. One woman made sure that her intentions would not go unnoticed: she went to the local police post to inform them that she intended to throw herself into the Seine, and was put under arrest.[26] Six of the eleven women were reported to have been drunk. All four cases in which the time of the attempt was given occurred late at night.[27]

The police were skeptical of the sincerity of these attempts. One woman was brought to a local police post by two concerned citizens, who had found her near the river in such despair that they feared for her life. The police recognized her as "only a prostitute" who feigned despair in order to gain sympathy (and probably a coin or two). They locked her up.[28] The police were cynical, but perhaps with reason. There was a dramatic contrivance to these drowning attempts, for all were staged in the shadows of Notre Dame, the Conciergerie, the Palais de Justice, or the Prefecture of Police. The "contagion" of suicide, a phenomenon noted by contempo-

[25] AN F⁷ 4172, report of 3-4 October 1826; AN F⁷ 3881, report of 29 June 1827.

[26] AN F⁷ 4168, report of 14-15 July 1820.

[27] At 9:00 p.m., 10:00 p.m., 11:45 p.m., and 2:00 a.m. Here is a complete list of reports on the eleven attempted drownings: AN F⁷ 4172, report of 23-24 July 1825 (Seine); AN F⁷ 4172, report of 3-4 October 1826 (Canal Saint-Martin); AN F⁷ 4173, report of 1-2 March 1827 (stabbed first, then Seine); AN F⁷ 3881, report of 20 June 1827 (well); AN F⁷ 3881, report of 8 July 1827 (Seine); AN F⁷ 4173, report of 24-25 November 1827 (Seine); AN F⁷ 4173, report of 29-30 May 1828 (Seine); AN F⁷ 4174, report of 15-16 July 1829 (Seine); AN F⁷ 4174, report of 29-30 November 1829 (Seine); AN F⁷ 4174, report of 22-23 May 1829 (Seine).

[28] AN F⁷ 4180, report of 11-12 October 1816.

raries and by historians,[29] led also to a contagion of suicide attempts; the threat to go into the river was an expression of despair.

It is possible, too, that notice by the police is what many women wanted above all. Accommodations in the police posts were not comfortable, but they were often better than sleeping outside. A certain Rose Boucher was released from the Prefectural Depot in February 1825. She had no home, no money; she went to a post on the Left Bank, at the place Maubert, to ask for shelter for the night. She appeared several days later at a nearby post; she stood just outside and declared that she had taken an overdose of emetics in order to kill herself. She was sent to the Hôtel-Dieu. Nearly eight months later she was found at 2:00 a.m., wandering along the quai des Orfèvres, declaring her intention to throw herself into the river. She was arrested.[30] Her suicide attempts were a means of obtaining recognition and help in an unfriendly city.

The police often tried to establish a motive for the suicide cases in which they became involved, even though the motives seldom went beyond the standard ones of "misery" or "disappointment in love." In the cases involving prostitute suicides, the police noted the motives if they were readily available but did not exert themselves in the matter. Women's motives were usually sexual in nature or, perhaps better, represented a combination of sexual dishonor and economic distress. The

[29] Chevalier, *Classes laborieuses,* pp. 343-345; Richard Cobb, *Death in Paris: The Records of the Basse-Geôle de la Seine, October 1795–September 1801* (New York: Oxford University Press, 1978), pp. 44-56. Even the police commented upon suicide "trends" at certain times of the year. A prefectural bulletin in 1845 noted: "As [occurs] every year at the same time, spring brings about strange and sad phenomena. In three days there have been to our knowledge twelve suicide attempts, of which six were fatal, and sixteen *aliénés* have been taken to the prefecture in the past two days." AN F⁷ 3393, *Bulletin de Paris,* 26 March 1845.

[30] AN F⁷ 4172, reports of 1-2 February, 4-5 February, and 17-18 September 1825.

fifteen-year-old shoe stitcher who was abandoned by her lover, the twenty-four-year-old linen worker who was pregnant, the twenty-three-year-old gauze maker who poisoned herself because of "misery, the result of her misconduct"—these cases were clear. So too was the case of the young woman who attempted suicide because she was two months pregnant and had been abandoned by her seducer. She was brought back to life only to hear a lecture from the *commissaire* about the sinfulness of suicide and, according to the reports, "showed herself to be repentant."[31]

Prostitutes had violated the code of chastity, and they were often in economic distress; perhaps that was all that needed to be said, for the policeman as well as for the historian. The city fathers were inclined to congratulate women for their superior staying power in the face of difficulties, noting that many more men than women committed suicide: "The greater fickleness of character in the organization of women, and consequently less violent passions, a greater resignation, [and] greater ability to support physical and mental ills are, without doubt, the reasons for the difference that one notes in the number of suicides of the two sexes."[32]

ANGER, OUTRAGE, AND FRUSTRATION

Jeanne Dessuel, dressmaker, was arrested at 2:00 a.m. . . . in the markets with a certain Louis Lenoir, shoemaker. These two individuals were drunk and were locked up at the police post Lingerie by the patrol. The woman Dessuel insulted the gendarmes of the post and did not cease her flood of odious words, repeating with a sort of fury that her dear Emperor Napoleon would soon return, that a lot

[31] AN F⁷ 3839, report of 12 March 1819; AN F⁷ 3839, report of 13 January 1819; AN F⁷ 3839, report of 11 December 1818; AN F⁷ 3839, report of 31 July 1819.

[32] Moléon, *Rapports généraux,* I:306.

of people of her opinion, whom she did not want to name, knew it as well as she did; that she was a Bonapartist and gloried in it, that she mocked the gendarmes and the government, who were *canaille*.

Report of 22-23 May 1816[33]

The clerk who copied the above report apparently felt that such ramblings were significant; he drew boxes around the words "Emperor Napoleon" and "Bonapartist" to catch the eyes of his superiors, who had to read and sign the daily summary of events.

The verbal insult had little in common with the violence of suicide; on the other hand, insulting the king was as much a rhetorical convention as the declaration of suicidal intentions. The late-night, early-morning phenomenon of getting drunk and invoking Napoleon was not limited to old soldiers on half-pay or even to the prostitutes whose statements are of most concern here; rather, it served for a number of people as a satisfying method of venting hostility against the gendarmes who were supposed to be keeping the king's law and order. Invective of this kind played upon the nervousness and suspicion of bureaucrats who had survived several administrations; failure to report an incident was almost as serious as the incident itself.

Marie Louise Laisse, a prostitute working out of the Palais Royal, turned up uninvited one night at the local police post (drunk, according to the reports) and there "vomited a thousand insults against the king and the Bourbons," compounding her problems by shouting "Vive l'Empereur!" The year was 1816; old wounds were still sensitive, and it was noted darkly that the *chef du poste* had not even forwarded an account of this incident until the following day.[34] Two prostitutes were arrested on the place des Victoires singing songs

[33] AN F⁷ 4166.
[34] AN F⁷ 4166, report of 26-27 November 1816.

against the government, including one whose refrain, reported in full, was: "Nous ne sommes pas royalistes, nous n'aimons pas les Bourbons. A bas la calotte. Vive Napoléon."[35] Julie Edouin was observed strolling on the place du Châtelet at noon (drunk, said the report) carrying a bust of Bonaparte and causing a crowd to gather. The notoriety of this event caused her to be sent to the prefecture.[36] Another night, a little after midnight, the police, led by repeated cries of "Thief! Murderer!" arrested three women (all drunk), including two prostitutes, who were fighting and trying to rob each other. They were held at a local police post until morning. Louise Aimée Huberty, one of the prostitutes, was presumably sober by then; but upon hearing that she was to be taken to the prefecture, she jumped on the camp bed and "outraged the bust of the king," striking it repeatedly and trying to turn it over and smash it.[37] Robbery was one thing, lese majesty was another; a separate *procès-verbal* had to be filled out for this incident.

Too much (or too little) should not be read into these events; antiroyalist statements did not represent political consciousness or contain a threat of potential action.[38] It is true that prostitutes, unlike their male counterparts the vagabonds, did have the advantage of being able to move up in society by their association with relatively stable workers in steady employment; and, though it was unlikely that talk in the tiny *cabinets* of the hotels often turned to politics, there were other opportunities to meet. Prostitutes frequented cafés, as did

[35] AN F⁷ 3838, report of 11 October 1815.
[36] AN F⁷ 4175, report of 6-7 May 1832.
[37] AN F⁷ 4181, reports of 27-28 June and 28-29 June 1820.
[38] Recent scholarship, particularly the many works by George Rudé, has replaced the traditional notion of a mob of prostitutes, vagabonds, and thieves with a respectable revolutionary crowd of artisans and shopkeepers. See, for example, Rudé, *The Crowd in History: A Study of Popular Disturbances in France and England, 1730-1840* (New York: Wiley, 1964).

workingmen; they drank with these men, talked, learned antiroyalist songs, and sometimes developed long-term relationships. Prostitutes did not show a simple-minded loyalty to the king, but they were not shouting "Vive la république!" either. Napoleon was an easily understandable symbol of resistance, and calling his name was a proved method of angering the authorities with whom they dealt—just as individuals arrested during the Revolution frequently angered their captors with "Vive le roi!"[39] The repeated anti-Bourbon statements noted in the police reports were expressive of nothing more complicated than anger, outrage, and frustration. The police seem to have accepted them as such. Apparently only one prostitute was arrested and tried for "sedition" during the Restoration,[40] despite numerous provocative statements aimed directly at the police. Their outrage had some legitimacy. Records suggest that Huberty, who had tried to smash the bust of the king, eventually became a *chiffonnière,* or ragpicker, a profession even more precarious than that of prostitute.[41]

VIOLENCE IN PUBLIC PLACES

Hallard, prostitute, found running at midnight in the rue des Filles-Dieu.
Report of 7-8 May 1819[42]

[39] See Appendix B: Letters from Revolutionary Prisons.

[40] "Mlle. Sophie Delaude...âgée de 25 ans, fille publique, condamnée par le tribunal de police correctionnelle du département de la Seine, le 17 novembre 1818, à 13 mois de prison, 50 francs d'amende et aux frais, pour avoir, étant prise de vin, invoqué le nom de Napoléon." Auguste Imbert, *Biographie des condamnés pour délits politiques, depuis 1814 jusqu'en 1828* (Paris: n.p., 1828), p. 101. My thanks to Deborah Perry for this citation.

[41] *Louise Aimée Huberty:* AN F^7 4181, report of 28-29 January 1820; AN F^7 4170, report of 20-21 May 1822; AN F^7 4159, reports of 28 July 1824, 24 September 1824, and 5 July 1825; AN F^7 3894, report of 9-10 August 1832; AN F^7 4163, report of 27 May 1842, and AN F^7 3897, report of 28-29 May 1842 (same arrest); AN F^7 4163, report of 27 May 1842; AN F^7 3897, report of 21-22 August 1844.

[42] AN F^7 4180.

Police reports were often terse, and the ambiguities in the evidence were many. Often, only parts of the stories were told. This was especially true of the quick, transitory violence characteristic of the street and public places; it often exploded so quickly that even the victims did not know quite what had happened to them. There was, to be sure, no great pressure to resolve these cases.

Aggressiveness was often combined with consumption of alcohol. Indeed, drinking was a problem for the prostitute, for she spent much of her time in the cafés and cabarets where she picked up her customers. Alcohol unfortunately broke down her usual wise inhibitions with regard to the police. Toinette Simon, a previously undiscovered prostitute, was caught when she invaded the police post, "completely drunk," to demand that they arrest the individual with whom she had been drinking all day; all she got for her trouble was a free trip to the prefecture and registration as a new *fille publique*. Josephine Barre showed up at 1:00 a.m., drunk, to get her *souteneur* out of jail (he had been arrested for fighting); she was arrested.[43]

Most drunken behavior was pointless, undirected, and noisy. Annette Bernard caused a rather large crowd to gather, and was arrested; at the police post she made such a racket, wrote the irritated clerk, that she was sent straight off to the prefecture. Two prostitutes stationed themselves near the river and shouted insults at passers-by.[44] Virginie Benoit was found asleep on the street "completely drunk"—as were Brigitte Leboeuf; Aimée Bonami, with one man; a certain Durouchant, with two men; and countless others, alone or in groups.[45]

[43] AN F⁷ 4175, report of 14-15 May 1832; AN F⁷ 4174, report of 22-23 November 1830.

[44] AN F⁷ 4180, report of 10-11 June 1819; AN F⁷ 4172, report of 28-29 April 1826.

[45] AN F⁷ 4171, report of 2-3 July 1824; AN F⁷ 4182, report of 21-22 June 1824; AN F⁷ 4173, report of 8-9 May 1827; AN F⁷ 4173, report of 13-14 June 1828.

Thérèse Adam was scooped off the street completely drunk and covered with mud; she had been struck by a cart and had been unable to right herself. Angelique Lafarge was found sleeping in the middle of the rue Faubourg Saint-Antoine with a storekeeper, and—here the endless drunkenness becomes much less benign—her head had been bloodied. A drunken thirty-six-year-old prostitute went to the window to empty some water, overbalanced, and fell three stories. Another prostitute was found dead in the street, as a result of a fall while drunk, and a woman named Leroux suddenly dropped dead from excessive consumption of alcohol. The woman Merlin became embroiled in a dispute with a soldier in a cabaret. He killed her with a saber thrust, probably without realizing it; he was "completely drunk," according to the report.[46]

Physical abuse, often apparently unmotivated, was always a possibility. The woman Largemain, suddenly attacked by four men, received sympathy but little else; the police believed she had been "cruelly mistreated," but her assailants had vanished as quickly as they had come. Adele Beaupré was picked up at 11:30 p.m. shouting for help. Her bonnet and shawl had been stolen, but she had saved her two gold pieces of 20 francs each by hiding them in her mouth.[47] One prostitute suffered what was probably a stunning financial loss when a drunken butcher tore her clothing, and another was stabbed in the hand when she refused a man.[48]

[46] AN F⁷ 4171, report of 20-21 October 1824; AN F⁷ 4168, report of 8-9 October 1820; AN F⁷ 3876, report of 20 February 1822; AN F⁷ 3882, report of 8 August 1828; AN F⁷ 3882, report of 9 January 1828; AN F⁷ 3839, report of 24 September 1818.

[47] AN F⁷ 3875, report of 8 September 1820; AN F⁷ 4173, report of 30-31 July 1828.

[48] AN F⁷ 4168, report of 16-17 January 1820; AN F⁷ 3838, report of 23 July 1817.

It would be wrong to see prostitutes always as victims. They had knives, and they sometimes used them in anger or passion. Marie Junon, who was drinking one afternoon with two firemen, became angry with one of them and stabbed him between the nose and the left eye; he was not expected to live. The woman Deraine stabbed a man named Delis and fled; she was later picked up in the *cave* of a tavern, trying to hide the murder weapon in the straw.[49] These were exceptions, for the usual motive behind a stabbing was theft, and most prostitutes left their victims alive, if not well.

Theft was a routine part of prostitution and seems often to have been settled unofficially at the street level by the neighborhood police. Theft compounded by aggravated assault was likely to be viewed rather more seriously by the authorities, and so most prostitutes preferred the more subtle method of picking pockets. The notation that something had been *pris dans la poche* by a prostitute cropped up with distressing regularity in police reports. The circumstances, as recounted by the victims who brought the complaints, were always the same: a man innocently walking down the street had been approached by a prostitute who solicited him physically—that is, she had grabbed his arms, perhaps, or his lapels—distracted him with a line of patter, and in the meantime extracted his purse, his watch, and his handkerchief. Some prostitutes carried cutting tools for the purpose of clipping the ribbons or cords that tied watches and other valuables.[50] As this suggests, prostitutes often preferred to steal from men they did not know intimately, reasoning that the

[49] AN F⁷ 3877, report of 9 October 1828; AN F⁷ 3881, report of 28 June 1827.
[50] AN F⁷ 4181, report of 23-24 August 1820; AN F⁷ 4182, report of 25-26 January 1824.

victim of a brief encounter would have difficulty identifying someone who had merely distracted him for a few moments on the street. The aggressive style of solicitation in these times, brazen, open, and vulgar, facilitated this kind of crime. The man might be shocked, he might be diverted; only later would he discover that he had also been robbed.

Probably the most rewarding pocket was one picked in 1825 by Clementine Clément, also known as Madame Léger. Grégoire, an ex-sailor, had broken into the home of the Princesse de Rohan and robbed her of 4,000 francs and some jewels. It was a bold crime, and Grégoire celebrated by going to a rooming house with Clément, whom he had met in a tavern. When he fell asleep, Clément made a routine search of his pockets. Instead of transferring the discovered treasure to her own attire, she simply dressed herself in his clothes and left. Grégoire awoke the next morning a far poorer man. He began combing the area for Clément and would probably have found her eventually for, as the police report commented, she "made herself stand out" by her expenditures.

Sentimental contemporaries, certain that prostitutes had hearts of gold, liked to think that their money was spent on orphans and the aged.[51] Clément began throwing parties and buying drinks for her friends; she made some major purchases as well, from the practical (furniture) to the extravagant (a gold penholder). Her explanation of this sudden wealth provided an insight into her aspirations. An "immensely rich" captain had become her lover; she lived with him in a mansion in Vincennes, a suburb of Paris. She was waited on hand and foot by "Negroes from the antipodes," who served her, on bended knee, from golden dishes. Moreover her captain was "as generous as he was rich" and kept her in ready money.

---

[51] Even Parent-Duchâtelet believed that this might be true. See *De la prostitution,* I:143.

By this time Grégoire had concocted some sort of story in order to enlist the police in his search. Clément's profligate ways had drawn attention in her neighborhood (the Cité) and she was arrested while ordering a banquet for twenty. Both she and Grégoire were tried, and Clément got two years in prison for her part in the affair.[52] The story is atypical both in the scale of the theft and in the amount of coverage given to the activities of the prostitute involved. This attention was due to the involvement of the Princesse de Rohan. Nevertheless, despite the exalted status of her indirect victim, it was Clément's words and actions that dominated the affair. Deference, exacted from the captain's exotic servants, played a curiously prominent role in her fantasy, perhaps indicating a strong desire on her part for respect, perhaps indicating nothing more than her notion of how well-to-do people behaved. In any case her reaction to sudden prosperity was an unabashed determination to live it up, and her daydreams were equally extravagant.

Customers were not always so obliging as to fall asleep, and when prostitutes were caught in the act of picking a pocket—as they often were—they seemed to feel that the best defense was a good offense. The notation that a couple was found *s'accusant mutuellement de vol* is a frequent one in the reports; the police were continually breaking up battles waged over a few francs. In some cases the prostitutes probably had legitimate grievances. One woman justified her claim to the disputed sum by declaring, with an effrontery that apparently shocked the police, that it was "money she had

---

[52] *Gazette des tribunaux,* 25 December 1825. When she was arrested Clément still had 2,000 francs in bank notes, 560 francs in silver, a gold watch and two chains, and several jewels. AN F⁷ 3879, report of Tuesday, 28 June 1825. Vidocq (*Voleurs,* pp. 142-146) gives a more detailed account.

earned honestly with an individual."[53] The danger of picking pockets (danger, that is, from the victims, who were likely to fight back if they noticed) led some prostitutes to work in teams. Sometimes these teams resorted to brute force[54] but usually, as in the case of prostitutes who worked alone, they preferred to rely on finesse and sleight of hand. A cook, for example, suddenly found himself poorer by 15 francs. He pursued the two prostitutes who had just solicited him, but they had nothing; they had passed the money to a third woman standing innocently nearby. In this case a witness had apparently observed the switch, and all three women were arrested.[55]

Association with male confederates usually entailed the use of force and intimidation. The victim, lured by the women, his supicions lulled, was easily caught off guard by the men. A certain Dumouzat was returning home late one night when he was accosted by several prostitutes who tried to draw him toward a dark alley. He suddenly found himself surrounded by a group of men, armed with clubs, who began to beat

[53] "A 1ʰ, les cris à la garde s'étant fait entendre dans la rue Guerin Boisseau, la Garde s'y est aussitôt transportée et y a arrêté Prosper Maître, cocher du cabriolet n° 317, disant demeurant cul de sac Ste.-Opportune n° 3 et la fille [publique] Emelie Mamelet, demeurant chez Madam Boucher logeuse rue Guerin Boisseau n° 37, qui se battaient. La femme était échevelée et couverte de boue et l'homme avait les mains écorchées et en sang. Ils s'accusaient reciproquement d'avoir voulu soustraire 2 pièces de 5 francs que Maître disait être la fruit de son gain pendant la journée et que la femme disait avoir gagnée *honnêtement avec un particulier.*" AN F⁷ 4182, report of 23-24 January 1824.

[54] For example, two prostitutes assaulted a sixty-one-year-old merchant, inflicting a serious head wound. AN F⁷ 3879, report of Sunday, 16 January 1825.

[55] A rare domestic note intruded into this vignette. One of the prostitutes claimed to be nursing a four-month-old child who was waiting alone in her apartment. The police escorted the woman home and asked only for her prostitution *carte* as security. AN F⁷ 4181, report of 23-24 July 1820.

him. Fortunately Dumouzat's screams had awakened the neighborhood and the attackers, *filles* and all, vanished into the alley.[56] In this as in other cases prostitution served as a cover for other crimes. The women in this incident were not soliciting at all, in reality, but were using the guise of prostitution to cover up the very real crime they were trying to commit.

It is difficult to know whether the prostitutes were considered full partners in these gangs of *malfaiteurs* or whether they themselves suffered from the brutality of their male colleagues. The latter seems more likely, yet the muscle of the men who worked with prostitutes came in handy on occasion, for it could be used against the police. Two guards escorting Josephine Vitou to the prefecture were "attacked at 9:30 p.m. on the rue Saint-Honoré by *souteneurs des filles publiques,* around twenty in number, lying in wait at the establishment of Leblanc, tavernkeeper." Reinforcements, too few and too late, were "gravely insulted" and Vitou was free, though something of a fugitive.[57] These outpourings of popular support for the prostitute seldom surprised the police, for they knew they were in enemy territory; but they were often angry at the extent of this support, particularly since their own procedures made such incidents routine.

The usual procedure in an arrest required a wait of several hours at a police post before the walk to the prefecture. The walk introduced publicity into the affair, and the delay at the post gave the prostitutes' associates time to plan the escape. The circumstances were always the same. One or more prostitutes, conducted to the prefecture by at least two guards, were suddenly attacked by *une troupe de bandits,* by *sept ou*

---

[56] AN F⁷ 4180, report of 7-8 September 1819.
[57] AN F⁷ 4174, report of 23-24 November 1830.

huit mauvais sujets, or simply by *jeunes gens.*[58] These variously described characters provided the strength and the diversion; it was up to the prostitute to make good her escape. Some lovers or *souteneurs* were even bolder than this, braving the police on their own grounds. A young cabinetmaker sneaked into a police post to help a prostitute escape and was himself arrested; a marblecutter claimed a recently arrested prostitute as his wife and was arrested for being without identity papers.[59] There were others who helped, and particularly enraged the police, by whistling or shouting warnings at the approach of a patrol.[60] The police were constantly reminded that the streets were not theirs alone.

LOVERS AND BORDELLOS

There is in the rue [Vieille] place aux Veaux a house of prostitution whose master is currently being detained at the prefecture. He is a real cutthroat. A day does not go by that a crime is not committed there, and it was there that the riot with the soldiers began two days ago. It is said that several Prussians have already been killed; all the neighbors demand the closing of this house.

Report of 8 October 1815[61]

The people with whom prostitutes most frequently associated were those who made money from them in some way. Some

[58] AN F⁷ 4172, report of 29-30 April 1826; AN F⁷ 3877, report of Saturday, 2 August 1823; AN F⁷ 4172, report of 31 January–1 February 1825. In the largest such incident a five-man guard, escorting eight prostitutes, claimed to have been attacked by about sixty individuals. The pitched battle yielded curiously meager results: one prostitute was freed, and one of the "sixty" was captured. AN F⁷ 4174, report of 13-14 May 1829.

[59] AN F⁷ 4173, report of 1-2 August 1827; AN F⁷ 4171, report of 27-28 June 1823.

[60] The police commented that in some neighborhoods people were posted so that they could whistle in warning at the first sight of a patrol. AN F⁷ 4181, report of 4-5 August 1822.

[61] AN F⁷ 3838.

of these people were dangerous, and there was a natural tension in such relationships. An unnamed *maître de maison* had two of his prostitutes arrested for stealing from a customer.[62] One Langot, who ran a house on the rue Sainte-Barbe, asked the police to arrest an unruly customer who was beating the women, "and even"—revealing here his priorities—"threatened to break the furniture."[63] When houses were run by women there was perhaps a greater willingness on the part of prostitutes to take up arms against the oppressors; complaints from madams about assaults committed against them by prostitutes were not unknown.[64] One *fille de maison,* arrested for creating a public disturbance, tried to extricate herself from the situation by informing on her madam, telling the police (wrongly) that there was an arsenal hidden in the brothel.[65]

In retaliation, the madam could use the authority she held by virtue of her "contract" with the police, who were naturally inclined to side with her in any dispute. Beyond that, the favored device for control was the madam's nominal ownership of everything in the bordello, including the clothing.

[62] AN F[7] 4173, report of 15-16 April 1827.

[63] AN F[7] 4180, report of 6-7 September 1816.

[64] See, for example, AN F[7] 4173, report of 20-30 August 1827; AN F[7] 4176, report of 28-29 December 1829; and AN F[7] 4170, report of 22-23 August 1822, when five prostitutes attacked "the woman Dufoi," their madam.

[65] "Cette fille leur [guards] ayant dit qu'elle avait des révélations à faire, conduite chez le commissaire de police de la rue Mezière n° 7 où elle a déclaré à ce magistrat que des armes étaient cachées chez la femme Gros rue du Coeur Volant n° 20, maison de prostitution. Le commissaire avec deux gardes s'est rendu chez la femme Gros, où il a trouvé un poignard et un sabre de cavalerie appartenant au Sieur Denancourt, vivant en concubinage avec cette femme...." AN F[7] 4175, report of 6-7 July 1832. Another prostitute arrested for attacking her madam spoke of a certain "Alfrede," *souteneur,* and of another prostitute who, she hinted, knew something about a recently committed murder. AN F[7] 4175, report of 1-2 October 1832.

If a prostitute decided to leave, she could be arrested for "stealing" the clothes on her back;[66] if she became angry, she could be arrested for disturbing the peace;[67] if she became violent, she could be arrested for destruction of property.[68] She could even be physically mistreated with relative impunity, as happened in the case of one prostitute who came to her local commissariat "covered with blood" and declaring that her *maîtresse* had her beaten by two men.[69] Nothing, apparently, was done in this case; the police were too uneasy about their compromise with vice to risk stirring up trouble.

In addition to their official tolerance of the brothels the police granted a semiofficial recognition to lovers, *amants* or *souteneurs,* because they realized that these individuals sometimes had an important stake in the prostitute's earnings. When the women were in brothels the bonding was often emotional, with little gain on either side. More questionable were the cases of *filles isolées* who "lived with" lovers (particularly if these lovers were unemployed), or women who began their careers as single women, married, and yet continued to work as prostitutes; in these latter cases the husbands were exploiting their wives.

It was a tense relationship, and fury could easily engulf both partners. A medical student shot himself in the room of a prostitute who lived on the rue Saint-Honoré; it was believed that this "act of despair" was due to jealousy.[70] A

[66] See, for example, the report of a woman "prévenue d'avoir enlevé des effets d'habillement qui lui avaient été confiés." AN F⁷ 4170, report of 13-14 July 1822; also see AN F⁷ 4173, report of 21-22 June 1827, and AN F⁷ 4167, report of 12-13 February 1819.

[67] Three bordello prostitutes were arrested for fighting among themselves. AN F⁷ 4175, report of 7-8 May 1832.

[68] One woman was arrested "à la requisition de la maîtresse de maison pour lui avoir déchiré un bonnet de la valeur de 22 francs." AN F⁷ 4172, report of 27-28 July 1828.

[69] AN F⁷ 4170, report of 26-27 February 1822.

[70] AN F⁷ 3839, report of 19 June 1818.

gendarme became jealous of his prostitute-girlfriend; after killing her, he shot himself in the head.[71] A man named Blanvillain, unemployed and without a trade, was separated from his wife. He went to a brothel on the rue de la Calandre, on the Cité, to find her. Not allowed to enter the house, he armed himself with "four large stones" which he heaved through the window, incidentally hurting the madam of the house and her servant. *Ce furieux,* as the police report called him, threatened to burn down the house and was taken into custody.[72] And again in a house on the rue de la Calandre: a prostitute was struck by an individual with whom she lived; she grabbed a knife on the table and stabbed him three times, killing him.[73] An unemployed journeyman butcher, Bary, who lived with the madam of a house, hanged himself at her place of business. He was a *très mauvais sujet,* according to the police, who were not unduly disturbed by his passing.[74] Finally, there was Louise Deleau, who accepted her lover's foibles with a degree of stoicism. A police officer who was conducting a routine search of her building was at first refused admittance by her; when he asked why, she replied that she had believed him to be Tabouret, the man with whom she had lived for several years and who had adopted the unpleasant habit of making a scene outside her door every time he got drunk.[75]

There was a pattern in these random acts of violence. The salient factor in the relationships between prostitutes and their lovers was lack of possession: privacy was hard to come by. This was a serious problem for all poor couples, married or unmarried, and it was a particular problem for the single and mobile, who often lived in rooming houses. As prostitutes

[71] AN F⁷ 3877, report of Friday, 7 March 1823.
[72] AN F⁷ 3882, report of 16 September 1828.
[73] AN F⁷ 3878, report of Tuesday, 24 August 1824.
[74] AN F⁷ 3838, report of 3 November 1817.
[75] AN Y 13143, report of 18 November 1790.

knew, lodging houses were vulnerable to a police invasion at any time. Further, though the police often spoke of a prostitute as "living with" someone, this phrase usually implied only that the prostitute had accepted the man as a lover rather than as a customer; when the woman was a *fille de maison* the couples were subject to periods of physical separation.[76] The violent Blanvillain was denied access to his wife in a house where all sorts of men routinely passed through, and he reacted with rage. A different kind of denial was evident in the case of a soldier who brought his friends from the regiment to a house of prostitution to see his girlfriend. They were all shown up to her room; she and one of the other soldiers recognized each other as old acquaintances. Outraged, the boyfriend stabbed her.[77]

There were certain, no doubt unspoken, standards of fidelity that both partners were expected to observe: standards of place, time, and emotional involvement. The jeweler who brought two loaded pistols to a house of prostitution because he suspected his mistress of infidelity was clearly not talking about physical fidelity; at the same time, neither the police nor anyone else involved found anything bizarre in his concern that she might have transferred her affections to someone else.[78] A prostitute identified only as Lemaire stabbed her lover Richard, a locksmith, when she found him with another woman. She went straight for the heart, inflicting a dangerous wound in the area of the left shoulder.[79]

This peculiar concept of fidelity could be violated in different ways. Bocquet, a *fille isolée* living in lodgings, hurled

---

[76] According to Parent-Duchâtelet, prostitutes who had just left prison or the hospital were allowed twenty-four hours with their lovers before they had to go back to "work for the house." *De la prostitution,* I:153.

[77] AN F⁷ 4180, report of 4-5 November 1819.

[78] AN F⁷ 3879, report of 24 July 1825.

[79] AN F⁷ 3875, report of Wednesday, 4 July 1821.

herself out of a second-story window because the man she lived with had found her in bed with a butcher—an easily understood professional occurrence, but one that was shocking when confronted.[80] Conversely, some men were taught that the relationship was merely business. A gendarme (again) became despondent over a certain Virginie Vanier, with whom "he had some intimacy." The relationship was apparently less intimate than he had believed. She did not want to receive him during the day, outside business hours; she had clearly relegated him to the ranks of her customers. He forced his way into the room, threw her out, barricaded the door, and shot himself.[81]

The violence, murder, and mayhem all suggested that, in spite of their professions, prostitutes had personally significant and emotionally important relationships with men; their contemporaries found that hard to believe and could not comprehend the motives of the men involved, except by ascribing them to greed. These relationships were not in any sense typical, and they were subject to unusual stresses and strains. Prostitutes were forced by lack of space to play out the most intimate scenes of their lives on relatively public stages, both the beginnings of affairs—and their endings:

> Yesterday, at three o'clock in the afternoon, Gaury, age 22, laborer . . . was in the back room of a tavern with Guénard, the prostitute with whom he lives; at the end of a heated discussion between the two, who were both drunk, she stabbed him in the stomach. According to the surgeon this is a grave wound. This man was taken to his parents' home. The girl Guénard protested that she had had no intention of stabbing her lover, but that he

[80] AN F⁷ 3875, report of Sunday, 10 December 1820.
[81] AN F⁷ 3875, report of Monday, 4 June 1821.

had threatened to leave her; she, wanting only to frighten him, held out the knife and he impaled himself on it.[82]

THE PROSTITUTE AND THE POLICEMAN

A certain Henry, laborer . . . has been pointed out as a very suspicious character. He frequents cabarets, where he makes infamous statements against the king. He is also immoral and violent. A number of people believe that he is a police agent.

Report of 30 October 1815[83]

Respect for the police was not high in this period, as they themselves were aware. The reports were full of outrageous characters who brought off credible impersonations of agents from the prefecture, sometimes for extended periods, before they were caught.[84] The actions of these imitators were seldom flattering to the guardians of law and order. One man got himself admitted as an inspector into a *maison,* where he began to commit acts of "arbitrary authority." He overplayed his hand, fortunately; the madam got suspicious, realized that she had never seen him before, and contacted the local police, who put him out of business immediately.[85] Two prostitutes became so irritated with a certain Bard, who professed to be a police inspector, that they denounced him to the local *com-*

---

[82] AN F[7] 3875, report of Thursday, 19 April 1821.

[83] AN F[7] 3838.

[84] They were able to get away with this because police inspectors and agents did not wear special uniforms. In March 1829 about one hundred inspectors were organized into the Sergents de ville, a uniformed group meant to be visible. The gendarmes, an army unit, had been created in 1813 to replace several regiments of the infantry and dragoons as the special guard of the city of Paris. There were about 1,528 gendarmes during the Restoration, of whom about 611 were mounted; they wore uniforms and carried sabers. See *Compte d'administration des dépenses de la Préfecture de police* (1830), pp. 5-6, 43.

[85] AN F[7] 4168, report of 18-19 May 1820.

missaire: "[He] introduces himself into certain homes and seeks to play the role of conciliator and busybody among persons who are having difficulties."[86]

Prostitutes were involved with the police on at least two levels. In an abstract sense, their involvement stemmed from the ever-growing pile of regulations, ordinances, and *arrêtés* that defined their rights as *filles publiques*. But on a practical, personal level, they knew the police, cooperated with them, and were abused by them; occasionally they were befriended by them, and sometimes they were forced to depend on them.

For the prostitute this relationship may well have been the most critical in her life, both in its concrete effect on her circumstances and in its effect on her integration into the greater society. Sometimes intimate relationships developed— proximity alone caused this to happen occasionally—and the paradoxes of such a love affair could lead to tragedy at worst, charges of corruption and favoritism at best. One woman, Angelique Thullon, found her position on the margin graphically illustrated as two rivals, a gendarme and a convict, fought for her.[87]

The policeman was the most powerful person in the prostitute's life, much more powerful than the king; yet, unlike the king, who could be vilified only from afar, the policeman was touchable. He could be kicked, stabbed, or spat on. When arrest was inevitable, the prostitute could make the arrest as unpleasant as possible by "vomiting insults," as the police liked to phrase it, biting, or breaking windows at the police post. Passive resistance could also be effective. Marie Valleran, arrested on the Pont au Change, simply refused to walk. The two guards had to carry her and, since it was still early, they attracted a jeering crowd.[88]

[86] AN F⁷ 3838, report of 9 August 1817.
[87] AN F⁷ 4182, report of 23-24 January 1824.
[88] AN F⁷ 4176, report of 29-30 January 1835.

If the police answered violence with violence, there was little evidence of this in police reports, though it did occasionally appear. One prostitute, accused by the *chef du poste* of having struck him, responded that she had been stabbed with a saber and struck several times on the arms. Marie Bachet, described as a cook, was caught in bed with two soldiers. She was sent to the commissariat, where she complained that her guards had not allowed her to dress before they escorted her through the streets and that they had struck her several times.[89] On occasion interdepartmental rivalries caused one branch of the police to reveal the misdeeds of another. When a *chef du poste* roughed up a prostitute who refused to tell him her name, he was immediately challenged by an agent of the Bureau of Morals who, "taking the side of this girl, said to the chief that he had no right to ask her name, that it was not his business, and that he was wrong to use violence against people consigned to his post." The prostitutes in custody agreed with this and decided to revolt, making an unsuccessful raid on the gunrack to arm themselves. The noise caused a crowd to gather outside, but the incident was reported only because the local police were angry with the agents working out of the Bureau of Morals at the Prefecture.[90] If cases of deliberate abuse were seldom reported, however, there were suspicious cases. One drunk and disorderly prostitute attempted to stab one of her captors, but fortunately pierced only his clothing. That night, however, she wound up at the hospital, not at the post; she had "seriously injured her head by falling," said the report. It might

[89] AN F⁷ 4166, reports of 3-4 March 1817 and 17-18 January 1818.

[90] AN F⁷ 4171, report of 20-21 October 1823. This kind of clash between local and prefectural officials occurred repeatedly: local post officials felt that prefectural agents made free with their posts and did not show the proper respect, "sortant et rentrant à tous momens sous divers prétextes, et s'étant conduits insolemment envers lui [chef du poste]." AN F⁷ 4171, report of 26-27 December 1823.

have happened as written. No one was going to check on it in any case.[91]

This was the dark side of the relationship between the prostitute and the policeman. There was hatred and contempt on both sides, for each was forced into contact that was too intimate. Their language and actions often reflected disgust. "The *commissaire*," wrote one clerk, "decided to end the frightful libertinage . . . and arrested eighteen filthy prostitutes." Marie Honorine Valour, a prostitute, was arrested for denigrating the police as *mouchards*.[92] A woman came to a police post to ask for help: a friend, she said, had thrown her out of her apartment and threatened to beat her up. She was sent to the *commissaire* first, and the commissaire, "having recognized her as a prostitute," sent the police back to their post, taking no further action.[93] Denise Maset, arrested for drunk and disorderly conduct in a cabaret, kicked the *chef* and broke the jail window. The police angrily demanded payment for the broken glass, but Maset enjoyed the triumph of the destitute: she had no money.[94] The public was alarmed by reports of an unknown horseman who had attacked and gravely wounded a woman on the street; gun sales were said to have

[91] AN F⁷ 4172, report of 10-11 June 1826. Angelique Masson, a cook in a house of prostitution on the rue Quincampoix, was also arrested for drunk and disorderly conduct: "elle s'est blessée à la tête en se laissant tomber sur le lit de camp du corps de garde." AN F⁷ 4166, report of 16-17 January 1817.

[92] AN F⁷ 3838, report of 8 August 1816; AN F⁷ 4176, report of 24-25 October 1837.

[93] "Vers minuit Emilie Carlier, demeurant rue de Seine nº 60, s'est présentée au poste pour requerir la garde, disant que son bon ami était renfermée chez elle, qu'il refusait de lui ouvrir, et qu'il l'avait menacée dans la journée de la maltraiter; 2 hommes et un caporal ont été envoyées avec cette femme chez le commissaire du quartier, qui l'ayant reconnu pour une femme prostituée, a renvoyée les hommes à leur poste sans faire d'autres recherches." AN F⁷ 4174, report of 1-2 July 1829.

[94] AN F⁷ 4172, report of 12-13 July 1825; AN F⁷ 4171, report of 4-5 May 1824.

risen. The police tried to calm public fears. The victim, they said, was only a prostitute, harmed by her own kind.[95] Rose Dessaux "revolted" against her guard, tore his cape, and bit his arm; Angelique Lemoine insulted her guard "grossly"; a group of *filles de maison* "vomited" all sorts of insults against the guard, and one "wanted to join actions to her words."[96]

The police used prostitutes as informers. This relationship was a natural one. Their marginally criminal lives put prostitutes in touch with many suspicious characters. In addition, the official requirements concerning regulated prostitution allowed many perfectly ordinary contacts with the police, so that the opportunity and the motive were there for the prostitutes to give information.[97] The police also seem to have used prostitutes as auxiliary policewomen on at least one occasion. In late 1819 there was some concern over the problem of *piquers,* a name given to young toughs who roamed the streets stabbing people with long needles. The wounds were never serious, but the ever-present threat of being stuck started to make people nervous. Since the victims of these attacks were almost always women, the police recruited twenty *filles de maison* to act as bait; each was shadowed by an officer. The women were paid 5 francs apiece per day for their trouble and were taught how to walk like honest women (eyes down). After eight days none of the prostitutes had been attacked,

[95] "Il est bien avéré d'après la déclaration même de la femme trouvée renversée et blessée rue du Cadran que c'est une femme publique victime des mauvais traitements de quelques mauvais sujets." AN F[7] 3880, report of Friday, 17 November 1826.

[96] AN F[7] 4173, report of 22-23 December 1828; AN F[7] 4171, report of 23-24 March 1824; AN F[7] 4180, report of 14-15 August 1816.

[97] Data on police informants are scanty. Generally the police did not keep records such as the following: "La nommée Rayer, fille publique logée rue de la Mortellerie n° 96 signale confidentiellement comme voleur d'habitude le nommé Jean Antoine Boulanger, âgé de 36 ans, ciseleur, rue de la Mortellerie n° 96." AN F[7] 3838, report of 20 July 1816.

and the expense of the operation brought it to an unsatisfactory end.[98]

Cooperation in crime solving was likely to be involuntary: prostitutes were the creatures of the police, vulnerable to arrest at any moment and thus susceptible to pressure. A further opportunity for abuse rested in the fact that policemen got *primes,* or bounties, awarded according to the number of violations of the prostitution regulations that they were able to establish. This bonus system was not unique to the Bureau des mœurs, for agents of the Sûreté also received bonuses based on the performance of certain of their duties.[99] But the Sûreté had to be able to prove its charges in a court of law; the Bureau des mœurs acted as judge and jury—as well as legislator and enforcer—regarding prostitutes. Thus there was room for the charge that the police sometimes rounded

[98] For accounts of various attacks see AN F⁷ 3839, reports of December 1819. The details of the prostitute decoy operation are from M. Froment, *La Police dévoilée, depuis la Restauration et notamment sous Messieurs Franchet et Delavau,* 4 vols. (Paris: Lemonier, 1829), I:224-226. Tulard believes that this work, credited to an *ex-chef de brigade,* was actually written by the same Guyon who wrote the *Biographie des commissaires.* Tulard, *Paris et son administration,* p. 429.

The police of Paris had their own theory about the *piquers:* "Les personnes sensées sont dans l'opinion au sujet des piqûres, que ces manoeuvres ont pour but de compromettre et de vexer l'autorité en décriant la police. Elles pensent encore qu'on ne doit les imputer qu'à ceux qui en juillet 1815 jettaient de l'eau forte sur les schalls des femmes dans les lieux publics; . . ." AN F⁷ 3839, report of 17 December 1819. One can only hope, for the sake of the women of Paris, that these *malveillants* soon got over their anger with the police.

[99] *Primes* paid to the Brigade des mœurs amounted to 3,588 francs in 1836, 3,904.75 in 1837, and 6,200 in 1838. See the *Compte d'administration des dépenses de la Préfecture de police* for the appropriate years. Gabriel Delessert became prefect in September 1836 and remained in that position until the downfall of the monarchy. He was a strong official and took a personal interest in prostitution; his wife was cosponsor of a rescue society for young girls and ex-prostitutes. The large jump in the amount paid out in *primes* reflects a change in enforcement policies.

up women indiscriminately to earn extra money, knowing that the burden of proof of prostitution would not be very heavy. Josephine Creton, a young woman arrested for street-walking, was given moral support by her landlady, who made an angry complaint. She declared that "police inspectors arrest without distinction all women that they find walking alone on the boulevards after a certain hour." The official commanding the post gave some consideration to these accusations, apparently, but decided that Creton would have to be charged after all—for resisting arrest.[100]

In return prostitutes demanded much from the police, using them as informal judges in disputes that arose in the streets. A prostitute and a soldier appeared at midnight at the post Palais de Justice, each with a complaint against the other, she of having been struck, he of having been robbed (they both probably had a case). But "they explained themselves so badly," wrote the irritated clerk, "that it was impossible to understand precisely what they meant." Both were sent to the prefecture; the men at the local post wanted nothing more to do with them. Josephine Poirion arrived at the post, drunk, demanding that the guard accompany her—though when pressed, she could not say why, the original grievance having been lost in an alcoholic haze.[101]

[100] AN F⁷ 4166, report of 30-31 July 1816. The *commissaire* in effect confirmed the landlady's suspicions about police policy, though he did not condemn that policy in principle: "Cette nuit à 11 1/2ʰ une femme qui étoit pourchassée par une patrouille de militaires s'est refugiée, comme dans un asile, au corps de garde du petit pont de l'Hôtel-Dieu; mais la patrouille y entra brusquement sans s'être fait reconnaître. Delà une altercation entre les gardes nationaux du poste et les militaires; ceux-ci réclamaient la femme pour l'emener en disant qu'il leur avait été donné pour consigne d'arrêter toutes les femmes qu'ils trouveraient dans les rues après 11 heures. Cependant celle dont il s'agit n'étoit point femme publique et l'on voit par là une preuve des abus et inconvénients auxquel peut donner lieu une mesure, bonne an elle-même, quant l'exécution en est confiée à des hommes sans discernement." AN F⁷ 3838, report of 28 July 1817.

[101] AN F⁷ 4180, report of 30 April–1 May 1819; AN F⁷ 4166, report of 5-6 August 1816; AN F⁷ 4174, report of 27-28 June 1829.

The police regarded prostitutes, on the whole, as an irritating group, by turns quarrelsome, violent, profane, noisy, and suicidal. Nor were the prostitutes much taken with the police, as they showed on numerous occasions. Yet the police were the constituted authorities; they replaced a family, a community, a church, a priest, older brothers, and they had the virtue of always being there:

Rosalie Allair, prostitute, came to ask for refuge at the pointe Saint-Eustache during the night, held overnight;

Heloise Ravisard, prostitute, came to the post drunk and wounded in the hand, held overnight;

Julie Bonai, prostitute, came at midnight to the marché Saint-Martin to ask for refuge, held overnight;

Adele Hubert, prostitute, came to the place du Châtelet for refuge during the night, claiming to be pursued by individuals with whom she did not want to go, held overnight;

An unknown, prostitute, came to the post Petit Pont, saying she had been released from the [Petite] Force that day and had no place to go, held overnight;

Honorée Montieu, prostitute, came to ask for refuge at the marché Saint-Martin, completely drunk, held overnight;

Marie Bureau and Reine Marchand, prostitutes, came to Petit Pont to warm themselves, held overnight;

Françoise Mousseau, prostitute, came to the place Maubert to ask for refuge, claiming to be pursued by some men and insulting the royal family, held overnight;

Marie Louise Etienne, prostitute, came to the Lingerie at midnight to ask for refuge, claiming to have been pursued by several individuals in the rue de la Feronnerie, held overnight;

Josephine Boulanger, prostitute, came during the night to the pointe Saint-Eustache to ask for refuge, held overnight;

Marianne Olivier, prostitute, came during the night to the post Palais de Justice, to ask for refuge, held overnight;

Reine Piolet, prostitute, came to the post to ask for refuge, to avoid abuse by Joseph Theodore Charlot, worker, held overnight;

Josephine Pautre, prostitute, who came to the post drunk, making a terrible racket, claiming she wanted to avoid a man she had been with earlier, held overnight;

Adele Beaupré, prostitute, came at 1:15 a.m. to ask for refuge, held overnight;

Julie Pinaut, prostitute, came to the Rotonde de la Villette at 10:30, drunk, held overnight;

Louise Ravisard, prostitute, came to the post Palais Royal at 11:30, declaring that she was without refuge and without means of subsistence, held overnight.[102]

The undeniable instances of kindness by the police were all but lost among the more frequent instances of abuse. The legal situation of prostitutes lent itself to corruption, although it was difficult to find solid proof of this in the early nineteenth century. The police did not keep records of internal affairs

[102] AN F⁷ 4170, report of 5-6 February 1822; AN F⁷ 4173, report of 19-20 November 1828; AN F⁷ 4174, report of 21-22 March 1829; AN F⁷ 4172, report of 23-24 July 1825; AN F⁷ 4172, report of 21-22 July 1825; AN F⁷ 4180, report of 20-21 January 1822; AN F⁷ 4170, report of 8-9 January 1822; AN F⁷ 4171, report of 31 November–1 December 1823; AN F⁷ 4168, report of 11-12 November 1820; AN F⁷ 4173, report of 6-7 November 1828; AN F⁷ 4173, report of 20-21 January 1826; AN F⁷ 4182, report of 27-28 July 1824; AN F⁷ 4174, report of 5-6 May 1829; AN F⁷ 4173, report of 13-14 November 1828; AN F⁷ 4171, report of 16-17 October 1823; AN F⁷ 4173, report of 16-17 January 1828.

of this nature. There were unconfirmed rumors, newspaper exposés, and more or less serious books by disgruntled former police employees, all hinting at bribery, payoffs, and protection extended to obliging women. Guyon's biography of the *commissaires* hinted of numerous special relationships between madams and policemen, of special banquets in bordellos; there was some gossip about women who were released in return for special favors,[103] payments, or other *condescendances equivalentes,* and these stories would not die down. "The stories of these illicit transactions are particularly widespread at Saint-Lazare. . . . [T]hey are so consistent that one is forced to assume that they rest on facts," wrote Frégier.[104] There was only one reported case of attempted bribery, by a prostitute, held overnight in a cell, who offered her guard 2 francs to let her go.[105]

The daily relationship of prostitutes with the police illustrated, perhaps more graphically than the rules and regulations, the extent to which prostitutes were truly victims. Their contemporaries, to be sure, were eager to embrace this unthreatening view of them. The police commissioner J.-L. Rey was relentless in his determination to portray their passivity. Prostitutes rarely committed acts of violence, he asserted, and when they did, it was out of jealousy. "Pressed by need," he admitted, "they could, perhaps, forget themselves so far as to search a man's pocket, even to steal his watch; but for all

---

[103] Guyon, *Biographie des commissaires,* pp. 215-216. The extortion of sexual favors was mentioned briefly: "On a vu des militaires de la Légion de police se rassembler au nombre de sept à huit, se former des patrouilles, quoique n'étant pas de service, et arrêter les femmes publiques, qu'ils mettent ensuite en liberté, quand ils leur ont fait payer du vin et fait la débauche avec elles." Report of 4 Pluviôse Year IV (24 January 1795), in François Victor Alphonse Aulard, ed., *Paris pendant la Réaction thermidorienne et sous le Directoire,* 5 vols. (Paris: Leopold Cerf, 1898-1902), II:701.

[104] Frégier, *Des classes dangereuses,* I:263.

[105] AN F⁷ 4172, report of 27-28 February 1825.

that, one cannot consider them to be professional thieves." He found prostitutes to have excellent hearts and discovered that they "rarely refuse alms to the poor."[106]

Such an interpretation of their behavior was almost comically inaccurate, and did little justice to the many evidences of resourcefulness and toughness in individual prostitutes. Unfortunately, all their strength was expended in a situation in which they could scarcely expect to triumph; their poverty, their legal segregation, their estrangement from others (especially women) in their class, all worked against them. As the daily police reports revealed, prostitution was a very bad business indeed.

[106] J. L. Rey, *Des prostituées et de la prostitution en général* (Le Mans: Julien, Lanier et Cie., 1847), pp. 21-23. The image of passivity has persisted into the twentieth century, in defiance of all observations. Note, for example, the following passive characterization of what a prostitute does: "For practical, law-enforcement purposes, the definition of prostitution has usually not been too difficult. The prostitute defines herself when she agrees to have sexual intercourse with a person (not her husband) who offers her money for engaging in the intercourse, which may be coital or extra-coital. The prostitute is usually considered to have agreed to the intercourse, and so to have defined herself, once she has accompanied the other person to the place where the act is to take place and has accepted money for its performance. Payment is usually made in advance of the sexual act." Harry Benjamin and R. E. L. Masters, *Prostitution and Morality* (New York: Julian Press, 1964), pp. 21-22. In contrast, a more recent work has correctly emphasized the "verbal sexual aggression" required by prostitution. See Barbara Sherman Heyl, *The Madam as Entrepreneur: Career Management in House Prostitution* (New Brunswick, N.J.: Transaction Books, 1979), p. 120.

· 6 ·

Criminal Marginality

ONE peculiar benefit of being employed along the Seine was the opportunity to make extra money by pulling bodies out of the river. An *arrêté* of 1836 had set the price at 25 francs for victims who were "recalled to life" and 15 francs for those brought up as corpses. "In allowing these sorts of bounties, the authorities have had the principal goal of encouraging acts of self-sacrifice, and of offering an indemnity to courageous citizens who often do not hesitate to throw themselves into the current to aid persons in danger," stated an 1841 clarification of the original circular. Moreover, "the recovery of those submerged is of a high importance for the families of these individuals, who often have a great interest in establishing their decease legally." Unfortunately, the original good intentions of the measure had been swamped by fishermen bringing in the bodies of fetuses and stillborn infants for the full 15-franc indemnity. These kinds of recoveries, of infant bodies encountered in the river "by chance," could not be compared to the often dangerous work of recovering adults. Nevertheless, "since the discovery of these fetuses is ordinarily made by fishermen, or by workers, and it is useful to compensate them for the time away from their work," the prefecture concluded that 5 francs would be paid if the finder would take the body to the morgue.[1]

[1] Circular of 20 July 1841, *Recueil des circulaires,* I:381-382.

The precariousness of life was sometimes obscured by the language of administrative routine, but it could never be entirely forgotten. A great many people lived under the constant threat of destitution. They were marginal in society, on the border between poverty and nonexistence. The essence of their condition was vulnerability; they had nothing to rely on if wages were interrupted. Women on their own were particularly vulnerable because of their weak economic position, and their solution in this case was so obvious that it appeared in contemporary proverbs: poor women were exhorted to remember that they were women, reminded that they were "sitting on a fortune." This was one kind of marginality, stemming from economic distress and often leading to the decision to become a prostitute.

The marginality that characterized the registered prostitute, however directly it may have stemmed from this cycle of unemployment and poverty, was a different phenomenon. It arose from the prostitute's unusual and virtually unique relationship to the prefecture. Once her inscription had been accomplished, she was vulnerable to frequent arrests and short prison terms. This series of interruptions imposed a kind of criminal marginality on her, a cycle of imprisonment, impoverishment, and crime. Her deviance from society, a result of her actions as a prostitute, was aggravated by actions of the administration that served to separate her even more completely from ordinary existence. The lives of prostitutes were shaped by both kinds of marginality: one of them economic, a commonplace in the popular mentality; the other of administrative origin, the effects of which contemporaries were scarcely aware.

THE THREAT OF ECONOMIC FAILURE

Women often resorted to prostitution because they did not earn enough money to survive otherwise, but beyond this deceptively simple statement their situation was less clear.

The only clues to the conditions shared by prostitutes before they entered this phase of their lives were provided by Parent-Duchâtelet. He collected information on 3,120 women inscribed during the years 1828-1832, apparently expecting to find a few key professions that would account for most prostitutes; instead he found over six hundred different occupations listed, a confusion of trades that led him to abandon the taxonomic table he had planned to draw up and simply to group them together.

Parent's groupings had predictable results. A great many of his prostitutes (1,559, or 50 percent) came from the overcrowded and sweated clothing trades, including *couturières,* seamstresses, breeches makers, coat makers, glove makers, lace makers, and artificial-flower makers. Next came an odd group of 859 (27.5 percent) domestic servants, day laborers, servants from dairies, farms, and vineyards, shop clerks, street peddlers, and acrobats. A third category (285, or 9.1 percent of the total) was composed of women whose skills in the cloth and clothing trades were more specialized than those of women in the first category; these included various workers in the wool, silk, cotton, and linen industries as well as gauze makers, fringe makers, and furriers. Next came 283 women (9.1 percent) in a variety of occupations apparently grouped together because they did not involve textile manufacturing: hatters, helmet makers, shoemakers and bootmakers, brush makers, laundresses, and ironers. The smallest group comprised 98 women (3.1 percent), all of them involved with metal goods in some way, including jewelers, clockmakers, enamelers, burnishers and polishers, engravers, and others. Parent also had a group of 36 women (1.2 percent) in miscellaneous professions, including actresses and *figurantes* of the stage, music teachers, and even a few *rentières* with solid incomes.[2]

[2] Parent-Duchâtelet, *De la prostitution,* I:78-81.

Parent-Duchâtelet had the rare virtue of publishing every-thing, even (as he considered this survey to be) his failures. The table just described, though at first glance quite inform-ative, did not prove the sorts of things that Parent had ex-pected it to. The most vulnerable occupations (and also probably the ones that accounted for the greatest number of workers) were in the first and second categories, but even this result was suspect because of his rather indiscriminate groupings. (Why, for example, were laundresses not included in the first or second category?) The failure to pinpoint several partic-ularly vulnerable trades was, however, significant in itself, for what it seemed to prove was that *no* occupation was entirely safe from the threat of prostitution: it was not the occupation itself but rather the conditions surrounding the job that made the difference. Parent did pinpoint one problem, the danger of periodic and seasonal unemployment; factories or work-shops might shut down for two or three months, leaving the employees with no resources.[3]

Other variables included the degree of skill a woman brought to her trade, especially if she were engaged in piecework, as well as the particular branch of the trade she was in. An industrial survey of Paris in 1853 revealed the wide range of conditions and salaries, even within a single occupation. Seam-stresses engaged in making sleeves and collars could earn a maximum of 2 francs a day and a minimum of 50 centimes, depending on the employer and on the quality of work. *Cor-setières,* with a low of 1 franc a day, could go up to 5 francs if they were fast and worked on *corsets de luxe.* Wages for *culottières,* or breeches makers, ranged from 1 to 3 francs daily, although the earnings of women who worked at home were decreased by the amount spent for materials. Embroi-derers who worked in gold or silver thread were listed as earning a maximum wage of 7 francs a day, but the survey

[3] Ibid., I:82.

warned that such income had been artificially elevated for a time because of a change in the style of military uniforms; since the change had been accomplished, the maximum had diminished by half.[4]

The same survey, in an effort to make a rough determination of the standard of living, also included the prices of certain essential goods. A half-kilo of "medium quality" beef cost 45 centimes; a chicken of medium size, 2.39 francs; a kilo of bread, 28 centimes.[5] There was also rent to consider, as well as clothing, wood, and coal. The comparison of these prices with the wages of the least advantaged workers in the lowest paid trades—seamstresses, for example—led to the unavoidable conclusion that some women did not earn enough to support themselves.

When a woman's earnings were merely supplemental to the family income, her low wages could be tolerated; but many women were not a part of a family unit. A further contributor to the vulnerability of women, then, lay in their separation, whether geographical or otherwise, from relatives. Women who came to Paris in the hope of work or in pursuit of a lover were taking a dangerous gamble: they might earn enough to keep themselves, but they might also find themselves in risky isolation. Of the 12,707 women inscribed from 1816 to 1831, Parent-Duchâtelet discovered only 4,469 from the Department of the Seine; the rest had migrated to Paris. The nearby departments of Seine-et-Oise and Seine-Inférieure furnished the largest contingents, each contributing more than 300 women to the total,[6] indicating that migrations from even these relatively close areas had serious consequences.

[4] *Statistique de la France: prix et salaires à diverses époques* (Strasbourg: Imprimerie administrative de la Veuve Berger-Levrault, 1864): p. 87 (seamstresses), p. 86 (*corsetières* and *culottières*), p. 85 (embroiderers).

[5] Ibid., pp. 120-121.

[6] Parent-Duchâtelet, *De la prostitution,* I:39-44. Of the total, 12,201 came from France.

Many women who came to Paris eventually found themselves in contact with the administration. The prefecture's
records of mendicity passports, issued to help indigents return
to their homes, reveal many stories of failure that led to
prostitution. Victorine Basset, a twenty-two-year-old embroiderer, had been in Paris for four years and had held three
positions before turning to prostitution. The prefecture issued
a passport, and she was arrested eight days later for soliciting:
"She alleges as her excuse for not going to Melun that she
did not dare present herself to her parents, in the state of
destitution she was in."[7] Eighteen-year-old Caroline Picard
had been in Paris for several years, brought there by her
parents, who had left her with her older brothers; she went
to the prefecture voluntarily, after three days of unemployment, to request her inscription. Her brother, a shoemaker,
declared himself unable to help her and told the prefecture
to send her back to her widowed mother in Arras.[8] Louise
Dubray, an eighteen-year-old *couturière* arrested for prostitution, called on her cousin, a tailor; he refused to claim her,
since he had already accepted responsibility for her once and
she had left his home. She was sent back to her parents.[9]
Louise Guilleminot, an eighteen-year-old worker in cashmere
who was arrested for prostitution, called on her uncle, a
doctor, and on Crussair, an attorney. The uncle had moved
without leaving a forwarding address. Crussair stated that
she was merely a former client who had engaged him to
recover a sum of money owed her by an uncle; it was
only a small sum, he explained, "which had been absorbed

[7] AN F⁷ 11892, report of 22 September 1826. She was born in Melun,
Seine-et-Marne.

[8] AN F⁷ 11892, report of 25 November 1826. She was born in Arras, Pas
de Calais.

[9] AN F⁷ 11892, report of 11 December 1826. She was born in Villers-
Cotterets, Aisne.

by the expenses of recovering it."[10] She, too, was sent home.

There were other cases, more suspect perhaps from the point of view of morality, but no less definite from the standpoint of economic need. Seventeen-year-old Victorine Thierry, arrested and treated for syphilis, had come to Paris under the supervision of an older sister who "had announced that she had made her fortune in the capital." The two sisters had soon parted because of "incompatability of humor," and Victorine had been without a job for fifteen days when she was caught. The police were temporarily unable to find the older sister, but knew that she "had kept several houses of prostitutes, and had continued her illicit commerce with a certain Sieur Gros."[11] Clementine Bréard, a twenty-year-old laundress, had been in Paris for two years; when arrested for prostitution, she was discovered to be six months pregnant. She was kept in a shelter until she was able to be brought back to the prefecture, this time with "a male infant of seven months," and was then sent back to the Seine-Inférieure.[12] There were, finally, a number of women who declared they had come to Paris specifically to be registered as prostitutes, selecting in advance what became an unavoidable choice for so many. The prefecture usually managed to talk them out of the idea.[13]

All these stories were variations on a familiar theme, whether the deciding factor was the loss of a job or the inability of a

[10] AN F⁷ 11892, report of 28 September 1826. She was born in Chablis, Yonne.

[11] AN F⁷ 11891, report of 9 May 1826. She was born in Blois, Loir-et-Cher.

[12] AN F⁷ 11891, report of 2 August 1826. She was born in Havre, Seine-Inférieure.

[13] For example: AN F⁷ 11910, report of 18 September 1830, concerning Marie Françoise Lucie Albanésie, age eighteen, *brodeuse,* born Buemps, Pas de Calais; report of 16 September 1830, concerning Victoire Noëme Marie Eleanore Boudot, age eighteen, *ouvrière en tulle,* born Saint-Quentin, Aisne.

relative to provide anticipated support. Economic failure was always a possibility, given the persistently low wages of women and the low priority placed on educating women for a lucrative trade. Too many young women were sent off with only rudimentary skills. It was usually the combination of factors, the loss of a job and isolation from relatives, that left women vulnerable to prostitution. Once registered, moreover, they found added to their economic marginality the equally serious criminal marginality of the *fille publique*.

The Meaning of "Publique"

The inscription of the prostitute, in itself a rather simple act, had implications that changed (by contemporary interpretations) the legal status of the woman involved. It was, according to one authority, "the transformation ipso facto of a woman, enjoying until then all rights, into a woman *soumise*, following the consecrated expression, submitted to the administrative actions of the police, subject to certain police regulations, subject to the corporal examination, and riveted by official patent to the most abject prostitution."[14] Once the decision to inscribe had been made, the act itself was preceded by a ceremony of sorts: the new prostitute was brought before the *agents des moeurs* so that they could "engrave her features and demeanor on their memories, in order to recognize her in every circumstance."[15] She then signed the register, an action that was conveniently interpreted as an agreement to obey the rules.

Prostitutes were divided into "lots," each taken by an officer. Thus, each new prostitute was placed under the sur-

[14] Alfred Fournier, "Prophylaxie publique de la syphilis," *Annales d'hygiène publique et de médecine légale* 18, 3rd sér. (1887):74.
[15] Trébuchet and Poirat-Duval, editors' comment in Parent-Duchâtelet, *De la prostitution,* I:89.

veillance of a specific morals agent; the size of his bonus depended on the degree of compliance he could exact from the women in his group.[16] The strictest adherence to the rules meant that a prostitute was not permitted to do certain things that were not illegal in themselves—she was not allowed to congregate with her friends in a group, for example—but, perhaps more important, she was forced to keep in contact with the prefecture, checking in at regular intervals for her medical examination. In addition, her acquaintance with police agents virtually ensured that her new profession would not remain unnoticed by those around her.

The introduction of this element of notoriety into the prostitute's life was a painful consequence of inscription, one that made it difficult for her to escape that life. In other circumstances, the implications of constant surveillance were not lost on the administration. Thus the prefect expressed some concern, in a circular of 1833, about the effects of intrusive surveillance on ex-convicts. When police measures were too obvious, he warned, the status of these former prisoners became known to all, branding them with "a sort of universal reprobation" and making it impossible for them to improve their conduct.[17] Such solicitude (rare as it was) was not extended to prostitutes; the full weight of the prefecture was extended against them.

Just as important as the loss of her good name was the sheer amount of time the prostitute spent in custody. Each arrest subjected the prostitute to a series of more or less

[16] Lecour, *Paris et Londres,* p. 57. Lecour noted that early in the dispensary's history, inspectors had had to be able to show that 75 percent of their women had reported for the examination; if their lot fell below 70 percent, they were to lose three days' salary. This policy had "destroyed solidarity" among inspectors. The bonuses were then calculated differently, with 3 francs for the discovery of each *disparue* and, as of 1830, a bonus of 15 francs for clandestine places of debauchery.

[17] Circular of 15 August 1833, *Recueil des circulaires,* I:232-233.

prolonged stays in a series of institutions. She spent several hours, perhaps the night, at the commissariat. She was walked to the depot, a gendarme on either side; this sight attracted catcalls and sympathy from various passers-by, a problem that the prefecture attempted to remedy with the occasional use of the *voiture fermée,* or closed carriage. (These carriages were not an ideal solution, for "cries and bursts of scandalous gaiety" could be heard from the outside.) If she arrived at the prefecture before 4:00 p.m., she was taken to the dispensary to be examined; if not, she was examined at the depot by a doctor on night duty at the dispensary.[18] In the Prefectural Depot she was housed in a room that measured forty feet by twenty-five feet; it was thought to be able to accommodate fifty women, all of them prostitutes (other women were held in a separate cell). Accommodations consisted of wooden planks attached to the wall, furnished with straw mattresses; the room was washed down every two days.[19] The room in which the medical examination was performed at the dispensary was also large, divided into stalls by a series of partitions which, in the normal manner of public places, were neither quite high nor quite low enough.

After the examination, the prostitute faced a hearing before

---

[18] Lecour, *Paris et Londres,* pp. 74, 83. The closed carriage did not represent an attempt to isolate prostitutes from the populace but rather was an attempt to solve the vexing problem of transport. This problem was explained in a circular that extended the *voiture spéciale* to other kinds of criminals. The escorted walk, according to the prefect, had numerous disadvantages: "tantôt, la pitie publique s'égare sur des individus peu dignes d'intérêt, mais habiles à exciter l'emotion dans les rues"; men arrested for trivial crimes were embarrassed; and "de véritables malfaiteurs trouvent dans le trajet du commissariat à la Préfecture, soit des occasions d'évasion, soit le moyen de prévenir leurs complices ou de se débarrasser d'objets compromettants." Circular of 30 January 1857, *Recueil des circulaires,* II:158-159.

[19] BN 8° Z. Le Senne 10.876(3), *Notice sur la Préfecture de police* (Paris: n.p., 1828).

the chief of the Bureau of Morals. If there had been a great many arrests, she might have to wait as long as three days to hear sentence pronounced. The schedule of punishments was not rigid, but there were certain guidelines. Imprisonment was generally one month for a first offense, two or three months for "more or less frequent" subsequent arrests, and six months for women who had "shown themselves incorrigible" by the frequency of their arrests or the severity of their offenses. But even these imprisonments were not fixed, since the prefect received a list of those imprisoned each month and made the decision about whether or not they should be released before their sentence was up.[20]

The Petite Force was established as the prostitute prison in 1801, and the mere fact that a woman had been in the Force was enough to brand her as a prostitute. Even though *filles publiques voleuses,* or prostitute-thieves, were sent to Saint-Lazare, the Petite Force was still a disorderly place. According to one contemporary report, the inmates manifested "the most indecent gaiety," causing the halls to resound with "laughter and filthy songs." Madelonnettes was established as the prostitute prison in 1826, to be replaced in 1836 by Saint-Lazare. Both prisons set aside special wings for those prostitutes who wished to repent and enter the Bon Pasteur convent; from 1837 on, this wing was known as the *quartier pour les jeunes filles repentantes,* a sign that the prefecture could temper justice with mercy.[21] There was always some uncertainty about the exact day of their release; aside from monthly commutations of sentences, the authorities might decide to release them sooner, or later, according to administrative needs.

[20] AN F⁷ 9305, *Compte rendu à son Excellence le Ministre de l'intérieur sur la prostitution publique* (12 May 1819). Also see Parent-Duchâtelet, *De la prostitution,* II:180-182.
[21] Lecour, *Paris et Londres,* pp. 60-62.

STATISTICS OF MARGINALITY

A series of more or less prolonged stays in prison, combined with the prostitute's high visibility, must have added much uncertainty to an already precarious economic situation. Prostitution was probably more profitable, on a daily basis, than many of the occupations open to women. But the *fille publique*'s employment was frequently broken up by police intervention; she was constantly in the position of having to start all over again. Because punishments were so common, and so flexible, records of them were not kept up in any systematic way. However, it is possible to see how often prostitutes were arrested, if not how long they were in jail, through the prefectural reports of daily arrests; these lists, unlike the *arrondissement* reports of the gendarmerie, noted those whose misdeeds had not been dismissed at the commissariat level. These records, available in an unbroken series only for the eight-year period from the beginning of 1839 to the end of 1846, form the basis for the following examination of the effects of the regulatory system. During this period, there were 1,765 prostitutes with five or more arrests recorded at the prefecture. From these records, I compiled an individual arrest sheet for each of the 1,765 individuals, showing the number of arrests, their dates, and their causes.[22] Locations of arrests were not given consistently enough to permit any conclusions, though it is possible to trace the personal geography of some prostitutes. What these records offer, besides an insight into individual lives, is a report of the effect of administrative action on those individuals, indicating (more accurately than police claims or abolitionist charges) the extent of police efficiency and the human costs of maintaining it.

[22] The individual records were compiled from daily police reports in AN F⁷ 3896-3899.

TABLE 13

Arrests of Parisian Prostitutes for Having Venereal Disease,
1839-1846

Number of Women	Number of Times Arrested
345	1
242	2
162	3
104	4
105	5
55	6
39	7
28	8
22	9
4	10
2	11
3	12
5	13
2	14
3	15-20
TOTAL 1,121 (63.5%)	

SOURCE: AN F⁷ 3896-3899.

In order to understand more fully the effects of surveillance on individual prostitutes, it is necessary first to establish the outlines of the total group. A surprising number—about 69 percent—were under police control for more than four years.[23] This continuity in the métier is somewhat surprising: the common image of the nineteenth-century prostitute was of a workingwoman driven, on occasion, to supplement a

[23] Of the 1,765 prostitutes 94, or 5.3 percent, were under police control for two years; 203, or 11.5 percent, for three years; 248, or 14.1 percent, for four years; 277, or 15.7 percent, for five years; 301, or 17 percent, for six years; 348, or 19.7 percent, for seven years; and 294, or 16.7 percent, for eight years.

meager wage. Yet this image was probably true, for by far the greatest number of prostitutes simply disappeared after a single arrest. On the other hand, the multiple arrests, as well as the time spent in the profession, suggest that for the 1,765 women in the group prostitution represented more than just hard times. It was, at the very least, a habitual resource; at most, it was a livelihood.

The professionalism of the métier was underlined by the fairly high degree of compliance with the requirements of the system. Women had to report regularly for their examinations, or they were judged *insoumise*. More than half (55.7 percent) of the 1,765 had no arrests for *insoumission;* 25.5 percent had one such arrest; 12.2 percent had two arrests; 5 percent had three arrests; and 1.6 percent had four.[24] This adherence to the system was noteworthy, especially considering the widely noted unpopularity of the examination; in a few short years, the police had imposed a remarkable discipline.

The purpose of the system, the control of venereal disease, seemed to be justified by the results. A rather astonishing number of women, 63.5 percent, had been arrested at least once for having a *maladie,* a proportion that fed the paranoia of the authorities about the problem. (See Table 13.) Individual records reveal that the length of time set aside for treatment was not very long; a contemporary study showed an average of forty-five days in treatment.[25] Limitations of

[24] While it is true that a great number of women simply disappeared (and thus never showed up on the arrest records again) it is also true that the *insoumise* category included a number of first arrests. In any case, those women who made up the sample were in compliance for the duration of their career.

[25] Note by Trébuchet and Poirat-Duval, in Parent-Duchâtelet, *De la prostitution,* II:35. This was one figure for the 1850s. In the eighteenth century, patients had been ejected from Bicêtre at the end of six weeks, regardless of their state of health.

TABLE 14
Arrest Record of Marie Catherine Ringers

Date of Arrest	Cause	Number of Weeks since Last Arrest
7 November 1839	Syphilis	
4 January 1840	Syphilis	8
11 March 1840	Syphilis	9
5 September 1840	Syphilis	25
26 January 1841	Malady	20
19 February 1841	Contravention	3
5 January 1842	Malady	46
15 March 1842	Syphilis	10
13 August 1842	Malady	22
21 February 1843	Malady	27
25 July 1843	Malady	22
27 November 1843	Syphilis	18
26 March 1844	Syphilis	17
14 May 1844	Malady	7
5 July 1844	Malady	7
30 August 1844	Malady	8
31 December 1844	Malady	18
25 April 1845	Malady	16
25 August 1845	Malady	17
24 October 1845	Malady	9
30 January 1846	Malady	14
1 December 1846	Malady	44

SOURCE: AN F⁷ 3896-3899.
NOTE: Total arrests, 22; average interval between arrests, 4 months.

space and budget (for all the poor, not just for prostitutes) resulted in a constant shuffling of patients.

The theoretical end product of the dispensary system was not meant to be a Marie Catherine Ringers. (See Table 14.) She illustrates the impotence of the system in this regard; she could be neither cured nor stopped. (The dispensary could have revoked her card, but they preferred to keep her under surveillance.) The venereal prostitute, of which Ringers represented the worst extreme, was not uncommon, as the number of prostitutes with multiple arrests because of disease indicates. Their arrests tended to be rather close together; they were expelled from the hospital to make room for new arrivals, only to be returned at the next arrest. Women at this extreme of the spectrum seemed to fall under police supervision primarily because of their state of ill-health. For these women, the medical aspect of regulated prostitution may have seemed a genuine benefit, as medical care that did not have to be competitively wrested from the "honest poor" of the city.[26]

For those women who were not primarily syphilitic, a greater measure of integration into the profession was the length of time between trips to the prefecture. Arrests came at rather frequent intervals, as Table 15 indicates: about half of all the women were arrested at least once in six months, and each arrest might lead to an imprisonment of several months. This is only an average, for arrests might come much more or much less frequently than this. Some prostitutes vanished from the records for entire years, only to reappear in a series of arrests that followed one another in rapid succession. This pattern of recurring arrests forced them into a rootless, disrupted existence; it is probable that most could afford only the impermanent *garni*. Fortunately, these arrests in series did not last long. Their occurrence seems to point to cycles of

[26] The poor had to report to the Bureau of Charity, where a rapid examination determined whether or not they were sick enough to merit a bed. Incredibly, Parent-Duchâtelet had a hand in this, too: "De tous les désagréments inséparables du service médical du bureau central des hôpitaux, il n'en est pas, à notre avis, de plus grand que celui que procure le spectacle des malheureux qui viennent réclamer des secours, mais que le défaut de place met dans la nécessité de renvoyer." Parent-Duchâtelet, "Recherches sur la véritable cause des ulcères," p. 237.

TABLE 15
Intervals between Arrests of Parisian Prostitutes, 1839-1846

Average Number of Months between Arrests	Prostitutes		Average Number of Arrests at This Interval	Highest Number of Arrests at This Interval
	Number	Percentage		
2	42	2.4	6.6	13
3	139	7.9	11.8	30
4	237	13.4	11.0	24
5	252	14.3	10.4	18
6	236	13.4	9.4	15
7	173	9.8	8.6	12
8	167	9.4	7.7	12
9	137	7.7	7.0	11
10	110	6.2	6.5	9
11	92	5.2	6.1	8
12	57	3.2	6.0	8
13	52	3.0	5.5	7
14	24	1.4	5.6	6
15	28	1.6	5.3	6
16-19	19	1.1	5.0	6
TOTAL	1,765	100.0		

SOURCE: AN F⁷ 3896-3899.

relative independence and extreme vulnerability (not only signaled by, but also caused by, arrests). This independence may be illusory, however: the long periods of "freedom" could conceivably have been spent in bordellos—prostitutes were known to enter bordellos in winter and leave in the summer—where the freedom from arrest was more than compensated by the authoritarianism of the madam.

It is easier to visualize the distribution of arrests by examining the records of individuals. (See Tables 16 through 20.) These women were chosen at random, with the exception of Reine Baglin, whose thirty arrests (the largest number) seemed to merit special consideration. A total of 172 women, or 9.7 percent, had more than fifteen arrests; these women represent the extreme limits of enforcement. Yet even those with the minimum number of five arrests reveal the characteristically irregular distribution of entanglements with the police, with arrests coming in short bursts followed by periods of relative tranquillity. Despite the many dissimiliarities between these women, the records all raise the question of what they were doing during those long intervals of silence.

FAILURE VERSUS DEPENDENCE

Aside from fortuitous escapes, there are at least two fairly persuasive hypotheses to explain the obvious gaps in each prostitute's record. One is that an arrest after a long period of silence marked a return to prostitution after a period of employment of some sort. This return may have resulted from an end to the employment, or retirement may have been involuntary, brought about by the arrest itself. Agents were paid bounties of 3 francs a head for finding prostitutes who had vanished from the fold; a woman who had simply disappeared, without making an official request to be expunged from the inscription rolls, was at risk. Once the arrest and imprisonment had taken place, the prostitute found herself at a loss. She could not return to her job after such a long absence. She was impoverished by her period of enforced unemployment, and was forced onto the streets, where she was once again in jeopardy of a new arrest. Each arrest and imprisonment served merely to increase the uncertainty of her position, and thus anchored her more firmly in the profession.

TABLE 16
Arrest Record of Reine Françoise Baglin, the Widow Guerin

Date of Arrest	Cause	Number of Weeks since Last Arrest	Location
28 October 1839	Contravention		—
8 February 1840	Contravention	15	—
19 May 1840	Contravention	14	—
18 November 1840	Contravention	26	—
27 December 1840	Contravention	6	—
8 April 1841	*Insoumise*	14	Cité
26 July 1841	Contravention	15	—
12 October 1841	Contravention	16	—
12 December 1841	Contravention	9	Arcis
14 January 1842	Contravention	5	—
10 March 1842	Contravention	8	—
24 June 1842	Contravention	15	—
8 August 1842	Insanity	6	Palais de Justice
6 September 1842	Contravention	4	—
30 September 1842	Contravention	3	—
9 October 1842	Contravention	1.5	—
8 November 1842	Contravention	4	—
8 December 1842	Contravention	4	Marchés
20 June 1843	Contravention	28	—
18 February 1844	*Insoumise*	35	Marché St.-Jean
11 May 1844	Contravention	12	—
10 November 1844	Contravention	26	Palais de Justice
1 May 1845	Contravention	24	—
2 August 1845	Contravention	13	—
1 September 1845	Contravention	4	Cité
10 October 1845	Contravention	6	—
29 November 1845	Contravention	7	—
11 January 1846	Contravention	6	—
12 April 1846	Contravention	13	Palais de Justice
27 December 1846	Contravention	37	St.-Jacques

SOURCE: AN F⁷ 3896-3899.
NOTE: Total arrests, 30; average interval between arrests, 3 months.

TABLE 17
Arrest Record of Annette Guillamette Tanguy

Date of Arrest	Cause	Number of Weeks since Last Arrest
15 January 1840	Contravention	
25 April 1840	Contravention	14
19 June 1840	Contravention	8
30 November 1842	Contravention	126
13 August 1846	Contravention	190

SOURCE: AN F⁷ 3896-3899.
NOTE: Total arrests, 5; average interval between arrests, 21 months.

TABLE 18
Arrest Record of Alexandrine Gabrielle Palais

Date of Arrest	Cause	Number of Weeks since Last Arrest	Location
11 July 1839	Contravention		—
23 September 1839	Contravention	11	—
28 March 1840	Syphilis	27	—
23 January 1841	Contravention	43	Palais Royal
12 March 1841	Contravention	7	—
12 May 1841	Contravention	9	—
6 August 1844	Theft	169	Sorbonne
2 November 1844	Contravention	12	—
2 April 1845	Contravention	22	—

SOURCE: AN F⁷ 3896-3899.
NOTE: Total arrests, 9; average interval between arrests, 8 months.

There is little direct evidence for this reconstruction, whatever its plausibility. Women left prostitution with varying degrees of formality and justification. Parent-Duchâtelet, and later Lecour, studied the inscription rolls in an attempt to discover the reasons women gave when they requested a

TABLE 19
Arrest Record of Henriette Caroline Lacrosse

Date of Arrest	Cause	Number of Weeks since Last Arrest	Location
19 November 1841	Contravention		—
29 March 1842	Contravention	18	—
7 July 1842	Contravention	14	—
23 September 1842	Contravention	11	—
17 June 1843	Contravention	38	—
9 December 1843	Contravention	25	—
19 December 1843	Contravention	1.5	—
8 July 1845	Contravention	29	Chaussée d'Antin
7 October 1845	Contravention	13	Chaussée d'Antin
10 December 1845	Contravention	9	—
28 January 1846	Contravention	7	—

SOURCE: AN F⁷ 3896-3899.
NOTE: Total arrests, 11; average interval between arrests, 5 months.

formal expungement *(radiation)* from the register. (See Table 21.) The largest single reason on Parent's list was new employment, but he expressed some doubt about this result; the prefecture did not have strict requirements of proof. Lecour's table seemed to confirm this suspicion, for by the 1860s those requirements had been tightened. From 1855 to 1860 an average of 94 women per year were expunged on the grounds of employment; for the period 1861-1869, this average dropped to 1.4 per year. A similar efficiency was shown in the number of deaths; the rise in this figure can undoubtedly be traced to better recordkeeping. The number of women brought to trial dropped in this later period, reflecting the century-long trend toward removing prostitutes from the formal court system. One might find slight evidence for frustrated upward mobility in the fact that only 95 women in the course of

TABLE 20
Arrest Record of Louise Veronique Luton

Date of Arrest	Cause	Number of Weeks since Last Arrest	Location
8 September 1839	Contravention		—
27 September 1839	Contravention	1.5	—
12 November 1839	Contravention	6	—
6 April 1840	Contravention	21	Palais de Justice
12 July 1840	Contravention	14	—
25 October 1840	Contravention	15	—
23 November 1840	Contravention	4	—
21 January 1841	Contravention	8	—
2 March 1841	Contravention	6	Palais de Justice
13 April 1841	Contravention	6	—
26 May 1841	Contravention	6	—
2 July 1841	Contravention	5	—
14 August 1841	Contravention	6	—
28 April 1842	Theft	37	Montrouge
9 June 1842	Trial	6[a]	—
12 August 1845	Contravention	9[b]	—
8 August 1846	Contravention	52	—
21 November 1846	Contravention	15	—

SOURCE: AN F⁷ 3896-3899; AN F⁷ 10142.

NOTE: Total arrests, 17; average interval between arrests, 5 months.

[a] Sentenced to 3 years in prison.

[b] Nine weeks after release from prison.

fifteen years, compared with 108 over the earlier course of ten years, rose to the rank of madam.

As complete as this information seemed to be, Parent was not willing to stop with the official statistics; he had a sense of where he thought retired prostitutes ought to be on the social scale, and he made appropriate inquiries. He found that a number of women had become the concubines of street

TABLE 21

Parisian Prostitutes Removed from the Inscription Rolls

Reason	1817-1827		1855-1869	
	Number	Percentage	Number	Percentage
Regular job	1,572	30.9	579	11.9
Serious illness	177	3.5	0	0
Death	428	8.4	1,503	31.1
Marriage	121	2.4	331	6.8
Concubinage	101	2.0	0	0
Claimed by parents or husband	282	5.6	0	0
Departure from Paris with passport/aid	1,206	23.7	2,121	43.7
Sent home by *dames de charité*	239	4.7	0	0
Sent to depot of Saint-Denis	91	1.8	0	0
Escorted from Paris by gendarmerie	138	2.7	0	0
Sentenced in court to prison	185	3.6	109	2.2
Admission to house of refuge	319	6.3	111	2.3
Authorized to keep bordello	108	2.2	95	2.0
Independent means, pension	114	2.2	0	0
TOTAL	5,081	100.0	4,849	100.0
Disappeared	5,433[a]		7,890	

SOURCE: A.-J.-B. Parent-Duchâtelet, *De la prostitution dans la ville de Paris,* 2 vols. (Paris: J.-B. Baillière, 1857), I:584-587; C.-J. Lecour, *La Prostitution à Paris et à Londres, 1789-1871,* 2nd ed. (Paris: Asselin, 1872), p. 123.

[a] This number is for the years 1820-1828 and was therefore not counted in the 1817-1827 total. Likewise, *disparues* were not figured in the 1855-1869 total; if they had been included, they would constitute 61.9 percent of that total.

sweepers; 48 others had become ragpickers. Over half of the women reclaimed from prostitution by their parents had been living at home during the period of their prostitution; nearly half of those who had married and were removed from the rolls had chosen men who lived on the same street, sometimes even in the same building, and who could not have been ignorant of their intended's profession. This, Parent thought, was "sad proof" of the small importance of chastity in working-class life. Parent's most significant discovery had to do with the high rate of recidivism. He found that 2,126 women, or 39.1 percent, of all those who had "disappeared" and were dropped from the rolls were retaken—over half of them within nine months.[27]

Parent's information indicates that some women had attempted to leave prostitution (or at least the regulatory system) and failed, a fact that gives weight to the first hypothesis. The second hypothesis, in contrast, is based on the notion of dependence rather than of failure and vulnerability. It is possible that prostitutes became familiar with public institutions and learned to manipulate them for their own benefit. When times were hard, prostitutes used their knowledge to arrange for their own support, at the expense of the city. Their absence from the arrest records is explained by their presence in public institutions.

Parent-Duchâtelet was, as always, the first to notice this phenomenon. A number of prostitutes, he noted, seemed to consider prison as "a retreat prepared for them by the public munificence." As soon as they were freed, they committed other crimes (but only those peculiar to prostitution) to get themselves readmitted. On the outside, they were unable to survive, and ended by becoming destitute; the police found them sleeping on the streets. Imprisonment was in these cases

[27] Parent-Duchâtelet, *De la prostitution,* I:578, 594-595, 588-589, 599.

an act of mercy: "one is especially indulgent in their regard at the approach of winter and bad weather."[28]

Though Parent-Duchâtelet was always scrupulous in regard to facts, it is not necessary in this case to rely entirely on his word. A number of surveillance reports reveal the same pattern that Parent noted. These reports dealt with a rather small group of prostitutes who, in addition to their periods of administrative detention, had also served time in prison as a result of a regular court conviction. Once surveillance had been triggered by a court conviction, the officials also registered the prostitute's detentions as a *fille publique*. In almost all these cases the prostitution had preceded the entanglement with the law; in a few, the women turned to prostitution after a long stay in prison. Whatever the exact circumstances, however, prostitution was for these women a part of the cycle of poverty, crime, and uncertainty.

One of the best-documented examples of dependence on prison as a way of life was the case of Elizabeth Gabrielle Doizant, a native of Paris born in 1782. Her first recorded Restoration arrest was on 11 January 1817; the arrest report noted that she had left the Petite Force only the day before. She was arrested again on 27 January 1817 as a night prowler; it was reported that she had left the Prefectural Depot only two days before her new arrest, an indication that she had spent about a week in the depot. Not surprisingly, she had

---

[28] Ibid., I:580-581. Jeannel noticed the same phenomenon among the lowest class of prostitutes: "Ces femmes abruties ne redoutent guère la prison. Lorsqu'on les condamne, elles ont presque toujours oublié déjà le méfait qui a motivé leur arrestation. D'ailleurs la prison a l'avantage de les reposer, de les nettoyer, d'interrompre l'alcoolisme qui les dévore et par là d'améliorer leur santé. Quelques-unes, comme certains voleurs et vagabonds finissent par préférer la détention à la liberté et recherchent l'occasion de se faire arrêter." Julien Jeannel, *De la prostitution dans les grandes villes aux dix-neuvième siècle et de l'extinction des maladies vénériennes* (Paris: J.-B. Baillière, 1874), p. 261.

"the most outrageous words" for the guardsmen who captured her, and on 4 March 1817 she was duly tried in court
for "outrage"; she received a sentence of three months.

At some point, Parent's description suggests, Doizant apparently ceased to dread imprisonment and came to regard
it as a kind of institutional relief. In May 1824 she was arrested
for vagabondage, given a three-month sentence, and put at
the "disposition of the government," an open-ended surveillance that legally allowed the government to keep watch on
her for as long as they wished. Instead of three months she
remained for two years and three months, the period beyond
her sentence having been granted in "hospitality." She was
freed on 15 September 1826. On 14 October, she was back
and this time stayed until 6 July 1827; her sentence required
her to stay until she had earned enough in the prison workshop to live on for two months. This kind of sentence was
common and of obvious practical value, even though the exact
amount of the *pécule* was never determined.

Doizant's freedom did not last long. She was back the day
after, 7 July 1827, requesting readmission on the grounds that
she had given her sick mother all that she had earned during
her detention and was again destitute. She left on 20 October
1827 and "disappeared" (that is, gave a false address). On the
night of 24 October she was arrested as a night prowler, and
on 30 October 1827 was sent back to Saint-Denis to stay there
until 1 May 1828; the length of the sentence, and the release
date, suggest that she may have been granted sanctuary for
the winter. She was duly released on 1 May 1828. Her life
outside was punctuated by a few minor arrests for drunkenness and vagabondage, and on 25 May 1832 she was found
wandering the streets at 1:30 a.m. "without papers, home, or
means of livelihood." The surveillance reports listed her once
more on 28 February 1834, on her release from Saint-Lazare.
She was dropped from the surveillance rolls but continued

to figure in the police arrest records throughout the 1830s and 1840s. Her final arrest was on 15 May 1846.[29]

Other cases, less complete than this, are nevertheless equally suggestive of prison dependency and familiarity. One woman in the mendicity prison requested a transfer to Saint-Lazare so that she could work in the laundry.[30] Another prostitute, acquitted in court of a theft charge, nevertheless was immediately imprisoned at Saint-Lazare for two months.[31] A similar case involved Henriette Prieur, who was acquitted but sent to Saint-Denis to earn enough to live on for two months. She earned 62 francs and was released on 14 October 1830. About two weeks later, "having dissipated what she had," she came voluntarily to Saint-Lazare on 2 November and was readmitted.[32]

Justine Pioche entered Saint-Lazare at her own request to spend the winter.[33] Eleonore Poplet (also known as Lucrece Liberté) asked to remain until the return of the *belle saison*. She earned 107 francs, a sum that testified to her industriousness; nevertheless, she preferred to work inside rather than to take her chances with the outside world.[34] This apparent

---

[29] AN F⁷ 4166, reports of 11-12 January and 27-28 January 1817; AN F⁷ 10001, Tribunal de la première instance, report of the 1st trimester 1817; AN F⁷ 10194, reports of the 3rd trimester 1826, the 4th trimester 1826, the 3rd trimester 1827, the 4th trimester 1827, and the 2nd trimester 1828; AN F⁷ 4174, report of 30 September 1830; AN F⁷ 4175, reports of 1 February 1831 and 25 May 1832; AN F⁷ 10193, report of the 1st trimester 1834; AN F⁷ 3899, report of 15 May 1846. (These are only the arrests listed in the text.)

[30] AN F⁷ 10193, report of the 3rd trimester 1831 (see Marie Fauconnier).

[31] AN F⁷ 10193, report of the 3rd trimester 1831 (see Antoinette Hypolite Gayetan). Though she was acquitted of theft, her entry into Saint-Lazare was nevertheless "en punition."

[32] AN F⁷ 10194, report of the 2nd trimester 1829; AN F⁷ 10193, report of the 4th trimester 1830.

[33] AN F⁷ 10194, report of the 4th trimester 1823.

[34] AN F⁷ 10193, report of the 1st trimester 1830. Her sobriquet is reported in F⁷ 10193, report of the 2nd trimester 1831.

emotional dependence was sometimes seconded by physical weakness. Rosalie Fournier first entered the records on a conviction of vagabondage. Her next arrest, as a prostitute, caused her to be sent to the Saint-Denis mendicity prison late in 1825; it was noted that she was to stay there "until further orders." She was released on 3 October 1827. Arrested on 14 March 1828, she spent another fourteen months in Saint-Denis. During this long stay she was able to accumulate only 20 francs because she was often sick; though this was an inadequate *pécule,* she was released in May 1829. On 29 September 1829, she was given three months in prison for theft, served her time, and was sent immediately on her release (on 30 December) to Saint-Lazare, where she remained until 1 June 1830.[35]

Some women seemed unable to survive outside; prison represented a kind of discipline that they were unable to maintain for themselves. Georgette Legris entered the records on 28 October 1824 after a three-month sentence for vagabondage. She was sent directly to Saint-Denis, where she stayed until 1 April 1827; she was back on 24 August 1827 (again in Saint-Denis) and stayed through the winter to 1 March 1828, when she was released. On 27 March 1828, she requested readmittance, claiming that she was "without resources." By 11 July 1829 she had earned 40 francs; her husband vouched for her. She took a passport to go to the Department of Seine-et-Oise, claiming that she was called there by *affaires de famille,* a reason that might have had something to do with her husband's sudden appearance. She returned to Paris on 30 July 1829 and reported her return to

[35] AN F⁷ 2310, report no. 317; AN F⁷ 10194, reports of the 4th trimester 1825, the 4th trimester 1827, the 1st trimester 1828, the 2nd trimester 1829, and the 4th trimester 1829.

the prefecture, in an obvious attempt to maintain correct relations with the authorities.

On 20 October 1829 Legris was arrested as a night prowler and sent to Saint-Denis to earn enough for two months. By 22 April 1830 she had 106 francs from her work and from a sale, and she was released—only to be arrested again on 13 May 1830 as a night prowler, "having dissipated in a few days everything she possessed." She was released in late March 1833 with 98 francs. She lasted longer outside than usual this time, but on 4 October 1833 she was sentenced to one month of prison for vagabondage. On 6 January 1834 she again requested entry into Saint-Denis, "on account of her state of impoverishment."[36]

Reports of such detail were rare, arising from a certain combination of offenses, judgments, and decisions about the individual. Moreover, in the usual way of archival sources, these sets of records do not overlap with the others. This made it impossible to find such direct evidence of the activities of any of the 1,765 prostitutes. Nevertheless, these histories provide some clue that others, less subject to official scrutiny, may have been forced into similar dependence on the prison system.

The two hypotheses for the gaps in the records suggest different orientations on the part of the prostitute. In one, she was looking away from prostitution, attempting to escape but, because of the rigors of the economy or of the police, unable to do so entirely. The other suggests an acceptance of prostitution as a way of life, as well as a comfortable feeling

[36] AN F⁷ 10194, reports of the 1st trimester 1827, the 3rd trimester 1827, the 1st trimester 1828, the 3rd trimester 1829, and the 4th trimester 1829; AN F⁷ 10193, reports of the 2nd trimester 1830, the 1st trimester 1833, the 4th trimester 1833, and the 1st trimester 1834.

vis-à-vis the administration, and a more or less conscious acceptance of the fact that she was on the fringes of society.

OPENING THE GATES

The plight of the registered prostitute was not a popular focus of commiseration. Contemporaries preferred instead to extend their sympathies to a more obvious victim, the "honest" workingwoman arrested by mistake. This happened often—the thousands of single-arrest prostitutes testified to the ease with which arrests were made—and undoubtedly was devastating for the individual. This emphasis upon the innocent ignored the equally devastating effect of a series of arrests and imprisonments on the "guilty," who may have been guilty only through bad luck or chance or an unfortunate combination of circumstances.

In perspective, the city's problem was not so serious as the anguished rhetoric suggested. A total of 1,765 career prostitutes in the last years of the July Monarchy does not lend support to the extravagant estimates of many thousands of prostitutes crowding the city streets. The numbers appeared greater than they were because a growing Paris was itself crowded and because much of the activity of prostitution was condensed into the central areas of the city, on both banks and on the Cité. And these 1,765 career prostitutes do not provide an adequate measure of the impact of prostitution for another reason: many part-time or one-time prostitutes were never caught.

If the effects of the career prostitute on the city appear to have been exaggerated, however, the effects of the city's regulatory system on them were substantial, even considering the fact that most prostitutes had relatively few arrests and imprisonments. (See Table 22.) An assessment of the effects of the regulatory system on prostitutes has to begin with a consideration of the impact of the registration itself. The

TABLE 22
Concentration of Prostitution Arrests, 1839-1846

Number of Arrests	← Intervals in Months between Arrests →							
	2	3	4	5	6	7	8	9
5	18	26	32	41	41	24	30	30
6	7	21	28	24	20	19	32	29
7	8	11	25	26	22	21	24	22
8	2	11	18	20	20	22	22	23
9	2	4	23	10	21	19	16	27
10	1	10	12	11	17	25	22	5
11	2	7	13	16	21	20	18	1
12	1	2	6	15	19	15	3	0
13	1	4	10	16	19	8	0	0
14	0	4	9	14	24	0	0	0
15	0	3	6	17	12	0	0	0

SOURCE: AN F⁷ 3896-3899.

inscription set the prostitute apart from others. It is probable that this action had psychological consequences; it is certain that it had legal ones.[37] In addition, the registration system

[37] A large body of sociological literature has developed on the subject of deviance and, more to the point here, on the effects of "labeling" an individual as deviant. The regulatory system, with its practice of labeling and even carding the individual, is a perfect field for this kind of work. See, for example, Howard S. Becker, *Outsiders* (New York: Free Press, 1963); Edwin M. Lemert, *Human Deviance, Social Problems, and Social Control* (Englewood Cliffs, N.J.: Prentice-Hall, 1967); and Earl Rubington and Martin S. Weinborg, eds., *Deviance: The Interactionist Perspective* (New York: Macmillan, 1973). Judith Walkowitz has also examined the integration of prostitutes with their community, noting the high degree of support many women received from their families (especially from female relatives); she suggests, however, that the fact of being legally segregated from the rest of the population by the Contagious Diseases Acts had the overall effect of isolating prostitutes, economically and socially, from the working-class community. Walkowitz, *Prostitution and Victorian Society,* pp. 201-213. Corbin's *Les Filles de noce* stresses the government's deliberate "marginalization" of the prostitute.

frequently had the effect of creating a cliental relationship between the prostitute and the administration. This expressed itself in the relatively low number of arrests for *insoumission* as well as in the impressive voluntary rate of compliance with the medical exam (see Appendix A, Table 28). On the administrative side, this special relationship led the prefecture, on occasion, to mix compassion with repression, allowing prostitutes to use the various prisons as refuges. This was a privilege, in the traditional sense of the word, to which these women were entitled because they were known to the authorities.

The prefecture was not, of course, engaged primarily in providing relief. Moreover, the state of destitution that caused women to seek refuge was in part attributable to the policies of the prefecture. Though prostitutes probably earned more on a daily basis than other workingwomen, they were no less vulnerable to irregular employment. In addition, single arrests frequently seemed to set off periods of high vulnerability. Upon release from the initial imprisonment, the prostitute, impoverished, was forced back on the streets immediately. Unless she had been especially thrifty, it was not likely that she had any money from her work in Saint-Lazare. The *masse de réserve*—that fraction of workshop wages kept back by the authorities in other prisons—did not exist at Saint-Lazare; the women were given their wages immediately, to buy extras in the prison store.[38]

---

[38] Lecour, *Paris et Londres,* p. 65. The mendicity depot was set up so that two-thirds of the wages earned by the inmates went to the establishment; one-half of the remaining third went to the inmate during his stay, and the rest was held for him until his release. Law of 24 Vendémiaire Year II (15 October 1793), in Duvergier, *Collection,* VI:229-233. Walkowitz has commented upon the hierarchical wage scales of prostitutes, noting that the poorest prostitutes found their earnings tied to the varying wages of the casual laborers who were their customers; while the better class of prostitutes could probably save money, the lowest barely earned enough to live on and "had to resort to the workhouse and to other forms of casual

They could scarcely avoid a resumption of their lives as prostitutes, and reminders were there from the very moment of their release from prison. Parent-Duchâtelet recalled that the wardens customarily had freed prostitutes simply by opening the gates, but that had become unsatisfactory: "As the number [of prostitutes] rose to 100, 150, in some cases 200, there resulted a disorder, augmented by *mauvais sujets* who, always aware of the hour when the gates would be opened, flocked in advance from all points of Paris, forming an obstruction in the streets." This manner of operation had to be altered, but the improvement, the staggering of releases in small groups, proved little better. This time the problem was internal: "The release of 10 to 15 women signaled to the others that a selection was taking place.... This idea of approaching freedom filled all heads, resulting not only in an almost complete abandonment of the workshops, but also in turbulence, a true lack of discipline." This problem resulted in yet another reform. A list was made at the end of each month (no one was particular about sentence length) of women who were the "least vicious" and who were also near release. The gates were opened at one- or two-hour intervals, releasing small groups of women into the world, there to start again the cycle of prostitution, arrest, and impoverishment.[39]

---

employment." *Prostitution and Victorian Society*, pp. 23-24. Finnegan's study focuses entirely upon the stunning destitution of this lowest class of prostitutes and indicates that the poverty of prostitutes can be linked to the poverty of their working-class clientele. *Poverty and Prostitution*, p. 134.

[39] Parent-Duchâtelet, *De la prostitution*, II:192-196.

PART THREE

The Problems of the Regime

o o o

° 7 °

Disease and Clandestinity

THE imposing edifice of the regulatory system, virtually complete by the middle of the century, had a built-in weakness—or strength, depending on one's point of view. It was pinpointed early by a police official who noted, with perfect accuracy and unconscious irony, that the creation by decree of the registered prostitute had resulted in the simultaneous creation of the clandestine prostitute. Once some women had been defined by their relationship with the prefecture, others, the clandestines, were equally defined by the absence of such a relationship.[1] The definition of the clandestine was far hazier than that of the inscribed prostitute, and as the century wore on the clandestine came to overshadow the *fille soumise,* to the point that a leading abolitionist would write, with conscious irony, that a clandestine prostitute was simply any woman who had not been registered yet.[2] The cloudier the definition of the clandestine, the more pervasive she seemed to become. Prefect Anglès had estimated in 1820 that there were as many as nine thousand clandestine prostitutes operating in Paris. In 1878, the

[1] Félix Carlier, *Etude de pathologie sociale: les deux prostitutions* (Paris: E. Dentu, 1887), p. 19
[2] Guyot, *La Prostitution,* p. 152.

chief of the Bureau of Morals put the number of clandestines at somewhere between thirty thousand and forty thousand.[3]

OLD AND NEW

The concept of clandestinity, originally no more than a minor counterpart to registered prostitution, had changed over the course of the century; the first to pinpoint the change was Félix Carlier, a former officer with the dispensary. "The *insoumise* prostitute of thirty years ago . . . was encountered at the former barriers, outside the barracks, dressed in rags and seeking to deliver herself for a few sous," he wrote in 1871; "in the interior of the city, in the grand *quartiers* especially, she used a certain reserve and did not display her immoral luxury each evening to passers-by." Unfortunately, from Carlier's point of view, all that had changed: "[Clandestine prostitution] advertises itself and has become arrogant; as much as it was hidden before, it shows itself today."[4] Clandestine prostitutes had undergone a change, not only in behavior but, even more important, in the ways they were perceived by contemporaries.

Just as clandestinity itself changed from a secret to a pervasive phenomenon, so the policing of clandestinity shifted from a concern with dangerous places to a concern about dangerous individuals. This was in fact the same kind of change: just as the police had worried early in the nineteenth century about the existence of certain areas in the city that were entirely given over to activities hidden from their surveillance, so did they worry later about the spread of these

[3] AN F⁷ 9305, report of 27 December 1820 from the prefect of police to the minister of the interior; Conseil municipal de Paris, *Procès-verbal,* p. 25.

[4] Félix Carlier, "Etude statistique sur la prostitution clandestine à Paris de 1855 à 1870," *Annales d'hygiène publique et de médecine légale* 36, 3rd sér. (1871):292-293.

illicit actions throughout society, with prostitutes as the carriers. (The changing images and concerns reflected the central
dilemma of prostitution control: either prostitution was left
to fester by itself in restricted areas, or it was allowed to
spread throughout society—less innately threatening, but exposed to the entire population.)

Early in the nineteenth century, the prefecture was particularly concerned with the crowded, dark, clandestine places
into which they could not penetrate without risk. The two
policemen killed in the line of duty during these years had
both been attempting to invade the territory of the dangerous
classes: one, a *commissaire,* killed at the head of his troops as
he was reading an order to disperse; another, a *sergent de
ville,* shot in the head as he entered a café, "dead of his zeal
and intrepidity."[5] The worries about hidden prostitution owed
less to the threat of violence than to the threat to the moral
and physical well-being of the individual who sought out
prostitutes. The cabarets that catered to the lower classes were
places of open and indiscriminate sexuality; one disgusted
contemporary observer noted of the prostitutes that "they
dance, their pipes in their mouths, in the most indecent pos-
tures."[6] Parent-Duchâtelet observed that the *cabinets noirs* in
back were kept deliberately dark to hide the ravages of venereal disease from the customers.[7] The *pierreuses,* the lowest
and most dangerous of the clandestine prostitutes, worked at
night, away from light and surveillance, at construction sites,
along the river, in the shadows of public monuments, so that
no customer could see them well enough to turn away. One
morals agent had captured a sixty-five-year-old *pierreuse* prac-

[5] *Compte d'administration des dépenses de la Préfecture de police* (1832), pp.
29-30.

[6] Frégier, *Des classes dangereuses,* I:182; Parent-Duchâtelet, *De la prostitution,* I:512.

[7] Parent-Duchâtelet, *De la prostitution,* I:513.

ticing her trade behind the stone lions in front of a public fountain.[8] "The *pierreuses* or *femmes de terrain* are creatures repulsive in their ugliness," stated one writer. "They come out only at night and prowl around in dark and isolated places. . . . They practice onanism."[9]

The one event that fixed the early image of clandestinity was the cholera epidemic of 1832. After the worst was over, the famous public hygienist L.-R. Villermé (a friend of Parent-Duchâtelet's who read the eulogy at his funeral) reported on conditions in the lodging houses that the disease had passed through. It was a vivid survey, published in the *Annales d'hygiène publique* and quoted extensively by Parent-Duchâtelet and by Frégier, and it provided a sad and shocking insight into the living conditions of the poorest members of society. Villermé himself made no explicit connection between the places he described and clandestinity, but clandestines were naturally associated with slums, disease, and danger, and so the connection was an inevitable one.

The lowest kinds of *garnis,* according to Villermé, were the *logeurs à la nuit,* which provided nightly havens for "a mass of *gens sans aveu,* vagabonds, *femmes publiques,* thieves, living in a continual debauch and ordinarily having no other means of support than the uncertain product of their infamies. . . . [They] pass continually from one house or from one *quartier* to another, either to escape the surveillance of the police, or for another motive. Usually, they do not spend more than a single night in the same place, and this night, when they do not spend it in the haunts of prostitution, costs them from 5 to 15 sous."[10] But it was the sheer physical descriptions of the

---

[8] Béraud, *Les Filles publiques,* I:100.

[9] *Paris-Vivant: la fille* (Paris: Gonet, 1858), p. 32. His last rather cryptic comment may be explained by the fact that they were also called *manuelles.*

[10] L.-R. Villermé, "Note sur les ravages du choléra-morbus," *Annales d'hygiène publique et de médecine légale* 11 (1834):386-387. For a discussion of this article, see Coleman, *Death,* pp. 174-180.

places that proved most disturbing, particularly since it appeared that the worst places were also the ones inhabited by the most dangerous classes. The *garnis* of the Cité were the most filthy. "There were some [*garnis*] whose *cabinets* or rooms only got daylight, if one could call it that, from a courtyard three feet in diameter, others where the water from the household and the latrines infiltrated the rooms; another where one could see the filth from the toilets overflow onto the stairway, and where, in place of glass in the windows there was oiled paper." The inhabitants of these places, according to Villermé, were "fully the most depraved in Paris, and truly the dregs of society." These places were also impenetrable to the police, except at risk: "Several times the inspectors of police, whose duties call them into these sewers, have been almost suffocated when they entered the rooms and have been forced to leave momentarily to get some air."[11]

The anxiety about these places, as a menace both to health and to public safety, would abate only gradually over the course of the century, particularly as the worst areas were torn down. In the meantime, the police frequently exhorted *garni* keepers to keep adequate lists of those who stayed overnight. The Service des garnis kept careful watch of the rootless, migrating population, staging frequent late-night raids to capture dangerous individuals as they slept. And finally, the prefecture attempted to increase the number of tolerances. Prostitutes accounted for much of the dangerous population, and the police wanted to keep them out of places "where police operations can be neither certain enough nor active enough."[12]

As the physical conditions in the city improved, the anxiety over clandestinity gradually changed, becoming less a worry about unreachable places (though this never ended completely) and more a concern over uncontrolled individuals.

[11] Villermé, "Choléra," pp. 399-400.
[12] Béraud, *Les Filles publiques*, II:144.

The clandestine prostitute of the late nineteenth century made no attempt to hide her status or to conduct her trade in secret. That did not make the public authorities more confident on her account, for she was viewed as the agent chiefly responsible for the spread of venereal disease. Dr. Louis Martineau, a physician at the Lourcine charity venereal hospital in Paris, was convinced that most of his female patients were unsubmitted prostitutes. He recounted with both horror and fascination the results of an interview with one of his subjects, a twenty-four-year-old woman:

> She goes in the evenings to the *quartier* of the Bastille and stops passers-by, requiring 3 francs from those that she succeeds in capturing. Saturdays, Sundays, and Mondays, she "does" up to six of these *amants de passage*. She conducts her clients to the furnished hotels in the Bastille. The man pays 2 francs for the room. Then, according to the expression, she makes her *couchées,* that is to say, spends the entire night with the first comer; if not, she finishes the night at the Halles, where she encounters lovers of all sorts, the market gardeners, diners with whom she makes her *passes* on the banquettes of the private rooms in these restaurants. The price varies according to the more or less solvent appearance of these individuals; 3 francs for caps, 5 francs for top hats. . . . She avows that she practices sodomy and sapphism. She sleeps with another woman; finally, she lives with a worker, or so-called worker, who benefits from her prostitution.[13]

But Martineau had saved the worst for last. The woman, one of his patients, had a case of syphilis then in a contagious stage. She had entered the hospital voluntarily on the twenty-third of the month and had left on the twenty-seventh—a

[13] Louis Martineau, *La Prostitution clandestine* (Paris: Delahaye-Lecrosnier, 1885), pp. 72-73.

Saturday, and the beginning of three good workdays. "She demanded this discharge, and neither the administrator of the hospital nor the doctor had the right to refuse her."[14] She was free, as all of Martineau's patients were, to contaminate society; some of them, all in contagious stages, made 15 to 20 francs a day, in only 1- to 3-franc increments; another of his patients had boasted of being able to achieve ten "encounters" a day.[15] Martineau did not believe he was speaking of isolated cases.

By the late nineteenth century, clandestine prostitution had come to overshadow inscribed prostitution, both in numbers and in the perception of its danger to society. For Parent-Duchâtelet (who had devoted very little space to the subject, in contrast to his successors) clandestine prostitution had meant simply "secret" prostitution, most frequently involving the selling of minors; he believed that the numbers involved were very restricted, and he had emphasized primarily the lodging houses, cabarets, and other places that had fostered it. But Parent himself contributed inadvertently to the new, late-century concept of clandestinity by his findings. He had demonstrated the vulnerability of virtually all working-class women; contemporaries had taken this vulnerability and twisted it, using it as a reason for suspecting all working-class women of at least part-time prostitution. Indeed, Dr. Julien Jeannel turned Parent's argument inside out, suggesting that through their immorality working-class women were responsible for their own low wages:

> It is asserted that a young girl, a woman, can live only with great difficulty from the products of her labor in the large cities, and is led almost inexorably to procure additional income by debauchery; then these resources,

[14] Ibid., p. 74.
[15] Ibid., p. 76.

which are often greater than the principal salary, make possible on their part the acceptance of lower and lower salaries, so long as [these women] continue to work. Thus, before degrading workers to the point of definitive prostitution, debauchery plays an indirect role in intervening as an economic cause of the lowered salaries accepted by them and, reciprocally, of the salaries offered by patrons.[16]

The realization of universal vulnerability, the growth in estimated numbers, led to an increasing preoccupation with clandestinity everywhere. By the late nineteenth century, entire groups of working-class women were set aside as objects of suspicion. P.-A. Didiot advocated a special surveillance for all women who worked in cafés and restaurants, an extension of the traditional suspicion directed against any woman who entered a public house.[17] Waitresses were not alone in being maligned in such a manner; every woman whose job required contact with the public was open to suspicion. Writers of the period confidently assured their readers that hat shops, dress shops, glove merchants, novelty shops, bookstores, perfumeries, and various other establishments that used women behind the sales counter were "known" to be havens for clandestine prostitutes, covering up their activities in the back room with the appearance of ordinary business in the shop itself.[18]

[16] Jeannel, *De la prostitution,* p. 140.

[17] P. A. Didiot, *Etude statistique de la syphilis dans la garnison de Marseille suivie de généralités sur la prostitution et sur la fréquence des maladies vénériennes dans la population de cette ville et completée des reformes à apporter dans le service de la police militaire* (Marseille: Arnaud, 1866), pp. 30-31.

[18] For discussion of some of the clandestine *trucs* used by prostitutes, see A. Coffignon, *La Corruption à Paris* (Paris: Librairie illustrée, 1888), pp. 86, 89; Charles-Jerôme Lecour, *De l'état actuel de la prostitution parisienne* (Paris: Asselin, 1874), p. 19; and Gustave Macé, *La Police parisienne: gibier de Saint-Lazare* (Paris: G. Charpentier, 1888), p. 8. According to Virmaitre, the phony stores were known as *boutiques à surprises.* Charles Virmaitre, *Trottoirs et lupanars* (Paris: Henri Perrot, 1893), p. 7.

The *proxénètes,* the women who acted as paid go-betweens in the business of assignations, were said to be similarly ubiquitous, masquerading as merchants of toiletries, as fortunetellers, as flower sellers at public balls; they also served as *ouvreuses,* or ushers, in theaters. "I do not say that all ushers in general are procuresses," wrote one observer, with the air of one admitting a minor concession for the sake of perfect accuracy, "but there are a great many who exercise this profession."[19] Another authority went further, finding these intermediaries in the guise of *sage-femmes,* employment agents for domestic servants, and *arracheuses de dents* (tooth-pullers); they further escaped detection by calling themselves "seamstresses, dressmakers, laundresses, milliners, etc.," a series of occupational categories that included a great many of the women of Paris. "No one is unaware," he concluded, "that the guards of the stagecoach lines are, for the most part, agents of the madams of bordellos." These and similar accounts of coded advertisements in newspapers, of secret signals exchanged in public places, of buyers and sellers who knew each other on sight by instinct, portrayed (for the unwary consumer) an all-encompassing secret Paris that coexisted with the real one.[20]

The obsession with clandestinity clearly had its humorous side, if only because of what it revealed about the nineteenth-century preoccupation with sexuality. The mental transformation of Paris into a disguised pleasure bazaar was undoubtedly exciting, as was the imagined constant juxtaposition

[19] Carlier, *Les Deux Prostitutions,* p. 32; Charles Virmaitre, *Paris-Impur: les maisons de rendez-vous* (Paris: Alfred Charles, 1898), pp. 191, 193.

[20] Rey, *Des prostituées,* pp. 53, 78. Newspaper ads varied widely in style and content. For example, a notice for foreign language instruction that included the service of "correction" meant "whipping"; one procuress simply advertised "furnished apartments," a seemingly innocent phrase that apparently meant something special to *amateurs.* Virmaitre, *Paris-Impur,* pp. 75, 159.

of "honest" women in shops with the available women behind the counter. Unfortunately, the popularization of the idea of widespread clandestinity had dangerous effects for working-class women. It provided the motive and the incentive for the police to cut ever more deeply into the civil rights of these women, in the hope of finding as many prostitutes as possible. The treatment of registered prostitutes was justified by the regime by the fact that they had at least consented to lose a part of their liberty by signing the inscription book. But even this tenuous justification could not be made in regard to the thousands of *insoumises,* as they called them, who were arrested, examined, and sometimes imprisoned without ever having a trial of any sort. It was this single issue, or obsession, that made the essential illegality of the regime stand out most clearly.

THE MEDICAL VIEW

The medical establishment shared the popular anxiety over clandestinity. In 1867 the members of the International Medical Congress, meeting that year in Paris, addressed themselves to the issue of the government's role in the control of venereal disease. Their discussion ignored many aspects of the question that might have been explored, such as the education of citizens and the government funding of research and treatment; for, by this time, the problem was viewed almost exclusively in terms of the policing of prostitutes. The successive speakers outlined various methods of prostitution control in force in various major European cities, discussed the need to extend these regulatory systems to the rest of the world, and made the rather surprising assertion that clandestine prostitutes— that is, those who were unregistered—were primarily responsible for the spread of venereal disease. The obvious solution to this problem was to strengthen the regulatory system, particularly in regard to the administration's right to register women who did not want to be inscribed.[21]

Physicians did not make the mistake of assuming that only prostitutes were diseased. The "syphilitic poison," as one doctor noted, was "astonishingly widespread in all classes of society, and especially among young people."[22] Nevertheless, prostitutes were viewed as the chief means by which the disease was spread. The idea that syphilis permeated society from a single contaminated source was a necessary corollary to the only means of control then conceivable, controlling the prostitute. From this viewpoint, the prostitute became merely a link in the chain; if she were cleansed, the chain would be broken. "Syphilis rebounds from the most abject hovel to the most honest home," wrote the syphilographer Dr. Alfred Fournier. "The contamination of the virtuous spouse and the contamination of the child are often only the products of the syphilis of the prostitute. Consequently, to pursue the syphilis of the prostitute is to protect ipso facto the virtuous woman and the child."[23]

By the second half of the century clandestinity was viewed as an obstacle not only to the regulatory system but also to the health of nations. Prostitution and syphilis had become firmly intertwined in the late nineteenth century, both of them referred to as the "new leprosy" or the "new plague" of Europe. Uncertainty about the effectiveness of syphilis cures had placed most of the attention on prophylaxy, which was interpreted almost exclusively in a social rather than a personal sense. Individual hygienic measures were (when not explicitly

[21] See the discussion in *Congrès médical international de Paris: août 1867* (Paris: Victor Masson, 1868), pp. 306-442.

[22] Pelacy, "Rapport fait au Conseil de salubrité de la ville de Marseille, sur l'état et les besoins du service au dispensaire des filles publiques de cette ville," *Annales d'hygiène publique et de médecine légale* 25 (1841):299.

[23] Fournier, "Prophylaxie publique," p. 60.

repudiated)[24] lost in the flurry of regulations about public prostitution. Because of this approach, the specialists in the field had to concern themselves with the making of public policy and with the issue, in particular, of the conflict between the individual liberty of the prostitute and the public necessity of examining her. Individual liberty tended to weigh less heavily. The entrenched establishment of the regulatory system had led to an almost unquestioned faith in the efficacy of regular examinations; consequently, discussions of the control of venereal disease frequently turned on the question of clandestinity or, rather, on the question of determining the limits of the involuntary medical examination.

Indeed, a few medical extremists went further than even the police dared go, proposing to extend the examination to all working-class women, a suggestion that was an almost logical culmination of the universal suspicion and paranoia. An earnest young medical student, who studied Parisian prostitutes in 1851 for his thesis, made the inevitable proposal for universal surveillance. Dr. Davilo's plan was motivated by his concern about the high sickness rate among unsubmitted prostitutes. The best way to halt the spread of disease, he believed, would be to examine not merely those arrested as clandestines but also all those who were very likely to be clandestine. Thus his plan called for a mandatory monthly examination by a police doctor of every unmarried woman who did not live with her parents. *Commissaires* in each locality would collect detailed information on any single woman who lived alone and inform her of the regulation. She would be issued a card with her name, address, and physical description (to prevent substitution and fraud) as well as "good advice on hygiene."

[24] Barrier methods of birth control were known to provide some protection against the transmission of venereal disease but were not favored by the experts. One doctor spoke of "la dégoûtante capote," the "répugnant condom." *Congrès médical,* p. 375.

Any woman found with a venereal disease would be asked to go immediately to the Lourcine. If she refused, she would be taken to the Saint-Lazare prison infirmary.[25]

Davilo's proposal was not completely bizarre. From universal suspicion it was a relatively short step to the assumption of universal guilt, and a short step from that to the institution of universal preemptive registration. The implicit identity in the plan between young working-class women and clandestinity was underscored by Dr. G. Lagneau, who suggested that the mandatory examinations of working-class women be carried out by a doctor in each *arrondissement* who was already charged with the care of the poor. Lagneau further proposed to limit the examination to single women known to be promiscuous, since these were the most likely candidates for clandestinity. The *commissaire,* he suggested, would conduct a surveillance of the private lives of the single women in his area, sifting out the virtuous ones from the rest. After the collection of information on the others, and after subsequent confirmation of their "debauched lives," they would be formally required to report for inspection once a week.[26]

Dr. Jeannel proposed guidelines to judge these "debauched" lives, providing a list of "sufficient presumptions" of guilt. Most of Jeannel's determining causes were recidivist encounters similar to those specified by the police—in a *maison de passe,* in a public place—but he did not confine his rules to the public sphere. A woman "with no avowable means of support" caught bringing a man into her domicile should be arrested if he refused to vouch for her virtue. Even this slight protection, dependent on the man's good will, was denied her

[25] Davilo's *thèse* was summarized in an article by G. Lagneau, "Mémoire sur les mesures hygiéniques propres à prévenir la propagation des maladies vénériennes," *Annales d'hygiène publique et de médecine légale* 4, 2nd sér. (1855):315.
[26] Ibid., pp. 243-245

in other instances. "When, at close intervals, agents have encountered the same woman in the streets or in public places with different men, even though each one has declared himself to be her lover or her protector," she should be arrested for prostitution.[27] One specialist, who believed that the arrest by denunciation was carried out too infrequently, wanted every infected patient who entered a hospital—every male patient—to be interrogated about "the woman who had given him the disease"; this information would give the doctor "the authorization to make an immediate descent upon her home." Lagneau agreed, adding that "one could thus inscribe by office every woman convicted of having infected several men."[28]

A number of physicians attempted to prove their suspicions with scientific surveys. Dr. Charles Mauriac used his position as physician at the Midi venereal hospital to question his male patients. Out of 5,000 men, he discovered that 733 claimed to have been infected by *inscrites,* while 4,012 had been infected by *insoumises.*[29] Abolitionists questioned these surveys for a variety of reasons, but perhaps more to the point was the criticism of another physician (who happened to be on the regulatory side) who noted that the patient in such a survey might give false or mistaken information, or might be un-

---

[27] Jeannel, *De la prostitution,* p. 320. In a review of another study of prostitution, Jeannel criticized this kind of discretion in making an arrest: "La voie publique, le bal publique seront toujours, quoi qu'on fasse, le terrain des rencontres fortuites; d'ailleurs, qui oserait affirmer que les amours de hasard sont toujours ephémères? Quel moraliste, quel jurisconsulte entreprendra de définir la coquetterie reconnue légitimement séduisante, et la provocation indiscrète, scandaleuse et punissable?" Review of Hippolyte Mireur's *La Prostitution à Marseille,* in *Annales d'hygiène publique et de médecine légale* 50, 2nd sér. (1878):185-191.

[28] Lagneau, "Mémoire sur les mesures," p. 316.

[29] Fiaux discussed Mauriac's findings in Louis Fiaux, *Principaux pays de l'Europe,* pp. 318-319. See also Charles-Albert Vibert, "Premier rapport sur la prostitution dans ses rapports avec la police médicale, avec la transmission et la prophylaxie des affections syphilitiques," *Revue d'hygiène et de police sanitaire* 5 (1883):922. The remaining 263 men were infected by nonprostitutes.

aware of the incubation period of the disease and accuse the wrong person. This doctor's disillusionment with the method arose less from scientific purity than from disgust with bad results: he had been confronted with another survey of 873 men in which 625 had accused registered prostitutes of causing their illness, while only 46 had mentioned clandestines. This result, he claimed, was "completely in disaccord with reality," and he threw it out.[30]

The statistics were often muddled by an inability to determine what clandestinity meant; women with venereal disease tended to be described as clandestines, whatever their occupation. One physician involved in the business of collecting disease statistics was honest enough to admit that he had made that assumption. "The column of clandestine prostitutes," he noted, "includes some women who have not gained their income exclusively in prostitution, but who have brought the medical examination on themselves, either by [being the objects of] a direct denunciation to the police, in the case of a well-established case of contamination, or by their general life style." Dr. E. Schperk, who prided himself on the accuracy of his statistical methods, formally differentiated clandestine prostitutes from other infected women at the beginning of his study, but tended to drop the distinction from his subsequent discussion. Thus he commented that within the mass of the female population "women cease to contract syphilis from the age of forty on, not because they are already syphilitic but because it is exceptional for a woman at that age to enter for the first time the path of clandestine prostitution."[31]

[30] J.-B.-A. Mougeot, "Question III du programme," in *Congrès médical,* p. 356.

[31] Adam Owre, "Quelques observations sur la question III," in *Congrès médical,* p. 414; E. Schperk, "Recherches statistiques sur la syphilis dans la population féminine de Saint-Petersbourg," *Annales d'hygiène publique et de médecine légale* 44, 2nd sér. (1875):296.

The insistence upon widespread medical examinations and the segregation of all infected women from society was increased by the very uncertainty of the cure. Doctors in the nineteenth century were not at all sure that the medicines and facilities at their disposal were adequate to the task. The history of the medical treatment of syphilis has been told elsewhere; it is most important here to point out that medical understanding of the disease, practically unchanged for over four hundred years, made some strides in the nineteenth century. Apart from some dead ends, such as syphilization (an attempt to inoculate for syphilis the way one inoculated for smallpox), physicians came to understand much more about the characteristics and behavior of the disease than they ever had before.[32]

Perhaps the most immediately significant discovery was made in 1838 by the American-born physician Philippe Ricord, who demonstrated the difference between syphilis and gonorrhea.[33] Once this distinction had been made and successfully established, more specific treatment for each illness could be provided. The accepted cure for syphilis was mercury, though there was no accepted standard procedure for its use; it was injected, ingested, and rubbed in. It was also

[32] Syphilization was not to be confused with autoinoculation (the reinoculation of an already diseased patient) which Philippe Ricord, among others, used as a diagnostic tool. At the 1867 Paris medical conference, Dr. Joseph-Alexandre Auzias-Turenne proposed syphilization of healthy or cured patients as a preventive measure. In one of the session's livelier debates, Ricord challenged Auzias-Turenne to prove the efficacy of the method by inoculating himself, and another physician sarcastically pointed out the opportunity to become a martyr to science. Auzias-Turenne did not carry the day. See Auzias-Turenne, "Question III du programme," in *Congrès médical,* pp. 375-380. A good recent overview of medical advances in this period, fully comprehensible to the layman, is John Thorne Crissey and Lawrence Charles Parish, *The Dermatology and Syphilology of the Nineteenth Century* (New York: Praeger, 1981).

[33] Crissey and Parish, *Dermatology,* pp. 84-85.

quite dangerous to the patient and had to be administered carefully, over a period of years, and with no guarantee of effectiveness. The arsenic-based Salvarsan, not discovered until 1909, would become the first improvement on mercury in four centuries, though, like mercury, it was sometimes fatal. Gonorrhea, once it had been recognized as a separate illness, was treated as a "local infection," by cauterization or by acid treatments of the sores. The breakthrough for both diseases would come in 1929, with the discovery of penicillin.[34] Before this breakthrough, doctors had not been able to guarantee to their patients that the disease had been eradicated.

Yet it was not always possible to translate even these imperfect cures into effective treatment. The stigma attached to venereal disease was so great that it reached even into the medical schools. Doctors were not well trained in the diagnosis of venereal disease, because the strict segregation of venereal patients ensured that nonspecialists would seldom see a case. Medical students in general were not tested on the subject for fear of embarrassing them. The Saint-Lazare prostitute prison, clearly the most concentrated laboratory for study, was closed to all but a few doctors on the grounds of decency; the prominent specialist Fournier had obtained entry there

---

[34] It was agreed that mercury should not be used except in cases of constitutional syphilis. See F. S. Ratier, "Mémoire en réponse à cette question: quelles sont les mesures de police médicale les plus propres à arrêter la propagation de la maladie vénérienne," *Annales d'hygiène publique et de médecine légale* 16 (1836):275. The variety of ways of using mercury in treatment are covered in chapters 9-21 of Alfred Fournier's massive study, which also includes a discussion of less common methods of treatment: *The Treatment and Prophylaxis of Syphilis,* trans. C. F. Marshall (New York: Rebman, n.d.). For a discussion of the treatment of gonorrhea, by the chief of the venereal hospital of Lyon, see J. Rollet, *Traité des maladies vénériennes* (Paris: Victor Masson, 1865), p. 27. On Salvarsan see Richard Lewinsohn, *A History of Sexual Customs,* trans. Alexander Mayce (New York: Fawcett, 1964), pp. 317-325, and Paul de Kruif, *Microbe Hunters* (New York: Harcourt Brace & World, 1926), pp. 308-330.

only with great difficulty, and his disgust with the atmosphere of the place was such that he did not want to return.[35]

It was also true that venereal hospitals made a poor showing against regular hospitals: "The beds, without curtains, have not the same linens; the wards are not scrubbed, the latrines are horrible; the patients have for their use crude earthenware dishes, a glass, and a tin spoon." The prejudice against those with venereal disease prevented any attempts to put venereal patients into better hospitals, to merge them with the victims of other illnesses. "Would there not be some disadvantages in placing near a young girl or a young man with an ordinary disease a girl or a man with a venereal disease?" asked the police official Trébuchet.[36] No doubt many physicians would have agreed with him.

Given the uncertain cures available, the policy of sequestration, moral as well as physical, took on a particular importance as the best means of controlling a dangerous disease. And in the end, it was always "prostitutes"—whether submitted or not—for whom the sequestration was recommended. In the peculiar politics of venereal disease, women were always the guilty transmitters, men (and the wives and children of these men) their hapless victims. One speaker at the 1867 medical congress, who likened such involuntary detention to military service, asked, "[Would one] hesitate to expropriate, for the sake of public health, some hours, some

[35] On the deficiencies in medical training and hospitals, see Fournier, "Prophylaxie publique," pp. 86-93, and Ratier, "Mémoire en réponse," pp. 262-296. Fournier commented that "Saint-Lazare n'est pas innocent de sa générale et triste rénommée."

[36] Ratier, "Mémoire en réponse," p. 272. The police official Adolphe Trébuchet (later one of the coeditors of the 1857 edition of Parent-Duchâtelet) commented on Ratier's work; Ratier (p. 272) quoted Trébuchet's belief in the need to segregate venereal patients from others. It was decided to place prostitutes in an entirely separate hospital, says Lecour, because of the "turbulence and undisciplined behavior" they displayed. *Paris et Londres,* p. 63.

days, some months, if it is necessary, of the freedom of a girl of *suspicious or contemptible morals* [emphasis mine]?" He added: "We have spoken of the [examination] of women; men escape completely, in this regard, all investigation. If the woman ... can fall, by this fact alone, under police action, it is not the same with the man, however debauched he may be.... [T]he private life of the man is screened from all investigations of this nature."[37]

The close association of guilt, disease, and clandestine prostitution led to a curious paradox in which medical concern was lavished upon men while medical care was forced upon women. Indeed, the paradox was even greater: while lower-class women were forcibly treated, as undeclared prostitutes, working-class men were frequently denied treatment. Workers' associations that provided medical aid frequently exempted venereal disease from their list of benefits. In some of the smaller towns, venereal men were denied a place in the local hospitals.[38]

Some of the middle-class specialists involved in the study of venereal disease wished to end this discrimination against workingmen, but they seemed unable to conceive of doing it in any but a regimented way. Dr. Jules Garin proposed to examine "all men over whom the administration exercises its power," including "soldiers, sailors, and prisoners." He suggested workers in state-operated factories as additional candidates. Dr. P. Didiot proposed to add customs officers and toll collectors to the list, as well as all single men in factories and workshops. With commendable evenhandedness, he wished all men entering tolerances to be stopped and checked. Police

[37] Mougeot, "Question III du programme," pp. 357-358.
[38] This was a common complaint and focus of criticism. The questionnaires sent out to local communities by Yves Guyot provide some indication of the community's provisions for treating men. See Guyot, *La Prostitution,* pp. 485-548.

Commissioner J.-L. Rey proposed that everyone arrested for vagabondage or mendicity be examined and, if found ill, sent immediately to an infirmary, whether convicted of the crime or not; this was essentially the procedure long followed for prostitutes.[39]

Some wished to extend surveillance to all celibate civil servants and to young men who entered the Grandes Ecoles, but these proposals bowed to bourgeois sensibilities. The men in question were not to be subjected to the indignity of regular examination by doctors of the administration; instead, these men were to present a certificate of good health from a doctor of their choice and only upon entry into the office or school.[40] Even such mild suggestions were not popular. The guiding principle behind most of the provisions for extending the exam was acknowledged overtly by a Norwegian doctor, who singled out for condemnation "the poor, the negligent, and the debauched," further warning of the danger of leaving them "without control, to themselves and their penchants."[41]

Even with the existence of such strong class bias, proposals to extend the mandatory exam to men were rare; most were content to leave the burden of venereal disease on the prostitute, not only the physical burden but the moral one as well. "The physical exam can be proposed for everyone," commented Dr. J. Rollet, "but it can be imposed on no one, for it is neither in the text nor in the spirit of the law." But Rollet's "no one" did not, apparently, include women, for he regarded the regular examination of prostitutes to be "the

[39] Jules Garin, "Des mesures prophylactiques à proposer aux divers gouvernements pour restreindre la propagation des maladies vénériennes," in *Congrès médical,* p. 397; Didiot, *Etude statistique,* pp. 25-26; Rey, "Question III du programme," in *Congrès médical,* p. 411.

[40] Lagneau, "Mémoire sur les mesures," p. 278.

[41] Owre, "Quelques observations," p. 415.

most important measure of international hygiene."[42] His careless comment was clear evidence of the lack of concern for the legal rights of women and, perhaps more important, of the tendency to forget about women when discussing the rights of the "people."

The attitudes expressed by many physicians represented, at base, a transformation of an obsolete idea. The old guilt traditionally associated with venereal disease, a guilt that had resulted in mandatory daily whippings for inmates of venereal hospitals, had been transferred entirely to women.[43] This old opprobrium was not always recognized for what it was; many defined it as a new concern for public health. In an attempt to reform the existing practice, Fournier asserted that syphilis, far from being a "certificate of debauchery," signified merely an "unfortunate encounter." At the same time he proposed involuntary detention for the *insoumise,* improving her condition only to the extent of removing her from the corrupting influence of the *soumise*: "What we want is that [the *insoumise*], simply *guilty of having contracted a venereal infection* [emphasis mine], be treated as simply a patient and, in this regard, interned in a hospital."[44] It was perhaps inevitable that some-

[42] J. Rollet, *De la prophylaxie générale des maladies vénériennes: réponse à la question III du programme du Congrès médical international de Paris, de 1867* (Lyon: Rapport présenté à la société impériale de médecine de Lyon, 1867), pp. 33, 144-145.

[43] "En 1785, les vénériens assiégèrent l'Hôtel-Dieu, ainsi que Bicêtre et la Salpêtrière, transformés en hôpitaux spéciaux. Ils s'y entassèrent littéralement, et c'était encore le plus petit nombre. Le même lit servait à plusieurs malades qui se relayaient pour l'occuper, et qui couchaient sur le carreau en attendant leur tour. Il fallait acheter le traitement par des châtiments corporels. On s'y résignait, tant le fléau sévissait avec gravité. On comptait alors à Bicêtre 600 entrées par an pour correspondre à plus de 2000 demandes d'admission." Lecour, *Paris et Londres,* p. 31. See also Ratier, "Mémoire en réponse," p. 265.

[44] Fournier, "Prophylaxie publique," pp. 59, 70.

one would propose to add visible stigmata to this guilt by infection. In cases of delay between examination and hospitalization, Lagneau proposed to mark every infected prostitute with a "perfectly visible" sign, on the stomach, thighs, or "elsewhere," to protect the unwary consumer.[45]

POLICING CLANDESTINITY

Perhaps the most disturbing aspect of all the recommendations by physicians, particularly those involving clandestines, was that they were not so very far from police practice. The prefecture often used the testimony of medical experts to bolster their position; at the end of the century, faced with particularly harsh criticism, they ultimately defended their activities on grounds of medical necessity. Physicians provided the rationale; all the police needed to do, then, was decide how to draw the limits of clandestinity.

The earliest pronouncements on the procedures to be taken in clandestine prostitution revealed the expected emphasis on policing places rather than individuals. An 1830 ordinance, published about a month before the revolution, granted a princely bounty of 15 francs to each inspector who discovered a *lieu clandestin de débauche,* a sum that was increased to 25 francs if the place catered to the prostitution of minors.[46] The difficulty of establishing the charge of "favoring debauchery" against tenants and landlords soon revealed some friction between the Morals Brigade, working out of the central prefecture, and the local *commissaires;* the *commissaires* had been refusing "under various pretexts" to execute the necessary *mandats de perquisition.* "This refusal, of which you, Messieurs, have undoubtedly not calculated the import," wrote Gisquet

[45] Lagneau, "Mémoire sur les mesures," p. 254.
[46] PP DB 407, ordinance of 21 June 1830; also published in Béraud, *Les Filles publiques,* II:138-139.

to his *commissaires,* "increases the already numerous difficulties that the establishment of a *flagrant délit* already presents.... A delay of a quarter of an hour can compromise the success of the operation."[47]

The difficulties involved in the question of trespassing on private property did not emerge in the treatment of the women arrested in these places, whether inscribed or not. Delessert, known for his (and particularly for his wife's) activities on behalf of wayward girls and repentant prostitutes, urged his officers to be very careful in the matter of arresting so-called clandestines: "Sometimes married women as well as young girls who have not lost all sense of honesty, blinded by a criminal passion or dominated by interest, abandon themselves to men.... [H]owever reprehensible they are, one cannot liken these women, these young girls, to shameful creatures, [to] these true prostitutes who solicit passers-by in the streets."[48] Women in these cases were to be processed by the *commissaire* and brought to the prefecture as quickly as possible, where their interrogation and, if necessary, their medical examination could be taken care of within a few hours. The purpose was to avoid a lengthy wait in custody that would be noticed by friends and families, a particularly serious matter if the women in question were not eventually inscribed. The ameliorative aspects of this measure could not hide the fact that women surprised in encounters that were possibly only romantic were nevertheless treated as if they were prostitutes, a procedure that made an illicit sexual adventure a very serious matter indeed for the working-class woman.

The seriousness was increased by the standard procedure to be followed in the arrest of an unregistered woman. In the general regulation of 1843 it was stated that the inspectors in

[47] Circular of 30 June 1836, *Recueil des circulaires,* I:263-264; repeated in circular of 10 October 1837, *Recueil des circulaires,* I:288-289.
[48] Circular of 24 March 1837, *Recueil des circulaires,* I:270-271.

these cases "will immediately verify that this woman is known at the address she has given, by the persons she claims to have served or worked for, and will gather with care all information pertaining to her conduct and her means of support." Though the police continually assured their critics that these inquiries were made with great discretion, they could not have gone unnoticed by the acquaintances of the arrested women.[49] The information collected formed the basis for the decision, pro or con, on inscription. The inscription was done automatically until 1878, when it was decided that recalcitrant women would be granted an administrative hearing before their registration.

In addition to the *garni* raids, which had the result of trapping women in unquestionably compromising situations, there were other less obviously incriminating causes for the arrest of clandestines, all of them left to the discretion of the arresting officer, and none of them routine grounds for the arrest of men. Public association with known prostitutes was sufficient reason for arrest. Women found by the police in the homes of *filles isolées* or in *maisons de débauche* were arrested, though theoretically only after several such encounters. Women picked up for public solicitation were formally charged, according to police guidelines, only after they had been observed several times on the street. In all of these cases, an inscription might be imposed by office.[50]

The police also arrested clandestines found by means of denunciations. Soldiers garrisoned outside Paris were inter-

[49] PP DB 407, *instruction réglementaire* of 16 November 1843.

[50] These guidelines were widespread and were included in numerous local regulations in addition to the 1843 and 1878 regulations in Paris. Their most public printing was probably in Albert-Jean de Sandouville, "Des mesures administratives à prendre dans le but d'empêcher la propagation des maladies vénériennes," *Annales d'hygiène publique et de médecine légale* 46 (1851):72-87. See also the appendices in the 3rd edition of Parent-Duchâtelet, *De la prostitution,* II:395-535.

rogated by military doctors, who passed along information to the police. Wrote Lecour: "Many of the indications furnished by soldiers are false or insufficient. Sometimes, these are acts of vengeance or jealousy, often intentional mistakes with the goal of not exposing to police measures women with whom the diseased soldiers desire to maintain relationships."[51] In addition to these routine reports, the prefecture received numerous complaints every day, some of them anonymous, that denounced women either as prostitutes or in some cases simply as carriers of venereal disease. Lecour noted that some of these complaints stemmed from "more or less legitimate bitterness," while others were "odious calumnies." Nevertheless, the Morals Brigade ignored none of them: "All these pieces of information are followed up with investigations, conducted with the greatest reserve, and with measures of surveillance."[52] If the women in the complaints were found to be registered prostitutes, they were immediately arrested and taken to Saint-Lazare.[53] If they were not already inscribed, the brigade then had the power to decide whether or not they should be.

Such a procedure provided disgruntled neighbors with potent ammunition against women who aroused social disap-

---

[51] Lecour, *Paris et Londres*, pp. 88, 90. A survey from 1845 to 1854, undertaken by Trébuchet and Poirat-Duval, indicates that the denunciations ranged from a high of 2,259 *filles,* denounced in 1850, to a low of 301 in 1854. A high percentage of the denounced women were not found, and most of those who were arrested were already inscribed. Totals for the ten-year period indicate that 13,007 women were denounced. Of these, 6,251, or 48 percent, were arrested, inscribed, and healthy; 95, or .7 percent, were arrested, *insoumise,* and healthy; 840, or 6.5 percent, were arrested, inscribed, and venereal; 48, or .4 percent, were arrested, *insoumise,* and venereal; and 5,773, or 44.4 percent, were never found. These figures indicate the relative ease with which inscribed women could be taken. Numbers by Trébuchet and Poirat-Duval, in Parent-Duchâtelet, *De la prostitution,* 1:574.

[52] Lecour, *Paris et Londres*, p. 88; *instruction réglementaire* of 16 November 1843.

[53] Lecour, *Paris et Londres,* p. 88.

proval. One of the few surviving written denunciations was from the owner of an apartment building who had rented a room to an embroiderer: "Since she has lived in the building, the other tenants have complained that she brings home unknown and suspicious-looking men." He believed that she was a clandestine prostitute, and the *commissaire* agreed to alert the Bureau of Morals to put her under surveillance. The ending in this case was a happy one, at least for the embroiderer: her landlord was told that there was no basis for his complaint and that he would have to use legal means if he wanted to evict her.[54]

When the decision was made to arrest a woman, treatment of her was likely to be heavy-handed. Though the police of Paris seldom acknowledged it in so many words, they nevertheless made no attempt to hide the fact that the unregistered woman received much the same treatment initially as the *fille en carte*. Legalities were handled semantically. Many nonprostitutes arrested for prostitution (as well as for other crimes) immediately became *filles non-inscrites* or *filles insoumises* and were, like the registered prostitute, submitted to the exam; the routine nature of this practice can be seen in Table 23. If the woman in question were found to have a venereal disease, she was sent immediately to the Saint-Lazare infirmary regardless of the subsequent disposition of her case. "The *insoumises*," according to one high-ranking police official, "are never sent in punishment to Saint-Lazare and they are only transferred there to be cared for in the infirmary, if they are ill."[55] The operating rules of Saint-Lazare contradicted even this modest denial, stating that "the second section [of the prison] is composed of *filles soumises*, under punishment or in treatment, of *filles insoumises* in treatment, of *filles in-*

[54] PP DB 407, complaint of 19 May 1836 from M. Olinger to the *commissaire* of Arcis.

[55] "Note de M. Grécourt," in Fiaux, *Commission extraparlementaire*, II:932.

TABLE 23

Nineteenth-Century Treatment of Unregistered Prostitutes
after Arrest

Year	Number Arrested as Insoumises	Found to Be Syphilitic no./%	Inscribed after Arrest[a] no./%
1816	412	107/26	—
1817	326	51/16	—
1818	290	58/20	—
1819	248	70/28	—
1820	340	83/24	—
1821	366	87/24	—
1822	159	48/30	—
1823	166	47/28	—
1824	164	64/39	—
1825	151	57/38	—
1826	72	35/49	—
1827	192	57/30	—
1828	224	50/22	—
1855	1,323	405/31	611/46
1856	1,592	551/35	652/41
1857	1,405	434/31	542/39
1858	1,158	314/27	443/38
1859	1,528	358/23	507/33
1860	1,650	432/26	338/24
1861	2,322	542/23	397/17
1862	2,987	585/20	443/15
1863	2,124	425/20	379/18
1864	2,143	380/18	364/17
1865	2,255	468/21	311/14
1866	1,988	432/22	323/16
1867	2,018	557/28	330/16
1868	2,077	651/31	340/16
1869	1,999	840/42	370/19

TABLE 23 (Continued)

Year	Number Arrested as Insoumises	Found to Be Syphilitic no./%	Inscribed after Arrest[a] no./%
1888	1,932	262/14	707/37
1889	2,511	401/16	691/28
1890	2,542	281/11	617/24
1891	2,408	277/12	665/28
1892	1,611	202/13	396/25
1893	3,208	448/14	787/25
1894	3,023	370/12	855/28
1895	3,288	380/12	860/26
1896	2,565	267/10	714/28
1897	2,968	295/10	702/24
1898	2,746	303/11	692/25
1899	2,456	290/12	622/25
1900	2,940	319/11	680/23
1901	3,608	353/10	1,574/44
1902	3,577	262/7	1,128/32
1903	2,821	192/7	781/28

SOURCES: For the years 1816-1828, A.-J.-B. Parent-Duchâtelet, *De la prostitution dans la ville de Paris,* 2 vols. (Paris: J.-B. Baillière, 1857), I:699; for 1855-1869, Félix Carlier, "Etude statistique sur la prostitution clandestine à Paris de 1855 à 1870," *Annales d'hygiène publique et de médecine légale* 36, 3rd sér. (1871):301; for 1888-1903, Henri Turot, *Le Prolétariat de l'amour* (Paris: Librairie universelle, 1904), p. 134.

[a] From 1816 to 1832, out of a total 12,544 inscriptions, only 720 (5.7 percent) were "by office." Parent-Duchâtelet, *De la prostitution,* I:363.

soumises detained in hospitality or by administrative measure."[56] The holding of an uninscribed woman "in hospitality

[56] "Règlement intérieur de la maison d'arrêt et de correction de Saint-Lazare, 29 November 1875," in Fiaux, *Commission extraparlementaire,* II:935.

or by administrative measure" was nothing less than imprisonment without trial or, indeed, without any legal formalities whatsoever. Having been declared *insoumise,* she was confronted by the familiar Catch-22 of prostitution, unable to deny the charge of prostitution because prostitutes were denied the protection of the law.

Throughout the nineteenth century, the prefecture made genuine attempts to ensure that clandestinity, the loophole in the regulatory system, would not be widened beyond recognition. Morals agents were reminded that they were not after women "who had only to reproach themselves for an act of private debauchery."[57] But the system was vulnerable to the good or bad intentions of the men who put it into operation; there were no structural, built-in safeguards for the women who were caught up in the system, and even the prefecture had to admit that abuses had occurred. Because the women involved were working-class women, because they were "badly dressed," as one morals agent described them,[58] the standard procedures were not subjected to any substantial reform throughout the century.

THE DISPENSARY AND THE REFORM

One result of the growing problem of clandestinity was the development of some hostility between the prefecture and the dispensary. Dr. Auguste Corlieu, a part of the dispensary staff in the 1870s and 1880s, was distressed at what he perceived as the prefecture's inattention to the advice of its doctors. "We do not run the administration, but nevertheless we are obliged to make common cause with it," he wrote in his 1887 study. "It is [the administration] that should support itself on us,

[57] BN 8° Z. Le Senne 14255, *règlement* of October 1878.
[58] Conseil municipal de Paris, *Procès-verbal,* p. 82.

not we on it."[59] The dissatisfaction evident in Corlieu's comment was not confined to him, and shortly after his book appeared the dispensary staged an abortive takeover of the *police des moeurs* from the prefecture. Nevertheless, whatever the friction between the prefect and the doctors, the dispensary was the locus of intersection between medicine and administration and thus naturally was drawn into the problem of the *insoumise*.

From its early troubled beginnings, the dispensary had grown into a stable, if not to say staid, institution. Dr. Denis held the position as *médecin en chef* for nearly a third of the century, from 1838 until his death in 1868, to be replaced by Dr. Pietri, who fell with the Empire. Dr. Cheron had made a short appearance in 1870, and he was succeeded by Dr. Clerc (who had refused to serve the Commune). Clerc died in 1886 and was followed by Dr. Passant.[60] The routine was as settled as the top personnel. The dispensary was open from 10:00 a.m. to 4:00 p.m. (expanded to 10:00-5:00 in 1882); the physicians divided their time between service in the dispensary and weekly trips to the *maisons de tolérance*. All tolerances in Paris had to be provided with a *fauteuil,* or examination bed, and "a box containing an assortment of speculums." This had been the procedure throughout the century, except briefly in 1848, when the temporary prefect of police François-Joseph Ducoux decreed that the *filles de maison* should report once a week to the dispensary and *isolées* once every ten days, a procedure that had proved unworkable.[61]

To the distress of the dispensary physicians, the routine had undergone substantial change in late 1882, when Prefect E. Camescasse (1884-1885) announced the expansion of the dispensary at no extra charge to the city. He hoped, he said,

[59] Corlieu, *La Prostitution à Paris,* p. 9.
[60] Ibid., pp. 51-52.
[61] Lecour, *Paris et Londres,* p. 83.

to find young doctors who would work for nothing—and he did. In addition to the sixteen dispensary doctors (the *titulaires*) there were now ten *adjoints* who worked for free, waiting for the chance to become a *titulaire*.[62] This, in addition to the fact that Camescasse had instituted an extra daily hour of service to the dispensary, accounted in no small part for the hostility of the physicians. Corlieu found this "exploitation" to be "unworthy of the dignity" of the medical profession. But the changes in routine, however galling they may have been, were not the chief cause for discontent. Instead, the dispensary doctors (and the medical establishment as a whole) were beginning to challenge procedures that had been standard at the dispensary for nearly a century, on the grounds that they had been established out of administrative rather than medical necessity.

There was, for example, particular worry about the examinations conducted on the premises of *maisons de tolérance*. Jeannel asserted that *filles de maison* had many ways of avoiding detection. Open sores could be covered by beauty marks; sores in the mouth could be masked by eating chocolate immediately before the examination; various powders and pastes could be used to patch the genital areas.[63] To avoid these tricks of the trade, Dr. Martineau proposed a requirement that all examinations be done at the dispensary: "The woman's trip from home to the dispensary, the wait for the examination, would eliminate the results of washes, of injections at the moment of the expected visit of the doctor."[64] Dr. Etienne Lancereaux believed that the examination should not be performed immediately after the arrival at the dispensary; in-

[62] Corlieu, *La Prostitution à Paris*, p. 55. Béraud had suggested the appointment of young doctors to serve a kind of apprenticeship. *Les Filles publiques*, II:166-167.

[63] Jeannel, *De la prostitution*, pp. 232-233.

[64] Martineau, *La Prostitution clandestine*, p. 183.

stead, he thought women should be made to wait for several hours and should be deprived of water during that time.[65]

There were further differences of opinion over the necessary frequency of the examination. The intervals sanctified by decades of police practice set the examinations at twice a month for *isolées* and once a week for *filles de maison*. Disputes over the adequacy of these procedures had continued throughout the century. Ricord wanted an examination of all prostitutes every three days, with the speculum. Dr. Félix-Séverin Ratier believed that the incubation period for venereal infections was four days and on that account wanted the examination to be made every four days, with the speculum.[66] Lancereaux wanted the examination to be done every two days, while Alfred Fournier, Jean-Joseph Crocq, and J.-B.-A. Mougeot wanted two examinations a week. Others worried that the examination itself created a false sense of security, for a woman whose symptoms appeared immediately after the examination could contaminate at will, with a clean bill of health from the dispensary. There was even some fear that the examination itself could spread disease; they hired "a woman to clean the instruments" rather late in the regime.[67]

It was the supposed guarantee of health granted by the examination that many doctors (particularly those outside the dispensary) found especially alarming. Many police officials seemed to regard the examination itself, however carried out, almost as if it were a totem against disease. In the provinces, the *visite sanitaire* was little more than a comforting ritual, a

[65] Emile Richard, "La Prostitution à Paris," *Annales d'hygiène publique et de médecine légale* 23, 3rd sér. (1890):391.

[66] Ricord quoted in Sandouville, "Des Mesures administratives," p. 73. (Sandouville himself believed that every four days was sufficient.) See also Ratier, "Mémoire en réponse," p. 282.

[67] Corlieu, *La Prostitution à Paris*, p. 119; PP DB 408, *Extrait du registre des procès-verbaux des séances du Conseil municipal de Paris, du 30 decembre 1888*.

blurred imitation of what was done in Paris. The specially designed *lit-fauteuil* was a luxury, replaced in at least one town, as Fournier reported, by an ordinary chair on a platform. In another village the examining physician did not use a speculum because the town did not have one.[68] Some towns were big enough to afford the equipment but, for one reason or another, did not use it. This was the case with Marseille, which had instituted what most experts regarded as an incomplete program of sanitary examination; though a number of *malades* were discovered, one physician wondered what would happen "if our colleagues used the speculum!"[69]

Aside from the doubts about administrative procedure, there may have been some uneasiness on the part of the dispensary doctors over the repressive role they were forced to play, especially in regard to the unsubmitted prostitute. Dr. Clerc, chief physician of the dispensary during the 1879 Municipal Council investigation, denied the rumor that violence was used against women who did not want to be examined: "The violence would, moreover, be completely useless; because if the woman is not in agreement, the examination becomes materially impossible. In cases of refusal, in fact very rare, we restrict ourselves to explaining to the recalcitrant ones that the examination is only a simple formality. If the woman does not yield to these exhortations, we simply mention her refusal on the report."[70] Clerc claimed that he "did not know" what happened to these women when they left the dispensary, that he was not sure whether they were sent to Saint-Lazare. A member of the Municipal Council, apparently (and correctly)

[68] A witness in the first town reported another breach of sound medical practice: "Ce sont les filles, raconte un témoin oculaire, qui, pour cet examen, écartent elles-mêmes les lèvres vulvaires avec leurs doigts (!)" Fournier, "Prophylaxie publique," p. 47.

[69] Melchior Robert, "Coup d'oeil sur la prostitution à Marseille," in Parent-Duchâtelet, *De la prostitution,* II:480.

[70] Conseil municipal de Paris, *Procès-verbal,* p. 53.

suspecting the worst, quickly jumped to the defense of the regime, arguing that "in sending these women to Saint-Lazare the prefecture is acting vigilantly. In fact, the woman who refuses to allow herself to be examined allows the existence of doubts about her state of health, and the prefecture only does its duty in examining her."[71] In any case Coué, head of the Bureau of Morals, had an answer to the problem. If a woman refused to allow herself to be examined after arrest, "the administration opens an inquiry into the past of this woman, and if it proves that she delivers herself notoriously to prostitution, at the third arrest she will be inscribed by office."[72] Most women understandably chose to undergo the examination.

But perhaps the most difficult of all practices for the doctors to accept was the fact that the administration made no real effort to cure their reluctant patients of a disease that was, in the final analysis, a life-threatening one. Though the fact was seldom explicitly acknowledged, there were two possible purposes for hospitalizing prostitutes. One was to try to cure them, a long procedure. Fournier, writing late in the century, expressed the belief that treatment should last at least several years, a substantial increase over the six to nine months that had long been considered adequate.[73] The other purpose was to sequester prostitutes only until the "primary symptoms" had disappeared and they were no longer contagious. Limited bedspace ensured that these two goals would be in conflict with each other, and administrative priorities ensured that the second goal would win. Additional resources for long-term treatment were simply not available. Abolitionists charged

[71] Ibid.
[72] Ibid., p. 29.
[73] Fournier, *Treatment and Prophylaxis,* p. 487.

that prostitutes were merely weakened, or "bleached," by their stay in Saint-Lazare.[74]

Dr. Corlieu of the dispensary acknowledged as much. He admitted that the dispensary's most serious concern was to stop young prostitutes, especially clandestine prostitutes, who were more likely to be in the contagious early stages of syphilis. Older prostitutes were often at the stage of "tertiary manifestations or secondary, nonsecreting manifestations."[75] If they were not cured, they were at least not likely to transmit the disease to another. The average forty-five-day hospital stay for venereal prostitutes[76] marked the time period necessary for the symptoms to disappear and the disease to go into a latent stage.

The abolitionist charge of sequestration rather than cure was true, but it was an open secret, available to anyone who cared to examine the policy statements of the administration. "The medical personnel at Saint-Lazare do their best to fight syphilis," stated Eugène Pottet, the historian of the institution: "They give permission to leave *only to prostitutes who are thought to present no further danger from the point of view of public health* [emphasis mine]." Rey openly acknowledged the divided goals and the reason behind them. He was disturbed that some prostitutes were being discharged too soon, some

[74] The phrase *traite des blanches* came to mean the body of complaints about prostitution, referring to everything from white slavery to the regulatory system. See the study by Paul Appleton, *La Traite des blanches* (Paris: Rousseau, 1903). Fiaux used the term in the sense I use here, as a complaint about the regime in Saint-Lazare: "Ce même bureau des moeurs, au lieu de guérir les filles comme la logique de son système l'exige, ne traite (et ne peut traiter en effet) que les manifestations actuelle de la maladie; il blanchit. . . ." *Principaux pays de l'Europe*, p. 345.

[75] Corlieu, *La Prostitution à Paris*, p. 23.

[76] Note by Trébuchet and Poirat-Duval, in Parent-Duchâtelet, *De la prostitution*, II:35. In the eighteenth century, patients had been ejected from Bicêtre at the end of six weeks, regardless of their state of health.

after as few as four days of treatment. "[It may] undoubtedly be objected," wrote Rey, "that the longer a woman remains in treatment, the more she costs the city, and therefore that she should be discharged as soon as the alarming symptoms have disappeared." He argued that expense should not be counted in such cases.[77]

Unfortunately, the dispensary was a municipally funded institution, and the cost of running it had to be a factor. It is likely that any attempt to intensify the treatment given to prostitutes would have been politically impossible. Indeed, it is easy to imagine the kinds of complaints that would have been raised, complaints about the wisdom and justice of curing prostitutes at public expense when other citizens were left to find their own treatments at their own expense. The impossibility of curing prostitutes, not only from the medical standpoint but also from the political one, accounted for the determination to submit all prostitutes to periodic examinations, so that they could be withdrawn if need be from circulation. It also accounted for the determination to capture as many clandestines, or "young debutantes," as possible. The working assumption was that clandestines were probably beginners in prostitution and thus, as Corlieu and others observed, likely to be in the most contagious stage. All the anxiety over clandestinity, all the obsession with the capture and examination of unsubmitted women, was based on nothing more complicated than this.

The administration's efforts had results opposite to those intended. The stigma attached to venereal disease caused even many men to be wary of treatment; for women, this reluctance was increased not only by the greater prejudice attached to venereal women but also by the danger of registration. Martineau admitted that the Lourcine hospital had for years pro-

[77] Eugène Pottet, *Histoire de Saint-Lazare* (Paris: Société française d'imprimerie, 1912), p. 52; Rey, *Des prostituées,* p. 112.

vided the police with the names of many of the women admitted for treatment. "Experience has demonstrated," asserted one specialist, "that it is in [the clandestine class] of prostitutes that attention to cleanliness is especially neglected, and we can affirm also that these are the ones whose company is the most dangerous and who propagate the gravest and most varied of the syphilitic maladies." Jeannel agreed that the *insoumises* were likely to require more time in the hospital than the others; the fear of inscription led them to delay treatment until their condition was too serious to be ignored.[78]

HAMPERS AND HANDBAGS

The concept of clandestinity served many functions. It was essential, first of all, to a medical establishment that accepted the examination of the prostitute as the best prophylactic means available. Clandestinity provided the proponents of the system with the illusion of control over venereal disease. This control was not in the present; rather, it rested on the promise of future control, in the sense that it provided a mandate for examining the female half, at least, of almost all venereal couples, whether the woman in question was a registered prostitute, a clandestine prostitute or (in the commonplace verbal carelessness of the day) a woman of "suspicious" morals.

The medical exam was justified by its proponents by the requirements of social hygiene, but it was also a means of punishing the sexual irregularities (whether alleged or real) of the women involved. This aspect was seldom recognized. During the hearings of the extraparliamentary commission on the *police des moeurs*, the abolitionist L. Bulot made a deliberately provocative proposal that every individual arrested "for any crime or offense whatsoever" be immediately

[78] Martineau, *La Prostitution clandestine*, p. 17; Didiot, *Etude statistique*, p. 28; Jeannel, *De la prostitution*, p. 202.

subjected to the exam. His proposal elicited a shocked response from one of his colleagues, who (thinking back, no doubt, on France's history) pointed out that such a procedure might result in the examination of men arrested for political offenses; he found this proposed indignity to be a "monstrous" suggestion. Bulot made a stinging reply:

> His modesty is revolted at the very thought of examining an arrested man! Why does this same modesty not revolt when one arrests a woman according to the simple caprice of an agent, when one examines her by force at the dispensary and when one inflicts on her the illegal torment of the speculum! [Is it] admissible that one humiliates, that one violates virtuous women, young girls, on the sole condition that one respects the man, that one does not touch the male? Such a system is abominable![79]

Abolitionists preferred to focus public attention on cases of mistaken arrest, for "innocent" women aroused more public sympathy than prostitutes; but on behalf of all women they complained of arbitrary behavior by the police, of "speculum rape," of the manifest inequality of the procedure.[80] In the face of these stirring images of violated womanhood, the regulationists evoked the innocent victims of syphilis, the chaste wife and child. To the virtuous woman they opposed

---

[79] Fiaux, *Commission extraparlementaire,* II:351-353.

[80] Portrayals of rough, drunken, bribe-taking policemen were common in abolitionist literature. A typical exposé, purportedly written by an agent but actually written by Yves Guyot, is *Lettres d'un ex-agent des moeurs* (Paris: Administration du journal *La Lanterne,* 1879). The worst aspect of this literature, of course, is that it was sometimes true: "Il est inutile de faire remarquer l'exagération de ces assertions que des erreurs regrettables et des abus de pouvoir ont fait paraître fondée." Dr. Auguste Lutaud, "La Prostitution en Angleterre," *Annales d'hygiène publique et de médecine légale* 16, 3rd sér. (1886):418.

the sexually promiscuous one; the erring husband who linked the two was allowed to drop quietly out of the picture.

Medical requirements thus imposed themselves on public policy. For the women who became tangled up in the administration of the *police des moeurs,* the danger of clandestinity was obvious. It meant that they could be treated as prostitutes (and thus denied the full protection of the law) without ever having been registered as prostitutes. But the danger to unregistered workingwomen was even more serious than this, for the threat of clandestinity effectively circumscribed their behavior, limited their hours, and made certain places, and certain types of places, off limits altogether. The chance of being arrested was small, but it was there; the result, as one contemporary noted, was that the streets did not belong to women at night.[81] Nor did their private lives, for in the ranks of the clandestines were placed not only women who accepted "a mob of men" for money but also women who "changed lovers frequently."[82] Clandestinity served, in this regard, as a means of curtailing the activities of lower-class women, whose lack of the card did not save them from arbitrary public judgments about their private behavior. The virtual hysteria that surrounded clandestinity and venereal disease cast suspicion on working-class women in general, since contemporaries seemed willing to believe that all those who were not *soumise* must be *insoumise.* A. Coffignon offered some assistance for those who had difficulty distinguishing registered prostitutes from clandestines. Clandestines, he suggested, carried small hampers or handbags when they walked the streets; registered prostitutes—did not.[83]

---

[81] Guyot, *La Prostitution,* p. 129.
[82] Vibert, "Premier rapport," p. 914.
[83] Coffignon, *La Corruption,* pp. 109-110.

· 8 ·

The Bordello and the
Business of Prostitution

"THE brothels where prostitutes live in common under the direction of *matrônes* or of *tenancières* who exploit them constitute the least troublesome system in terms of public decency and sanitary security," wrote Dr. Jeannel, in his thoughtful 1874 book. Included among the benefits: "no exhibitions, no public provocations, responsible direction." The security of the brothel was a well-worn theme among regulationists, for whom the *maison de tolérance* had long been an important part of the regime. Those troubled by the problem of clandestinity could find comfort in the notion of the controlled, geographically limited prostitution that was provided by the bordello. Indeed, it was the very opposite of uncontrolled, anonymous, scattered clandestinity. The outlook for the bordello inmates themselves, however, was not sanguine, as Jeannel noted: "Sequestered, exploited, brutalized, injured, they always hope to ameliorate their condition by changing their bordello or going to another part of the country. But they find everywhere the same reclusion, the same exploitation, the same disdain; everywhere the same punishments for their lack of foresight and their laziness."[1]

[1] Jeannel, *De la prostitution,* pp. 225-226.

Some would have quarreled with Jeannel's attribution of guilt in the last line, but few would have disagreed with his description of bordello life. Conditions in the *maison de tolérance* occasioned a rare harmony among those who opposed and those who supported the regulatory system: they all found bordello life horrible. The difference between the two sides, of course, lay in what they proposed to do about it. Jeannel and the regulatory side found the bordello reprehensible, but defended it from the standpoint of public health and public order. Their opponents argued that it was a morally indefensible institution, and they tried, as well, to challenge the claims to greater public safety. This argument was conducted no more dispassionately than the dispute over clandestinity. If clandestinity conveyed the notion of contagion, of a virus spreading through the ranks of working-class women, the dominant image of the bordello was that of a festering wound— contained, perhaps, but more awful for that very reason.

The attitude of the police, though they had implicitly conveyed a negative image of the bordello from the start, fell between these two extremes. The 1823 regulation, which can be viewed as the charter of the tolerance in Paris, had urged *commissaires* to establish bordellos in spite of their natural reluctance to do so. Prefect Mangin had unsuccessfully attempted to enclose all prostitution (though not all prostitutes) within bordellos in 1830; though his successors gave up that ambition, they continued to favor bordellos throughout the century, a fact that the periodically strict policing of *isolées* made obvious.

Nevertheless the brothel provided a focus for the tension that pervaded the regulatory system. It represented the one area in which prostitution ceased to be a simple problem of immorality among women, of *femmes folles de leurs corps,* and became a business. The professionalization of the selling of sex, the development of subsidiary business relationships and channels of communication, added an entirely new dimension to the problem. Financial interests, some of them considerable, hinged on the police system and gave the lie to claims that the police were merely exerting a neutral kind of control.

More important than that was the fact that the bordello came to symbolize the *régime des moeurs* in a way that no other single institution did. It was the subject of denunciations, heated invective, and semipornographic fantasies, and it unfortunately served to distract attention from the more fundamental inequities of the regime. It was also the most misunderstood aspect of the regulatory system. Though the colorful descriptions of the researchers disclosed endless details about the inner workings of the bordello—all in the interest of public health—there was never a clear understanding of what purpose the tolerated house served for the regime. This misunderstanding allowed the prefecture to preserve much of the substance of the tolerance even as its traditional style was being lost. It is necessary, then, to examine the bordello from a double perspective—to examine its essence, as revealed in the evolution of prefectural policy, as well as popular perceptions about it.

THE ECONOMICS OF THE BROTHEL

There was certainly money to be made in prostitution, but it is questionable whether the bulk of it, or even very much of it, went to the prostitutes themselves. It is, indeed, difficult to determine how much money was involved in tolerated houses, except through scattered references. In the 1820s, a madam forced to close down by the withdrawal of her *tolérance* lost the furnishings of her house, worth 1,800 francs.[2] Adolphe Trébuchet wrote of one bordello in the 1850s that, faced with a three-day punitive suspension, offered to donate

[2] Froment, *La Police dévoilée,* III:108.

200 francs to a local charity if the suspension were lifted (they were turned down).[3] Jeannel, writing in the 1870s, believed that the average price charged by the average house in the city was 5 to 10 francs for a more or less brief interlude (the *passe*) and 10 to 20 francs to spend the night (the *coucher*).[4] Prostitutes in the suburbs, according to Trébuchet and Poirat-Duval, worked for "incredible" low wages, charging workers 1 franc and soldiers 50 centimes.[5] The 1-franc houses catered to the lower classes, and no time was wasted on preliminaries. It was in these houses that one found men lined up outside doors: "In certain houses, each woman submits to fifteen, twenty, twenty-five contacts a day. Each man takes a number. One man follows another. The woman is a sewer, she plays no other role. She loses track of the number of the men, which allows the *maîtresse de la maison* to cheat her on the number of her *passes*."[6] On the other end of the spectrum were the houses that charged more than this—100 francs and up—and that provided more for their customers in the way of spectacle. Some houses staged *tableaux vivants* for their patrons; these were representations by the bordello inmates of various erotic themes, frequently with lesbian overtones.[7] Other houses were famous for their splendid and striking interiors, such as the mirrored glass palace of the Second Empire.

Virtually the only attempts to gauge the amount of money earned in bordellos were Louis Fiaux's survey for the years 1878-1888 and Félix Carlier's estimate for the years 1860-

---

[3] Note by Trébuchet and Poirat-Duval, in Parent-Duchâtelet, *De la prostitution*, I:305.

[4] Jeannel, *De la prostitution*, p. 241.

[5] Note by Trébuchet and Poirat-Duval, in Parent-Duchâtelet, *De la prostitution*, I:311.

[6] Guyot, *La Prostitution*, p. 207.

[7] Louis Fiaux, *Les Maisons de tolérance: leur fermeture* (Paris: Georges Carré, 1892), p. 143.

1870. Carlier's figures revealed that 94 percent of the tolerances still in business were earning in the relatively low range
of 4,000-15,000 francs per year, with only a little over 1 percent
earning a high of around 56,000 francs. Fiaux's figures for
the later ten-year period showed about 65 percent in the 6,000-
15,000-franc range and 12 percent in the highest income level,
which had risen to 120,000-250,000 francs per year. Despite
the uncertainty attaching to Carlier's figures there was, as
Alain Corbin notes, a fairly clear evolution in official tolerances: the rich got richer and the poor dropped out of the
business, in many cases becoming something else—a *garni* or
a *maison de rendezvous*.[8] In 1893, the *tenancières* of three houses
in the Paris suburb of Courbevoie were paid indemnities of
7,000, 4,000, and 3,000 francs for closing down their businesses
and returning the tolerance grants to the prefecture.[9]

There are no comparable financial surveys for the earlier
part of the century, though one of Parent-Duchâtelet's tables
provides some insight into the stability of bordellos. Parent
made a survey of changes in the personnel in control of the
bordellos, the madams, over the period 1818-1828. Only 7.7
percent of the bordello closings were due to bankruptcy, and
the largest number of changes (27.8 percent) came about because the tolerance was ceded from one person to another. A
survey drawn up by Parent-Duchâtelet's editors for the period
1842-1854 similarly revealed that only 7.9 percent of the changes

---

[8] The figures are in Carlier, *Les Deux Prostitutions*, p. 154, and Fiaux, *Les
Maisons*, p. 301. For Corbin's comparison of the two sets of figures and his
interpretation of that comparison, see *Les Filles de noce*, pp. 104-105.

[9] This was, Fiaux notes, a badly mixed-up case. The Prefecture of Police
had granted the tolerance, but the indemnities were decided upon by the
departmental prefect of the Seine and the mayor of Courbevoie. Further,
it was not at all a question of a departmental expropriation of the buildings
or land the tolerances were on, but simply a closing down of what probably
had been losing concerns since the reduction of the garrison at Courbevoie.
See Fiaux, *Son abolition*, I:716-718.

were attributable to "forced retirement" owing to misman-agement.[10]

Though it is difficult to say exactly how much money could be made from bordellos, it is possible to determine where the money went. At the top was the proprietor. According to an *arrêté* of 22 August 1816, no *maison de tolérance* was to be established in any building without the consent of the owner and of the principal tenant.[11] An 1870 survey of the proprietors of the buildings that housed the tolerances revealed that the greatest number of bordellos, about 68 percent, were owned by *rentiers,* followed by madams, who owned 15.4 percent of the buildings.[12] It was not completely respectable to own a brothel; a public scandal developed in 1888 when it was dis-covered that the secretary to the president of the republic was renting a building to a *maîtresse de maison.* (He explained that the property had come to him through inheritance and that he had felt obliged to honor the lease.)[13]

The potential objections of the property owner to the es-tablishment of a bordello was one reason for obtaining con-sent. Further, bordellos did strange things to property values, tending to lower the worth of those buildings around them even as their own value went up. The rise in value of a *maison de tolérance* derived, according to Parent-Duchâtelet, from the scarcity of buildings deemed fit (by the prefecture and es-pecially by the owners) for the purpose.[14] The prefecture's own rules prevented brothels from being closer than fifty meters from a church or school; by the 1850s, the prefecture was attempting to keep them out of busy, commercial, well-

---

[10] Parent-Duchâtelet, *De la prostitution,* I:304-306.

[11] Ibid., I:278.

[12] The 1870 survey is in Carlier, *Les Deux Prostitutions,* p. 153, and is cited in Corbin, *Les Filles de noce,* p. 101.

[13] Virmaitre, *Trottoirs et lupanars,* p. 23.

[14] Parent-Duchâtelet, *De la prostitution,* I:278-279.

traveled streets, though they were not always successful.[15] The police also had to face complaints from the neighbors. "There is no street," wrote Parent-Duchâtelet, "however dirty and disgusting, however bad the inhabitants may be, where the establishment of a public house of prostitution does not excite complaints on the part of all neighboring proprietors and tenants."[16] Buildings that were already devoted to prostitution became marked by it, so that established brothels were more likely, when the owner retired, to be ceded to another madam rather than closed entirely. The rent was elevated by scarcity.

The difficulties that necessarily accompanied the bordello— the noise, the violence, and the constant presence of prostitutes—made them undesirable neighbors. A certain Rigodet, proprietor of a building next to a *maison de tolérance,* carried on a correspondence with the government for more than two years; he was fearful of losing his principal tenant, Madame Vic, who ran a *bureau de loterie,* because her customers were being harassed and propositioned. The end result of his labors was a fifteen-day suspension of the house, an action described by the prefect as "severe punishment."[17]

After the owner of the building, the next individual to profit from the bordello was the madam. The women who ran the bordellos had a crucial importance in the scheme of things, for the solvency of the enterprise rested on the soundness of their judgment. Bordellos were businesses, which meant that supplies had to be bought at a good price, negotiations with employees had to be conducted successfully, and the location and style of the place had to be suited to the clientele

[15] Note by Trébuchet and Poirat-Duval, in ibid., I:283.

[16] Parent-Duchâtelet, *De la prostitution,* I:288.

[17] AN F⁷ 9305, series of letters between Rigodet, the *directeur de la police générale,* and the prefect of police, 22 July 1822–21 November 1824. The disorder was greater, in this case, because the *tolérance* in question was a *maison de passe* rather than a bordello.

it was designed to attract. The luxury bordellos, which might cost as much as 100,000 francs to equip, were not necessarily the most profitable ones.[18] Parent-Duchâtelet reported the case of one *dame de maison* who ran a house near a barracks on the rue de la Mortellerie. She had been successful enough to begin buying up property in Paris and, more important, to provide a dowry for her daughter, who married a former officer with the decoration of the Legion of Honor.[19]

The prefecture tried to keep these businesses small in scale and confined to a single bordello. During the Empire and early Restoration, some women, "truly born for enterprise and speculation," had been mistresses of as many as eight tolerances, as well as *maisons de passe* that were "packed with isolated prostitutes, from the *rez-de-chaussée* to the attic."[20] In 1816 the police had begun to prohibit this officially. They claimed that hired managers, or *sous-maîtresses,* could not provide adequate supervision, but they more than likely also recoiled before the spectacle of major enterprises being built on vice, and with police tolerance. It is also more than likely that the police could not entirely prevent bordello chains, operated by a single individual with others fronting for her (or him); the very existence of luxury bordellos suggests such large-scale enterprises.

Most madams made some money by renting *chambres de passe* on a short-term basis to *isolées,* clandestines and, for that matter, simply to consenting adults.[21] In addition, contemporaries were generally agreed on the fact that madams managed to get their hands on virtually all the money, both in wages and in tips ("glove money") earned by their regular *pensionnaires.* Arrangements differed from house to house.

[18] Parent-Duchâtelet, *De la prostitution,* I:459.
[19] Ibid., I:465-466.
[20] Ibid., I:414.
[21] Ibid., I:312.

Apparently some madams took all the money, providing the women only with food and clothing. In the majority of cases, however, the bordello prostitutes lived and worked in the tolerance, but with a contract of sorts: after the deduction of various expenses, for room, board, and clothing, they split their earnings with the madams, an arrangement that presumably provided some incentive for hard work—just as it provided penalties, in the form of indebtedness, if customers were lacking.[22] The rates charged by madams in these circumstances were high. Food cost from 4 to 6 francs a day. The room alone was perhaps 3 francs a day; furnishings—a bed, a mirror, a sofa—could bring the day's rent up to as much as 10 francs.[23] Then there were charges for a variety of things—perfumes, baths, carriages, sometimes even heating and lighting for the *chambre de passe*.[24] Fiaux reported the practice of a small charge, when a woman left the entry hall with her partner for the night, for a candle to light the way.[25]

There were other charges that were easily justifiable as professional expenses. The hairdresser, according to Fiaux, never cost less than a franc a day, part of which was kicked back to the madam; it took little encouragement to persuade women to rent jewelry, for they were eager to show themselves to their best advantage. Sometimes a bordello keeper insisted that her *pensionnaires* buy all their clothing from her, or from one of her agents, at inflated rates; or she might suddenly decide (if her employees were fairly well equipped) that all should be dressed alike.[26]

[22] Béraud, *Les Filles publiques*, I:144-145.
[23] Parent-Duchâtelet, *De la prostitution*, I:448. Jeannel also discussed this, estimating 3-10 francs a day for food. Jeannel, *De la Prostitution*, p. 229.
[24] Jeannel, *De la prostitution*, p. 229.
[25] Fiaux, *Les Maisons*, pp. 110-111.
[26] Ibid., pp. 92, 97-98.

Madams often rented out clothing, as they did everything else—a dress for perhaps 2 francs, a chemise for 8 sous, a pair of stockings for 6 sous.[27] Parent-Duchâtelet reported that prostitutes who became angry with their madams sometimes left secretly, wearing a fortune in clothing, worth from 100 to 150 francs and even up to 600 francs.[28] The police were called in by the madams in these cases, which usually ended with the return of the *fille* to the bordello. There was coercion implied in this kind of settlement, because prostitutes sometimes did not have any clothes that did not belong to the bordello. One *commissaire* during the 1830s insisted that all bordellos in his *quartier* be provided with a *vestiaire* of clothing that belonged to the prostitutes, so that they could leave without fear of pursuit.[29] The *marchande à la toilette,* the so-called *ogresse,* rented or sold clothing at exorbitant rates both to *isolées* and bordello inmates. A shawl or a ring might cost as much as 10 francs per day; a watch and chain, 30 francs. Some laundresses reportedly rented clothing before washing it and returning it to their bourgeois customers.[30] Laundering itself was a source of profit. Madams frequently enforced strict regulations about cleanliness:

> The question of personal and bed linen has a professional importance which is pointless to detail, so the *tenancière* makes one of her most significant profits by fantastic prices for laundry, or by peculiar conventions. In a great many houses, for example, the bed linen for the *chambre de passe* is changed only once every fifteen days; it is the woman's responsibility to keep it clean. If a change becomes necessary before the stated time, the laundering

[27] Parent-Duchâtelet, *De la prostitution,* I:448.

[28] Ibid., I:445.

[29] Frégier, *Des classes dangereuses,* II:261.

[30] Jeannel, *De la prostitution,* pp. 172-174, and Lecour, *Paris et Londres,* p. 227.

is charged to her. In the houses where the *chambre de passe* is also the woman's bedroom, the change is still made only every fifteen days![31]

Finally, Fiaux noted that money was used as a means of discipline. Madams could make any rules, however arbitrary, and assess a fine for their violation. Many rules were designed to protect the dignity of the head of the household. Numerous examples could be found: insolence at the dinner table in front of Madame, spilling on the tablecloth, or not standing up when the madam entered the dining room were all subject to a fine. If a woman refused a client for any reason, she had to pay her madam the price of the *passe*. The prostitute, herself the recipient of tips from customers, was at the mercy of the many domestics in service who expected tips for their services. Her *souteneur* or her lover—"soldier, goldbrick, *garçon* of a nearby café, Don Juan of the barracks or the gutter"—finally emptied her purse.[32]

Despite the many depredations of a variety of individuals, it was the madam who was generally cast in the role of chief villain in the prostitution drama, blamed for her rapaciousness and harshness to the women in her charge. Such sternness may have been due to the fact that most madams had worked their way up through the ranks. The many women who sought to make the move from *fille publique* to madam sought to impress the police with the respectability they had managed to bring even to their status as inscribed prostitutes. "Ask on my account the baker D——, the grocer P——, the butcher L——, the fruit seller M——," wrote one would-be madam; "all will tell you that you can in all security grant me what I am asking, and that I am liked, esteemed, and respected by all who know me." Another, who explained that two hernias

[31] Fiaux, *Les Maisons,* pp. 93-96.
[32] Ibid., pp. 110-111, 275.

and "other grave indispositions" had forced her into the ranks of the *filles publiques,* also called on her neighbors for support: "The testimony of the people of my *quartier* will prove to you, Monsieur le Préfet, that I have in some manner effaced, by my morality, my decency, and the regularity of my conduct, the abjectness of my state."[33]

The police preferred to grant tolerances to former prostitutes, reasoning that such women would have a better understanding of the problems of the business. If the would-be madam was married, she had to have written consent from her husband. Such consent would have been necessary anyway, since she was starting a business;[34] but Béraud emphasized the fear of the police that, without such written consent, husbands might later complain that the prefecture had allowed their wives to act independently. Husbands were allowed to live in tolerances only if they did not become involved in the business; many husbands ran nearby taverns or restaurants.[35] The police insisted that they never granted tolerances to men, but police records indicate that they did, at least during the Restoration.

In return for the right to hold a *tolérance* and to profit from the advantages and legal immunities that went with it, madams were held to a strict code of conduct. They were not to admit any woman, either as an inmate or simply for a *passe,* who was not registered. New prostitutes were to be brought to the prefecture within twenty-four hours to be registered and examined, and the madam had twenty-four hours to report departures. Madams were to make certain that all

[33] Parent-Duchâtelet, *De la prostitution,* I:432-434.

[34] Or perhaps not: the Cour royale of Paris, in a decision of 29 December 1835, decided that "une femme qui tient une maison de tolérance ne peut, à raison de l'industrie honteuse qu'elle exerce, être considérée comme commerçante, et que les billets souscrits par elle ne peuvent être regardés comme des actes de commerce." Parent-Duchâtelet, *De la prostitution,* II:266.

[35] Ibid., I:450.

prostitutes were present for the dispensary visit. Such administrative oversight meant that bordello inmates were much easier to control than *isolées,* a fact that generally prompted the police to deal rather leniently with madams when difficulties appeared.[36]

Nevertheless, occasions for punishment inevitably arose, and the police sometimes found themselves in a quandary over whether or not madams were to be considered along with prostitutes as standing outside the law. During the Empire and Restoration (and apparently the early July Monarchy as well) madams had been punished much as prostitutes were punished, with a short prison term or (owing to their relative affluence) a fine. By the late 1830s, the police had compelling reasons to reevaluate the madam's status: "A great number of these women, although born outside Paris, have lived here for fifteen, twenty, twenty-five years; some are principal tenants, others even proprietors; they sign leases for two, six, eight, ten thousand francs; they pay more or less heavy taxes and enjoy the protection of the law with others domiciled here."[37] Such considerations made it impossible to compare madams to propertyless transients, as prostitutes were likely to be.

Punishment for misdeeds thus had been shifted from the madams to the bordellos. By the late 1830s, virtually the only punishment that could be exacted was suspension of the tolerance. Parent-Duchâtelet regarded this as a more severe punishment than imprisonment would have been:

Let us suppose that a *dame de maison* is condemned to the lightest penalty that one could impose; for example,

---

[36] The rules appear in many places, but see PP DB 407, *instruction réglementaire* of 16 November 1843, and BN 8° Z. Le Senne 14255, *règlement* of October 1878.

[37] Parent-Duchâtelet, *De la prostitution,* II:260-261.

the closing of her establishment for eight days. Not only would her rent still run during this time that she was earning nothing, but she could not keep any prostitutes with her, because the administration would expel all of them in closing the house, and these latter, in order not to die of hunger, would be obliged to place themselves elsewhere.

Closing the bordello, even for a short time, forced madams to start all over again; closings for long periods could bring "total ruin."[38] Few of their contemporaries would have pitied them. Just as prostitutes were blamed for transmitting syphilis to "virtuous women," so madams were blamed for corrupting minors and exploiting their *pensionnaires*. In both cases, the man who transmitted the syphilis, who made the exploitation profitable, was quickly removed from the equation.

Madams had obvious motives for attempting to get from the *filles* all that they possibly could, but they also tried to get prostitutes to run up a debt, by tempting them with special foods, wines, and entertainments. By this means prostitutes were tied to the life. There was no likely way, if they wished to return to an ordinary working-class existence, for them to pay off such a debt; and so this "debt of honor," as Jeannel referred to it,[39] served to repress any inclination to leave. It was possible to transfer to another bordello; indeed, it was desirable from the madam's point of view, as well, since it amounted to a renewal of her business. When a woman transferred, the new madam paid the former one the amount of the debt, thus assuming it herself. Jeannel thought that about 400 francs was the highest desirable amount; if the prostitute owed more than that, then her new madam was

[38] Ibid., II:262.
[39] Jeannel, *De la prostitution,* p. 230.

obliged to sink an enormous amount of capital into her at the very beginning, before realizing any profit.[40]

Prostitutes made the necessary contacts to transfer from one bordello to another through *entremetteuses,* or go-betweens, who brought together madams and *filles,* and constituted yet another group that profited from prostitution. Either party could initiate the contact. Jeannel had a collection of *entremetteuse* letters, from madams seeking new faces and from prostitutes expressing a willingness to go almost anywhere except a working-class brothel. "Madam," began one of the letters, "I am sending you my photograph so that you can place me. I owe 400 francs; I have my own linen and some toiletries. I believe myself agreeable. Thus, Madam, I beg you to try to place me in any town except in a *maison à 1 franc.*"[41]

Some go-betweens had national and international scope; but Frégier, in his 1840 study, noted that even *entremetteuses* who operated on a restricted local scale profited quite handsomely. Parisian madams sent them into placement bureaus and hospitals—especially venereal hospitals—in search of women who were unemployed and without resources. If negotiations went well and the recruit agreed to enter the brothel, she was likely to be given a present, perhaps a dress and a shawl, to seal the bargain, as well as 4 or 5 francs a week until she left the hospital or prison. The go-betweens in these cases were paid on commission, according to the quality of the find, and might receive up to 50 francs per acquisition. Less prosperous madams simply sent their agents to the prison gates to offer shelter to the women being released.[42] The fee paid to the agent marked the beginning of the prostitute's indebtedness, for it was charged to her.[43]

[40] Ibid.

[41] Ibid., p. 155.

[42] Frégier, *Des classes dangereuses,* I:174; Parent-Duchâtelet, *De la prostitution,* I:431-432.

[43] Fiaux, *Les Maisons,* pp. 90-91.

Entremetteuses were generally despised because of their use of white-slave tactics. The authorities did not restrict their actions unless they became involved in the transportation of minors. Indeed, a note from the prefect in 1846 revealed just how limited was the action taken, since it affected only girls being sent outside Paris. The circular, addressed to the *commissaires* of the city, reported that the prefect had been

> struck with the ease with which the *fauteurs* of prostitution obtain passports representing as adults the young girls that they recruit for houses of prostitution in the departments and in foreign countries, where they send them, deceiving them about the true reason for their voyage. These *courtiers à la débauche,* who exploit the inexperience of young girls delivered to them by misery, often have as accomplices the conductors of public coaches, who sometimes act on their own account.[44]

The young women, made vulnerable by their poverty and isolation from their families, were then sold by the *entremetteuses*. But the only action recommended by the prefecture was that the *commissaires* should make certain that young women applying for passports were as old as they claimed.

A final figure in the shadows of prostitution, a deceptively obscure one, was the *sous-maîtresse,* or assistant madam. It was her job to see to the daily drudgery of keeping the bordello functioning, and her duties varied according to the wealth of the establishment. In lower-class houses, she seems to have been little more than a domestic servant with a title. In upper-class houses, her opportunities for earning money were surprisingly varied, as this letter, from a madam explaining her terms to a would-be *sous-maîtresse,* hinted:

> Every day, in addition to turning over to me the daily earnings for the house, you are to give me 2 francs; you

[44] PP DB 407, circular of 25 July 1846.

are obliged to clean the salons every evening. In short, it is necessary to work. You may well imagine, Mademoiselle, that if I make you give me 2 francs it is because I know what *sous-maîtresses* earn at my place, and I am reasonable with employees. I insist that the *sous-maîtresses* be very amiable and polite to the Messieurs, as to the women.[45]

In some well-to-do bordellos the assistant madams were apparently paid a regular salary, estimated by one writer at 2,000-6,000 francs per year;[46] in others, they paid for the privilege of being in a position to earn money. *Sous-maîtresses* frequently held a monopoly on the sale of cigarettes, oranges, and other such items.[47] Prostitutes as well as clients tipped the assistant madam for her discretion in pairing clients with *filles*—and, presumably, in *not* pairing them, since bordello prostitutes were not allowed to refuse any customers.[48]

All writers who examined the bordello system agreed that the inmates were shamefully exploited, but few came up with a theory as comfortable as that espoused by Jeannel. He agreed that madams (and others) cheated the prostitutes of their earnings; but that fact merely demonstrated their complete inaptitude:

> The *filles* who people the *maison de prostitution* would almost all be incapable of regulating their expenses themselves; they would fall into the most wretched misery if their material life were not governed and ensured by the *matrônes*.[49]

[45] Jeannel, *De la prostitution,* p. 163.
[46] Coffignon, *La Corruption,* p. 52.
[47] Jeannel, *De la prostitution,* p. 239.
[48] Coffignon, *La Corruption,* p. 53.
[49] Jeannel, *De la prostitution,* p. 228.

Those who were capable of caring for themselves proved it by doing so.

BORDELLO LIFE

Life within the bordello was almost universally acknowledged to be tedious; it occurred to few writers that such "tedium" might well have seemed attractive to working-class women. Inmates rose very late in the morning, or even in the early afternoon, their late risings a product of their late working hours. They spent the days in a variety of light activities of their own choosing—talking, singing, playing the piano, and reading. (Parent-Duchâtelet asked to see their books, expecting to find them engrossed in pornography; he was surprised to discover that they preferred light romances.)[50] After an early supper they prepared themselves to appear in the salon for an evening of "comings and goings," as one writer delicately expressed it.

Days such as this compared favorably to those of domestic servants or seamstresses, for example, from whose ranks prostitutes were largely recruited. But the middle-class writers who described their lives preferred to stress the indisputable aimlessness of such an existence:

> See how the interminable afternoon passes—the gloomy emptiness of endless hours marked by boring rounds of drinks, smoked packs of cigarettes, mechanical games of cards and lotto, the session with the coiffeur, after dinner finally the long session of dressing and makeup that readies the troops for battle.

The days could become almost unbearable in the houses that catered to the middle and popular classes: their business fluc-

[50] Parent-Duchâtelet, *De la prostitution,* I:128.

tuated according to paydays, and inmates might go several days without even customers, undesirable though they sometimes were, to ease the tedium.[51]

The monotony was reinforced by the physical appearance of the brothel. Police regulations required closed shutters; this resulted in stuffy shelters made oppressive by the presence of too many women:

> Let us see the collective retreat, the "dog kennel," the "henhouse," the "cupboard," all characteristic terms: a large room, a pine floor covered with stains, with tobacco ash, with matches; in the middle, a rickety table on which are haphazardly thrown some combs, sugar, coffee grounds, greasy playing cards; in the corner, a little stove with an open grill on which clothes irons and curling irons are heating; on the wall, trails left by black smoke and traces of cork burnt for makeup. An indefinable atmosphere pierces the odor of coffee, alcohol, bully tobacco, burnt hair, ironed linen. A striated half-day filters through the blades of the venetian blinds.[52]

The dismal surroundings were usually untempered by any glimpse of the world at large, for prostitutes were supposedly allowed outside only once every two weeks. And, as a final slap at nature, day and night were reversed; this completed the divorce from reality and took its toll on the emotional health of the inmates: "Who could withstand this claustration during the day, this eternal false illumination of the nights,

---

[51] Fiaux, *Les Maisons,* pp. 265, 130-131. Dr. Level, a member of the Municipal Council, was quoted by Fiaux as having estimated that the *fille de maison* had about seven or eight *passes* in a twenty-four-hour period. This kind of regularity, while accurate for those houses with a wealthy clientele, was not typical, according to Fiaux, of those tolerances which catered to the middle and popular classes.

[52] Fiaux, *Les Maisons,* p. 266.

this imprisonment prolonged for a week, two weeks, a month?"[53]

The living conditions in luxury bordellos were little better, for despite the richness of their surroundings, the *filles* themselves were housed in the garrets. "Let us imagine an attic furnished with two or three iron beds," wrote one observer, "where the *filles* sleep sometimes two by two. Large tin basins full of dirty water show how these women prepare themselves. Along the length of the walls, with hanging strips of loose wallpaper, one perceives long trails of the soot that forms part of the [prostitute's] makeup."[54]

The juxtaposition of richness and poverty was not the only unusual feature of the bordello; even more striking to contemporaries was the fact that the bordello was a house whose residents were all women. No men other than the husbands of madams were allowed to live in the tolerances, though some argued that madams might need others for protection. Brothels had to be alert to the possibility of mass attacks by men, motivated sometimes by simple drunken rowdiness, frequently by vengeance on the part of those who believed they had been infected by an inmate. Each bordello had a peephole in the front door so that the madam or her assistant could look over those who sought admittance; young men in groups might be denied entrance. In at least one instance, a group of young men silently lined up along the wall, making it appear that only one man was seeking to get in. The opening of the door served as the signal for the assault, and "the six prostitutes, the *matrône,* the *sous-maîtresse,* all were over-

[53] Ibid., p. 267.
[54] Coffignon, *La Corruption,* p. 51. During the Municipal Council investigation of 1879, Naudin of the Bureau of Morals acknowledged that there were two sets of rooms: one luxurious, where the *filles* slept with clients, and one set of plain rooms, where they slept alone. Conseil municipal de Paris, *Procès-verbal,* p. 109.

whelmed with kicks and fists, thrown lightly clad into the mud, and rolled in the gutters."[55] Béraud recalled a similar invasion in 1838 by five students; they declared that they were seeking vengeance against the house, and to that end were attempting to throw the prostitutes out the windows. They had to be stopped by the police, and Béraud noted that no *souteneurs*—who had unrestricted access to houses at that time—were active in the defense of the women.[56] Whatever the dangers faced by the women, however, the police barred male companions from the houses; for it was feared that the presence of *souteneurs* could turn bordellos into veritable dens of death for patrons with some money. "Even in our day," wrote Béraud, "it has happened that men of all ages, young men of all ranks, have disappeared, murdered in a cowardly fashion in *maisons de débauche* by the *souteneurs* of prostitution."[57]

The measures taken for the safety of male customers had the unfortunate effect, according to contemporaries, of leaving women entirely to their own devices; the tedium within the house was relieved by various kinds of deviant sexual behavior. Bordellos seethed with internal rivalries (according to most middle-class observers, who simultaneously insisted that the inmates were apathetic and heedless of their surroundings). Real companionship within the brothel was virtually nonexistent; the inmates enjoyed only the company of those who "wallow in the same mudhole," engaging each other in petty but violent disputes and competing against each other in beauty contests notable only for their vulgarity.[58]

All that was available in human fellowship was the dubious

---

[55] Jeannel, *De la prostitution,* p. 238. This incident occurred in Bordeaux.
[56] Béraud, *Les Filles publiques,* II:149.
[57] Ibid., I:190. *Souteneurs* were forbidden to stay in a brothel, even for a single night, by a circular of 3 October 1838. Note by Trébuchet and Poirat-Duval, in Parent-Duchâtelet, *De la prostitution,* I:153.
[58] Fiaux, *Les Maisons,* pp. 272, 137.

comfort of what most people in the nineteenth century regarded as perversion. The houses were nests of lesbianism or, to use the favored contemporary terms, of *tribadisme* or *saphisme*. Fiaux was typical in blaming the *maison* not merely for sheltering lesbianism but for creating it.[59] He asserted that no one was born a lesbian, just as no one was born a pederast; lesbianism arose, as did pederasty, from premature and excessive sexual activity, and lesbian relationships were inevitable for all women who became inmates.[60] Most women felt disgust at the rampant tribadism when they first entered the house. Familiarity soon wore away the initial shock, and cramped conditions frequently led to the forced cohabitation—called "doubling" in the argot—of two women in the same bed. What usually followed was a seduction and conquest, of sorts. The unending parade of men combined with the fevered closeness of the house to create a receptiveness to greater intimacy; a new recruit would become intoxicated with the strong liquor served in the houses, and succumb. The custom of all houses decreed that a woman who had successfully seduced one of her comrades had to purchase two bottles of champagne for the next meal, one to be placed before herself, the other to be placed before her "new friend."[61]

Madams encouraged these relationships, according to Fiaux, for they tranquilized the women and made them more amenable to the difficulties of life in the bordello. Many madams were themselves lesbian and preferred to have a whole troop willing to satisfy them. Moreover, there was a strong desire

---

[59] Parent-Duchâtelet blamed the prison and the hospital instead: "Une opinion généralement admise parmi ceux qui ont été à même d'étudier les prostituées, c'est qu'elles contractent dans la prison et dans l'hôpital les vices affreux qu'on leur connaît, *et qu'elles en sortent toujours plus libertines et plus dégoûtantes sous ce rapport qu'elles n'y étaient entrées.*" Parent-Duchâtelet, *De la prostitution,* II:151.

[60] Fiaux, *Les Maisons,* pp. 154-156, 141.

[61] Ibid., pp. 141, 245, 141.

to bring some life to the *tableaux vivants,* the sexual exhibitions performed by the inmates to whet the appetites of customers: "The sapphic pantomime plays a considerable role in the scenes they offer to clients; the women who practice [sapphism] bring much more skill into the paid exhibitions or rather show less repugnance about appearing in such scenes."[62] Then, too, sapphism was sometimes an integral part of the job. Being "for women" as well as "for men" was an expected duty, a fact that Fiaux did not seem to understand; nor did he seem to understand that women might have female as well as male lovers whom they preferred to their clients. "It is curious," he wrote, "that the women of the brothels, so ready to practice sapphism among themselves, show less eagerness and agree to practice it with women they do not know—the customers from outside—only for a good price." The repugnance of the prostitutes was easily explained, however: "These are not only young women who come to the tolerance to give themselves up to the sapphic vice—but women of fifty, sixty, and seventy years!"[63] He apparently paid little attention to the ages of male customers.

The nineteenth-century outrage over such relationships led all writers to describe a final outcome for prostitutes that their own research should have told them was incorrect. According to this scenario, the hardship of the life, the sterility of lesbianism, led to death; there was no way out. Women could change brothels, but this was a mere change of scene; it could not change the ultimate ending of this familiar nineteenth-century morality tale:

Maddened, ragged, dying of hunger, young at least, they entered; now worn-out, dishonored, offering only the outline of precocious, repugnant old age, incapable of

[62] Ibid., p. 143.
[63] Ibid., pp. 146-147.

attracting trade to the lowest house, rotted with all the putrefaction amassed since nubility, they are thrown into the street and doors are shut against them.[64]

There were variations on this, of course. One writer saw them "brutalized by misery and drunkenness, covered with filthy rags."[65] Or they ended in the hospital, "completely devoured by the contagion they had pitilessly sown around them." The luckier ones, having viewed "the depth of the abyss," returned home or settled into a bittersweet tranquillity, as the house-keeper-mistress of an aged government official or a *petit rentier* (apparently the highest level to which they could aspire).[66]

The most vivid portrayal of the sexual iniquities of the bordellos appeared in Louis Fiaux's *Les Maisons de tolérance,* published in 1892. Dr. Fiaux was a feminist, one of the most sympathetic of the abolitionists, and a long-time activist (he continued to write after World War I). Perhaps in part because of who he was, the work was startling. All of what Fiaux said about the *maison de tolérance* had been said before, mostly by writers who had uttered self-conscious professions of disgust for the way in which the house was run even as they endorsed it for its utility. Fiaux's physical description of the house (the trail of burnt cork down the walls) as well as his description of the tedium that reigned within had been inspired by a similar account by Coffignon, one published shortly before his own.[67] The alcoholism and lesbianism of the *filles de maison* had been mentioned in virtually every other study of prostitution, from Parent-Duchâtelet on. There was nothing in Fiaux's presentation that would have been new to his audience, not even his rhetorical flights. Earlier works had matched, if not surpassed, the salaciousness of his

---

[64] Ibid., pp. 54-55, 287.
[65] Jeannel, *De la prostitution,* p. 258.
[66] Coffignon, *La Corruption,* pp. 100, 102, 107-108.
[67] Ibid., pp. 50-51.

imagery. But never before had the house been dissected with such concentrated fury as in Fiaux's work, and never had the collected information been assembled in such a powerful way.

Nor had a serious work ever treated prostitutes—bordello prostitutes—to such scatological abuse. The *filles de maison* were described by Fiaux as "animated filth," as "a heap of excrement encased in human skin"; their relations with each other became "pitiful friendships that excrete tribadism." The constant parade of men left women "glutted to the point of vomiting." Saint-Lazare, the prostitute prison, was a place of "gangrenous promiscuities," a "laboratory of interfeminine immoralities."[68] Prostitutes were characterized by "a primitive lack of mental and emotional development." Madams who handed down a tolerance to a daughter or niece revealed "a precious type of atavism ... where the spirit of *próxènetisme* is hereditary."[69] Of prostitutes again: "Among almost all of them the psychology of the child, the inattention of the young savage, the mobility and emptiness of a prehistoric brain still bathed in animality."[70] Even the customers came in for a share of abuse: the richer houses were more notorious for their perversions than the popular houses of the suburbs, where "the more rudimentary cerebrospinal system of most clients contents itself with less capriciously shameful depravity."[71]

Les Maisons was a curious paradox, a truly pornographic work dedicated in all sincerity to the preservation of purity; but it was unusual only in its power. The popular literature of prostitution throughout the nineteenth century had increasingly become an amalgam of realistic social commentary and fantasy escapism. This body of work, quite apart from

[68] Fiaux, *Les Maisons,* pp. 135, 281, 272, 136, 270.
[69] Ibid., p. 21.
[70] Ibid., p. 279.
[71] Ibid., p. 160.

the serious scientific and sociological studies of prostitution, varied widely in kind and quality, including partisan writings of activists, the streetwise memoirs of policemen, gritty pieces of investigative journalism, and guidebooks written to help foreigners make their way through Paris. The work varied as widely in quality as it did in style. Much was clearly inflammatory, meant to enrage rather than to inform; some was based on hearsay and unresearched guesswork. Much of what passed for accepted truths were nothing but stereotypes, taken by one writer from another, repeated in book after book until they finally attained a status akin to that of fact.

At its best, prostitution literature was solid, relatively un-biased, factual; at its worst it was soft-core pornography, not only in its depiction of sexual violence and enslavement but also in its tendency to dwell on the sordid and unclean. Studies of prostitutes often reveled in descriptions of the hovels in which they lived, the filth of their surroundings, the humil-iation inflicted on them by customers. Often this information was revealed with an outward show of great reluctance. "Al-though we decided at the beginning of this monograph to use information received on the morals of the *filles de maison* only with extreme reserve, we cannot omit..." apologized Fiaux at the beginning of his discussion of sexual practices in brothels. Twenty-one pages later: "In spite of the nausea that these turpitudes would bring forth in a doctor himself, and the regret of having to touch pen to paper to write such filth, it is indispensable to complete here the tableau..." Finally, after nearly fifty pages had been devoted to the un-speakable, the end came: "This is enough of this repugnant matter."[72]

This brand of voyeurism, drawn from the works of sci-entists, energized by anecdotes and true confessions, was meant

[72] Ibid., pp. 137, 158, 183.

[305]

for public consumption. Studies by Fiaux and others were written out of a self-consciously assumed sense of duty. The middle classes did not merely want to know about the prostitute's world, they felt an obligation to know; one work began its chapter on prostitution with a peremptory command: "Ladies, do not close the book."[73] The literature provided thoroughly respectable titillation, a combination of sex and violence with moral guidance; the sad stories of individual prostitutes were cautionary tales for young girls tempted to err.

Bordello literature, the work of Fiaux and others, provides a remarkable glimpse into the dark side of the nineteenth-century obsession with prostitution, the frightened vision of the monsters created by misery and want. Bordello prostitutes, the most fully integrated into the regime, became the scapegoats of this fear. To an extent the horror of moral and physical corruption was shared by abolitionists and regulationists alike; they differed only in their proposed methods for handling it. The regulationists—though not the police— would shut the contagion away from the rest of the world in bordellos; the abolitionists would destroy the houses and disperse the inhabitants.

Most of what was written about the inner workings of prostitution was based on fact; nevertheless, the discussions of life within the bordellos should be taken with a grain of salt, as most clearly indicative of the anxieties of those— mostly middle-class professional men—who studied them. The careful research methods of the prostitution specialists, so evident elsewhere, frequently failed them when they were called upon to discuss something so delicate as the question of the relationships of bordello inmates. Consequently they relied on reports brought to them by "Monsieur X," passed along rumors, and confidently served up old chestnuts—the

---

[73] Grisson, *Paris horrible et Paris original,* p. 294.

husband and wife who encountered each other in the bordellos, the old gentleman-voyeur who had an apoplectic fit when he found himself watching his daughter from the peephole in the bordello—as fresh insights. Exaggeration was not necessary; the bordello by definition was bad enough.

The Maison de Rendezvous

Late in the nineteenth century the problem of the bordello seemed about to be solved without any official action at all. The decline in the number of brothels, first apparent in the 1850s, became increasingly rapid in the 1880s, accelerating as the century drew to a close. Fiaux asserted, with some exaggeration and some accuracy, that only perversion kept them alive at all: "Without the current practices of public tribadism, of pederasty, of sodomy, and of bestiality, all houses of prostitution would have disappeared long ago."[74] Lépine, prefect of police at the turn of the century, said that tastes had changed, causing clients to prefer the apparently more impromptu encounters on the street, consummated in the new *maisons de rendezvous* (*garnis* devoted entirely to prostitution).

It is undeniable that the number of bordellos dropped dramatically, but it is doubtful that this decline represented a significant change in consumer desires, as was generally thought. Rather, this steady fall in the number of bordellos seemed to reflect a change in administrative policy or, better, a shift from one aspect of the system to another, less politically volatile one. The new emphasis in administrative practices arose in turn from several legal changes early in the 1880s. In order to understand the new developments, it is necessary to place them within the context of the entire nineteenth century.

Houses of prostitution evolved along with the society, from

[74] Fiaux, *Les Maisons,* p. 135.

the small-scale artisanal stage of the Restoration (particularly in the mid-1820s) to large, industrial-scale houses appropriate to capitalist society and the luxurious tastes of the nouveau riche. (See Table 24.) This evolution was far less exaggerated than it appeared. The police of the Restoration, in their count of the tolerances, had routinely included *maisons de tolérance, maisons de passe,* and *maisons à partie.* Many establishments could be classified under more than one category. Most madams who maintained traditional brothels also rented out some rooms to *isolées,*[75] sometimes on a regular basis; because of the difficulties involved in renting, some prostitutes lived in bordellos, though not under the regime of the madam, and were not counted as *filles de maison.*

Some madams rented *chambres de passe* on a short-term basis. Houses used exclusively in this way were called *maisons de passe;* though these were counted on the police rolls as *maisons de tolérance,* they housed no prostitutes at all. This kind of house, the ancestor of the late-nineteenth-century *maison de rendezvous,* for a time seemed to be gaining rapidly on the traditional bordello. A dispensary officer noted in 1823 that 48 of the 150 bordellos—nearly a third—did not have even one prostitute in residence.[76]

And finally, the *maison à partie* most clearly resembled the lavish showplace bordellos, the *lupanars* of the late nineteenth century. An evening at a *maison à partie* apparently included a feast and gambling, as well as "orgies and the most unbridled debauchery," a description similar to the accounts of the turn-of-the-century brothels; the women who attended did not all live in the bordellos and were generally left alone by the police, unregistered and unexamined.[77] The long tradition of discretion in regard to women at the highest levels of pros-

[75] Parent-Duchâtelet, *De la prostitution,* I:312.
[76] Ibid., I:319.
[77] Ibid., I:320-321.

TABLE 24

The Changing Size of the Parisian Maison de Tolérance

Year	Filles de Maison	Maisons de Tolérance	Prostitutes per House
1812	700	205	3.4
1813	700	216	3.2
1814	695	205	3.4
1815	692	202	3.4
1816	659	205	3.2
1817	600	196	3.1
1818	468	180	2.6
1819	470	179	2.6
1820	453	178	2.5
1821	395	182	2.2
1822	321	169	1.9
1823	287	150	1.9
1824	258	148	1.7
1825	275	145	1.9
1826	277	142	2.0
1827	304	153	2.0
1828	334	167	2.0
1829	706	182	3.9
1830	1,052	198	5.3
1831	1,071	205	5.2
1832[a]	1,019	202	5.0
1842	—	229	—
1843	—	235	—
1844	—	235	—
1845	—	235	—
1846	—	231	—
1847	—	230	—
1848	—	220	—
1849	—	219	—
1850	—	212	—
1851	—	219	—
1852	—	217	—

TABLE 24 (*Continued*)

Year	Filles de Maison	Maisons de Tolérance	Prostitutes per House
1853	—	213	—
1854	—	212	—
1855	1,852	204	9.1
1856	1,978	202	9.8
1857	2,008	199	10.1
1858	1,714	195	7.9
1859	1,912	192	10.0
1860	1,929	194	9.9
1861	1,823	196	9.3
1862	1,807	191	9.5
1863	1,741	180	9.7
1864	1,639	179	9.2
1865	1,519	172	8.8
1866	1,448	172	8.4
1867	1,412	167	8.5
1868	1,341	158	8.5
1869	1,206	152	7.9
1870	1,066	152	7.0
1872	1,126	142	7.9
1873	1,143	138	8.3
1874	1,109	136	8.2
1875	1,149	134	8.6
1876	1,145	133	8.6
1877	1,168	136	8.6
1878[b]	1,278	138	9.3
1879	1,188	137	8.7
1880	1,041	133	7.8
1881	1,057	125	8.5
1882	976	118	8.3
1883	988	101	9.8
1884	901	101	8.9

TABLE 24 (*Continued*)

Year	Filles de Maison	Maisons de Tolérance	Prostitutes per House
1885	833	91	9.2
1886	822	86	9.6
1887	778	83	9.4
1888	772	69	11.2
1889	691	66	10.5
1890	663	64	10.4
1891	682	61	11.2
1892	596	57	10.5
1893	540	56	9.6
1894	580	53	10.9
1895	536	53	10.1
1896	485	50	9.7
1897	496	49	10.1
1898	479	49	9.7
1899	490	49	10.0
1900	504	112[c]	4.5
1901	429	108[d]	4.0
1902	382	107[e]	3.6
1903	387	123[f]	3.1

SOURCES: For the years 1812-1832, A.-J.-B. Parent-Duchâtelet, *De la prostitution dans la ville de Paris,* 2 vols. (Paris: J.-B. Baillière, 1857), I:668-669; for 1842-1854, note by Trébuchet and Poirat-Duval, in ibid., I:306-309; for 1855-1883, Louis Fiaux, *La Police des moeurs en France et dans les principaux pays de l'Europe* (Paris: E. Dentu, 1888), pp. 102, 298; for 1884-1887, A. Coffignon, *La Corruption à Paris* (Paris: Librairie illustrée, 1888), p. 69; for 1888-1903, Henri Turot, *Le Prolétariat de l'amour* (Paris: Librairie universelle, 1904), p. 134.

[a] Information not available for all years.
[b] Exposition universelle.
[c] Including 64 *maisons de rendezvous*.
[d] Including 60 *maisons de rendezvous*.
[e] Including 60 *maisons de rendezvous*.
[f] Including 76 *maisons de rendezvous*.

titution was reaffirmed by Prefect Lépine at the end of the century; he ordered the police not to trouble the women in the high-priced *maisons de rendezvous*.[78]

The term *maison de tolérance,* then, was used indiscriminately to cover a variety of arrangements. Only Béraud, in the late 1830s, attempted to separate the different types of houses. His survey revealed, out of 220 tolerances, 205 *maisons de tolérance* (bordellos with women in residence), 5 *maisons de passe,* and 10 *maisons à partie*.[79] The small numbers in the latter two categories were perhaps less surprising than the fact that they were still listed at all. Sometime during the early 1830s the police began to require each bordello to have at least two registered prostitutes in attendance; their presence allowed for a regular weekly visit by dispensary doctors and enabled the police to invade the premises at all hours.[80]

The most hotly debated measure taken by the police was the inauguration, with Mangin's ordinance on 14 April 1830, of the *maison close*. The policy of attempting to enclose all prostitution within bordellos was short-lived, occasionally contradictory, and far less extreme than contemporaries believed. Mangin's regulation prohibited prostitutes from appearing on the main streets or in the public gardens before 7:00 p.m., "on any pretext whatsoever." The emphasis given this point, both in the writing of the ordinance and in the enforcement policies of the regime, obscured the fact that the ordinance did not prohibit *isolées* from practicing their trade, but merely prohibited them from practicing it anywhere but in a *chambre de passe* in a bordello, in accord with common

[78] Lépine changed the policy later, even though he believed that distinction was a good one: "Les femmes qui fréquentent la catégorie des maisons de hauts prix, sont des demi-mondaines, des mondaines haut cotées, des petites actrices et même— ... des femmes mariées." Fiaux, *Commission extraparlementaire,* II:112.

[79] Béraud, *Les Filles publiques,* I:200-208.

[80] Parent-Duchâtelet, *De la prostitution,* I:318.

practice.[81] The policy, though shortly ended by revolution, had been subjected to a great deal of criticism, in part because it provided madams with a virtual monopoly. Not only could they control the space rented to *isolées,* but they could take advantage of this control to attract customers to their bordellos, where they would profit more directly from them.[82]

At least in part because of such criticism, another partial *maison close* policy appeared during the 1830s; by the new rule, madams were prohibited from renting rooms to *isolées,* a direct contradiction to Mangin's ordinance. This policy was abandoned in December 1842, for some houses, and the list of tolerances once again allowed to receive prostitutes *en passe* was gradually widened. In ending the policy, Prefect Delessert acknowedged the greater public disorder that would undoubtedly result, but announced that he was acting in the interests of public health. *Isolées,* forbidden to use the bordellos, were going instead to places the police did not know about or could not enter whenever they wished, as they could *maisons de tolérance.* Consequently they would once again be encouraged to come to bordellos, and madams were to be allowed to receive even unregistered women, so long as they later pointed them out to the police.[83]

This extended discussion of the ins and outs of bordello policymaking is meant to suggest that the bordello was a far more flexible institution than it appeared to be. The prostitutes who lived there were not prisoners, as they were portrayed in the literature. Indeed, Parent-Duchâtelet discovered that the "flightiness" so evident in prostitutes led them to change bordellos rather frequently during the year. (See Table 25.) The increased use of the punishment of suspension (see Table 26) would itself have forced a number of such changes, and

[81] PP DB 407, ordinance of 14 April 1830.
[82] Béraud, *Les filles publiques,* I:249-250.
[83] Circular of 26 December 1842, *Recueil des circulaires,* I:414-415.

TABLE 25

Mobility of Parisian Prostitutes in the Course of a Year,
According to Parent-Duchâtelet

Description	Number	Percentage
Remained in the same bordello	61	3.0
Went from the bordello to the street, from the street to the bordello, from one bordello to another		
Moved once	306	15.1
Moved twice	249	12.2
Moved three times	166	8.1
Moved four times	119	5.8
Moved five times	84	4.1
Moved six times	73	3.6
Moved seven or more times	164	8.0
SUBTOTAL	1,161[a]	56.9
Did not enter a bordello	821	40.1
GRAND TOTAL	2,043	100.0

SOURCE: A.-J.-B. Parent-Duchâtelet, *De la prostitution dans la ville de Paris,* 2 vols. (Paris: J.-B. Baillière, 1857), I:331.

[a] Of these, only 211 lived exclusively in bordellos during the course of the year.

it was noted by some observers that bordellos were used by prostitutes as a means of getting through bad weather; bordellos expanded in the winter and emptied out during the summers.[84] Lecour mentioned the impracticality of Dr. Jeannel's desire to "sequester" all prostitutes, *soumise* and *insoumise,* in bordellos; the "so-called" *filles de maison,* he noted, stayed there "impatiently, provisionally, and awaiting the moment when they can enjoy the relative liberty and chances for adventure that the *fille isolée* possesses."[85]

[84] Coffignon, *La Corruption,* p. 69.
[85] Lecour, *De l'état actuel,* p. 52.

TABLE 26
Changes in Leadership of Parisian Bordellos

Reason	1818-1828		1842-1854	
	Number	Percentage	Number	Percentage
Change of domicile	54	12.1	0	0
Death	47	10.6	75	3.7
Cession to another	116	26.1	242	12.1
Bankruptcy	32	7.2	55	2.7
Voluntary retirement	99	22.2	322	16.1
Expulsion	14	3.1	0	0
Closing	56	12.6	0	0
Suspension	27	6.1	1,313	65.4
TOTAL	445	100.0	2,007	100.0

SOURCES: For the years 1818-1828, A.-J.-B. Parent-Duchâtelet, *De la prostitution dans la ville de Paris,* 2 vols. (Paris: J.-B. Baillière, 1857), I:304; for the years 1842-1854, note by Trébuchet and Poirat-Duval, in ibid., I:306.

NOTE: In the years 1842-1854, 156 bordellos were newly created. Such bordellos are not included in the totals.

The increasing number of bordellos, clearly apparent through the mid-1850s, was also less a result of fashion than of prefectural policies aimed at increasing the number of places to which the police had instant access. Béraud, an officer of the Bureau of Morals during the Restoration, believed that *tolérances* should be given to any would-be madam who had at least two rooms at her disposal, on condition that the site not be too close to a church or school. "Any other locality," he believed, could be used for the purpose. He would refuse only to allow more than one tolerance in a building: "The gravest inconvenience would result from the existence of several bad places in the same building. Conflicts of rivalry and jealousy would be the source of great disorders." Noting that such a situation had existed in two or three locations during the Restoration, he added: "If I had been master of the situation, I would have disseminated these bazaars of libertinage whose gathering in a single place is incompatible with order and tranquillity."[86] Since public order was better served by increasing the number of bordellos and scattering them through the city, it was important that they be as unobtrusive as possible—thus the shuttered and curtained windows that made the bordellos so distinctive.

The police had many reasons for wanting to maintain the principle of the authorized house. They cared less about the form the tolerance took—whether it was a *maison close,* a *maison de passe,* or something in between—than they did about its capacity to provide them with information. The madam's dependent status made her cooperative, and the police used her as a source of intelligence on criminal activities as well as in the search for clandestine prostitutes and houses. The lists, of customers as well as prostitutes, provided the police with an entrée into the anonymous mass of the lower-class population, and their right to invade the tolerance at any time without legal formalities meant that they could apprehend suspicious characters on the spot.

Until the 1880s, holding a *tolérance* might have been considered an advantage. True, the authorized bordello was open to police intrusion day and night, and the madam had certain responsibilities in regard to the women in her charge; but prostitution could be practiced in bordellos with virtual impunity, and the police tended to side with madams in disputes. Several legal and administrative changes, beginning in the 1860s, made the tolerance less desirable. An 1866 decision by the Cour de cassation opened the way for *garni* prostitution by ending the traditional 200-franc fine imposed on lodging-

[86] Béraud, *Les Filles publiques,* II:156, 159, 163-164.

house keepers; they were now to be judged in the Tribunal de simple police, a change that reduced the penalty for violation to virtually nothing.[87] An 1883 ordinance reduced further the vulnerability of the lodging-house keepers, even to the arrest itself. The new ordinance prohibited them from receiving prostitutes "habitually," the imprecise wording providing an easy loophole. This regulation was used only rarely, according to one authority, and even then only when public protests against particular areas grew especially loud.[88] *Garni* keepers did well, trading off the minor losses in fines against the major profits to be made in prostitution.

Another kind of space was opened to prostitution in 1880, with a law ending the restrictions on *brasseries,* or taverns. They were now allowed to open with only the formality of a simple declaration of intent to the local authorities.[89] *Brasseries* had long been a natural haven for prostitutes, but the prefecture had previously been able to threaten owners with the closing of their establishments through the revocation of licenses; this threat was no longer available.[90] Coffignon attributed much of the decline in the number of *maisons* to the appearance of *brasseries* that employed women.[91] And indeed, by the mid-1880s the *maisons de tolérance* had been effectively deprived, by *brasseries* and *garnis,* of their exclusive rights to the practice of prostitution; all that was left to them was the list of traditional obligations. There was no longer any par-

[87] Circular of 10 April 1867, *Recueil des circulaires,* II:251-260. Also see Chapter 1.

[88] Ordinance of 25 October 1883, in Virmaitre, *Paris-Impur,* pp. 198-202.

[89] Law of 17 July 1880, in Coffignon, *La Corruption,* p. 95. Macé noted that many *marchands de vins* had immediately opened *chambres de passe.* Macé, *Gibier de Saint-Lazare,* p. 94.

[90] *Brasseries,* cabarets, cafés, and *débits de boisson* were forbidden to shelter prostitutes by virtue of the ordinance of 8 November 1780. A circular in 1874 reaffirmed the search for clandestine prostitutes in these places. See circular of 23 April 1874, *Recueil des circulaires,* II:303-304.

[91] Coffignon, *La Corruption,* p. 91.

ticular advantage to possessing a *tolérance,* and the number of authorized bordellos, particularly those which had been marginal, began to decline sharply.[92]

This decline in the number of *maisons de tolérance* was attributed by many contemporaries to a change in the public mentality. "The public has lost its taste for these official establishments," wrote Lépine around the turn of the century; "they are scarcely visited except by foreigners, provincials, and soldiers; the public instead goes to the *maison de rendez-vous,* where it encounters more discretion, and where, with a little imagination, it fancies itself to have found the charm of the unexpected." Lépine estimated the number of *maisons de rendezvous* to be "about one hundred";[93] another prefectural report, written about the same time, put the number at around two hundred and fifty.[94]

However extensively the *maisons de rendezvous* developed, they did not entirely replace the old-style bordellos. Further, from the 1850s on, the bordellos had taken on a more distinct form; they were larger, and had more inmates at any given time, though there were always major variations in the sizes of the different bordellos. One rather notorious place on the rue Chabanais kept a more or less constant population of twenty-two, though it had swelled to at least thirty-five women during the 1878 Paris International Exposition.[95] These changes in size were in addition to the geographical shifts of the

[92] As shown by Carlier and Fiaux: see fn. 8, above. Andrieux noted that the tolerance, once a benefit, had become a burden: "On se demande comment il se fait qu'il y ait encore des maisons de tolérance existant en vertu d'une permission administrative alors que cette permission, loin de leur attribuer comme autrefois une sorte de privilège, n'a pour effet que de les soumettre à la surveillance plus étroite de la police, à l'application des règlements et aux visites sanitaires." *Souvenirs,* II:27.

[93] AN ADXIX 150, *La Réglementation de la prostitution à Paris et dans le département de la Seine* (Melun: Imprimerie administrative, 1904), pp. 6, 10.

[94] PP DB 407, *Sommaire,* p. 26.

[95] Conseil municipal de Paris, *Procès-verbal,* pp. 21-22.

houses. An 1854 survey showed a cluster of bordellos in the center of the city, on both banks of the river, with a slight predominance in the area immediately to the southwest of the Cité. The notorious areas of old central Paris, with their narrow streets and dark alleys, were cleaned out by Haussmann; thirty years later bordellos had been shifted almost entirely away from these traditional areas and had been moved into the suburbs as well as the wealthier areas of the center-northwest. This shift also followed a growth in middle-class population in this area.[96]

It seems unlikely that these undeniable changes in the scale of the houses and in their geography represented as serious an evolution as contemporaries thought at the time. There had always been regular bordellos, some of them luxury bordellos, and there had always been *maisons de passe,* now called *maisons de rendezvous.* Prostitutes went from one to the other, despite anxious, overheated rhetoric about the sinkholes of corruption within. The police had once favored traditional bordellos; now, in large part because of the rhetoric, they favored the *maison de passe.* And as for the customers? Some still liked their debauchery regimented, others preferred it *à l'imprévu.* It was simply a matter of taste.

Indeed, given the difficulties that surrounded the traditional bordellos by the end of the nineteenth century, their continued existence can be explained only in terms of a continuing demand, either for "exotic" sexual practices or for the old-style ambiance of the brothel. There was only one reason for the existence of the business of prostitution, in the bordellos

[96] Louis Chevalier, *La Formation de la population parisienne au XIXᵉ siècle* (Paris: P.U.F., 1950), pp. 82-83. Chevalier's maps show only the Tenth and Eleventh arrondissements with a greater population growth, and the latter one was more heavily populated with workers. For another examination of the geography of the mid-century *maison de tolérance,* in relation to concubinage, see M. Frey, "Du Mariage et du concubinage dans les classes populaires à Paris (1846-1874)," *Annales, E.S.C.* 33 (août 1978):803-821.

as well as the *maisons de rendezvous,* and that was their prof-
itability. The police did not shore up the bordellos artificially,
nor did they attempt to abolish them; the prefecture's policy
was not characterized by such abrupt shifts. And, despite their
apparent capitulation to the *maison de rendezvous,* a surrender
presumably forced by the changing tastes of the Parisian
public, the police had given up neither the *arbitraire,* nor the
inscription, nor administrative detention. Prostitutes were still,
in legal terms, a class apart from everyone else.

The *maison de rendezvous,* the prefecture's self-proclaimed
"new solution" to the presumed unpopularity of the bordello,
was not very new. Prefect Andrieux noted that the *rendezvous*
had been around for a long time: "Formerly, although not
regularly authorized, they were nonetheless the object of an
active surveillance, and when their closing was not ordered,
it was because, on one hand, the police recognized that they
could be tolerated and, on the other hand, because the administration found there a sometimes useful source of delicate
and discreet information."[97] The decision to give *maisons de
rendezvous* an official and widely publicized sanction was essentially a political one: the *rendezvous* was an important part
of neoregulation, the late-nineteenth-century attempt to soften
the worst abuses of the *police des moeurs* so that the system
itself could be maintained.

The *rendezvous* was in fact nothing more than a *maison de
passe,* refurbished by the police with new rhetoric that emphasized its openness. The prefecture defined it as a "kind
of lodging house" and declared that the policing would be
done by the Service des garnis rather than by the morals
agents, who by this time had all been merged with the Sûreté.
The madam (or *patronne,* as she was now called) had to keep
an up-to-date file on each prostitute who worked for her,

[97] Andrieux, *Souvenirs,* II:27.

including biographical data and a photograph. The women did not have to be inscribed with the police, though they were treated as if they were registered; they had to be checked weekly by a police doctor and brought to the prefecture if they were ill. Contrary to what was generally believed, prostitutes were allowed to live in the *rendezvous,* so long as the house in question occupied an entire building. There were numerous strictures designed to ensure that the establishment would not intrude into the neighborhood. As for the interior regulations, these were listed in an unusually careless fashion, as if the official who drafted them suffered from the tedium of a century's experience: "No gambling, no bars or restaurants, no 'voyeurs,' no turpitudes. No minors."[98] In sum, the *rendezvous* was no more than a successful sleight of hand on the part of a prefecture that was increasingly conscious of public relations.

The bordello, in the traditional closed sense, occupied a peculiar position within the ideology of the regime. Regarded by most prostitution specialists and regulationists as the center of the *régime des moeurs,* as the one essential aspect of the system, it drew a great deal of abolitionist fire. The police, on the other hand, saw the maintenance of the traditional brothel as a distinct second to the possibility of making inroads—they lost all hope of complete control—against clandestinity. They may have regretted their inability to close all prostitutes within bordellos, but they also accepted the impracticality of such a plan. Throughout the nineteenth century, they manipulated the size and form of the bordello to suit perceived needs; and, when the *maison de tolérance* became a liability, in part because of bad publicity, in part because of legal changes, the police simply adjusted their policies and

[98] PP DB 408, circular of 14 February 1900.

rhetoric to suit the new situation. The decline of the *tolérance* and the rise of the *rendezvous* were less attributable to changing tastes than they were to the canniness of the police, who bent all their energies to the preservation, in some form at least, of the *régime des moeurs*.

· 9 ·

Neoregulation and the
End of the Regime

The *police des moeurs* no longer exists; it is dead.
Prefect of Police Lépine, 1904[1]

LEPINE's epitaph was composed in equal parts of irony and
accuracy. To be sure, each passing year of the new century
found the *régime des moeurs* of the nineteenth century more
inappropriate, more out of tune with contemporary mores,
more a liability than an asset. The days of the regime as it
had existed were clearly numbered, the result of nearly three
decades of agitation against it; and yet the partisans of the
regulatory system remained strong enough to help dictate the
terms of the transition. Indeed, the antiregime activism had
in some ways proved beneficial to the system. The attacks
against it had drawn the police together; they had been forced
to articulate their goals. By the end of the century the *régime
des moeurs* had ceased to be presented as a necessary evil, as
it had been regarded early in the century, and had become a
positive good.

[1] Fiaux, *Commission extraparlementaire,* I:490.

ABOLITIONISM

The abolitionist movement in France had not become a co-hesive group until 1874, the year of Josephine Butler's visit. Butler, who spearheaded the repeal campaign against the Contagious Diseases Acts in Britain, made Paris her first stop on a European tour meant to publicize opposition to the system of regulated prostitution and to symbolize the degree to which this system represented a threat to working-class women everywhere. The international scope of the problem was further underlined in 1875, when the first meeting of the British and Continental Federation for the Abolition of the Governmental Regulation of Prostitution was held in Liv-erpool.[2] Butler's campaign would not achieve the repeal of the Contagious Diseases Acts in England until 1886, nor did she achieve very much of a concrete nature in France. Never-theless she had provided a positive, coherent outlet for all those who disliked the *régime des moeurs;* from the 1870s on, the group would gain increasing momentum.

The French faced a number of obstacles to reform, both inherent and accidental. Though there were many active, energetic writers and spokespersons, France unfortunately lacked a single prominent leader, a native Josephine Butler, to focus both the intellectual and the emotional energies of the abolitionists. Yves Guyot and Louis Fiaux were the most prominent writers, publicists, and theoreticians of abolition-ism, each able to move effortlessly from the yellowest hue of journalism to thoughtful, moderate, reasoned analysis; the French feminist Maria Deraismes was active in the French section of the international abolitionist movement.[3] None of

[2] Nancy Boyd, *Three Victorian Women Who Changed Their World* (New York: Oxford University Press, 1982), p. 48.
[3] Bidelman, *Pariahs Stand Up!,* p. 61.

THE END OF THE REGIME

them was able to rise above the sum of their works to embody the movement, as Butler had.

But, to be fair, all would-be Butlers in France, male or female, faced a much more complex battle than the one in England. Butler had a clear goal in the abolition of the Contagious Diseases Acts.[4] French reformers, undecided about the most effective political strategy, divided their efforts between the national and the local level. At the national level abolitionist efforts were virtually without result; the introduction of the topic of prostitution had traditionally been the signal for numerous pleasantries in the Chamber of Deputies. When abolitionists chose to struggle at the more accessible local level, however, it meant that the battle had to be fought over and over again, in each separate municipality. Regulationists were protected by the very fact that prostitution was not in the Penal Code. The Prefecture of Police had recognized this advantage early in the Restoration and had resisted all attempts to pass a law on the subject. Prostitution was an administrative matter and, as such, was virtually impervious to reform attempts.

Nevertheless, those who opposed regulation seemed to be in a much stronger position after the fall of the Second Empire, for it was especially under a republic, with its guarantee of civil rights for all, that the denial of fundamental rights to prostitutes could be viewed as an anomaly. In fact this denial of civil rights was more than that to the abolitionists: it was for them a revived Bastille, a stubborn survival from the old regime. "The former monarchy conceived this matter in a way that can be explained and even justified by the mentality of the epoch," stated Procureur général L. Bulot, "but to maintain this mentality in the institutions of a republic,

[4] For a discussion of Butler, see Walkowitz, *Prostitution and Victorian Society,* pp. 90-112.

of a modern democracy, is a dangerous and unacceptable anachronism."[5]

In their arguments the abolitionists tended to link the regulatory system with what they regarded as another anachronistic survival, the Church's influence in government and society. Thus the abolitionist movement in France, along with the French feminist movement, had a strong anticlerical flavor. In feminist organizations this anticlericalism stemmed from concern about the Church's monopoly over the education of girls, and its presumed monopoly over their thoughts. The traditional hostility of Church leaders to the republic caused many French feminists to demand education for women before they demanded the vote; they feared that granting women the vote too early would simply deliver a large bloc of voters into the hands of their conservative opponents.[6]

The anticlericalism of the abolitionists was an important part of their outlook and provided them with a vocabulary for their grievances. Louis Fiaux cleverly used clerical imagery to describe the *régime des moeurs*. He made Parent-Duchâtelet into "the apostle of regulatory claustration" for his support of the bordellos. Parent's book became the "gospel" of the regulatory system. The theory behind regulated prostitution was its "dogma," with the prefect Mangin as chief apostle.[7] Inscription was the "sacrament" of legalized promiscuity, the

---

[5] Fiaux, *Commission extraparlementaire*, I:449. Corbin makes an important distinction between the "prohibitionism" of Butler's imported variety of abolitionism, with its emphasis on a rigid single standard of morality, and the campaign of the Paris radicals, based on the principle of individual liberty. This latter group, led by Guyot, also hoped to transfer the power of the Prefecture of Police to the elected Municipal Council. Corbin, *Les Filles de noce*, pp. 324-331.

[6] See Bidelman, *Pariahs Stand Up!*, pp. 6-9, and James F. McMillan, *Housewife or Harlot: The Place of Women in French Society, 1870-1940* (New York: St. Martin's Press, 1981), pp. 84-89.

[7] Fiaux, *Commission extraparlementaire*, I:cclxxxviii-cclxxxix; Fiaux, *Les Maisons*, p. 5.

counterpart of the sacrament of marriage. Pronouncements on procedures made by the police were said to be made *textuellement et sacramentallement.* There was an absolute "concordance" in the spirit of all the police regulations and in all the books of the police doctors.[8] The regulatory church was not without its saints and martyrs, as the history of the disease statistics of the *maisons* was in part a "pathological martyrology of the unfortunate creatures interned there during a century." Saint-Lazare, the prison hospital for prostitutes, became the Maison de Géhenne, the place of propitiatory sacrifices for the good of the system. And of course prostitutes could look to their own fearsome Trinity: "the inspectors who arrest them, the doctor who examines them, the *chef de bureau* who condemns them."[9]

The rhetoric had some immediate triumphs. The *Lettres d'un ex-agent des moeurs,* published anonymously in 1878 and 1879, as a supposed confession by a former police officer, detailed the various forms of blackmail, corruption, and illegalities that were routine in the Brigade des moeurs. It was only later that Guyot revealed himself as the author; and this was after the forced resignation of Lecour as head of the Bureau of Morals, a resignation motivated at least in part by Guyot's pamphlet.

Lecour, already the author of several intelligent studies of the regime, took up his pen again to examine what he referred to as a campaign against the Prefecture of Police that, "for several years and notably in 1878, [had] taken on the proportions of a genuine hostility."[10] He was not worried about the British and Continental Federation, "these foreign de-

---

[8] Fiaux, *Principaux pays de l'Europe,* p. 167; Fiaux, *Les Maisons,* pp. 12, 86.

[9] Fiaux, *Commission extraparlementaire,* I:cclxxxviii, xxi; Fiaux, *Principaux pays de l'Europe,* p. xvi.

[10] Lecour, *La Campagne,* p. 1.

fenders of public debauchery and their adherents." His concern was with unfavorable publicity:

> I mean the campaign led by M. Yves Guyot against the Prefecture of Police and whose first and principal attacks had as their object the Service actif des moeurs. It offers the curious spectacle of individual action—laborious, tenacious, violent, vulgar, full of ignorance, [et cetera]— managing, by these proceedings and thanks to circumstances, to associate diverse newspapers with his hostility, to impassion to a certain degree public opinion, to stir up the Chamber [of Deputies], and to constitute a force before which the superior authority, proceeding by means of concessions, appeared for a moment to be on the point of bending.[11]

Lecour's attempt to diffuse Guyot's attack throughout the prefecture, suggesting that the Bureau of Morals was merely and accidentally the first target, was indicative of a clever holding action that the police would maintain for a number of years, implying that the prefecture itself would stand or fall with the Bureau of Morals. This kind of insinuation, combined with the general fear of venereal disease, created a powerful argument in favor of the status quo. But perhaps a greater asset to the regime than its defenders was the nature of the abolitionist rhetoric.

By the late nineteenth century, antiregime propaganda had, for better or worse, settled into two well-worn tracks: the mistaken arrest and the iniquities of bordello life. For the mistaken arrest there was an ever-growing catalogue of examples, collected with gleeful efficiency by the abolitionists; the more tragic the story's end the better. There was Marie Ligeron, for example, a young worker arrested on her own

[11] Ibid., pp. 99-100.

doorstep "at the very moment she left the embrace of her fiancé"; she was held in prison until the intervention of an abolitionist journalist obtained her release. Her short imprisonment had affected her profoundly, both physically and mentally, and she died a short time after, *victime de la police des moeurs*. There was also the case of Amelie Renault, a registered prostitute who left her home at a late hour to get medicine for her sick child. She was arrested and held overnight, unable to persuade anyone to listen to her. Gendarmes escorted her home the next day to verify her story; the child was found dead. She was visited later by an *agent des moeurs,* "who threatened her with the vengeance of his colleagues if she dared to speak of this affair."[12]

This trend in abolitionist literature was essentially a healthy one: the abuses that occurred in the prostitution arrests went to the heart of the regime's denial of the legal rights of women. And, notwithstanding a tendency to slant these stories away from the constant difficulties suffered by prostitutes and toward the plight of innocent women arrested by mistake, there was nevertheless an emphasis on the way in which the regulatory system discriminated against women.

The bordello literature, in contrast, gave free rein to attitudes that bordered on misogyny. The discussions of bordello life, though often based on direct observation, usually went too far at some point. Often, their anxieties about what went on in these housefuls of women alone together sounded suspiciously like worried contemporary insistence on the need to maintain woman's isolation in the home, away from other women. And, too, the bordello literature was as likely to come from the regulatory as from the abolitionist camp. Louis Fiaux's *Les Maisons de tolérance* was probably the strongest example;

[12] Congrès de Genève, Fédération britannique continentale & générale, *Fascicule D: Actes rélatifs à la police des moeurs en France* (Neuchatel: Bureau du bulletin continental, 1877), p. 22.

the next most powerful study was that of Dr. Jeannel, one of the staunchest defenders of the regime. The concentration upon the turpitudes of brothel life, however titillating, served to draw attention away from the regime of exception to which prostitutes as a group were subject. Even more significant, the destruction of the brothel came to the forefront of the abolitionist cause, distracting attention from other, more fundamental issues.

THE EXTRAPARLIAMENTARY COMMISSION

By the turn of the century, the abolitionists considered themselves on the verge of triumph. The abolitionist movement itself, in decline for a number of years, had recently regrouped and intensified its activities. The Prefecture of Police and the Bureau of Morals had been badly scarred by the Forissier affair of 1903, yet another case of mistaken arrest. The affair had resulted in an immediate investigation by the Paris Municipal Council and, more important, in the appointment of an Extraparliamentary Commission to study the *police des moeurs* and draw up a draft proposal for a law. This development seemed to promise, at long last, the inclusion of prostitution in the Penal Code and, consequently, the entry of the prostitute into the common law.

The Extraparliamentary Commission included longtime activists on both sides of the issue (Fiaux, Guyot, Fournier) as well as public functionaries who had shown particular interest in the question: Senator Bérenger; Victor Augagneur, mayor of Lyon; Henri Turot, a member of the Paris Municipal Council; Prefect of Police Lépine (1893-1897, 1899-1913); and Procureur général Bulot, of the Cour d'appel of Paris. Along with these luminaries were some equally distinguished lawyers, deputies, physicians, professors—and one lone woman, Avril de Sainte-Croix. An abolitionist, she also ran the Oeuvre Libératrice, a shelter for prostitutes.[13] The commission's mandate to investigate the regulatory system as well as to draw up a law seemed to promise a wide hearing for the inequities of the regime. Abolitionists took heart from the fact that the commission began on a note of unusual harmony. By unanimous vote, it was declared that "prostitution by women does not constitute a legal offense [*délit*] and does not come under the application of the Penal Code."[14]

It seemed to be a good beginning, but some were not hopeful. During the first session, Augagneur commented with much truth (if little optimism) that "each member already has his mind made up on the question of regulation or abolition;... even the most extended inquiry will modify no opinion." The following November Bulot complained that "the commission talks a lot and never votes."[15] And the unanimous vote on the first proposition was virtually meaningless. It had been drawn up as a simple declarative statement, and in that sense it was, of course, true. Prostitution was not in the Penal Code; to have voted against the resolution would have been to vote in defiance of simple fact. Abolitionists attempted to claim this vote as a victory, and Augagneur later defined it as a repudiation of the *police des moeurs,* which it certainly was not.[16] For the moment, everyone preferred to ignore the fact that regulationists wanted prostitution to be a criminal offense no more than abolitionists, though their motives were different.

Nevertheless, despite the divisions, they struggled through four years and thirty-seven meetings, adjourning on 28 December 1907—and, surprisingly, they came out with a co-

---

[13] See Fiaux, *Commission extraparlementaire,* I:641-647, for a list of commission members.

[14] Ibid., I:13.

[15] Ibid., I:6, 560.

[16] Ibid., I:423.

herent legislative proposal. It explicitly ended administrative internment, the inscription list, and the mandatory medical examination. *Provocation à la débauche* became a crime under certain specified conditions. Soliciting in groups of more than two people, by means of "obscene words," or "with words contrary to public decency," as well as soliciting minors of either sex younger than fifteen years were all forbidden; finally, it was forbidden to solicit near military and maritime establishments, near schools and public assistance offices, or near churches. Those arrested for any of these offenses were to be tried before the Tribunal de police correctionnelle and punished with imprisonment of from six days to two months and a fine of from 16 to 200 francs.

The issue of venereal disease revealed the most obvious cracks in the commission. The bulk of the debate dealt with the reforms to be brought into medical schools and hospitals. Senator Bérenger and Dr. L. Butte of the dispensary had insisted upon including Article 32, which went against the majority of the commission and against the spirit of the proposed law:

> Any individual condemned for solicitation on the public streets or in places freely open to the public or for an offense against morality, who is discovered to have a contagious venereal disease and is unable to prove his voluntary submission to treatment, will be conducted by order of the judge to a hospital and will be kept there until his state of health no longer offers any danger of contagion.[17]

This section seemed to represent a revival of the old regime of mandatory examination and treatment; but it did, after all, include the participation of a judge, and the mandatory

[17] Ibid., III:513

[332]

treatment was to be exacted only against someone who had already been condemned for public debauchery. The abolitionists' rejection of what was, at base, no more than a sensible determination to cure an already imprisoned individual of an ailment showed their extreme sensitivity to the issue; the refusal to cure a prisoner of any other disease, or to cure any other prisoner of venereal disease, would have been regarded as inhumane.

Another area of controversy had to do with the punishment of those who transmitted venereal diseases. This proposal was the embodiment of the concept of *contamination intersexuelle,* long discussed—and not always favorably—in abolitionist circles. It was usually conceived of as a means of combatting the charge that abolitionists were heedless of the dangers of venereal disease; it also clearly had strong moral overtones. Though the details of different proposals varied, the offense of *contamination intersexuelle* would provide the means by which someone who had contracted a venereal disease from another could initiate legal proceedings. The accused would be charged with willful injury, thus permitting the crime to be covered by the Penal Code.[18]

This was the essence of the new draft proposal, and despite the anxiety over Article 32, it represented the abolitionist point of view. The spirit of the law was summed up by this near slogan: "Even when it is admitted that prostitution is not by itself a *délit,* it must be recognized that there are nevertheless some *délits de prostitution.*"[19] In other words, prostitutes were no longer to be condemned for what they were but for what they did; "prostitution," with all its implications as a style and way of life, was replaced with the more specific offense of "provocation." (It should be noted that all provisions of

[18] For the text of the proposal, see ibid., III:503-515.
[19] "Rapport de M. Feuilloley ... sur le projet de loi générale," in ibid., III:516.

this proposal applied to both sexes; men who made obscene remarks to women on the streets would be equally as liable to arrest as professional prostitutes, though it was doubtful that such a law would have been enforced in this way.) The treatment of venereal disease was to be brought into the twentieth century. It was hoped that the stigma would gradually disappear and that this would encourage everyone to seek treatment. This, it was believed, would be far more efficient than attempting to cure everyone through control of the prostitute.

The bill as it was presented to the deputies was a unified whole. It did not attack the problem piecemeal, suggesting minor changes here and there. Rather, it represented an attempt to rethink the problem of prostitution from the beginning; viewed in this light, it was an admirable piece of work. It goes without saying that the bill had not the slightest chance of passage—at least not directly. At about the same time, two related laws were passed, one on *proxénètisme*—the closest lawmakers were able to come to restraining the *maison de tolérance*—and another on the protection of minors. These were the two perennially controversial aspects of the regime, and the two that had from the beginning been subject to changes and reinterpretations.

The failure to pass a law having a direct bearing on prostitution—the Marthe Richard Law, abolishing controlled bordellos, was not passed until after World War II—was discouraging.[20] It seemed that the attempt to bring prostitution within the legal system had failed, justifying the predictions of those who had argued the impossibility of legislating morality. In fact, the abolitionists had been outflanked, even before the investigations began, by something called *néo-réglementarisme*.

[20] Corbin, *Les Filles de noce,* pp. 507-510.

HOLDING THE LINE

Neoregulation was, at base, a determination to retain police control over prostitution, whatever the cost. That was how Fiaux defined it, and it was the basic guiding principle behind all the somewhat diverse modifications collected under this heading.[21] In part, it was an effort to smooth over the worst abuses of the old regime. For example, the 1878 codification of the rules of the *police des moeurs* had provided the means by which a prostitute could appeal her sentence, or an uninscribed woman her inscription. The value of this right of appeal was questioned by some who doubted that prostitutes would get a fair hearing before the police board.[22] Shortly before the Extraparliamentary Commission began to meet, Lépine reformed the *maison de tolérance,* decreeing that no prostitute could be kept in a tolerance against her will simply because of the debt owed to her madam.[23] The most visible and highly publicized reform of neoregulation was the decline of the *maison de tolérance* and the corresponding rise of the *maison de rendezvous.* Lépine's public embrace of the *rendezvous* in 1900 was viewed as a defeat for the prefecture, and it was hailed by most abolitionists as proof that the public had finally developed a healthy revulsion for regulated prostitution.[24] In fact it was a successful public relations gambit on the part of the prefecture, whose policies concerning tolerated houses had never been fully understood; the way had been prepared for this by years of increasingly hysterical rhetoric about the *maison de tolérance.*

There were some qualms about the changed policies of the prefecture. The fundamental problem with the neoregulatory efforts, as critics began to point out, was that all were purely

---

[21] Fiaux, *Commission extraparlementaire,* I:cii-ciii.

[22] Ibid., I:34-35.

[23] Fiaux, *Son abolition,* I:389.

[24] PP DB 408, *règlement* of 14 February 1900.

administrative changes, subject to interpretation by the police and thus free, as always, to be revoked or changed. Even more important was the increasing recognition that neoregulation was less a matter of substantive change than it was a matter of public relations. The changes emerged primarily from dialogues with the Paris Municipal Council, and they were generally no more than sufficient to blunt the demands of the councillors—or so it seemed to the increasingly frustrated abolitionists. The regulatory administration was less Macchiavellian than it occasionally appeared. Throughout the last two decades of the century the administration was fighting a simple holding action, designed to preserve at least a part of the regime.

The prefecture's stance on the *régime des moeurs* was called into question most publicly in 1903-1904, during the investigations by the Municipal Council and the Extraparliamentary Commission; in fact, though, the changes in policy were prefigured in two earlier Municipal Council investigations, one in 1879 and another in 1890. Despite the similarities, the three Municipal Council investigations were quite different in their expectations of the regime—or, perhaps better, of what could be done to change the regime—and this, with their essentially antiregulatory bias, revealed the rapid progress of the abolitionist mentality in the last two decades of the century. All three municipal investigations rested on the council's control over the dispensary budget, a new and threatening tactic. As Dr. Clerc of the dispensary testified, the administration had always shown a "grand liberality" to this establishment, fulfilling "all requests for material or instruments that were made."[25] The threat to stop the flow, combined with a certain assertiveness on the part of the Municipal Council, forced the prefecture to bend.

[25] Conseil municipal de Paris, *Procès-verbal,* p. 54.

The first of these, the investigation that began in 1878, allowed one day to Yves Guyot and another to Emilie de Morsier, who proposed to establish a shelter for girls; aside from these two sessions, the council was excessively deferential to the police. The prefect was allowed to refuse to send six lower-ranking morals agents to testify (on the grounds of a need to preserve "respect for the rules of hierarchy"). Morsier's proposed shelter, to be established with 20,000 francs taken from the regulatory budget, was attacked as having been conceived "in a spirit of hostility to the *police des moeurs*."[26] The council found itself able to achieve agreement only on a single issue, the need to change the personnel of the Bureau of Morals; the morals agents were thus made the scapegoats for the difficulties inherent in the regime itself.[27] Dr. Clerc made a similar suggestion regarding the personnel of the dispensary, suggesting that a competition be held for the appointments or that preference be given to those who had interned at Saint-Lazare, the Lourcine, or other venereal hospitals—in other words, to those students who were likely to know something about venereal disease.[28]

The call for reform was answered almost immediately, though not precisely in the manner envisioned by the council. They had voted in late December 1880 for the disbanding of the Morals Brigade, to be accomplished by 1 January 1882; they made no specific recommendations about what should replace it.[29] On 19 March 1881, Prefect Andrieux (1879-1881)

---

[26] Ibid., pp. 38, 133.

[27] Ibid., session of 7 July 1879.

[28] Ibid., p. 54. This demand was repeated in every subsequent reform proposal. Many specialists suspected that misdiagnosis was common and that the inexperience and lack of training of most dispensary doctors caused them to label as venereal diseases many cases of simple skin rash. William Acton, "De la prostitution considérée au point de vue de l'hygiène publique," *Annales d'hygiène publique et de médecine légale* 46 (1851):39-44.

[29] Fiaux, *Son abolition*, I:635.

issued an *arrêté* that suppressed the Morals Brigade and merged all those officers with the Sûreté. His investigations had convinced him, Andrieux later wrote, that Auguste-François Lerouge, chief of the Morals Brigade at the time of the council inquiry, had allowed "grave abuses" in the service. The real problem, as he noted in his memoirs, was that the Morals Brigade had become a damaging institution from the standpoint of public relations. Its bad reputation hampered its own ability to function, and Andrieux hoped to bolster its activities with the help of the Sûreté: "The truth is that, in suppressing the unpopular denomination of the Brigade des moeurs, I hoped to reinforce at the same time the two services, thus united, and composing a force of 320 men, under the direction of an intelligent as well as experienced chief. The *agents des moeurs* were making only a pretend exit [*fausse sortie*]."[30]

Andrieux's confession of his clever maneuver was included in his memoirs, published only a few years after the events described had taken place. Perhaps in part because of this, later reformers insisted on more substantial proposals, drawing on the accumulated discontent of the medical community, in particular, and to a lesser extent on the increasing attacks on the legality of administrative detention.[31] A proposal for an overhaul of the regulatory system was finally put before the Municipal Council in 1890. The proposal, a compromise distilled from the suggestions of Prefect of Police Henry Lozé (1888-1893), several dispensary physicians, and moderate abolitionists, was eventually voted down by the full council. It is nevertheless of interest because of the indications it provides of what each side was willing to settle for.

The chief aim of the measure was to humanize the treat-

---

[30] Andrieux, *Souvenirs,* II:22-23.

[31] The Académie de médecine, for example, conducted an extensive debate on the subject of regulated prostitution in 1888. See Fiaux, *Son abolition,* I:419-435, 659-662.

ment of venereal disease. The fear that had resulted in wholesale arrests of so-called *insoumises* in an almost blind attempt
to capture contaminated women was giving way, slowly, to
a more scientific approach. According to this new proposal,
prostitutes were to be subjected to one or two weekly examinations.[32] Those discovered to have a venereal disease were
no longer to be conducted immediately to the Saint-Lazare
prison, as they had always been; instead they were to be given
twenty-four hours to report, voluntarily, to one of the new
"sanitary asylums" to be created, under the direction of Public
Assistance rather than the Prefecture of Police. Once in the
hospital, they were to be treated not as prisoners but as regular
patients. And after they had been released, they were to be
directed to the various outpatient venereal clinics to be established in the regular hospitals, where they would receive
free medication and instructions for further treatment. The
clinics, to be open from 9:00 to 11:00 p.m., were a part of a
serious new attempt to provide care for the poor population
in general: "There is a very great interest in permitting an
entire class of patients, low-level clerks, workers who cannot
lose a morning's work to wait in a hospital clinic, to receive
care after the day's labor."[33]

On this basis alone, the proposal marked a clear improvement on past procedures; nevertheless, the habits of thought
created by eighty years of the regulatory system could not be
easily abandoned. Emile Richard, who drew up the draft
proposal for the Municipal Council, found that the system
inexorably re-created itself. It was necessary, Richard believed,

[32] Two for bordello prostitutes, one for *isolées*. For a summary of and
commentary on the proposed revisions, see H. Feulard, "La Question de
la prostitution devant le Conseil municipal de la ville de Paris," *Annales de
dermatologie et de syphiligraphie,* 1, 3rd sér. (1890):932-940. Also see Fiaux,
Son abolition, I:638-642.

[33] Feulard, "La Question," p. 940.

to continue to subject prostitutes to a special surveillance; given that, he decided that the inscription was the only way to ensure that all prostitutes were examined. Then the rest fell into place: "The inscription and the sanitary visit would evidently have no utility if they did not have as a sanction the ability to constrain habitual prostitutes, recognized as diseased, to enter the hospital where they will receive the care that their state requires and from which they can leave only when they no longer offer any danger of immediate contagion."[34] To ensure that everything went as planned, the dispensary would have at its command a new "Sanitary Brigade" of sixty officers, whose principal purpose would be to seek out women who missed their examinations or who failed to report to the sanitary asylums: "These agents should inform themselves of the reason for the delay, inquire, if necessary, about their new address and bring the women to the dispensary." The affairs of the Sanitary Brigade were coordinated through the prefecture, but they were at least meant to be different from the Morals Brigade, in that they were presumably to take into custody only those women in default in medical matters.[35]

This was the extent of the projected improvement. The proposal to end the practice of administrative internment was voted down, and the inscription by office was to be maintained on much the same basis as before, despite an attempt to suppress it. Most important of all, however, was the agreement of the prefect. The only real difference between the proposal as eventually formulated and the version originally proposed by Prefect Lozé was that he suggested the continued treatment of prostitutes in Saint-Lazare. (Lozé's proposal, which in several instances merely repeated standard regime practices, would

[34] Richard, "La Prostitution à Paris," pp. 386, 388, 394.
[35] Fiaux, *Son abolition,* 1:638-642.

further have had the effect of gaining Municipal Council sanction for these activities.) Neither Lozé's nor the Municipal Council's project was passed by the full council, a fact that Fiaux attributed to political maneuverings having little to do with the innate worth of the proposals themselves.[36]

Still, this series of debates had resulted in a new and workable system of venereal disease control. Because of that, the 1890 proposal could only be adjourned, however final its defeat appeared. Another serious discussion of the matter in the Muncipal Council was inevitable; the spark that set it off, in 1903, was the Forissier affair.

A complicated, messy business, the Forissier affair was so covered over with lies and partisan reporting that it is difficult to get to the bottom of it. Two young women had been arrested for solicitation on the street. There was nothing unusual in this, except that the two women were middle class, the sister and fiancée of a young man, Antoine Forissier, who saw the whole thing. Forissier also happened to be a journalist employed by the abolitionist *Lanterne,* Guyot's old newspaper. Forissier publicized the incident, adding that one of the arresting officers was drunk.

The two policemen, in the meantime, had come up with another story. As they told it, they had been conducting a routine arrest in the vicinity of the two young women, who had become agitated at the sight. Thinking that the women were about to faint, the agents had run to their assistance, inadvertently causing them further panic; to corroborate their story, the officers brought in the two registered prostitutes whom they claimed to have been arresting. Prefect Lépine at first backed up the story told by his agents, no doubt suspicious about the coincidence of Forissier's employment, but shortly

---

[36] See ibid., pp. 643-645, for Lozé's proposal; ibid., pp. 383-389, for Fiaux's discussion of the vote on the 1890 proposal.

thereafter he publicly withdrew his support, claiming that he had been deceived.[37]

Lépine did not suffer for this politically; indeed, he played a major role in the Municipal Council investigation, which began immediately, as well as in the Extraparliamentary Commission that followed shortly thereafter. (Not everyone trusted his motives; Henri Turot, a municipal councillor, attributed Lépine's "volte-face" to his sudden realization that the abolitionists were determined, this time, to bring matters to a definitive end.)[38] The truth about the Forissier incident did not really matter, since it provided an excuse for the long-overdue examination of the system. The fact that outrage of this magnitude could only be generated by the arrest of middle-class women was, of course, one of the major problems of the regime.

The Municipal Council debates were in large part motivated by a determination to have something concrete to present to the Extraparliamentary Commission. The hope of many of the abolitionists, at least, was that Paris could take the lead in the nationwide suppression of the *régime des moeurs,* just as that city had led in its creation. The resulting proposal, voted on 18 March 1904, revived the medical proposals suggested in 1890, including treatment in a "sanitarium" rather than in Saint-Lazare prison as well as the establishment of free venereal clinics in as many hospitals as possible. The council further voted to set up special dispensaries for distributing medicines in the most populated areas of the city. Even more encouraging was the fact that the two most critical aspects of the regime were addressed for the first time. The

---

[37] Ibid., pp. 390-394. The two policemen were fired and brought before the Tribunal correctionnel; two years later they were rehired by the prefecture, one to guard a cemetery, the other to guard the morgue.

[38] Henri Turot, *Le Prolétariat de l'amour* (Paris: Librairie universelle, 1904), p. 339.

prefect agreed to end both the practice of administrative detention and the inscription.

The regime apparently was over; but once again, it displayed a tendency to re-create itself. Instead of the inscription it was decided that each prostitute would make a *déclaration* (to the Prefecture of the Seine) of her intention to become a prostitute. Instead of the old, discredited inscription *carte*, she would carry a *certificat de santé*, verifying her state of health. She had to be examined twice a week if she was younger than twenty-five, once a week if she was under thirty, and twice a month beyond that age. The key to the reform was, of course, the problem of whether or not the *déclaration* was to be voluntary rather than imposed. This issue was left undefined by the Municipal Council; questions as narrow as this, of course, had always been administrative matters.

Nevertheless, the promised end of administrative detention (for offenses involving public order), the end of the prison hospital, and the beginning of outpatient medical care, were unmistakable improvements. Neither side was completely happy with the final proposals, but the sessions ended in an atmosphere of rare good feeling. The abolitionists believed that they had brought prostitutes back "within the law," in that the offenses they committed, offenses against public order, would be handled no differently from the same offenses committed by anyone else.[39]

In fact, there was only one remaining issue of serious contention: the *maison de tolérance,* a particularly controversial subject because of the way it had been portrayed through several decades of abolitionist literature. The problem was discussed most completely in the Extraparliamentary Commission, whose hearings for a time overlapped those of the Municipal Council. The discussions were heated. Avril de

[39] Fiaux, *Son abolition,* I:390-417, and for a copy of the resolutions, I:646-651.

Sainte-Croix was inevitably rebuked for "thinking like a woman," in her "emotional," instinctive dislike of the bordello. "What dominates her sentiments more than her argument," her critic wrote, "although she does not forget the question of hygiene, is a sentiment of disgust and revulsion against the legal existence of establishments where, for the needs and pleasures of the man, women are maintained in the most degrading conditions, such that their recovery is impossible."[40]

It was a curious defense to make of the institution. More to the point was the speech by Lépine, who launched into a skillful defense of the prefecture's "new" institution, the *maison de rendezvous.* He used a shrewd marketplace technique, first making an impossible bid and then revealing his final offer. His impossible offer was the enclosure of all prostitutes in closed *maisons de tolérance,* or *prostitution à huis-clos.* This, he suggested, was the ideal solution, since bordellos offered the surest guarantee of public health; he asserted that not a single case of venereal disease had been discovered among bordello prostitutes during the previous year. Bordellos were also superior from the point of view of public order, since they kept women off the streets. Faced as he was with a draft proposal whose wording would have deprived him not only of the *tolérance* but also of the *rendezvous,* Lépine tried not altogether successfully to convey the disaster that would result:

> *Lépine:* Supposing the *maison de tolérance* suppressed, what will become of the dispersed *pensionnaires?* They will inundate our streets. . . .
> *Turot:* There are 380 women in bordellos in Paris. . . .
> *Lépine:* And they are just so many more recruits for

[40] Fiaux, *Commission extraparlementaire,* II:68.

the sidewalks, soliciting young men, scandalizing virtuous young women, young girls![41]

Having made his impossible offer, Lépine then skillfully retreated to the conditions he wanted:

There is between the *maison de tolérance* and the *maison de rendezvous* a major difference, which the speaker cannot stress too much: it is that one is an *internat,* and the other is an *externat.* From this definition, from this organization, flow considerable consequences. In the *maison de tolérance,* the *fille* is lodged there and, the speaker agrees, kept there several days or several weeks at a time; . . . here prostitution is, in some sense, imposed. In the *maison de rendezvous,* on the contrary, the women simply come to make their *passes;* they come if they want and only as much as they want; if for whatever reason they no longer want to return, they do not return. It is an entirely free and voluntary place of prostitution.[42]

[41] Ibid., II:110.

[42] Ibid., II:110-111. Corbin believes (to compress almost unmercifully his complex and skillful argument) that the change in the *maison de tolérance* was a result of changing consumer tastes: "La maison, 'égout séminal' où l'on vient satisfaire un besoin physiologique, n'attire plus guère; en revanche le besoin de séduction s'est considérablement développé. Dans les milieux populaires comme au sein de la petite bourgeoisie, la clandestine séduit chaque jour davantage, tandis que les nudités et les oripeaux des bordels suscitent désormais le dégoût." *Les Filles de noce,* p. 175. Consequently the regulatory system suffered a defeat, insofar as it was forced to accept the *maison de rendezvous* and to agree to the "relative opening up" of all tolerated houses. Ibid., p. 178. As I have tried to show, the apparent decline of the *maison de tolérance* (never as "closed" as popular opinion would have it) is explained primarily by two factors: the changing legal situation, which made the tolerance undesirable, and the manipulation both of statistics and of public pronouncements by the prefecture, as it attempted to adjust the system to changing times. Public acceptance of the *maison de rendezvous* was far from a defeat for the prefecture, for the essentials of the system had been preserved: registration, carding, and instant accessibility to people and places.

But what had been gained in freedom, Lépine suggested, had been lost in disease control; the public's health was not so well protected as in the "old *maison de tolérance,*" but it was more protected than with the prostitution of *isolées* or clandestines. Further, Lépine added, he had ended all the regulatory instructions that had formerly guided bordellos—except one: "The prefecture remains intransigent on the hygiene question, on the question of the obligatory visit."[43] He had, he admitted, made one change in his original pronouncement on the *rendezvous.* Those *maisons de rendezvous* which cost at least 40 francs a night had been off-limits to the police; now, they too were to be subjected to regular surveillance, in order to protect the public health. (The new circular noted that "undoubtedly these expensive houses are frequented by a smaller and more specialized public, but one that, *apart from the question of the restraint to be observed in certain cases* [emphasis mine], nonetheless has the right to protection . . . in the matter of health.")[44]

Further defenses were made of bordellos, including the right of prostitutes to live together, if they so desired,[45] but the central defense of the regime was the argument in behalf of the public health. The regulationists were now in a far stronger position than they had been for a long time, particularly in terms of public relations. The changes made by the prefecture, and its apparent willingness to entertain reforms, meant that the regulationists by this time had made a strategic retreat to a position that was more defensible than any they had ever held. They now insisted primarily on the regular medical examination and on the inscription as the obviously necessary means of carrying out the examination. Even the

---

[43] Fiaux, *Commission extraparlementaire,* II:110-111.

[44] PP DB 408, note of 31 March 1900.

[45] Fiaux, *Commission extraparlementaire,* II:116. This defense was made by Senator Bérenger.

abolitionists, particularly moderates, found it difficult to reject this position completely.[46]

In return for relatively minor sacrifices—including the *maison de tolérance*—the regulationists now occupied a position at least as attractive as that of the abolitionists. Since the modifications made in the *maison de tolérance* had presumably stripped the Paris regime of its most offensive and least defensible aspects, the "insalubrious industry" argument could be presented with greater force. It was true, admitted the regulationists, that prostitutes were not the only ones with venereal disease. They were, however, the only ones who engaged in sexual commerce for a living, and they would clearly have more sexual contacts than a private individual. A government that would allow prostitutes to go unchecked would be abrogating its responsibility. Against this logic the abolitionists could only make the probably accurate but rather lame-sounding assertion that if the venereal disease hospitals were no longer prisons, more prostitutes would go to them voluntarily. During the testimony of the Extraparliamentary Commission, Lépine suggested that this belief took no account of the realities of the situation. "Can one believe that they would go to the hospital if the *souteneur* needed . . . to keep them at home?" he asked. Moreover, the abolitionists seemed to assume a higher degree of education than actually existed; the women of the lowest classes, he argued, would not even conceive of the possibility of curing themselves.[47] Consequently the police would do it for them.

---

[46] Dr. Fournier and Senator Bérenger (in a law proposed, but not passed, in 1895) suggested very similar legal reforms that would have brought the *police des moeurs* into the legal system. Both proposals preserved intact the two major supports of the old system: the inscription and medical surveillance through the mandatory examination. See the discussion of both proposals in Dolléans, *La Police des moeurs,* pp. 49-60. The prefecture around the turn of the century, under Lépine, particularly stressed the inscription; note the inscription rate for *insoumises* in Table 23.

[47] Fiaux, *Commission extraparlementaire,* I:379-380.

A CHANGE OF ATTITUDE

Only two laws concerning prostitution were passed at this time, one before and one after the commission's hearings, and neither bore directly on the treatment of prostitutes. The 1903 law was against *proxénètes* and *souteneurs,* and it essentially repeated Articles 334 and 335 of the Penal Code against the prostitution, or "incitement to debauchery," of minors. The purpose was to prevent the selling of minors in bordellos; but legal prohibitions against this practice had been available and unenforced throughout the century. *Souteneurs* were also to be punished for conducting their trade, by imprisonment from three months to two years, by a fine of from 100 to 1,000 francs, and by "banishment" from their locality for five to ten years.[48]

The second major law to be passed around this time was the Law of 11 April 1908, concerning the prostitution of minors. It codified long police practice, providing for the notification of the parents of prostitutes younger than age nineteen, and also allowed the parents to request the administrative detention of wayward children. However, young prostitutes were no longer to be inscribed; instead, their cases would come before a civil tribunal, where it would be decided whether to put the prostitute in the custody of her parents or to send her to a special reform institution.[49]

Both laws included overdue reform measures; but the control of prostitution had always been a matter of administration

[48] Ibid., II:914-917. The new law included Lépine's reform of the bordello: "Quiconque aura, par les mêmes moyens [violences, menaces, abus d'autorité], retenu contre son gré, même pour cause de dettes contractées, une personne même majeure, dans une maison de débauche où l'aura contrainte à se livrer à la prostitution."

[49] Ibid., III:529-533. Fiaux believed that the police of Paris deliberately tried to sabotage the law for the protection of minors by refusing to arrest or take any responsibility for minor girls, thus allowing the situation to deteriorate. III:79-80.

rather than law, and administrative procedures in contrast showed little change, particularly in the critical matter of administrative detention. In an interview published shortly after the beginning of the commission, the *chef de service* revealed little of the new attitude that had supposedly accompanied Lépine:

> Today I saw the following case. A *fille inscrite,* recognized as syphilitic several months ago, was arrested and sent to Saint-Lazare to spend fifteen days in administrative punishment for having refused to come to the examinations. At Saint-Lazare she again refused to allow herself to be examined. When she finished her prison term, she was taken to the dispensary; she still refused to allow herself to be examined. There is every reason to suppose that she carries an infectious disease. Someone asked me what to do. I responded: "You will take her to the depot; you will try to reprimand her; you will tell her that I will send her to Saint-Lazare again if she does not want to be examined."[50]

Ironically, the woman in question was suffering largely because of an earlier reform. A regulation of 1878 had advised physicians to proceed no further if a woman resisted medical examination; the police in these cases simply held the woman in jail until she became "reasonable."[51]

It is possible to cite many examples of this sort, but the following exchange, during the thirteenth session of the Extraparliamentary Commission, reveals not only the continued existence of arbitrary practices but also an astonishing lack

[50] Quoted from the *Bulletin de la Société des prisons* (janvier 1904):62-63, in ibid., I:584-585. The *chef* denied having said this.

[51] BN 8° Z. Le Senne 14255, *règlement* of October 1878. "Bien qu'il ne se soit produit aucun cas où la visite corporelle ait été faite de force, il sera recommandé au service médical de s'abstenir d'y procéder dans le cas où il rencontrerait une résistance."

of sensitivity, perhaps stemming from confidence, on the prefect's part:

> *Sainte-Croix:* [I] would like to pose a question to M. Lépine: What do you do, M. le Préfet, when there is a denunciation against a particular woman in a *maison de rendezvous?* Do you have her arrested?
> *Lépine:* Certainly, I arrest her first of all, then have the denounced woman examined.
> *Sainte-Croix:* ... But, M. le Préfet, if the woman you have arrested is healthy, in what juridical situation do you find yourself in regard to her, since prostitution, even before the vote of the commission, was not considered a *délit?*
> *Lépine:* I quite simply have the right to arrest this woman because she prostitutes herself, because she has been reported to me as prostituting herself.[52]

After the excitement of the investigations was over, the prefecture quietly returned to other practices of the old system. The inscription—they still called it that—was still involuntary, as was administrative detention for reasons of health. An *arrêté* of August 1908 established a new *Tribunal administratif* to hear the cases of prostitutes and *insoumises,* replacing the Commission spéciale first instituted in 1878. The change admittedly was for the convenience of the prefecture rather than for the women: instead of pulling several regular officers off active duty to sit on the commission, the tribunal would now hire retired police officers.[53]

But it was the *maison de rendezvous* that showed the greatest

---

[52] Fiaux, *Commission extraparlementaire,* II:112.

[53] PP DB 408, *arrêté* of 4 August 1908. The two new *assesseurs* on the commission were to be chosen "parmi d'anciens Commissaires de police de la ville de Paris ou d'anciens employés supérieurs de la Préfecture de police." The Conseil d'état abolished the new tribunal in 1911. Corbin, *Les Filles de noce,* p. 472.

continuity. A routine regulation of 4 April 1912 showed just how little it differed from the regular *tolérance*. *Tenancières* (no longer authorized, but merely required to make a declaration) were held to the following rules, among others:

V. *Tenancières* are forbidden to cause to stand in front of the door, for purposes of solicitation, either *pensionnaires* [*sic*] or domestics of the establishment. . . .

VIII. The *tenancière* of the *maison de rendezvous* is provided with a *livre de police* [*sic*] on which will be inscribed the surnames, first names, and ages of the *pensionnaires*. They will be required to indicate with the greatest care the dates of entry and departure of each of them.

IX. Without exception, the *pensionnaires* of the *maisons de débauche* [*sic*] will be subject, each week, to a medical examination. The discovery of illness will be immediately reported by the doctor to the Bureau administratif des moeurs [*sic*], and the *tenancières* should bring venereal *filles* to the dispensary.[54]

The regulation was signed by Lépine.

The evident transformation of the *maison de rendezvous* into the *maison de tolérance* was perhaps the clearest betrayal by the neoregulationists. Lépine had in the beginning made much of the freedom and anonymity of these places, portraying them as the harbingers of a new era in prostitution control. When he had "discovered" that *maisons de rendezvous* kept registers of the women who worked in them, he had ordered these registers destroyed.[55] Fiaux remembered Lépine's enthusiasm in this regard during the Municipal Council debates: "As for the registers, photographs, statistical albums of the *maisons de rendezvous,* we have destroyed them, we threw

---

[54] PP DB 408, *règlement* of 4 April 1912 concerning *maisons de rendezvous.*
[55] Turot, *Le Prolétariat,* p. 329.

them into the fire when the investigation began!"[56] In the absence of a law, it was easy for the prefecture to fall back into old administrative habits.

Neoregulation had achieved what Prefect Anglès had wanted at the beginning of the Restoration; it provided the *police des moeurs* with an official sanction outside the Prefecture of Police. In this case the approval had been granted by the Municipal Council, rather than by the French government, but the general discussion of prostitution in the Extraparliamentary Commission contributed to the impression that the problem of prostitution had been thoroughly aired. And in a sense it had: no longer were there regulationists on one side and abolitionists on the other; instead, there was an entire spectrum of positions. On the regulatory side, there were still those who preferred the status quo. Senator Bérenger and Dr. Fournier favored something called legal regulation, a system that would have written into law the existing regulations but would have required a judge to preside over all matters of punishment and inscription. Libertarians claimed for prostitutes the freedom from all special measures, and *suppressistes* wanted to forbid all prostitution entirely, imprisoning prostitutes for the fact of their occupation alone and driving them all off the streets. This group was on nobody's side, although somebody must have noted, in this precedent-laden issue, that their ideas were reminiscent of the capitularies of Charlemagne.[57]

Many would-be reformers attempted to place the *régime des moeurs* in some kind of historical context, usually to emphasize its obsolescence in modern society. "We have revived, for prostitutes, the *lettres de cachet* of the old regime," noted one such critic, "and we have made them more terrible, in

[56] Fiaux, *Son abolition,* I:403.

[57] Ibid., I:626. For further discussion of the proposals of Fournier and Bérenger, see Dolléans, *La Police des moeurs,* pp. 49-60.

that they are delivered by a subaltern."[58] The historian Edouard Dolléans emphasized that the regulatory system represented a kind of traditional discrimination: "The *police des moeurs* is a vestige of the antagonisms of sex and class that are perpetuated in the social state as in the collective conscience; . . . Enacted in the interest of the man . . . the regulationist measures strike only the woman by reason of sex. But, by reason of class, the police strike only poor women, only the feminine proletariat." The *police des moeurs*, continued Dolléans, was a singular holdover from earlier eras. It was a remnant of a time when women were property, when physical strength was the most important determinant of status; and, perhaps most relevant here, it was an unsightly remnant of the old regime:

> The politics of the old regime in the matter of morals conformed to the general spirit of the legislation, which took classes and persons into consideration; privilege and the *arbitraire* were principles of public law. The Revolution proclaimed the principle of civil equality and declared that henceforth people would be punished because of their actions and not because of their *qualité*. However, the *police des moeurs* was reorganized in 1802 and prostitutes remain submitted to the same regime of exception and *arbitraire*. . . . The law should strike people not because of their *qualité* but because of their actions.[59]

This kind of criticism implied that the *régime des moeurs* was merely a remnant of the old regime and could simply be abolished. But perhaps more to the point was Dolléans' further contention that the regulationist controversy represented two distinct tendencies in French life and thought,

[58] Jules Justin, *La Liberté individuelle et la police des moeurs* (Dijon: Carré, 1894), p. 120.
[59] Dolléans, *La Police des moeurs,* pp. 4-6, 11, 17.

both of them very much a part of contemporary life. The first such tendency, authoritarian and paternalistic, was marked by its adherence to traditional roles and values, its devotion to rigid codes of behavior. The other stemmed from the revolutionary tradition, embodying the ideals of liberty, individuality, and equality before the law. Though Dolléans was clearly partisan, he nevertheless managed to provide a judicious analysis of the motives of both sides. "The ideas of social justice, of liberty, and of sexual equality," he wrote, "inspire abolitionism, while regulation supports itself on the concepts of public morality and social hygiene. . . . Regulation possesses an internal logic that is progressively developed in all its consequences. Circumscribed first of all to prostitution, little by little it extends its domain to extralegal sexual relations, then even to legal relations. This doctrine has as a final ideal the control of every sexual act that concerns the future of the race."[60]

It was a clearheaded analysis, but by the time it appeared (1903) the two sides had already begun to approach each other. Indeed, the very expansion of regulationist concerns to all issues of sexuality, foreseen by Dolléans, served to take some pressure off prostitution itself and, similarly, blunted abolitionist demands. Dr. Alfred Fournier, one of the most prominent regulationists not connected with the administration, was concerned enough to found his own organization in 1888, a group called the French Society for Sanitary and Moral Prophylaxis. The title was yet another reinvocation of the twin goals of the *régime des moeurs,* but with a difference. For Fournier, the problem now was not primarily that of prostitution but rather the erosion of respect for traditional values. "I hear little preaching about continence, chastity, virtue, respect for women, early marriages," he wrote, com-

[60] Ibid., p. 12.

plaining that literature and the theater glorified adultery and sexual freedom. "There still remain among the middle classes a few family circles in which the mother, by her example and guidance, supervises the moral education of the child. But among the people, where the hard struggle for daily bread keeps the father and mother away from the household, what becomes of the moral education of the child, and still more of the young man?"[61]

Such a complaint was not uncongenial to abolitionists; they had long protested the double standard at the base of the regulatory system, implied by the very fact of setting apart certain women for the illicit sexual use of any man.[62] There were other ways in which some abolitionists and some regulationists approached each other, in their common desire to end open soliciting on the streets, in their common concern to strike against those *souteneurs* who made too obvious a business of prostitution. The prefecture's long-term uneasiness over its role in the prostitution of minors was partially assuaged by the new law that allowed for administrative detention of wayward girls, also a reform desired by abolitionists.

And, too, there was increasing cynicism over the extent to which reforms were genuinely possible. The abolitionist protest against the *tolérance* had apparently been answered by the *rendezvous*, a reform soon shown to be an empty one. The problem of the arbitrary arrest and detention, long the most serious abuse of the system, could only be solved by the proposal to bring all cases involving prostitutes before the

[61] Fournier, *Treatment and Prophylaxis,* p. 491.

[62] During the Municipal Council investigation of 1879, for example, Guyot had attacked Lecky's famous characterization of the prostitute as the "priestess of humanity," set apart so that other women could remain pure. See Conseil municipal de Paris, *Procès-verbal,* p. 90. And see William Edward Hartpole Lecky, *History of European Morals,* 2 vols. (New York: D. Appleton and Co., 1898), II:282-283.

appropriate judicial tribunals. A law professor at the University of Paris, while upholding the principle of this reform, suggested that it would make little difference to the prostitutes themselves, whatever coherence and consistency it might lend to the legal system of France:

> What is going to be changed in the current state of affairs? Without doubt, we will have rendered homage to the principle of judicial competence; we will have charged the tribunals with one more duty, a duty they do not want, that they are badly prepared to fill; and if we are persuaded that they will bring to these cases a spirit of justice and humanity, we know very well that they will have no other basis on which to rest their judgments than the testimony and the depositions of the policemen, before which they will bow, as today the administration bows.[63]

Even in the midst of all the doubts, however, no one would have argued that the neoregulatory regime that was taking shape in the early twentieth century, similar in so many ways to that of the nineteenth century, was identical to it. The greatest difference between the two was also the most intangible, the hardest to pin down: namely, the change in attitude on the part of those who did the policing. The peculiar moral intensity of the nineteenth century had marked the regime, providing it with a distinctive edge, despite procedural similarities to the past and present. The regulatory system had seemed to provide a practical means of controlling venereal disease and maintaining order; and yet the disease statistics and the crowded streets showed that neither was being done. The failures had been attributed not to the impossibility of the task but rather to insufficient zeal on the part of the

---

[63] R. Saleille, "Opinion," cited in Fiaux, *Son abolition,* I:627.

agents and, later, to the moral support granted prostitutes by the abolitionists. Those responsible for controlling prostitution had lived with the constant desire for more money, more effort, more agents, more cooperation, more efficiency—all of which would allow them to achieve the goal they had set themselves, the moral and physical prophylaxy of society.

This sense of urgency was gone by the twentieth century. The change was attributable to a number of things, both major and minor—changing attitudes toward women, toward sexuality, and toward the proletariat, the rebuilding of parts of the city during the Second Empire, and a more practical approach to disease control. The years spent by the Prefecture of Police jousting with the abolitionists had resulted in a softening of positions, and an exchanging of ideas, on both sides. The abolitionists came to accept the "insalubrious industry" arguments as the regulationists stopped insisting upon the need to exclude prostitutes from civil law.

But perhaps most important was the fact that, for both sides, the problem of prostitution moved off center stage and became a peripheral issue, no longer able to stand alone as a symbol of social control and the relations between sexes and classes. The police had once believed they were cleansing society when they arrested prostitutes. Somehow, for whatever combination of reasons, they had stopped believing it; and when they stopped believing it, the *régime des moeurs* of the nineteenth century was over.

APPENDIX A

Arrest and Inscription
Statistics

o   o   o

TABLE 27
Size of the Inscription List in Nineteenth-Century Paris

Year	Inscribed	Filles Isolées		Filles de Maison	
		Number	Percentage	Number	Percentage
1812	1,293	593	45.9	700	54.1
1813	1,676	976	58.2	700	41.8
1814	1,905	1,210	63.5	695	36.5
1815	1,854	1,162	62.7	692	37.3
1816	2,185	1,526	69.8	659	30.2
1817	2,412	1,812	75.1	600	24.9
1818	2,586	2,118	81.9	468	18.1
1819	2,606	2,136	82.0	470	18.0
1820	2,746	2,293	83.5	453	16.5
1821	2,913	2,518	86.4	395	13.6
1822	2,902	2,581	88.9	321	11.1
1823	2,709	2,422	89.4	287	10.6
1824	2,653	2,395	90.3	258	9.7
1825	2,623	2,348	89.5	275	10.5
1826	2,495	2,218	88.9	277	11.1
1827	2,472	2,167	87.7	304	12.3
1828	2,663	2,329	87.5	334	12.5
1829	2,843	2,137	75.2	706	24.8
1830	3,028	1,976	65.3	1,052	34.7
1831	3,261	2,189	67.1	1,071	32.9
1832	3,558	2,539	71.4	1,019	28.6
1833[a]	3,723	—	—	—	—
1834	3,782	—	—	—	—
1835	3,813	—	—	—	—
1836	3,818	—	—	—	—
1837	3,875	—	—	—	—
1838	3,990	—	—	—	—
1839	3,969	—	—	—	—
1840	3,928	—	—	—	—
1841	3,886	—	—	—	—
1842	3,841	—	—	—	—

TABLE 27 (*Continued*)

Year	Inscribed	Filles Isolées		Filles de Maison	
		Number	Percentage	Number	Percentage
1843	3,821	—	—	—	—
1844	3,862	—	—	—	—
1845	3,967	—	—	—	—
1846	4,160	—	—	—	—
1847	4,285	—	—	—	—
1848	4,275	—	—	—	—
1849	4,168	—	—	—	—
1850	4,358	—	—	—	—
1851	4,410	—	—	—	—
1852	4,302	—	—	—	—
1853	4,218	—	—	—	—
1854	4,232	—	—	—	—
1872[b]	4,242	3,116	73.5	1,126	26.5
1873	4,603	3,460	75.2	1,143	24.8
1874	4,567	3,458	75.7	1,109	24.3
1875	4,545	3,393	74.7	1,152	25.3
1876	4,493	3,333	74.2	1,160	25.8
1877	4,297	3,127	72.8	1,170	27.2
1878	4,157	3,030	72.9	1,127	27.1
1879	3,991	2,648	66.3	1,343	33.7
1880	3,582	2,475	69.1	1,107	30.9
1881	3,160	2,103	66.6	1,057	33.4
1882	2,839	1,723	60.7	1,116	39.3
1883	2,825	1,786	63.2	1,039	36.8
1884	2,917	1,956	67.1	961	32.9
1885	3,911	2,998	76.7	913	23.3
1886	4,319	3,405	78.8	914	21.2
1887	4,681	3,755	80.2	926	19.8
1888	4,591	3,819	83.2	772	16.8
1889	4,951	4,260	86.0	691	14.0
1890	4,770	4,107	86.1	663	13.9

TABLE 27 (*Continued*)

Year	Inscribed	Filles Isolées		Filles de Maison	
		Number	Percentage	Number	Percentage
1891	5,020	4,338	86.4	682	13.6
1892	5,004	4,408	88.1	596	11.9
1893	4,793	4,253	88.7	540	11.3
1894	5,104	4,574	89.6	530	10.4
1895	5,750	5,214	90.7	536	9.3
1896	5,700	5,215	91.5	485	8.5
1897	5,233	4,737	90.5	496	9.5
1898	6,018	5,539	92.0	479	8.0
1899	6,180	5,690	92.1	490	7.9
1900	6,222	5,718	91.9	504	8.1

SOURCES: For the years 1812-1854, A.-J.-B. Parent-Duchâtelet, *De la prostitution dans la ville de Paris,* 2 vols. (Paris: J.-B. Baillière, 1857), I:32, 36, 668-669; for 1872-1900, Henri Turot, *Le Prolétariat de l'amour* (Paris: Librairie universelle, 1904), pp. 131, 134, 172.

[a] Full information not available for all years.

[b] The numbers given as totals may vary from source to source, depending upon whether those gathering the data took the total at the beginning or the end of the year or whether, as Parent-Duchâtelet did, they averaged the monthly totals.

Table 28
Voluntary Dispensary Examinations
(no. visits/no. sick)

	Sunday	Monday	Tuesday	Wednesday	Thursday	Friday	Saturday	Total
August 1821								
First week	—		—	—	58/1	85/5	62/3	250/11
Second week	45/2		73/5	60/4	71/7	46/2	48/2	304/22
Third week	6/2		80/6	55/7	a	74/4	50/2	323/21
Fourth week	64/2		91/6	93/6	65/3	57/2	78/8	384/20
Fifth week			156/9	161/3	141/3	136/4	101/3	695/22
TOTAL VISITS/SICK								1,956/96
September 1821								
First week	43/4		86/10	70/5	59/2	57/3	58/2	435/23
Second week	62/1		65/6	66/3	40/0	56/4	42/1	317/17
Third week	48/3	13/2	88/5	70/1	71/2	68/3	77/1	448/15
Fourth week	61/1		103/3	125/4	126/3	122/5	125/2	762/20
TOTAL VISITS/SICK								1,962/75
October 1821								
First week	—		58/6	80/4	68/1	50/3	53/5	354/22
Second week	45/3		72/8	62/4	81/5	47/0	52/5	370/24
Third week	56/2		78/3	63/7	—	58/2	58/2	313/18
Fourth week	62/4		101/4	95/1	73/5	85/3	103/1	587/17
Fifth week	130/3		117/0	118/5	89/2	—	—	324/7
TOTAL VISITS/SICK								1,948/88

	Sunday	Monday	Tuesday	Wednesday	Thursday	Friday	Saturday	Total
November 1821								
First week					46/1	54/4	51/4	112/6
Second week	61/2		85/5	50/6	39/2	56/0	52/3	339/21
Third week	52/2		66/3	38/6	63/5	60/5	38/4	291/18
Fourth week	54/3		87/4	77/2			75/2	461/19
Fifth week	99/1		135/4	140/6	141/6	164/4	—	580/20
TOTAL VISITS/SICK								1,783/84
December 1821								
First week	55/8		72/6	65/0	62/4	63/3	43/4	420/29
Second week	60/4		79/4	60/5	59/4	64/2	—	315/15
Third week	53/0		61/6	67/4	—	—	—	
Fourth week	36/3		134/3	—	138/6	127/4	112/3	804/28
Fifth week	151/3		142/9	—	—			
TOTAL VISITS/SICK								1,703/85

Source: AN F⁷ 3875.

Note: The report for each day actually listed the women who were examined the day before. The dispensary was closed on Sunday.

a Dispensary closed on August 15 to celebrate Assumption of the Virgin Mary.

TABLE 29

Prostitution Arrests, 1857-1894

Year	All Arrests[a]	Insoumise Arrests	
		Number	Percentage
1857	7,471	1,405	18.5
1858	6,206	1,158	18.7
1859	8,071	1,528	18.9
1860	9,696	1,650	17.0
1861	7,382	2,322	31.5
1862	9,843	2,987	30.3
1863[b]	6,774	2,124	31.4
1867	6,620	2,018	30.5
1868	7,500	2,077	27.7
1869	6,788	1,999	29.4
1870	7,841		
1871[b]	7,967		
1873	11,218	3,319	29.6
1874	12,608	3,338	26.5
1875	15,415	3,152	20.4
1876	12,757	2,349	18.4
1877	12,147	2,582	21.3
1878	12,094	3,599	29.8
1879	9,173	2,105	22.9
1880[b]	10,232	3,504	34.2
1885	12,761	2,989	23.4
1886	17,643	2,707	15.3
1887	20,009	2,218	11.1
1888	16,746	1,932	11.5
1889	20,242	2,511	12.4
1890	22,161	2,542	11.5

Year	All Arrests[a]	Insoumise Arrests	
		Number	Percentage
1891	21,977	2,408	11.0
1892	16,122	1,611	10.0
1893	22,797	3,208	14.1
1894	29,695	3,023	10.2

SOURCES: For the years 1857-1871, PP DB 408, *Statistique d'entrée au Dépôt des filles publiques;* for 1873-1880, Louis Fiaux, *La Police des moeurs en France et dans les principaux pays de l'Europe* (Paris: E. Dentu, 1888), p. 174; for 1885-1894, PP DB 408, *Renseignements demandés par M. Fiaux,* 22 October 1895.

[a] Prostitutes sent on to Prefecture of Police.

[b] Information not available for all years.

APPENDIX B

Letters from
Revolutionary Prisons

THE following letters were written by prostitutes detained in prison in the 1790s and have been included here because of the rarity of such communications from lower-class women. The arrest records, inevitably filtering the actions and words of prostitutes through the eyes of the police, emphasized the unusual violence that punctuated the prostitute's life. The letters that follow, sent from Parisian prisons during the Reign of Terror, paradoxically suggest the normality, the prosaic matter-of-factness, of their authors' lives in the face of extraordinary circumstances.

No great claims can be made for these letters; they were preserved randomly, scattered among the correspondence of people from all ranks of life. The letters are biased, for all were written by imprisoned women anxious to get out of jail. Still, they are valuable as firsthand statements. The women wrote what they believed the authorities wanted to hear, but inadvertently they revealed many other things as well. If nothing else, these letters highlight the continuity of the problems faced by prostitutes, even through war, revolution, and the changing attitudes of their betters.

Despite the fact that most of the prostitutes to be discussed here were arrested during the high point of the Revolution, their misadventures were not overtly political, though they may have been considered "counterrevolutionary" in the heat of the moment. The one exception among these nonpolitical prisoners was Marie Antoinette Bartellemy, a laundress who drunkenly managed to turn a routine morals arrest into an affair of state. She was lucky. Had the timing of her offense been different, she might well have gone before the Revolutionary Tribunal.

Bartellemy was a thirty-year-old native-born Parisian, arrested as a prostitute on the night of 1 Messidor Year II (19 June 1794) during a regular *visite de nuit*. She was taken to a local police post where, "seeing that she was going to be conducted to the Salpêtrière prison, she asked instead to go to the Petite Force; on being refused, she flew into a rage, crying 'Long Live the King!' and saying that she would rather be guillotined." Her reaction to the Salpêtrière was extreme, but not altogether unwarranted; the place had a terrible reputation. It was inextricably linked with prostitution and venereal disease, and all inmates later bore the stigma of having stayed there.[1]

Bartellemy's obstreperousness achieved her purpose, at least momentarily. She was taken to the Petite Force (and almost immediately was transferred to the Salpêtrière). Unfortunately her "political" statement had come on the heels of the Law of 22 Prairial, which expedited the work of the Revolutionary Tribunal in disposing of those disloyal to the *patrie;* this fact prevented her case from being handled routinely.[2] She was not the only ordinary citizen to be held for invoking

[1] AN F⁷ 3299¹. See Parent-Duchâtelet, *De la prostitution,* II:12-21, for a discussion of the treatment of venereal disease in the 1780s.

[2] Jacques Godechot, *Les Institutions de la France sous la Révolution et l'Empire* (Paris: Presses universitaires de France, 1951), pp. 119-120. The law is also discussed in Emile Campardon, *Le Tribunal révolutionnaire de Paris,* 2 vols. (Paris: Henri Plon, 1866), I:335-339. During Messidor Year II (19 June–18 July 1794) 1,005 people were brought before the tribunal, of whom 796 were executed. Campardon, *Le Tribunal,* II:221.

the king's name, nor was she even the only *fille publique* to be so charged. Two prostitutes arrested eight months earlier, for offenses virtually identical to hers, had both been condemned to death. One had been executed on the day of her sentencing; the other, reprieved by pregnancy, outlived the Terror and eventually was released.[3]

Bartellemy appeared for trial on 29 Thermidor, shortly after the fall of Robespierre (9 Thermidor), and the case was sent on to the Comité de sûreté générale, apparently because of its political implications. Subsequently her case was ignored; the pertinent documents had been lost in the shuffle of papers, perhaps because the Comité had been reorganized just two days before her trial was to take place.[4] The inaction on her case led Bartellemy to write a series of letters of protest. The first surviving letter, written with two other women, was dated 23 Nivôse Year III (12 January 1795), about seven months after her arrest:

> Marie Antoinette Bartellemy, age thirty, native of Paris, laundress, was arrested on 1 Prairial [*sic*] and conducted to the commissariat of the section Bonne Nouvelle, then to the Force where I have endured the greatest misfortune possible, having been imprisoned for three months at the end of which I was called to the Tribunal correctionnelle, where I was accused of statements against the republic, of which I have no memory in that I was drunk at the time of my arrest; and I do not at all believe what they have accused me of because my sentiments have never approved the conduct of the *ci-devant*.
>
> Marguerite Levaseure, age thirty-two, native of Nan-

---

[3] For a discussion of the two women, see Henri Wallon, *Histoire du Tribunal révolutionnaire de Paris,* 6 vols. (Paris: Hachette, 1880), II:244-245, and Campardon, *Le Tribunal,* I:216-217.

[4] Godechot, *Les Institutions,* p. 279.

terre, merchant at les Halles, under arrest since 19 Messidor, conducted to the section Poissonnière, then to the Salpêtrière from which I was called to the Tribunal correctionnelle seventeen days after my arrest, accused of statements against the republic of which I have no memory in that I was drunk at the time of my arrest.

Jeanne Quantain, age thirty, native of Nogent le Rotrou... linen worker, living in Paris, rue de Rats no. 7, arrested in Germinal by the Revolutionary Committee, conducted to the [headquarters of] the Revolutionary Committee and then to the Force and to Plessis; currently at Salpêtrière in chains.

All three of us beg you, Citizen [of the Comité de sûreté générale], to bring us to judgment as soon as possible or to transfer us [to another prison], in that we are deprived of everything, having sold all that we had to write letters, from which we have had no response; being in the greatest misery, we beg you to take notice of our sad position, and to have us judged as soon as possible or transfer us immediately if this is possible.

Her next two letters, dated 30 Floréal Year III (19 May 1795) and 21 Prairial Year III (9 June 1795) were both addressed to the Comité de sûreté générale:

Citizen,

Permit the citizeness Marie Antoinette Bartellemy, laundress, age thirty, native of Paris, to be so bold as to send you a few lines begging your consideration for the long sojourn I have suffered in slavery. I was arrested 1 Messidor of the second year, nightly round, sections Bonne Nouvelle and Droits de l'Homme, conducted to the Petite Force, having appeared before the *correctionnel* on 29 Thermidor without having appeared since that time; being accused of having shouted "Long Live the King," of

LETTERS FROM REVOLUTIONARY PRISONS

which I have no memory since I was drunk; believing
myself to have been forgotten I address myself to you,
Citizen, with confidence, to beg you to put an end to my
misfortune or to have me called into court to decide my
fate. I trust everything to your humanity and justice.

Salut et fraternité,
Marie Antoinette Bartellemy

Citizen,

I am taking the liberty of writing to you to express
my sorrow. For a year I have suffered in chains, and no
one has yet decided my fate. The documents of my case
were sent to your committee on 9 Fructidor. . . . Several
days ago you sent word to me to be patient, but I can
be patient no longer. I am crushed under the weight of
my chains. I prefer death than to be captive as I have
been for so long, living in the depths of misery. Worthy
Citizen, imagine my unfortunate lot; I throw myself at
your feet, bathing them in my tears. I hope that in your
goodness and humanity you have the means to make my
pain cease and to decide my fate more quickly. I am
obliged to sell my rations to have my letters written so
that you can judge my cruel position. I do not believe
you inhuman enough to leave me to perish in chains.

Salut et fraternité,
your very submissive *concitoyenne,*
Marie Antoinette Bartellemy

Although it is not always possible to determine the intended
recipients of these letters, it appears that Bartellemy had wisely
not concentrated all her efforts on the Comité de sûreté générale she also sent pleas back to the Tribunal de police correctionnelle, the court that had inadvertently cast her into
administrative oblivion. A letter written four days after the
immediately preceding one indicates that she finally received

some word, probably not as a result of this last letter—the interim was too short—but in reply to an earlier one. She seemed to have been immeasurably cheered by that reply. The relatively businesslike, recapitulative tone is in sharp contrast to that of the weepy missive written just four days before:

> 25 Prairial Year III [13 June 1795]
> Citizen,
>
> I am taking the liberty to write to assure you of my very humble respect and at the same time to beg you to take pity on my cruel situation. You have had the goodness to write me that I should write to the Comité de sûreté général. I have written several letters and had no response. It is very cruel to see that, since 1 Messidor, I have been imprisoned without being judged; and sent to the Comité de sûreté générale on 29 Thermidor, charged with saying "Long Live the King." Knowing you to be filled with goodness and humanity for the unfortunate, I dare implore your pity. Deign to bestow a look of commiseration on the pain that I endure. After the Supreme Being I have only you as a recourse. Deign to shorten my detention and give the order [so that a wretch does not perish in prison].
>
> Marie Antoinette Bartellemy

This letter managed to stir up a rather sluggish search for the records of her case, although (perhaps incidentally) Bartellemy was again transferred from the Salpêtrière to the Petite Force, her third prison transfer in less than a year.[5] Still undaunted, she sent yet another letter. It took the form of a thinly veiled bribe in a currency that was peculiarly appropriate to the spirit of the time:

---

[5] Her numerous transfers were not at all unusual, as Soboul has commented. Albert Soboul, *Les Sans-culottes parisiens en l'an II* (Paris: Clavreuil, 1962), p. 802.

5 Thermidor Year III [23 July 1795]

To the Comité de sûreté générale:

Citizen, I am taking the liberty to write to you in order
to assure you of my very humble respect and at the same
time to pray you to have the goodness to call me before
you as soon as possible. In view of the fact that I have
something very interesting to tell you [*dénoncer*], I dare
to hope that you will not refuse me; I can say no more
about the subject of which I am speaking. I hope to have
the honor to explain myself before you.... I pray you to
call me before you as soon as possible.

Marie Antoinette Bartellemy

The promise of a denunciation was probably less likely to
move the authorities now, when the Thermidorian Reaction
was in force, than it would have been during the Terror. But
Bartellemy's appeal to the informer's mentality was understandable: she had been in prison for more than a year, and
in a crowded prison the old spirit doubtless survived. Moreover, the fear of prison rebellions, much on the minds of the
authorities, may still have had an effect. So far as the historian
is concerned, however, the case of Marie Antoinette Bartellemy must end here. There are no further documents.

There is, however, more on one of the coauthors of Bartellemy's first letter, Marguerite Levasseur. Almost immediately, she was transferred with three other women from the
Salpêtrière to the Luxembourg prison. There she and her
three companions, of whom at least one, Elizabeth Lenoir,
was a prostitute,[6] had made their presence unbearable by 25
January 1793, less than two weeks after their arrival. At the

---

[6] Lenoir was described in a note dated 10 Nivôse Year III (9 January
1795): "Agée de 30 ans, native de Longui [Longuy,] département de la
Meuse, arrêtée 5 Floréal an II [24 April 1795] par ordre Comité révolutionnaire de la section Contrat social comme suspecte et femme de mauvaise
vie." AN F⁷ 3299⁹.

end of what had obviously been a long day, the concierge at Luxembourg wrote a letter of complaint to prison authorities:

Citizens,

You transferred to the Luxembourg four women from the Salpêtrière, named Marguerite Levasseur, Claire Augustine Rivet, Elizabeth Lenoir, and Toinette Edmond, wife of Dessée; since their arrival they have caused disorders, which increase every day, to the point that today, at about eight o'clock in the evening, Citizen Gaillard, prisoner, wanted to bring one of them into his room to sleep with him. His cell mates [*camarades de chambre*] opposed this, notably Citizen Perrin.... [There was a fight between Gaillard and Perrin, and the former was put in solitary confinement.] As for the four women, in order to avoid any further disorders I have decided to put them all together in one room where I will leave them until you have suggested what I should do with them.

The concierge received an answer a week later, approving his actions and suggesting that he simply leave the women where they were. But the four were not to be left forever quarreling with each other in a tiny cell. They were, according to the records, transferred at least twice during the next two months before they dropped from sight.

An unusual set of mother-daughter letters suggests the problems faced by wayward girls. Parents had the legal authority to cause their minor children to be imprisoned for promiscuity; and if parents did not act, the police might. Young girls—in practice, poor girls—caught loitering in the streets, in the company of young men, or out after a certain hour at night were arrested, and sometimes they were charged as prostitutes. The precise legal difficulties that the charge could entail did not, unfortunately, lead to a greater care in bestowing the title "prostitute." Parental rights could combine with the traditional carelessness about the rights of prostitutes to create complex problems for women who had not yet reached legal adulthood.[7]

One such case was that of Marguerite Grossaint, held in prison because her mother refused to take action:

15 Floréal Year III [4 May 1795]

Marguerite Grosin, sentenced during the month of Prairial to *réclamation* [that is, to remain in jail until claimed by her mother] was arrested at seven o'clock in the evening on the rue de la Vannerie. Although my domicile was with the citizeness Julien on the rue des Trois Canettes, in front of Notre Dame, where I was a fruit seller by profession, they came to arrest me in the above-mentioned street at the home of a friend whose name I do not recall. I was arrested as a *fille publique,* but I can protest that I have never practiced this vile profession. I beg you in the name of humanity to have me called back to court on appeal, in view of the fact that I have only my mother who could claim me and, as I do not know her address, I will be obliged to languish for a number of years in prison. I call upon your goodness and your charity to take me from this vile place. Please grant my request.

She restated her position more emphatically, if less clearly, a week later:

23 Floréal Year III [12 May 1795]

The woman Marguerite Grosin, detained by judicial decision since last Prairial in the Salpêtrière, demands

---

[7] The authority of the parents was diluted somewhat by revolutionary legislation. See Philippe Sagnac, *La Législation civile de la Révolution française* (Paris: Hachette, 1898), pp. 308-309.

her liberty; [on the grounds] that it is unjust that she was sentenced as a *femme publique,* having never practiced such a trade; that she is ignorant of the address of her mother, who could claim her.

The history of Grossaint's detention presents an illuminating case of good intentions gone astray. According to official reports, she had appeared before the Tribunal de police correctionnelle on 2 Messidor Year II (20 June 1794), charged with prostitution. Since she was a minor, the court had sentenced her to ten days of jail, to give her mother time to arrange a hearing (*tribunal domestique*) before the local justice of the peace. In this case, the apparent goal was to rescue Grossaint from a life of prostitution. There was some official confusion about the extent of the action, or inaction, of Grossaint's mother. Grossaint herself was brought again before the Tribunal de police correctionnelle in early Thermidor (late July) and was given an indeterminate prison sentence that would end as soon as her mother came to get her. But she had written on 5 Floréal Year III (24 April 1795) that "ma mère m'abandonne."

In the meantime Marguerite, who had been sent to the Salpêtrière in July 1794 for treatment of a skin disease, finally suggested that they try to reach her mother again through her former landlady, the citizeness Julien. The application to Julien was successful, and on 6 Germinal Year III (24 July 1794), more than a year after Grossaint's imprisonment, Marguerite's mother answered an invitation to appear in the chambers of the tribunal:

Citizen,

The citizeness Julien has just brought the letter that you were kind enough to write. I am very sorry that I cannot respond to your invitation, but I cannot walk. Since I cannot see any other motives [for the invitation] than those which concern Marguerite Grossaint, my young daughter, I am respectfully forced to remind you that she was sentenced by the Tribunal de police correctionelle to be held until a *bureau de famille* had decided her case. The *bureau* was held before the justice of the peace of the Cité section, and it was determined that she would remain in prison for two years beginning 8 Messidor Year II [26 June 1794]. I perceive with sorrow that this judgment was only too just, and I would deem myself fortunate if during this time she made use of her time to reflect and to expose herself to no further reproaches.

It is impossible for me to receive her, although my tenderness for her is that of a good mother, but she has reduced me to the point where I have to live among strangers, and my faculties do not permit me to give her any aid, since I am infirm.

If, however, I am mistaken about the reason for your letter, please tell me and I will try to satisfy you.

femme Grossaint

As I would rather that the people with whom I live not know of my disgrace, my address is in care of the citeness Julien, rue des Trois Canettes no. 2, in the Cité.[8]

The two letters that follow express an identical and familiar concern. Neither of the writers was destitute, but both saw that their small resources would be lost during a long prison term. Charnet was arrested on 29 Fructidor Year II (15 September 1794) and wrote her letter on 25 Frimaire Year III (5 December 1794). Bellot was arrested on 18 Germinal Year III (7 April 1795) and wrote on 8 Thermidor Year III (26 July 1795). Both were clearly impatient, and each was placed in a somewhat ambiguous position; in neither case was the

---

[8] For the texts of all the preceding letters, see AN F[7] 3299[6].

word "prostitute" used by the arresting authorities. Charnet was arrested on suspicion of living a *mauvaise vie,* literally a wicked or bad life, and was sent to the prostitute prison. Bellot was arrested on suspicion of theft and "bad morals" (*mauvaise moeurs*), charges that were given equal weight by the arresting officer, and was sent to Pelagie:

> The citizeness Gilberte Charnet, age twenty-seven, native of Varenne sur Allier, Department of the Allier in Bourbonnois, was arrested on 29 Fructidor in the evening when she returned home. She was conducted . . . [to the commissariat in] the Chalier section, from which she was taken to the Salpêtrière, where she has been detained since that time without having received any news; though she has written about her unfortunate situation ceaselessly, she has received no information. This is why she addresses herself to you to beg you to take notice of her situation, not being at all guilty, and to take note of the fact that while she is in prison her rent still falls due and that she has, inevitably, to sell in order to pay her rent, having earned nothing for five months. She begs you to believe her your *concitoyenne,*
>
> Gilberte Charnet

Citizen,

> The citizeness Catherine Bellot, detained at Pelagie since 18 Germinal on a simple suspicion [charge] seeks recourse to your humanity so that you will order someone to interrogate her. She does not ask pardon, her innocence strengthens her, but asks that you shorten her afflictions, allowing her to leave. She is obliged to sell her furnishings [*meubles*] to pay her rent; she writes frequently to the section that arrested her, they responded that her *procès-verbal* was sent to the Criminelle. She begs you, Citizen, to have consideration for her long detention, to have

someone interrogate her so that it will be seen that she deserves her release. She was told to seek recourse from a constituted authority, but a wise friend told her to address herself to you. Have consideration for her just claim, have someone interrogate her.

Catherine Bellot[9]

As an authority on prostitution would later write, a prison term caused a great deal of anxiety for *filles:* "They think . . . about the rent that they cannot, perhaps, pay, of their personal effects, their clothes, their furnishings delivered up to the pillage of landlords who are often not very scrupulous."[10] Even the smallest bit of property was a hedge against destitution, for it could always be pawned for ready cash. Both Charnet and Bellot saw themselves slipping gradually into an unenviable state of misery; their letters serve as reminder of the precarious circumstances of life for the poor, and of the disasters that even a short prison term could bring.

Loss of property was not the only problem that could arise. A prison term did not end the family responsibilities carried by many women, responsibilities that in some cases followed them into the prison itself. Babet Sinard, apparently a *fille-mère,* wrote in late August 1795 to complain that she had been imprisoned since 15 June 1795:

Citizen,

The woman Babet Sinard, detained at Petite Force for three months, pregnant and with a sick child, has the honor to reveal to you that she suffers much without having deserved it—only because a person left some bedding with me as security for what she owed me, and this person was not married to the man that I believed to be

---

[9] For the text of these two letters, see AN F[7] 3299[3].
[10] Guyot, *La Prostitution,* p. 140.

her legitimate husband.... This is why I entreat you to take pity on my fate and on my child who is sick and to examine my case; if I am wrong, to punish me, but if not, to free me and my poor child.

As this somewhat tangled tale suggests, Sinard had been arrested for theft as well as for debauchery, though there may well have been extenuating circumstances in the theft charge. Nevertheless, the authorities were struck by her situation and sent an *officier de santé* to examine the sick child. He reported that the child was well, and Sinard was sent on 6 Messidor Year III (24 June 1795) before the grand jury. There is no record of the outcome of the case.[11]

As it has frequently been suggested, prostitutes were often arrested because of their *qualité* rather than for any specific offense. The following letter illustrates this confusion, not only in the arrest process but also later on, in charging and sentencing:

25 Messidor Year III [13 July 1795]

We are three unfortunates who throw themselves on your mercy, begging you to have pity on our misfortune. We were all arrested four months ago on the twentieth [actually 22 Ventôse (12 March 1795)] and conducted before Citizen Glodon, *commissaire* of police of the section Roule, on suspicion of stealing a purse. We don't know what they mean. We were conducted to the Petite Force, where we are now, without having yet appeared before any tribunal. We are describing ourselves this way in order to get someone to say something one way or another about us. We have received no response. Overcome with misery and sorrow, we considered that it would be appropriate to write to beg you, if this depends on you, to

[11] AN F⁷ 3299¹.

have the goodness to set our appearance [in court] so that our case can be decided and justice rendered. We can only think that we have been forgotten. We implore your goodness and honesty. You will oblige your very humble and very submissive co-citizenesses, Reine Maxsence, Genevieve Chalot, and I who take the liberty to write to you, Marianne Plit. I beg you, Citizen, to oblige me with a word in response to ease my disquiet.

What is most noteworthy in this letter (aside from the apparent comradeship, both in crime and in prison, of the three) was the difference between what the women, on one side, and the authorities, on the other, perceived to be the cause of the arrest. The women believed that they were being detained for a specific action, the theft of a purse; they sensed that they had a right to a hearing in this regard. The authorities, however, made no reference to the stolen purse in their remarks; instead, they claimed that the women were suspected of being *filles publiques* and *voleuses* and were being held as such in the Petite Force.[12] There was, to be sure, a frequent association in this period between theft and prostitution, and this further blurred the offenses. Still, a subtle but significant shift had occurred in the viewpoint of the authorities. The women were accused not of doing, but of being; not of stealing a pocketbook, but of being thieves and prostitutes.

Marie Louise Regis provided a further example of the confusion concerning prostitution and theft. Arrested on 27 October 1792, Regis was still in jail in June 1795—and had not yet had a trial. The chief reason for the delay rested in the fact that the overworked, and temporarily clerkless, *juge de paix* who had jurisdiction over her case had never heard of

<hr>

[12] AN F⁷ 3299³. Maxsence, incidentally, had the unfortunate name of Reine Leroi, which she prudently changed to Reine Maxsence.

her (and neither, he added, had his predecessor in the post). Her letter prompted a search for the missing documents, which had been forwarded elsewhere.[13] In the meantime she had written a plaintive protest:

12 Prairial Year III [31 May 1795]

Citizen,

The woman Marilouisse Regisse, age nineteen, laundress by profession, was arrested on 27 October old-style at the Courtille, from which I was conducted to the justice of the peace at Passy, where my testimony was taken, and from there sent to the Conciergerie, where I remained three months. Then I was taken to the Petite Force, rue Pavée, where I remained for eighteen months; there I was afflicted with scabies, and they transferred me to the national hospital [Salpêtrière], where I remained two months, and then to Vincennes, where I remained for three months. I have now been at Pelagie for five months and, Citizen, you will have the goodness [to hear] that I have not yet [had a trial]; and I wrote to two justices of the peace in Paris, and I have not yet had any response. I beg you to have regard for my youth and my long detention; I commend myself to your goodness and pray you to have me appear [in court] as soon as possible. I am fearful of importuning you and, awaiting a little word of response, I will be very obliged to you.[14]

[13] AN F^7 3299[11]. This was a continuing problem throughout the early years of the Revolution. The ground rules and the personnel were constantly changing, and there was a shortage of clerks. "Seul sans aide je ne puis tout faire," complained one *commissaire* when he was reproached for his slowness in a case involving two prostitutes. AN BB^3 82.

[14] Regis understandably seemed to have kept a rather more complete record of her detention than the authorities. Her figures came out exactly right: Conciergerie from November 1792 to January 1793; Petite Force from February 1793 to July 1794; Salpêtrière from August to September 1794; Vincennes from October to December 1794; Pelagie from January to May 1795. AN F^7 3299[11].

Originally, Regis had been charged with the theft of a gold watch from the citizeness Julienne, her landlady. The watch had been recovered when Regis' lover pawned it, and she confessed when confronted with the evidence. Through the long years of her case, however, the original charge of theft had dropped out of the picture to be replaced with that of prostitution. One official stated, in a note dated 22 Ventôse Year III (12 March 1795), that she had been arrested as a *femme publique*.

This interpretation had much circumstantial evidence, if no hard evidence, to back it up. Though not more than seventeen at the time of her arrest, Regis had a lover who abetted her in criminal activities. She lived away from her family. Her occupation was laundering, an often vulnerable trade. Regis had, as she stated, been arrested at the Courtille, an area of Belleville notorious as a haven for *filles*. There were, in short, a number of facts in her situation that would have left her open to suspicion. The long stay in prison may have been due to the inevitable confusion caused by constantly changing city officials—in prison at the beginning of the Reign of Terror, she was still there almost a year after it ended—but Regis was also handicapped, as were Marianne Blé and the others, by the vagueness of the charges brought against her. The plight of these women was not an unusual one during the Revolution; unfortunately, the uncertainties in their situation would continue for prostitutes throughout the nineteenth century.

Equally unfortunate was the fact that uncertainty did not carry over into police practice. Prerevolutionary ordinances had been superseded by new constituent laws that granted sweeping powers to the police.[15] This meant, in practice, that traditional procedures were carried out under a new aegis. The next five cases to be discussed grew out of arrests made

[15] The justification in this period for the arrests of prostitutes (as such) was the Law of 16-24 August 1790.

solely because the woman involved was considered to be a *fille publique*. Consequently, the circumstances that led to these arrests provide clues to the types of behavior likely to get poor women in trouble.

Marianne Lavale and Marie Catherine François were both taken in routine roundups. The *commissaire* in charge of their arrests had gone to the area around the markets of Paris to find "thieves, evaders of military service, and prostitutes"; this area, whose restaurants and cabarets were open all night for the benefit of market workers, had traditionally served as a haven for ne'er-do-wells. (François had been found in Le Roi Yvetot, a rowdy cabaret that later achieved notoriety as the subject of a song by Pierre-Jean Beranger.) Both women had been in the wrong place at the wrong time, and they demanded a trial or, at the very least, a transfer from the Salpêtrière:

22 Floréal Year III [11 May 1795]

Citizen,

A trial is urgently requested by Marianne Lavale, native of Coutanse in Normandy [Coutances in Manche], age twenty-one, breeches maker, residing on the rue de l'Arbresec, section Gardes Françaises, [and] Marie Catherine François, age twenty-three, native of Ilier [Eure], dressmaker, residing on the rue des Prêcheurs at the home of Citizeness Lefebvre. [We] were arrested sometime in Pluviôse [1 Pluviôse Year III (20 January 1795)] in the arrests of the Halle au Blé; we were conducted to the Salpêtrière to be cured of a minor illness that we had contracted. Citizen, cast a look of commiseration over our cruel situation; we have languished in prison for four months without deserving it. . . . [W]e are overcome with sorrow to see ourselves among all sorts of contagious illnesses; we lack everything without aid, obliged to sell the little that we have. . . . We pray you, Citizen, to send us before a tribunal.[16]

The above letter provides indirect evidence that the women had been given a routine medical exam shortly after their arrest. Similar indications are provided by the official notes that were attached to the next letter, from Marie Catherine Rortan:

Salpêtrière, Floréal Year III [April-May 1795]

The unfortunate Catherine Rortan, age sixteen, native of Caleux in Picardy, Department of the Somme. . . . I pray you, Citizen, to cast a look of commiseration on my cruel position. For nearly two years I have not known what is in store for me, being abandoned by everyone, without receiving any aid from anyone, stripped of everything; I have been obliged to rid myself of everything to aid myself during a serious illness that I have just had, since we lack everything. I pray you to have me appear [in court] as soon as possible in order that you may decide my fate one way or another, [and surely] you will render me the liberty of which I have been so unjustly deprived. . . .[17]

Rortan was a *terrassière*—earth worker, digger, navvy—who had been arrested as a *fille publique* on 23 May 1794, about a year before her letter was written. Her claim of two years (not one) in uncertainty suggests that her arrest may have put an end to a long period of vagabondage brought on by her lack of skills, her youth, her provincial origins, and her isolation. She was discovered after her arrest to have a venereal disease and was sent to the Capucins, a venereal hospital. She was pronounced cured on 3 November 1794

---

[16] For the letter and the *commissaire*'s report, see AN F[7] 3299[8].
[17] AN F[7] 3299[12].

and was sent to the Salpêtrière to await trial. In the meantime, her *procès-verbal* had been sent on to the Tribunal correctionnel. The documents relating to her case had been put aside for some reason, and Rortan found herself in prison, apparently forgotten, with no end in sight. The facts are meager, but her vulnerability speaks for her. She was young and alone, she had no secure means of earning a living, she had contracted a shameful disease—these were enough to cause her to be branded a prostitute.

Similar personal circumstances surround the case of Marie Claudine Martin:

Pelagie, 8 Floréal Year III [28 April 1795]

Citizens,

Marie Claudine Martin, age twenty-two, orphan, was arrested while walking through the Palais Egalité eighteen months ago as a *femme publique*. Although I had some work in my apron that I was carrying back to the section Butte des Moulins, I was taken to the *commissaire* of police of the same section; telling him I was ill, I asked to go to the Capucin hospital, where I spent two months. From the hospital I was transferred to Salpêtrière, from there to Vincennes and then Pelagie; after that to Salpêtrière and finally to Pelagie, where I am now. [All this occurred] without a trial, although I wrote several times sending word of my jail entries. I beg you, Citizens, to have the goodness to give me my liberty. I have never been in prison except for this. The ordeal has been rather rigorous for me. I have done nothing against honor and probity. I repent my shortcomings and leave everything to you. My gratitude will be infinite.

Marie Claudine Martin

Martin was arrested in what was to become known in the nineteenth century as a *rafle*. She had been arrested with

twenty-one other women, all of whom had been charged with
prostitution, though it is hard to conceive that the evidence
against all twenty-two could have been firmly grounded.[18]

Youth did not have a monopoly on vulnerability, as Angelique Dehaie's letter reveals:

> Salpêtrière, 15 Frimaire Year III [5 December 1794]
>
> Angelique Dehaie, widow of DeLille, age forty-eight,
> appeals to your humanity and your justice. She was ar-
> rested by the *commissaire* of the section Chalier at ten
> o'clock in the morning in her apartment. The *commissaire*
> told me that he was arresting me because someone had
> told him that I was a *femme publique*. They took me to
> the Salpêtrière, where I have suffered for four months
> in the greatest misery. I was never a *femme du monde.*
> The occupation that I [have] practiced for twenty years
> is sick nurse. Citizens, I appeal to your humanity; don't
> allow to languish any longer in prison the unfortunate
> widow DeLille.[19]

Dehaie portrayed herself as the victim of a simple denunciation, and nothing in the official notes attached to her file
contradicts this. She had been arrested on 26 Thermidor Year
II (13 August 1794), fifteen days after Robespierre's fall, and
thus spent only a few months in prison before her wish to
be released was seconded by the desire of the authorities to
empty the jails. Dehaie stated that she had never been a *femme
du monde*—not "I am not," but "I was never." Perhaps the
phrasing was accidental. But it may have reflected an unspoken, perhaps unconscious, recognition on her part of the
exigencies of life for the poor, and an understanding that
many poor women may well have had a past that had to be
hidden.

[18] See AN F⁷ 3299⁹.
[19] AN F⁷ 3299⁴.

One last letter, by Rose Lefevre, seems to reflect a determination to hide nothing:

Salpêtrière, 22 Floréal Year III [11 May 1795]
Citizen,

The unfortunate Rose Lefevre, age twenty, native of Saint-Menous, diocese of Chalon, laundress, residing on the rue du Chantre no. 623, in the home of Citizen Gayant, café keeper, section Oratoire, for drinking a bottle of beer at a café with only three defenders of the fatherland. I beg you, Citizen, to cast a look of commiseration on my cruel situation. For twenty-two [actually twenty] months I have not known what is in store for me ... stripped of everything, with recourse to no one, having been obliged to sell my clothes to aid myself during a serious illness that I just had, since we lack means of subsistence. I was sentenced to three months of police detention at the Petite Souri of Paris; I appeared at my appeal, where I was given six months. There it is—a year since my term was finished (and I know it was finished), but someone told me that I had not been sentenced. I have been told since that time that the record of the decision was lost; thus I beg you, Citizen, to have me appear [in court] as soon as possible so that you can decide my fate one way or the other....

I know that you are the protector of all unfortunates and will not leave me to languish any longer in slavery....

The woman Rose Lefevre respectfully urges you to remove me from slavery or to give me justice.

Lefevre had been arrested on 28 September 1793. The reasons for her arrest differ from one account to another. Lefevre herself admitted to sharing a beer with (only) three soldiers, an action to which she contrived to give a patriotic aura. The concierge of the Petite Force was under the impression that she had been arrested for brawling. The tribunal tried her for theft and prostitution; the theft charge was dropped, but they imprisoned her anyway because she was thought to be a prostitute.[20] The records show nothing on the final outcome of her case.

[20] Lefevre was a native of Sainte-Menehould, Marne. From her description it appears that she was tried before the Tribunal de police correctionnelle. The "Petite Souri" probably refers to the Petite Force, since that is where she spent the early part of her imprisonment. "Souri" perhaps was meant to be "Souricière," or mousetrap; this was a common term of reference to the *cachot* where prisoners were held immediately after they were brought to the prisons before being taken to their cells. Throughout the early nineteenth century, the police used the term to designate places, particularly at les Halles, where roughnecks congregated and could be trapped in an arrest. AN F^7 3299^8.

Select Bibliography

Archives de la Préfecture de Police (PP)

DB 407-413. Prostitution.

F^7 3845-3873. Reports of the Prefecture of Police, 1802-1830.

F^7 3874-3893. Bulletins of the Prefecture of Police, Restoration–July Monarchy.

F^7 3894-3899. Daily record of arrests at the Prefecture of Police, 1830-1846.

F^7 4159-4165. Reports of the Gendarmerie of the Seine, 1821-1847.

F^7 4166-4182. Reports of the Gendarmerie royale, Garde municipale, and Garde nationale, 1816-1846.

F^7 9304-9305. *Femmes publiques.*

F^7 10193-10194. Surveillance reports, 1820-1835.

F^7 3299^1-3299^{13}. *Détenus par mesure de la haute police.*

F^{15} 2811. *Police des moeurs et mendicité.*

Aulard, François Victor Alphonse, ed. *Paris pendant la Réaction thermidorienne et sous le Directoire.* 5 vols. Paris: Leopold Cerf, 1898-1902.

Bloch, Camille, and Tuetey, Alexandre, eds. *Procès-verbaux et rapports du Comité de mendicité de la constituante, 1790-1791.* Paris: Imprimerie nationale, 1911.

Campardon, Emile. *Le Tribunal révolutionnaire de Paris.* 2 vols. Paris: Henri Plon, 1866.

Caron, Pierre, ed. *Paris pendant la Terreur: rapports des agents secrets du Ministère de l'intérieur.* 6 vols. Paris: Société de l'histoire contemporaine and Société de l'histoire de France, 1919-1958.

Collection officielle des ordonnances de police (1800-1848). Paris: Boucquin, 1880.

Commission ministerielle permanente pour la prophylaxie des maladies vénériennes. *Documents fournis par M. le Préfet de police mais non publiés.* Paris: n.p., 1902-1903.

Compte d'administration des dépenses de la Préfecture de police (1817-1845). Paris: Imprimerie royale, 1818-1845.

Compte général de l'administration de la justice criminelle en France (1825-1850). Paris: Imprimerie royale, 1825-1850.

Conseil municipal de Paris. *Procès-verbal de la Commission de la police des moeurs.* Paris: n.p., 1879.

Defert, Louis. *Code de police: textes des ordonnances de police depuis l'origine.* Paris: Giard & Brière, 1905.

Delamare, Nicolas. *Traité de la police.* 4 vols. Amsterdam: n.p., 1729.

Duvergier, Jean Baptiste. *Collection complète des lois, décrets, ordonnances, règlements, et avis du Conseil d'état.* 30 vols. Paris: Guyot, 1834-1838.

Elouin, Trébuchet, A., and Labat, E. *Nouveau dictionnaire de police.* 2 vols. Paris: Béchet Jeune, 1835.

Hennequin, Felicien. *Annexes au rapport général présenté par M. F. Hennequin, . . . sur les travaux de la Commission extraparlementaire du régime des moeurs.* Melun: Imprimerie administrative, 1908.

Isambert, François-André. *Recueil général des anciennes lois françaises, depuis l'an 420 jusqu'à la Révolution de 1789.* 29 vols. Paris: Belin-Leprieur, 1821-1833.

Parnet, M. *Recueil analytique des circulaires de la Préfecture de police.* Paris: Paul Dupont, 1895.

Rabasse, M. *Manuel portatif des commissaires de police*. Paris: Boucquin, 1825.

Recueil officiel des circulaires émanées de la Préfecture de police. 2 vols. Paris: Imprimerie Chaix, 1882.

Sabatier. *Histoire de la législation sur les femmes publiques et les lieux de débauche*. Paris: Gagniard, 1830.

Tuetey, Alexandre. *Répertoire général des sources manuscrites de l'histoire de Paris pendant la Révolution française*. 11 vols. Paris: Imprimerie nouvelle, 1900.

Wallon, Henri. *Histoire du Tribunal révolutionnaire de Paris*. 6 vols. Paris: Hachette, 1880.

OTHER PRIMARY SOURCES

Acton, William. *Prostitution*. Edited by Peter Fryer. London: MacGibbon & Key, 1968. Originally published in 1870.

Andrieux, Louis. *Souvenirs d'un préfet de police*. 2 vols. Paris: Jules Rouff, 1885.

Appleton, Paul. *La Traite des blanches*. Paris: Rousseau, 1903.

Barthèlemy, Toussaint. *Etude d'hygiène sociale: syphilis et santé publique*. Paris: J.-B. Baillière, 1890.

Béraud, F. F. A. *Les Filles publiques et la police qui les régit*. 2 vols. Paris: Desforges, 1839.

Canler, M. *Mémoires de Canler*. 2 vols. Paris: Roy, 1882.

Carlier, Félix. *Etude de pathologie sociale: les deux prostitutions*. Paris: E. Dentu, 1887.

Cinquante années de visites à Saint-Lazare par M. d'A. Paris: Librairie Fischbacher, 1889.

Claude, M. *Mémoires de Monsieur Claude*. 2 vols. Paris: Jules Rouff, 1881.

Claveau, A. G. *De la police de Paris, de ses abus, et des reformes dont elle est susceptible*. Paris: A. Pillot, 1831.

Coffignon, A. *La Corruption à Paris*. Paris: Librairie illustrée, 1888.

Commenge, O. *Hygiène sociale: la prostitution clandestine à Paris*. Paris: Schleicher, 1897.

Congrès de Genève: septembre 1877. Neuchatel: Bureau du bulletin continental, 1877.

Congrès médical international de Paris: août 1867. Paris: Victor Masson, 1868.

Corlieu, Auguste. *La Prostitution à Paris.* Paris: J.-B. Baillière, 1887.

Dictionnaire de l'argot moderne. Paris: E. Gazel, 1844.

Didiot, P. A. *Etude statistique de la syphilis dans la garnison de Marseille suivie de généralités sur la prostitution et sur la fréquence des maladies vénériennes dans la population de cette ville et completée des reformes à apporter dans le service de la police militaire.* Marseille: Arnaud, 1866.

Dolléans, Edouard. *La Police des moeurs.* Paris: Librairie de la Société du recueil général des lois et des arrêts, 1903.

Du Camp, Maxime. *Paris, ses organes, ses fonctions et sa vie dans la seconde moitié du XIXᵉ siècle.* 6 vols. Paris: Hachette, 1869-1875.

Dufour, Pierre [Paul Lacroix]. *Histoire de la prostitution chez tous les peuples du monde depuis l'antiquité la plus reculée jusqu'à nos jours.* 6 vols. Paris: Seré, 1851-1853.

———. *History of Prostitution.* Translated by Samuel Putnam. 3 vols. Chicago: Covici, 1926.

Esquiros, Alphonse. *Les Vierges folles.* 4th ed. Paris: Delavigne, 1844.

Fiaux, Louis. *L'Armée et la police des moeurs: biologie sexuelle du soldat.* Paris: Félix Alcan, 1917.

———. *L'Integrité intersexuelle des peuples et des gouvernements.* Paris: Félix Alcan, 1910.

———. *Les Maisons de tolérance: leur fermeture.* Paris: Georges Carré, 1892.

———. *La Police des moeurs devant la Commission extraparlementaire du régime des moeurs.* 3 vols. Paris: Félix Alcan, 1910.

———. *La Police des moeurs en France et dans les principaux pays de l'Europe.* Paris: E. Dentu, 1888.

———. *La Police des moeurs en France: son abolition.* Paris: Félix Alcan, 1921.

———. *La Prostitution réglementée et les pouvoirs publics.* Paris: Félix Alcan, 1902.

Fournier, Alfred. *Leçons sur la syphilis, étudiée plus particulièrement chez la femme: clinique de l'hôpital de Lourcine.* Paris: Adrien Delahaye, 1873.

————. "Prophylaxie publique de la syphilis." *Annales d'hygiène publique et de médecine légale* 18, 3rd sér. (1887):55-108.

Frégier, H. A. *Des classes dangereuses de la population dans les grandes villes.* 2 vols. Paris: J.-B. Baillière, 1840.

Froment, M. *La Police dévoilée, depuis la Restauration et notamment sous Messieurs Franchet et Delavau.* 4 vols. Paris: Lemonnier, 1829.

Garin, J. *De la police sanitaire et de l'assistance publique dans leurs rapports avec l'extinction des maladies vénériennes.* Paris: Victor Masson, 1886.

Gisquet, Henri-Joseph. *Mémoires de M. Gisquet, ancien préfet de police, écrits par lui-même.* 4 vols. Paris: n.p., 1840.

Granveau, A. *La Prostitution dans Paris.* Paris: vendu par l'auteur, 1867.

Grisson, Georges. *Paris horrible et Paris original.* Paris: E. Dentu, 1882.

Guyon, Louis. *Biographie des commissaires de police et des officiers de paix de la ville de Paris.* Paris: Goullet, 1826.

Guyot, Yves. *Etudes de physiologie sociale: la prostitution.* Paris: G. Charpentier, 1882.

[Guyot, Yves]. *Lettres d'un ex-agent des moeurs.* Paris: Administration du journal *La Lanterne,* 1879.

Jeannel, Julien. *De la prostitution dans les grandes villes aux dix-neuvième siècle et de l'extinction des maladies vénériennes.* Paris: J.-B. Baillière, 1874.

Justin, Jules. *La Liberté individuelle et la police des moeurs.* Dijon: Carré, 1894.

Leblond, Albert, and Lucas, Arthur. *Du tatouage chez les prostituées.* Paris: Société d'éditions scientifique, 1899.

Lecour, Charles-Jerôme. *La Campagne contre la Préfecture de police.* Paris: Asselin, 1881.

————. *De l'état actuel de la prostitution parisienne.* Paris: Asselin, 1874.

————. *La Prostitution à Paris et à Londres, 1789-1871.* 2nd ed. Paris: Asselin, 1872.

Macé, Gustave. *La Police parisienne: gibier de Saint-Lazare.* Paris: G. Charpentier, 1888.

————. *Le Service de la sûreté*. Paris: G. Charpentier, 1884.

Manuel, Pierre. *La Police de Paris dévoilée*. 2 vols. Paris: J.-B. Garnery, Year II [1794].

Martineau, Louis. *La Prostitution clandestine*. Paris: Delahaye-Lecrosnier, 1885.

Mireur, Hippolyte. *La Prostitution à Marseille*. Paris: E. Dentu, 1882.

Moléon, V. de, ed. *Rapports généraux sur la salubrité publique*. 2 vols. Paris: Bureau du recueil industriel, 1840-1841.

Parent-Duchâtelet, Alexandre-Jean-Baptiste. *Hygiène publique, ou mémoires sur les questions les plus importantes de l'hygiène*. 2 vols. Paris: J.-B. Baillière, 1836.

————. *De la prostitution dans la ville de Paris*. 2 vols. 3rd ed. Edited by A. Trébuchet and Poirat-Duval. Paris: J.-B. Baillière, 1857.

Pottet, Eugène. *Histoire de Saint-Lazare*. Paris: Société française d'imprimerie, 1912.

Potton, A. *De la prostitution et de la syphilis dans les grandes villes, dans la ville de Lyon en particulier*. Paris: J.-B. Baillière, 1842.

Pradier, F.-H. *Histoire statistique, médicale et administrative de prostitution dans la ville de Clermont-Ferrand*. Clermont-Ferrand: n.p., 1859.

Puibaraud, Louis. *Les Malfaiteurs de profession*. Paris: Flammarion, 1893.

Restif de la Bretonne, Nicolas-Edme. *L'Oeuvre de Restif de la Bretonne*. 9 vols. Edited by Henri Bachelin. Vol. 3: *Le Pornographe, ou idées d'un honnête homme sur un projet de règlement pour les prostituées*. Paris: Trianon, 1931.

Reuss, Louis. *La Prostitution au point de vue de l'hygiène et de l'administration en France et à l'étranger*. Paris: J.-B. Baillière, 1889.

Rey, J. L. *Des prostituées et de la prostitution en général*. Le Mans: Julien, Lanier et Cie., 1847.

Richard, Charles. *La Prostitution devant le philosophe*. Paris: Ghio, 1881.

Sainte-Marie, Etienne. *Lectures relatives à la police médicale, faites au Conseil de salubrité de Lyon et du département du Rhône pendant les années 1826, 1827, et 1828.* Paris: J.-B. Baillière, 1828.

Sanford, Henry S. *The Different Systems of Penal Codes in Europe.* Washington, D.C.: Tucker, 1854.

Sue, Eugène. *Les Mystères de Paris.* 2 vols. Paris: Charles Goşselin, 1843.

Turot, Henri. *Le Prolétariat de l'amour.* Paris: Librairie universelle, 1904.

Valbel, Horace. *La Police de sûreté en 1889.* Paris: E. Dentu, 1889.

Vidocq, Eugène François. *Les Voleurs.* Paris: Editions de Paris, 1957.

————. *Les Voleurs: physiologie de leurs moeurs et de leur langage.* Paris: chez l'auteur, n.d.

————. *Les Vrais Mystères de Paris.* 4 vols. Paris: Alexandre Cadot, 1844.

Villermé, L.-R. "Note sur les ravages du choléra-morbus." *Annales d'hygiène publique et de médecine légale* 11 (1834):385-409.

Virmaitre, Charles. *Paris-Impur: les maisons de rendez-vous.* Paris: Alfred Charles, 1898.

————. *Trottoirs et lupanars.* Paris: Henri Perrot, 1893.

SECONDARY SOURCES

Ackerknecht, Erwin H. "Hygiene in France, 1815-1848." *Bulletin of the History of Medicine* 22 (March-April 1948):117-155.

Bertier de Sauvigny, Guillaume. *Nouvelle Histoire de Paris: la Restauration, 1815-1830.* Paris: Hachette, 1977.

Bidelman, Patrick Kay. *Pariahs Stand Up! The Founding of the Liberal Feminist Movement in France, 1858-1889.* Westport, Conn.: Greenwood Press, 1982.

Bloch, Camille. *L'Assistance et l'état en France à la veille de la Révolution.* Paris: 1908. Reprint ed., Geneva: Slatkine-Megariotis, 1974.

Boucheron, Véronique. "La Montée du flot des errants de 1760 à 1789 dans la généralité d'Alençon." *Annales de Normandie* 21 (mars 1971):55-86.

Bullough, Vern, and Bullough, Bonnie. *The History of Prostitution.* New York: University Books, 1964.

Burford, E. J. *Bawds and Lodgings: A History of the London Bankside Brothels, c. 100-1675.* London: Peter Owen, 1976.

Chevalier, Louis. *Classes laborieuses et classes dangereuses à Paris pendant la première moitié du XIXe siècle.* Paris: Plon, 1958.

Cobb, Richard. *The Police and the People: French Popular Protest, 1789-1820.* Oxford: Oxford University Press, 1970.

Coleman, William. *Death Is a Social Disease: Public Health and Political Economy in Early Industrial France.* Madison: University of Wisconsin Press, 1982.

Cominos, Peter. "Late-Victorian Sexual Respectability and the Social System." *International Review of Social History* 8 (1963):18-48, 216-250.

Connelly, Mark Thomas. *The Response to Prostitution in the Progressive Era.* Chapel Hill: University of North Carolina Press, 1980.

Corbin, Alain. *Les Filles de noce: misère sexuelle et prostitution aux XIXe et XXe siècles.* Paris: Aubier Montaigne, 1978.

Cordelier, Jeanne. *"The Life": Memoirs of a French Hooker.* Translated by Harry Mathews. New York: Viking Press, 1978.

Finnegan, Frances. *Poverty and Prostitution: A Study of Victorian Prostitutes in York.* Cambridge: Cambridge University Press, 1979.

Flexner, Abraham. *Prostitution in Europe.* New York: Century Press, 1920.

Foucault, Michel. *The Birth of the Clinic.* Translated by A. M. Sheridan Smith. New York: Vintage Books, 1973.

———. *The History of Sexuality.* Translated by Robert Hurley. New York: Vintage Books, 1980.

Gegot, Jean-Claude. "Criminalité diffuse ou société criminelle?" *Annales de Normandie* 16 (juin 1966):103-142.

Godechot, Jacques. *Les Institutions de la France sous la Révolution et l'Empire.* Paris: Presses universitaires de France, 1951.

Gutton, Jean-Pierre. *La Société et les pauvres: l'exemple de la généralité de Lyon, 1534-1789.* Paris: Société d'édition, 1970.

Hillairet, Jacques [Auguste André Coussilan]. *Dictionnaire historique des rues de Paris.* 2 vols. Paris: Editions de minuit, n.d.

————. *Evocation du vieux Paris*. 3 vols. Paris: Editions de minuit, n.d.

Hufton, Olwen. *The Poor in Eighteenth-Century France*. Oxford: Oxford University Press, 1974.

La Berge, Ann Fowler. "A.-J.-B. Parent-Duchâtelet: Hygienist of Paris, 1821-1836." *Clio Medica* 12 (December 1977):279-301.

Levy, Darline Gay, Applewhite, Harriet Branson, and Johnson, Mary Durham, eds. *Women in Revolutionary Paris, 1789-1795*. Urbana: University of Illinois Press, 1979.

McHugh, Paul. *Prostitution and Victorian Social Reform*. New York: St. Martin's Press, 1980.

McMillan, James F. *Housewife or Harlot: The Place of Women in French Society, 1840-1940*. New York: St. Martin's Press, 1981.

Morris, Terence. *The Criminal Area: A Study in Social Ecology*. London: Routledge & Kegan Paul, 1957.

Nield, Keith, ed. *Prostitution in the Victorian Age*. Farnborough, Hampshire: Gregg International, 1973.

Paultre, Christian. *De la répression de la mendicité et du vagabondage en France sous l'ancien régime*. Paris: J.-B. Sirey, 1906.

Pollak, Otto. *The Criminality of Women*. Philadelphia: University of Pennsylvania Press, 1950.

Rosen, Ruth. *The Lost Sisterhood: Prostitution in America, 1900-1918*. Baltimore: Johns Hopkins University Press, 1982.

Rossiaud, Jacques. "Prostitution, jeunesse et société dans les villes du sud-est au XVᵉ siècle." *Annales E.S.C.* 31 (mars-avril 1976):289-325.

Sagnac, Philippe. *Le Législation civile de la Révolution française*. Paris: Hachette, 1898.

Smart, Carol. *Women, Crime, and Criminology: A Feminist Critique*. London: Routledge & Kegan Paul, 1977.

Terroine, Anne. "Le Roi des ribauds de l'hôtel du roi et les prostituées parisiennes." *Revue historique de droit français et étranger* 56 (avril-juin 1978):253-267.

Tulard, Jean. *Paris et son administration*. Paris: Commission des travaux historiques, 1976.

Vexliard, Alexandre. *Introduction à la sociologie du vagabondage.* Paris: Marcel Rivière, 1956.

Walkowitz, Judith R. *Prostitution and Victorian Society: Women, Class, and the State.* Cambridge: Cambridge University Press, 1980.

Weiner, Dora B. *Raspail: Scientist and Reformer.* New York: Columbia University Press, 1968.

Williams, Alan. *The Police of Paris, 1715-1789.* Baton Rouge: Louisiana State University Press, 1979.

Index

foles femmes et ribaudes communes, 58

Forissier affair, 341-42, 342n

Fournier, Dr. Alfred: on venereal disease, 251, 261, 272-74; on Saint-Lazare, 257-58; on Extraparliamentary Commission, 330; proposed reform of regulatory system, 347n, 352; French Society for Sanitary and Moral Prophylaxis, 354-55

Frégier, H., 161, 203, 244; *entremetteuses,* 294

French Society for Sanitary and Moral Prophylaxis, 354-55

Garde des sceaux, 75-76

Garde municipale, 158

Garin, Dr.: on mandatory venereal disease examinations, 259

garni. See lodging house

Gaultier de Claubry, C.-E.-S.: and Parent-Duchâtelet, 99n

Gendarmerie de la Seine, 158

gendarmes: Gendarmerie royale, 23, 25, 50, 89, 141-42, 151-53, 160, 165, 169, 177, 216, 329; armed escort of prostitutes, 51, 214; arrest reports, 136-38; organization of, 137-38, 137n, 194n; duties of, 138; personal relationships with prostitutes, 190-91, 193

General Health Council. See Conseil général de salubrité

gens sans aveu, 64, 85

Gisquet, Henri-Joseph (prefect of police): on judicial trials for prostitutes, xx-xxi; causes of administrative detention, 21; complaints about lodging houses, 34; advice to *commissaires,* 262

gonorrhea treatment, 257, 257n

grisette, 145

Guyon, Louis, 133

Guyot, Yves (abolitionist), 324, 326n, 337, 341; in conflict with Lecour, xxii, 327-28; sentenced to jail, 4n; on Extraparliamentary Commission, 330; attack on Lecky, 355n

Hallé, Jean Noël, 104n, 105n, 108

Halles, les (Paris), 163, 246

Haussman, Baron, 319

Hennequin, Felicien (author of 1902 survey), 81-91

Hôpital général and Parent-Duchâtelet, 72

Hôtel-Dieu, 171, 176, 261n

hôtel garni. See lodging house

Hugo, Victor, 110

Inscription, xvi, 23, 57, 91, 100, 213, 250, 276-77, 320, 326, 340, 346, 350; legal effects of, 6, 120, 206, 212, 234-37; changes in size of, 15-16, 16n; origins of, 19; information taken at inscription, 19, 114; "by office" (imposed by police), xvii, 19-20, 31-32, 264, 274, 335, 340; formula read to new prostitutes, 23-24; proposal to end, 332, 343; removal from, 24, 222; of minors, 24-29, 31; information collected by Parent-Duchâtelet, 113-16; disregarded for *maison de rendezvous,* 321

insoumise, 5, 15-16, 128-29, 242, 250, 254, 261, 270, 277, 279, 314, 339; arrests of, 5, 22-23, 30-32, 125n, 158, 218, 218n, 236, 266-69; defined, 6; inscription of, 31-32; *maisons de tolérance,* 46-47; Parent-Duchâtelet's lack of concern for, 113; venereal disease, 125; denounced by military, 265n. See also clandestinity, prostitutes

302; controversy about, 280-82,
302-307, 329-30; profits from,
282-96; lesbianism, 283, 300-304;
chambres de passe, 287; recruit-
ment for, 294-95; *sous maîtresse,*
295-96; changing size of, 307,
313-14, 318; Lépine's policies,
335, 344; discussed in Extraparliamentary Commission,
343-47; *maison de rendezvous,*
344-46, 351; defense of,
346-47
maison garnie, 33; arrests of *insoumises,* 22-23. See lodging
house
malades, 125. See also syphilis, venereal disease
mandats de perquisition, 262
mangeuses, 120
Mangin, Jean-Claude (prefect of
police), 51, 157, 326; attempt to
control *femmes galantes,* 18; inscription of minors, 25, 29; *maison close* policy, 41-45, 128, 281,
312-13
Manuel, Pierre: reported police
spying on *femmes galantes,* 19
marchande à la toilette, 289. See
also *ogresse*
marcheuse, 5-6, 47-48
marginality: defined, 206; illustrated by cases from police files,
216-34
Marseille, 273
Marthe Richard Law, 334
Martineau, Dr. Louis (of Lourcine
hospital), 276-77; interview with
clandestine prostitute, 246-47;
examinations in *maisons de tolérance,* 271
Mauriac, Dr. Charles, 254
medicine: clandestinity and venereal disease, 250-62. See also
dispensary, syphilis, venereal
disease

mendicants, 65, 78
mendicity, 42, 231; and venereal
disease, 260
mendicity depot, 68-69; described, 236n. See also Saint-
Denis
mendicity passports: issued to
minors, 28; examples of,
210-11
Mercier, 103
mercury treatments, 117; as cure
for syphilis, 256-57, 257n
Midi venereal hospital, 254
military denunciation of prostitutes, 264-65, 265n
minors, 91, 293, 334; legal protection of, xix-xx, 29n, 40, 40n, 83,
85, 332, 348, 348n; inscription
of, 24-29, 348; administrative
detention of, 27, 355, 376-77;
maison de tolérance, 28-29; clandestine prostitution, 247, 262;
recruited by *entremetteuses,* 294-
95; prohibited in *maisons de rendezvous,* 321
Miroir, H., 91
Moeurs. See Brigade des moeurs
morals agents. See *agents des
moeurs*
Morals Brigade. See Brigade des
moeurs
Morsier, Emilie de (abolitionist),
337
Mougeot, Dr., 272
Municipal Council of Paris, 30, 35;
1879 investigation of Brigade
des moeurs, 4, 4N, 273-74, 299n,
336-37, 355n; funding of dispensary, 10, 14; Forissier affair,
330; neoregulation, 336-43; disbanding of Brigade des moeurs,
337-38; 1890 reform of *régime
des moeurs,* 338-41; 1904 investigation, 342-43
murder, 140n, 166-68

Library of Congress Cataloging in Publication Data
Harsin, Jill, 1951–
Policing prostitution in nineteenth-century Paris.
Bibliography: p.
Includes index.
1. Prostitution—France—Paris—History—19th century.
2. Police—France—Paris—History—19th century.
3. Working-class women—France—Paris—Social conditions.
4. Women—Legal status, laws, etc.—France—Paris.
5. Sex discrimination against women—France—Paris—
History—19th century.   I. Title.
HQ196.P3H37   1985   364.1'534'0944361   84-42887
ISBN 0-691-05439-8 (alk. paper)

Jill Harsin is Assistant Professor of History at Colgate University.